המדריך

HaMadrikh
The RCA Lifecycle Guide

המדריך

HAMADRIKH
THE RCA LIFECYCLE GUIDE

THE RABBINICAL COUNCIL OF AMERICA

RABBI SHMUEL GOLDIN
RABBI LEONARD A. MATANKY

•

KOREN PUBLISHERS JERUSALEM

The RCA Lifecycle Madrikh
First Hebrew/English Edition, 2023
Nusaḥ Ashkenaz

Koren Publishers Jerusalem Ltd.
POB 4044, Jerusalem 91040, ISRAEL
POB 8531, New Milford, CT 06776, USA

Printed in the PRC

Standard Size, Hardcover, ISBN 978-965-7767-76-4

MRCA01

This new edition
of the Rabbinical Council of America's *HaMadrikh*
is dedicated in memory of

Rabbi Meyer Kramer *z"l,*

a long-time and devoted member of the RCA.

When Rabbi Kramer learned in Yeshiva University –
Yeshivat Rabbeinu Yitzchok Elchanan (RIETS) – in the 1930s and 40s,
and Orthodoxy was in steep decline in the United States, he embraced,
at the encouragement of his rebbe, Rav Dr. Samuel Belkin *zt"l,* Yeshiva University's
commitment to *kibbush hakehillot.* He settled in Philadelphia to attend law school,
met his wife, Rose *z"l,* at a Mizrachi meeting, and together made the decision to
consecrate their lives to the rabbinate in that city where Orthodoxy was in retreat.

Rabbi Kramer taught part-time in the University of Pennsylvania Law School,
but his full-time work was serving in congregations where many congregants,
like the city itself, were not religiously observant. He sought to bring them closer
to the ideals of *Yahadut,* and his wife was his full partner in these endeavors.
Rabbi Kramer not only worked with and related to his congregants, but also to Jews
of all backgrounds, whom he treated with great respect, as he did all human beings.
For him, life-cycle events were an especially meaningful opportunity to reach out
to other Jews in a caring, sensitive, positive, and personal manner.

This edition of *HaMadrikh* is lovingly dedicated by their son,
Rabbi Doniel Zvi Kramer, with his fervent prayer that it will enable
rabbis and chaplains and other *klei kodesh* to share, through their
life-cycle *avodat hakodesh,* the loving presence of השם יתברך
and His Torah whose דרכיה דרכי נועם וכל נתיבותיה שלום.

לזכר נשמות

Rabbi Meyer Kramer

הרב מאיר בן הרב חיים מנחם ז״ל

נפ׳ ז׳ תמוז תשע״ה

Mrs. Rose Schnabel Kramer

מרת רייזל בת ר׳ יהודה לייב ע״ה

נפ׳ ג׳ תשרי תשס״ז

ובנם היקר,

הילד משה שיה בן הרב מאיר ע״ה

נפ׳ כ״ז כסלו תשי״ג

תנצב״ה

CONTENTS

FOREWORD FROM THE RCA LEADERSHIP

The Torah tells us that Noah was so named because of the consolation that he brought to the world (Gen. 5:29). Rashi, echoing Ḥazal, states that actually two things occurred at the same time during Noah's lifetime: (1) Noah invented tools for plowing, which made it easier to work the soil. This brought comfort (*menuḥa*) to mankind. (2) Until Noah's generation, the soil itself was still manifesting the curse placed upon Adam, and thorns and thistles predominated every field that had been planted for grain. During Noah's lifetime, this vexing phenomenon diminished significantly, which brought great consolation (*neḥama*) to his generation.

Our world continues to accelerate at a dizzying pace. New technologies are constantly rendering old technologies obsolete even before we've had a chance to learn the old ones. The RCA has long recognized that just like every other profession, the rabbinate has its own "thorns and thistles," those inconveniences that can sometimes make our jobs cumbersome and unwieldy. As the world around us has succeeded in alleviating the inconveniences of the workplace, we in the rabbinate must strive to do so as well. Just as one needs the right tool for the right job, every rabbi needs the right tools to officiate and oversee various religious ceremonies and events.

Over thirty years ago, we published the first RCA *Madrikh*, a true classic, that alleviated many of the stresses that rabbanim out in the field undergo when presiding over life-cycle occasions.

We realized that we needed to bring a new *Madrikh* to the twenty-first-century, English-speaking rabbinate. This one would be even more robust than the previous one, taking into account that today's rabbi is called upon to preside over various events that were not addressed in the previous *Madrikh*. We also recognize that today's rabbi can benefit from additional pastoral and halakhic guidance and have created sections that address these needs. Finally, we are providing online resources to supplement our new *HaMadrikh* that will allow the rabbi to instantly access additional texts at www.rabbis.org/hamadrikh.

Those of us out in the field know what it's like to struggle through a funeral service in the middle of a rainstorm or blizzard. We've experienced the panic of realizing, at the *ḥatan's tisch*, that there's an error in the *ketuba*. Having a reliable toolbox like the new *HaMadrikh* will at least alleviate some of the job's stresses and will free our minds to remember the names of all the family members we're officiating for, and to have greater presence in the moment.

Thanks are not enough to express our *hakarat hatov* to the herculean efforts of Rabbi Leonard Matanky and Rabbi Shmuel Goldin in preparing this *HaMadrikh*. We must also express our great appreciation to Rabbi Reuven Bulka *zt"l*, who was the author of the previous RCA *Madrikh*, and who had started as one of the co-editors on this project before taking ill. His loss leaves a gaping hole in the hearts of his *ḥaverim* as well as the North American rabbinate.

Finally, an incredible *yasher koaḥ* to our *ḥaver* Rabbi Doniel Kramer, who came forward as a *gavra rabba* and dedicated this *HaMadrikh* in memory of his father, Rabbi Meyer Kramer *zt"l*.

May this new RCA *HaMadrikh* bring consolation and comfort. May it assist rabbis to be *mekadesh shem Shamayim* in all their efforts for Klal Yisrael.

Rabbi Binyamin Blau	Rabbi N. Daniel Korobkin
President	Honorary President

INTRODUCTION

For more than eighty years, one of the most important rabbinic resources has been a small volume known as a "Madrich." First composed and compiled by Rabbi Hyman E. Goldin *zt"l*, and then reimagined in the 1980s by Rabbi Reuven Bulka *zt"l*, these books have guided American rabbis through the often-complex task of officiating at life-cycle events. Each book is a masterpiece, and each has succeeded in having a meaningful impact upon American Jewry.

It is therefore with a deep sense of gratitude to these rabbis and a fair amount of trepidation that we present to you a new edition of this classic work, which we believe will address the ever-changing needs of the American rabbinate.

This new *RCA HaMadrikh, The Rabbi's Guide* offers, as did theirs, the complete texts for key life-cycle events. This volume, however, adds to those previous editions in several critical ways.

- **Fully Sourced and Expanded Halakhic Sections**

  The welcome literacy of today's Orthodox community has placed new demands upon its rabbinate. Questions of increased complexity are regularly posed, and the immediacy of modern communication raises the need for on-the-spot responses as never before.

  Considering these and other similar challenges, we have made every effort to provide rabbis with expanded and sourced halakhic information needed for their leadership at critical times.

  We are deeply indebted to Morenu HaRav Hershel Schachter *shlita* for his careful review of each halakhic section in this volume. HaRav Schacter's *piskei halakha*, insights, and edits have enabled us to present these halakhot with a confidence that would have been otherwise impossible.

- **"Rabbinic Road" Sections**
  Each chapter of this volume is introduced by a concise section of general guidance to the rabbi. These introductions are motivated by the conviction that a rabbi's greatest task is to serve as the pastoral guide for his congregants. At its best, this new edition of *HaMadrikh* should therefore aid rabbis in navigating the often-complex road ahead.

- **Added Content**
  Certain sections were deleted from the previous edition of the RCA Madrikh in order to limit its size. After consulting with our membership, we have expanded some of the sections and reinstated texts for both a *ḥanukat habayit* and a *hakhnasat sefer Torah*. These events reflect the changing needs of our communities as they seek to create a stronger bond between home and synagogue, and as more *sifrei Torah* are written and dedicated.

  In addition, we have included a wider selection of psalms, both within the chapters and at the end of this book. These chapters represent the key sections of Psalms that are recited in times of need.

- **Online Resources**
  In addition to material included in this book, the Rabbinical Council of America has prepared an online resource at www.rabbis.org/hamadrikh. There, rabbis will find additional forms (e.g., a *ketuba de'irkisa,* a replacement *ketuba* when signatures have faded, the prenuptial agreement, etc.), the entire *Vidui* service, which may be needed when the printed edition is not accessible, halakhic spellings of cities, and more. It is our hope that this resource will serve to support the dynamic needs of the rabbinate.

A few personal notes...

While participation in this project has been deeply meaningful for us both, it carries an additional layer of significance for Rabbi Shmuel Goldin. As noted, the original Madrikh of 1939 was conceived and authored by Rabbi Hyman E. Goldin, Rabbi Shmuel Goldin's grandfather. Rabbi Goldin is indebted to the RCA for enabling him to further his grandfather's legacy through this new publication.

Four years ago, when we met to plan this new edition, we were honored to have Rabbi Reuven Bulka join us and agree to serve as a co-editor. We looked to Rabbi Bulka, a prolific writer, a great rabbi, and editor of the first RCA *Madrikh*, for his sage advice and skillful writing. We were deeply saddened when his tragic illness and passing forestalled that possibility. Rabbi Bulka's presence is, nonetheless, felt throughout the pages of this volume, as much of the content is built upon the foundation of his earlier work.

One of the most important gifts provided by membership in the RCA is the *chavershaft* that develops over time. The editors of this volume met in the trenches of RCA leadership immediately before and during our respective terms as president of the organization. What began as a collegial relationship has blossomed over the years into a close, cherished friendship. This relationship informed our shared efforts on this project, enabling us to complement each other's strengths and augment each other's weaknesses seamlessly. We trust that the warmth of our partnership is reflected in the pages of this volume.

Thanks are certainly due to Caryn Meltz who, on behalf of Koren Publishers shepherded this effort to publication, and to Koren's publisher and our good friend, Matthew Miller. Their talented team, including Esther Be'er, Efrat Gross, Dvora Rhein, Rachelle Emanuel, and Debbie Ismailoff, and their patient acceptance of our continual emendations to the manuscript were invaluable in bringing the volume to reality. We thank our colleagues, Rabbis Shalom Baum, Mark Dratch, Chaim Poupko, Yona Reiss, Reuven Tradburks, and Michoel Zylberman for their review of portions of the manuscript. Their critiques and advice proved extremely helpful.

As always, we express our deep gratitude to our respective spouses for their patient support in this and other projects throughout our years of service to the Jewish community. We owe all to you, and you continue to inspire us in all we do.

Finally, we thank the leadership of the RCA, past presidents Rabbi Elazar Muskin and Rabbi Daniel Korobkin, president Rabbi Binyamin Blau, and executive vice president, Rabbi Mark Dratch for entrusting us with this critically important project. We hope that this edition of *HaMadrikh* will prove that confidence to have been well placed.

We close with a paraphrase of the talmudic prayer quoted in the name of Rav Nehunya ben Hakaneh upon entering the *beit midrash*:*

> "May it be Your will, Hashem, our God, that no mishap should occur because of us; that we should not err in a halakhic matter and that our colleagues will rejoice in us; that we should not declare the impure pure or the pure impure; that our colleagues should not err in a halakhic matter and that we will rejoice in them."

May this volume guide its readers and support the rabbis of our community *lehagdil Torah ulehaadirah*!

Rabbi Shmuel Goldin and Rabbi Leonard A. Matanky
Jerusalem/Chicago, 5783 (2023)

* Berakhot 28b.

המדריך

HAMADRIKH:
THE RCA LIFECYCLE GUIDE

THE RABBINIC ROAD: CHALLENGES AND OPPORTUNITIES

BRIT MILA

The preparations for a *brit mila* provide the rabbi with a wonderful opportunity to interact with a family – usually a younger family – against a background of deep joy and hectic preparation. Helping each family find a *mohel,* guiding the parents through a ceremony replete with honors for distribution, assisting in the determination of timing and venue, offering advice concerning the selection of a name, are just some of the areas of potential rabbinic involvement. As always, the *baalei simcha* will remember the assistance and guidance offered by the rabbi long after the event itself.

- The rabbi should maintain updated contact information of local *mohalim* for ready access. In particular, he should be able to identify those *mohalim* who will make themselves available over Shabbat or Yom Tov. The rabbi should familiarize himself with the professionalism of the *mohalim* he recommends; keeping in mind that, while the *brit* is a pivotal religious rite, it is a medical procedure, as well.
- The rabbi should be prepared to guide the celebrants regarding the halakhic issues surrounding the use of a clamp vs. a shield, and the proper way to perform *metzitza.*
- As early as possible, the rabbi should meet with the parents, in person or over the phone, to review the *brit* ceremony and the various honors for distribution. He will often be called upon to offer advice concerning the significance of each particular honor and to whom that honor should be given. The rabbi should also use this opportunity to gather personal information from the parents (concerning the child's name, family history, etc.) for inclusion in any remarks he may deliver (see below).

- If communal custom dictates that the *rabbi* be given a particular honor, the rabbi should feel free to delicately share that information with the parents. He should make it clear, however, that he is willing to forego the honor if the family feels the need to grant it to someone else. In this, and all related matters, sensitivity to each family's particulars and "politics" should be the order of the day.
- The rabbi should make every effort to attend the *brit mila* and, if possible, stay until the recitation of *Birkat HaMazon,* with its special inclusions, after the meal. The rabbi should also offer to speak, but, once again, indicate his clear understanding if the parents intend to limit any speeches to family members. All speeches, including the rabbi's, should be short, personal, and preferably delivered directly after the *brit* or early on during the meal. In this way, those attendees who must leave to "get on with their day" can do so comfortably.
- Concerning this and all other lifecycle events, the rabbi should carefully review his halakhic standards with the family as soon as possible.

HALAKHOT CONCERNING BRIT MILA

TIMING OF THE BRIT MILA

1. A *brit mila* is performed when a boy is eight days old, counting the day of birth as day one (יו״ד רסב:א).
2. If a *brit* was performed before the eighth day, the child must have *hatafat dam* performed after the eighth day (ערוה״ש יו״ד רסב:ה).
3. A *brit* must take place during the daytime (after sunrise and before sunset) and ideally in the morning because of the principle of זריזין מקדימין למצות (יו״ד רסב:א).
4. If the *brit* was performed after sunset, *hatafat dam* on a later day is required (ש״ך יו״ד רסב ס״ק ב).
5. The *brit mila* of a child born on Shabbat is held on the following Shabbat, unless the child was delivered by Cesarean section, in which case the *brit* is delayed until Sunday. Similarly, if the eighth day following a Cesarean section is a Yom Tov, the *brit* is delayed until after Yom Tov (יו״ד רסו:י).
6. If a child is born *bein hashmashot* (ע״ע משנה ברורה רסא ס״ק כג), the count of eight days begins that evening (i.e., the next halakhic day) (יו״ד רסב:ד).
7. If a child is born on Friday night *bein hashmashot*, the *brit* is delayed until the ninth day (Sunday). Similarly, a *brit mila* is not performed on a Yom Tov unless the child was definitely born eight days earlier, and not *bein hashmashot* (יו״ד רסו:ח-ט). However, if the eighth day is a *yom tov sheni shel galuyot*, the *brit* can take place, even when the boy was born *bein hashmashot* (נודע ביהודה מהדורא קמא או״ח סימן ל).
8. Twin boys (or two other boys having a *brit* at the same time) should not be brought into the room for the *brit* together. Rather, after the first *brit mila* is complete, the blessing of *HaMalakh*

HaGoel (Genesis 48:16) is recited, and then the second boy is brought into the room for his *brit mila* (פתחי תשובה יו״ד רסה ס״ק י). Between the two *britot*, it is appropriate for the father to deliver a *devar Torah* to further separate between the two sets of blessings.

POSTPONING A BRIT MILA

1. A child with a serious illness affecting his entire body does not have his *brit mila* until seven complete days (seven twenty-four-hour periods) have passed after his recovery (יו״ד רסב:ב).
2. A jaundiced child is typically not considered a *ḥoleh kol gufo* and may have his *brit mila* as soon as he has recovered (ציץ אליעזר ח״ג סימנים פא ופג). If, however, the child required a blood transfusion, then the *brit mila* should be delayed for seven days after his recovery (אג״מ יו״ד ח״ב סימן קכא).
3. Just as a doctor's expert advice is relied upon in circumstances of illness/emergency to suspend the laws of Shabbat, so too, a doctor's advice should be sought regarding a child's illness and the advisability of performing a *brit mila* (ערוה״ש יו״ד רסג:ד). There are, however, situations (e.g., after a child is removed from an incubator, or following a blood transfusion) when *halakha* requires a seven-day waiting period, despite the doctor's permission to immediately perform a *brit mila* (אג״מ יו״ד ח״ב סימן קכא).

SHALOM ZAKHAR

1. On the first Friday night following the birth of a boy, it is customary to host a *shalom zakhar* (יו״ד רסה:יב). This gathering can occur even when the baby is not in the location of the *shalom zakhar* (אוצר הברית ח״א ג:ב:ז).
2. If the child was born on Friday night after Shabbat began (causing his *brit mila* to be scheduled for the following Shabbat), there are different *minhagim* as to whether the *shalom zakhar* should take place on the first or second Friday night. The common *minhag*

is to hold the *shalom zakhar* on the second Friday night, i.e., the Friday night closer to the *brit mila* (חכמת אדם מט:כד).

3. If the *brit mila* must be postponed due to the child's illness, the *shalom zakhar* should still be held on the first Friday night after the child's birth. If, however, there is doubt as to whether or not the child will survive the illness, a *shalom zakhar* need not be held (אוצר הברית ח"א ג:ב:יא-יב).

TEFILLA ON THE DAY OF THE BRIT MILA

1. On the day of the *brit*, *Taḥanun* is not recited in the synagogue where the *brit* will take place or in any minyan which includes either the *mohel*, the *sandak*, or the father of the baby. If the *brit* takes place after *Minḥa*, *Taḥanun* is not recited at *Shaḥarit* or *Minḥa* if any of these men are present (אשי ישראל כה:כד).
2. The day of the *brit* is considered a holiday for the *mohel*, the *sandak*, and the father of the baby. These individuals, therefore, do not personally recite *Taḥanun* at *Shaḥarit* or *Minḥa* that day, no matter what time of the day the *brit* occurs (משנה ברורה קלא ס"ק כה).
3. If there is a later minyan in the same location as the *brit*, even after the *brit* has concluded and all of the participants have departed, the later minyan does not recite *Taḥanun* on the day of the *brit* (דברי משה או"ח ג). If, however, the later minyan is held in a separate sanctuary with its own *aron hakodesh*, *Taḥanun* is recited (משנה ברורה קלא ס"ק כד).
4. Just as *Taḥanun* is not recited when a *brit* falls on a weekday, *Av HaRaḥamim* and *Tzidkatekha Tzedek* are omitted when a *brit* occurs on Shabbat (או"ח קפד:ז).
5. While the *El Erekh Apayim* is recited prior to the reading of the Torah, the series of the *Yehi Ratzon* following the reading of the Torah is not recited(ש"ך יו"ד רס"ה ס"ק כד).
6. Those who are wearing *tefillin* prior to the *brit mila* should

continue to wear their *tefillin* for the *brit mila,* since both are referred to as an *ot* (ש"ך יו"ד רסה ס"ק כד).

7. It is customary in some communities for the *mohel* (or the rabbi) to lead the congregation in the responsive reading of the section of *Pesukei DeZimra* beginning with the words *vekharot imo haberit.* Some conclude this recitation with the words *kemo even bemayim azim,* while others continue until *Yishtabaḥ.*
8. In other communities, only the *mohel* and the *sandak* recite this section responsively aloud (דרך החיים ל:יד).

THE HONORS AT A BRIT IN ORDER OF SIGNIFICANCE

1. Many honors are available for distribution to those participating in the *brit mila.* The following is the list of honors, in order of significance.
   - A. *Sandak Meyushav*
     - I. Serving as the *sandak* is the most significant honor at a *brit mila.* The individual who receives this honor is referred to as the *baal brit.* This honor is given to a male family member or another righteous man (יו"ד רסד:א).
     - II. Halakhic authorities disagree as to whether the same person may serve as the *sandak* for more than one child in a family. Some forbid this practice (רמ"א יו"ד רסה:יא), while others permit a family member or the rabbi to serve in this role for multiple children of the same family (נודע ביהודה מהדורה קמא יו"ד פו, הגהות יד שאול יו"ד רסה).
   - B. *Amida laberakhot (Sandak Me'umad)*
   - C. *Berakhot*
   - D. *Keriat hashem (the naming)*
   - E. *Kiseh shel Eliyahu*
   - F. *Kvatter and kvatterin*
     - I. A husband and wife are chosen to serve as *kvatter* and *kvatterin* (אוצר הברית ח"א ג:יב:ד).

ii. In order to involve others in this important mitzva, multiple women can participate in bringing the baby to the *kvatterin,* and multiple men can take the baby from the *kvatter,* until one reaches the *kiseh shel Eliyahu* (אוצר הברית ח״א ג:טו:ח הערה כד).

G. *Min hakiseh leyad hasandak*

i. There are varying customs regarding this honor. Some have the father lift the baby and place him on the lap of the *sandak,* while others honor someone present to do this.

MOHEL

1. If the father himself is not the *mohel,* the father should seek a person who is experienced and righteous to serve as the *mohel* for the *brit* (יו״ד רסד:א).
2. If a *brit mila* was performed by a non-Jew, a Jew must later perform *hatafat dam* (יו״ד רסד:א).
3. A woman should not perform a *brit mila*. If a woman did the *brit mila,* however, *hatafat dam* is not required. In a situation where significant effort was made to find a male *mohel* to perform the *brit* on the eighth day, but none was found, a woman is permitted to perform the *brit mila* on the eighth day (לבושי שרד רס״ד ס״ק א, מגדל עוז יו״ד רסד ס״ק ה).
4. A *meḥalel Shabbat befarhesia* should not serve as a *mohel.* If such an individual performed the *brit mila* properly and on the eighth day, some authorities do not require *hatafat dam* (רעק״א יו״ד רסד ס״ק א), while others require *hatafat dam* (אות שלום רסד ס״ק ה).
5. Prior to the *brit mila,* the father must designate the *mohel* as his agent (*shaliaḥ*) to perform the *brit mila* (יו״ד רסה:ט).
6. A *mohel* should not perform his first *brit mila* on Shabbat, unless no other *mohel* is available, and the *mohel* is confident that he can perform the *brit mila* properly (שבות יעקב ח״ג סימן כה).

BERAKHOT

1. The *berakhot* of the *brit mila* should be recited while standing (שיבולי הלקט מילה ד).
2. Immediately prior to the *brit mila,* the *mohel* recites the *berakha* of *Al HaMila* (חכמת אדם קמט:יט).
3. Following the *berakha* of the *mohel,* and the circumcision, but before the *peria* is performed, the father of the baby recites the *berakha* of *LeHakhniso BiVrito Shel Avraham Avinu.* Sephardim recite this *berakha* before the *mila* is performed (ילקוט יוסף שובע שמחות ח״ב ח:ד).
4. If the father is not present at the *brit mila,* the *sandak* recites this second *berakha* (יו״ד קסה:א).
5. There are four different customs regarding drinking the cup of wine used for the *berakhot*: a) the *mevarekh* drinks the wine only after the baby is named; b) the *mevarekh* drinks the wine following the *berakha* but before the naming; c) the baby is given some of the wine to drink following the *berakha* but before the naming; and d) the *mevarekh* has intent for another person, who drinks the wine after the naming (אוצר הברית ח״א ג:טו:כה).
6. If one drinks the wine after the initial *berakha,* the cup should be refilled before the naming takes place (אג״מ ח״ג סימן ק).
7. When the *brit mila* takes place on Shabbat morning, a child is given the wine to drink, since *Kiddush* has not yet been recited (או״ח רעג:ה). If the individual reciting the *berakha* will drink at least a *revi'it* of wine, eat cake, or begin the regular Shabbat meal immediately afterward at the same location, the *berakha* for the wine can serve as the *Kiddush* for Shabbat morning (אור לציון ח״ב כ:כו).

SEUDAT MITZVA

1. Following the *brit mila,* it is customary to host a *seudat mitzva* with at least ten men (יו״ד רסה:יב) If, for some reason, the meal cannot occur on the day of the *brit,* it should be held on another day (פתחי תשובה יו״ד רסו ס״ק טז).

2. The *seuda* should include bread (חכמת אדם קמט:כד), and according to some authorities it should also include meat and wine (מג"א או"ח רמט:ו). Other authorities permit fish in place of meat (Rabbi J. David Bleich, *Tradition* 35, no. 2 [2001]: 55–60; תשובות והנהגות ח"ב סימן תפה, ע"ע).
3. There is a custom not to directly invite guests to the *seuda* of a *brit* so as not to obligate their attendance (פתחי תשובה יו"ד רסה:יח). If one is invited to a *brit* but has a conflicting responsibility, it is permitted not to attend the *brit* (שבט הלוי ח"ח סימן ריז).
4. Prior to the *zimun* of *Birkat HaMazon*, the *piyut* of *Nodeh LeShimkha* is recited (מג"א או"ח קסו ס"ק לג).
5. There are six special *HaRaḥaman tefillot* inserted toward the end of the *Birkat HaMazon*, after the paragraph of *BaMarom*. Typically, these passages are distributed among honored guests to recite out loud. However, the cup of wine used for *Birkat HaMazon* is not passed from one to the other for this honor.

BRIT ON SPECIAL DAYS

1. Rosh Hashana: In the synagogue, the *brit mila* takes place after Torah reading and before the blowing of the shofar (או"ח תקפד:ד). If the *brit* occurs at another location, it should take place after services are completed (משנה ברורה תקפד ס"ק יא).
2. Yom Kippur: The *brit mila* takes place after Torah reading and *Ashrei*. If the *brit mila* does not take place in the synagogue, it should take place after the Torah is returned to the Ark and before *Musaf* (או"ח פקכא:ב). The *berakha* for the wine is recited, the baby is given some of the wine, and no one else drinks from the cup (מג"א תרכא ס"ק ג).
3. Fast Days: The *brit mila* takes place as usual in the morning. At the *brit*, however, a young child is given the wine to drink (יו"ד רסה:ד). If the fast is *nidḥe* (postponed), the parents of the baby, the *sandak*, and the *mohel* do not complete the fast, and may drink the wine (משנה ברורה תקנט ס"ק לה). On *Taanit Esther*, even if the fast

is not *nidḥe*, the father of the baby, the *sandak*, and the *mohel* may drink the wine (i.e., they do not complete the fast).

4. Sukkot: Only the *seuda* of the *brit mila* should take place in the sukka. Due to health concerns, the *brit mila* procedure should take place indoors (אוצר הברית ח״א ג:יז:י:א).
5. Erev Pesach: The *brit mila* should preferably be performed before the time that *ḥametz* can no longer be eaten, so that a *seuda* with bread can be served (אוצר הברית ג:יז:כ:א).
6. *Sefirat HaOmer*: The father of the baby, the *sandak*, and the *mohel* may get haircuts in preparation for the *brit* (או״ח תצג:ב).
7. The Three Weeks: Until Rosh Ḥodesh Av, the father of the baby, the *sandak*, and the *mohel* may get haircuts in preparation for the *brit* (נודע ביהודה מהדורה קמא או״ח סימן כח).
8. The Nine Days: The father of the baby, the *sandak*, and the *mohel* may dress in freshly laundered Shabbat clothing, a young child is given the wine to drink, and the *seuda* of the *brit* can include meat (או״ח תקנא:א).
9. Tisha B'Av: The *brit* should take place after the conclusion of *Kinot*. Ashkenazim perform the *brit* before midday, while Sephardim perform it after midday (או״ח תקנט:ז). During the ceremony, the father of the baby, the *sandak*, and the *mohel* may wear Shabbat clothing. However, after the *brit* they should change back to Tisha B'Av clothing (או״ח תקנט:ח). A young child is given the wine to drink (או״ח תקנט:ז). The *seuda* is held after the conclusion of the fast (מג״א או״ח תקנט:יא).
10. During *Aveilut*:
    - A. *Aninut*: The *brit mila* takes place as normal, but the *onen* does not recite the *berakha* of *LeHakhniso*. The *sandak* recites that *berakha* in the *onen*'s place (כל בו על אבילות פרק ב ד:יב).
    - B. *Shiva*: The father of the baby may go to the synagogue for the *brit mila*, and he may participate in the *seudat mitzva* (זוכר הברית ז:לב).

THE BRIT MILA SERVICE

When the baby is brought in, all stand and say:

בָּרוּךְ הַבָּא Blessed is the one who has arrived!

The mohel says:

וַיְדַבֵּר The Lord spoke to Moses, saying: Pinehas the son of Elazar, the son of Aaron the priest, has turned My wrath away from the children of Israel, in that he was very jealous for My sake among them, so that I consumed not the children of Israel in My jealousy. Therefore say: Behold, I give to him My covenant of peace. *Num. 25*

The baby is placed on Elijah's seat, and the mohel says:

זֶה הַכִּסֵּא This is the throne of Elijah the prophet,
who is remembered for good.

The mohel says:

לִישׁוּעָתְךָ I wait for Your salvation, O Lord. *Gen. 49*
I hope for Your salvation, O Lord, *Ps. 119*
and I perform Your commandments.
Elijah, angel of the covenant,
the one who belongs to you is in your presence.
Stand to my right and be close to me.
I hope for Your salvation, O Lord. *Ps. 119*
I rejoice at Your word, like one who finds great spoil.
Those who love Your law have great peace,
and they have no stumbling-block.
Happy is he whom You choose and bring near, *Ps. 65*
that he may dwell in Your courts.

All present respond:

May we be sated with the goodness of Your House,
Your holy Temple.

סדר ברית מילה

When the baby is brought in, all stand and say:

בָּרוּךְ הַבָּא.

The מוהל *says:*

וַיְדַבֵּר יהוה אֶל־מֹשֶׁה לֵּאמֹר: פִּינְחָס בֶּן־אֶלְעָזָר בֶּן־אַהֲרֹן במדבר כה
הַכֹּהֵן הֵשִׁיב אֶת־חֲמָתִי מֵעַל בְּנֵי־יִשְׂרָאֵל, בְּקַנְאוֹ אֶת־
קִנְאָתִי בְּתוֹכָם, וְלֹא־כִלִּיתִי אֶת־בְּנֵי־יִשְׂרָאֵל בְּקִנְאָתִי:
לָכֵן אֱמֹר, הִנְנִי נֹתֵן לוֹ אֶת־בְּרִיתִי שָׁלוֹם:

The baby is placed on the כסא של אליהו*, and the* מוהל *says:*

זֶה הַכִּסֵּא שֶׁל אֵלִיָּהוּ הַנָּבִיא זָכוּר לַטּוֹב.

The מוהל *says:*

לִישׁוּעָתְךָ קִוִּיתִי יהוה: בראשית מט
שִׂבַּרְתִּי לִישׁוּעָתְךָ יהוה, וּמִצְוֹתֶיךָ עָשִׂיתִי: תהלים קיט
אֵלִיָּהוּ מַלְאַךְ הַבְּרִית
הִנֵּה שֶׁלְּךָ לְפָנֶיךָ, עֲמֹד עַל יְמִינִי וְסָמְכֵנִי.
שִׂבַּרְתִּי לִישׁוּעָתְךָ יהוה: תהלים קיט
שָׂשׂ אָנֹכִי עַל־אִמְרָתֶךָ, כְּמוֹצֵא שָׁלָל רָב:
שָׁלוֹם רָב לְאֹהֲבֵי תוֹרָתֶךָ, וְאֵין־לָמוֹ מִכְשׁוֹל:
אַשְׁרֵי תִּבְחַר וּתְקָרֵב, יִשְׁכֹּן חֲצֵרֶיךָ תהלים סה

All present respond:

נִשְׂבְּעָה בְּטוּב בֵּיתֶךָ, קְדֹשׁ הֵיכָלֶךָ:

The father of the baby says:

הִנְנִי I am ready and prepared to fulfill the positive commandment which the Creator, blessed be He, has commanded me to perform, to circumcise my son.

The mohel says:

אָמַר The Holy One, blessed is He, said to Abraham our father, "Walk before Me in integrity." I am ready and prepared to fulfill the positive commandment of circumcision which the Creator, blessed be He, has commanded us to perform. *Gen. 17*

The baby is placed on the knees of the sandak, and the mohel says:

בָּרוּךְ Blessed are You, Lord, our God, King of the universe, Who has sanctified us with His commandments, and has commanded us regarding circumcision.

Immediately after the circumcision, the father says:

בָּרוּךְ Blessed are You, Lord, our God, King of the universe, Who has sanctified us with His commandments, and has commanded us to bring him into the covenant of Abraham our father.

All present respond:

אָמֵן Just as he has entered into the covenant, so may he enter into Torah, the marriage canopy, and good deeds.

After the circumcision has been completed, the mohel (or another honoree) takes a cup of wine and says:

בָּרוּךְ Blessed are You, Lord, our God, King of the universe, Who creates the fruit of the vine.

בָּרוּךְ Blessed are You, Lord, our God, King of the universe, Who consecrated His beloved (Isaac) while still in the womb, and marked his flesh by means of the decree (of circumcision), and sealed his progeny with the sign of the holy covenant. Therefore as a reward for this act, dear living God Who is our Portion and our Rock, command (some say: Who has commanded) the salvation from destruction of our soul that is connected to our bodies, on account of His covenant that He has inscribed in our flesh. Blessed are You, Lord, Who establishes the covenant.

The father of the baby says:

הִנְנִי מוּכָן וּמְזֻמָּן לְקַיֵּם מִצְוַת עֲשֵׂה שֶׁצִּוַּנִי הַבּוֹרֵא יִתְבָּרַךְ, לָמוּל אֶת בְּנִי.

The מוהל *says:*

אָמַר הַקָּדוֹשׁ בָּרוּךְ הוּא לְאַבְרָהָם אָבִינוּ, הִתְהַלֵּךְ לְפָנַי וֶהְיֵה תָמִים. בראשית יז

הִנְנִי מוּכָן וּמְזֻמָּן לְקַיֵּם מִצְוַת עֲשֵׂה שֶׁצִּוָּנוּ הַבּוֹרֵא יִתְבָּרַךְ, לָמוּל.

The baby is placed on the knees of the סנדק*, and the* מוהל *says:*

בָּרוּךְ אַתָּה יהוה אֱלֹהֵינוּ מֶלֶךְ הָעוֹלָם
אֲשֶׁר קִדְּשָׁנוּ בְּמִצְוֹתָיו וְצִוָּנוּ עַל הַמִּילָה.

Immediately after the circumcision, the father says:

בָּרוּךְ אַתָּה יהוה אֱלֹהֵינוּ מֶלֶךְ הָעוֹלָם
אֲשֶׁר קִדְּשָׁנוּ בְּמִצְוֹתָיו
וְצִוָּנוּ לְהַכְנִיסוֹ בִּבְרִיתוֹ שֶׁל אַבְרָהָם אָבִינוּ.

All present respond:

אָמֵן. כְּשֵׁם שֶׁנִּכְנַס לַבְּרִית
כֵּן יִכָּנֵס לְתוֹרָה וּלְחֻפָּה וּלְמַעֲשִׂים טוֹבִים.

After the circumcision has been completed, the מוהל *(or another honoree) takes a cup of wine and says:*

בָּרוּךְ אַתָּה יהוה אֱלֹהֵינוּ מֶלֶךְ הָעוֹלָם, בּוֹרֵא פְּרִי הַגָּפֶן.

בָּרוּךְ אַתָּה יהוה אֱלֹהֵינוּ מֶלֶךְ הָעוֹלָם, אֲשֶׁר קִדַּשׁ יְדִיד מִבֶּטֶן, וְחֹק בִּשְׁאֵרוֹ שָׂם, וְצֶאֱצָאָיו חָתַם בְּאוֹת בְּרִית קֹדֶשׁ. עַל כֵּן בִּשְׂכַר זֹאת, אֵל חַי חֶלְקֵנוּ צוּרֵנוּ צַוֵּה (נ״א צִוָּה) לְהַצִּיל יְדִידוּת שְׁאֵרֵנוּ מִשַּׁחַת, לְמַעַן בְּרִיתוֹ אֲשֶׁר שָׂם בִּבְשָׂרֵנוּ. בָּרוּךְ אַתָּה יהוה, כּוֹרֵת הַבְּרִית.

The mohel (or another honoree) takes the cup of wine and says the following to name the baby.

For emendations to this paragraph due to special circumstances, see pages 22–23.

אֱלֹהֵינוּ Our God and the God of our fathers,
safeguard this boy for his father and mother.
He will be known among the Jewish people
as (*child's Hebrew name*) the son of (*father's name*).
May the father rejoice in the one who has come forth from his loins,
and may his mother be gladdened by the fruit of her womb.

As it is written: "Let your father and your mother be glad, and let her that *Prov. 23*
bore you rejoice." And as it says: "And when I passed by you, and saw you *Ezek. 16*
wallowing in your blood,

As a drop of wine is placed in the baby's mouth, the person naming the baby and all present say:

I said to you: 'In your blood, live; and I said to you: In your blood, live.'"

The one naming the baby continues:

And as it further says: "He has remembered His covenant forever, *Ps. 105*
the word that He has commanded to a thousand generations, which
He made with Abraham, and His oath to Isaac, and He confirmed it to
Jacob as a law, to Israel as an everlasting covenant." So too it says: "And *Gen. 21*
Abraham circumcised his son Isaac when he was eight days old, as God
had commanded him."

All present say

Give thanks to the Lord, for He is good, for His loving-kindness is forever. *Ps. 118*
Give thanks to the Lord, for He is good, for His loving-kindness is forever.

The honoree continues:

May this little one (*child's Hebrew name*) the son of (*father's name*). *(If the child has no halakhic father, mother's name is inserted)* become great.

All present respond:

Just as he has entered into the covenant, so may he enter into Torah, the marriage canopy, and good deeds.

The one who recited the blessings drinks some of the wine.

The מוהל *(or another honoree) takes the cup of wine and says the following to name the baby.*

For emendations to this paragraph due to special circumstances, see pages 22–23.

אֱלֹהֵינוּ וֵאלֹהֵי אֲבוֹתֵינוּ, קַיֵּם אֶת הַיֶּלֶד הַזֶּה לְאָבִיו וּלְאִמּוֹ וְיִקָּרֵא שְׁמוֹ בְּיִשְׂרָאֵל (שם הילד) **בֶּן** (שם האב).

יִשְׂמַח הָאָב בְּיוֹצֵא חֲלָצָיו וְתָגֵל אִמּוֹ בִּפְרִי בִטְנָהּ.

משלי כג / יחזקאל טז **כַּכָּתוּב: יִשְׂמַח־אָבִיךָ וְאִמֶּךָ, וְתָגֵל יוֹלַדְתֶּךָ: וְנֶאֱמַר: וָאֶעֱבֹר עָלַיִךְ וָאֶרְאֵךְ מִתְבּוֹסֶסֶת בְּדָמָיִךְ**

As a drop of wine is placed in the baby's mouth, the person naming the baby and all present say:

וָאֹמַר לָךְ בְּדָמַיִךְ חֲיִי, וָאֹמַר לָךְ בְּדָמַיִךְ חֲיִי:

The one naming the baby continues:

תהלים קה **וְנֶאֱמַר: זָכַר לְעוֹלָם בְּרִיתוֹ, דָּבָר צִוָּה לְאֶלֶף דּוֹר: אֲשֶׁר כָּרַת אֶת־אַבְרָהָם, וּשְׁבוּעָתוֹ לְיִשְׂחָק: וַיַּעֲמִידֶהָ לְיַעֲקֹב לְחֹק, לְיִשְׂרָאֵל**

בראשית כא **בְּרִית עוֹלָם: וְנֶאֱמַר: וַיָּמָל אַבְרָהָם אֶת־יִצְחָק בְּנוֹ בֶּן־שְׁמֹנַת יָמִים, כַּאֲשֶׁר צִוָּה אֹתוֹ אֱלֹהִים:**

All present say

תהלים קיח **הוֹדוּ לַיהוה כִּי־טוֹב, כִּי לְעוֹלָם חַסְדּוֹ:**

הוֹדוּ לַיהוה כִּי־טוֹב, כִּי לְעוֹלָם חַסְדּוֹ:

The honoree continues:

(שם הילד) **בֶּן** (שם האב). (אם מבחינה הלכתית אין אב לבן, קוראים לו על שם אמו)

זֶה הַקָּטָן גָּדוֹל יִהְיֶה.

All present respond:

כְּשֵׁם שֶׁנִּכְנַס לַבְּרִית, כֵּן יִכָּנֵס לְתוֹרָה וּלְחֻפָּה וּלְמַעֲשִׂים טוֹבִים.

The one who recited the blessings drinks some of the wine.

The mohel says:

מִי שֶׁבֵּרַךְ May He Who blessed our fathers, Abraham, Isaac, and Jacob, bless this tender circumcised boy (*child's Hebrew name*) the son of (*mother's name*), sending him a complete recovery in the merit of his having entered into the covenant. And just as he has entered into the covenant, so may he enter into Torah, the marriage canopy, and good deeds, and let us say, Amen.

The mohel and father then say the following prayer:

רִבּוֹנוֹ Master of the Universe, may it be Your will that he be worthy, favored, and acceptable before You as if I had offered him before the throne of Your glory. May You, in Your abundant mercy, send through Your holy angels a holy, pure soul to

mohel says:	*father says:*
(*child's Hebrew name*) son of (*father's name*) (*If the child has no halakhic father, mother's name is used*)	My son (*child's Hebrew name*) son of (*father's name*)

who has just been circumcised for the sake of Your Great Name, and may his heart be as open wide as the entrance to the Sanctuary to Your holy Torah to learn and to teach, to observe and to fulfill. Bestow upon him length of days and years, a sin-fearing life, a life of abundance and honor, a life in which his heart's wishes are fulfilled for the good. Amen, and thus may it be Your will.

The מוהל *says:*

מִי שֶׁבֵּרַךְ אֲבוֹתֵינוּ אַבְרָהָם יִצְחָק וְיַעֲקֹב, הוּא יְבָרֵךְ אֶת הַיֶּלֶד הָרַךְ הַנִּמּוֹל (שם הילד) **בֶּן** (שם האם) **וְיִשְׁלַח לוֹ רְפוּאָה שְׁלֵמָה בַּעֲבוּר שֶׁנִּכְנַס לַבְּרִית, כֵּן יִכָּנֵס לְתוֹרָה וּלְחֻפָּה וּלְמַעֲשִׂים טוֹבִים. וְנֹאמַר אָמֵן.**

The מוהל *and father then say the following prayer:*

רִבּוֹנוֹ שֶׁל עוֹלָם, יְהִי רָצוֹן מִלְּפָנֶיךָ, שֶׁיְּהֵא חָשׁוּב וּמְרֻצֶּה וּמְקֻבָּל לְפָנֶיךָ, כְּאִלּוּ הִקְרַבְתִּיהוּ לִפְנֵי כִּסֵּא כְבוֹדֶךָ. וְאַתָּה, בְּרַחֲמֶיךָ הָרַבִּים, שְׁלַח עַל יְדֵי מַלְאָכֶיךָ הַקְּדוֹשִׁים נְשָׁמָה קְדוֹשָׁה וּטְהוֹרָה

The מוהל *says:*

(שם הילד) **בֶּן** (שם האב).

(אם מבחינה הלכתית אין אב לבן, קוראים לו על שם אמו)

The father say:

לִבְנִי (שם הילד)

הַנִּמּוֹל עַתָּה לְשִׁמְךָ הַגָּדוֹל, וְשֶׁיִּהְיֶה לִבּוֹ פָּתוּחַ כְּפִתְחוֹ שֶׁל אוּלָם, בְּתוֹרָתְךָ הַקְּדוֹשָׁה, לִלְמֹד וּלְלַמֵּד, לִשְׁמֹר וְלַעֲשׂוֹת. וְתֵן לוֹ אֲרִיכוּת יָמִים וְשָׁנִים, חַיִּים שֶׁל יִרְאַת שָׁמַיִם, חַיִּים שֶׁל יִרְאַת חֵטְא, חַיִּים שֶׁל עֹשֶׁר וְכָבוֹד, חַיִּים שֶׁתְּמַלֵּא מִשְׁאֲלוֹת לִבּוֹ לְטוֹבָה, אָמֵן, כֵּן יְהִי רָצוֹן.

ALTERNATIVE VERSIONS FOR NAMING IN SPECIAL CIRCUMSTANCES

The mohel (or another honoree) takes the cup of wine and says the following to name the baby.

אֱלֹהֵינוּ Our God and the God of our fathers,
safeguard this boy for
say (skip if child has no father): his father and
say (skip if child has no mother): his mother
if child has no parents say: Israel.
He will be known among the Jewish people
as (*child's Hebrew name*)
the son of (*father's name*). *(If the child has no halakhic father, the mother's name is inserted)*

If the father is naming the baby, he says:

May it be God's will
that I rejoice in the issue of my loins,
and may his mother be gladdened by the fruit of her womb.

If the child's father is deceased, this is said:

May the father rejoice in Paradise
in the issue of his loins,
and may his mother be gladdened by the fruit of her womb.

If the child's mother is deceased, this is said:

May the father rejoice
in the issue of his loins,
and may his mother be gladdened in Paradise by the fruit of her womb.

If the child's parents are deceased, this is said:

May the father rejoice in Paradise
in the issue of his loins,
and may his mother be gladdened in Paradise by the fruit of her womb.

Continue the naming ceremony from the words, "As it is written: "Let your father and your mother be glad" – page 18.

ALTERNATIVE VERSIONS FOR NAMING IN SPECIAL CIRCUMSTANCES

The מוהל *(or another honoree) takes the cup of wine and says the following to name the baby.*

אֱלֹהֵינוּ וֵאלֹהֵי אֲבוֹתֵינוּ, קַיֵּם אֶת הַיֶּלֶד הַזֶּה

אם אין לבן אב מדלגים "לאמו": **לְאָבִיו**

אם אין לבן אם מדלגים "לאביו": **(וּ)לְאִמּוֹ**

אם אין לבן אב ואם, אומרים: **לְיִשְׂרָאֵל**

וְיִקָּרֵא שְׁמוֹ בְּיִשְׂרָאֵל (שם הילד)

בֶּן (שם האב). (אם מבחינה הלכתית אין אב לבן, קוראים לו על שם אמו)

If the father is naming the baby, he says:

יְהִי רָצוֹן שֶׁאֶשְׂמַח בְּיוֹצֵא חֲלָצַי
וְתָגֵל אִמּוֹ בִּפְרִי בִטְנָהּ.

If the child's father is deceased, this is said:

יִשְׂמַח הָאָב בְּגַן עֵדֶן בְּיוֹצֵא חֲלָצָיו
וְתָגֵל אִמּוֹ בִּפְרִי בִטְנָהּ.

If the child's mother is deceased, this is said:

יִשְׂמַח הָאָב בְּיוֹצֵא חֲלָצָיו
וְתָגֵל אִמּוֹ בְּגַן עֵדֶן בִּפְרִי בִטְנָהּ.

If the child's parents are deceased, this is said:

יִשְׂמַח הָאָב בְּגַן עֵדֶן בְּיוֹצֵא חֲלָצָיו
וְתָגֵל אִמּוֹ בְּגַן עֵדֶן בִּפְרִי בִטְנָהּ.

Continue the naming ceremony from the words, כַּכָּתוּב: יִשְׂמַח־אָבִיךָ וְאִמֶּךָ, וְתָגֵל יוֹלַדְתֶּךָ *– page 19.*

PIYYUT FOR THE SEUDAT MITZVA

Some say the following during the seudat mitzvah.

יוֹם לְיַבָּשָׁה On the day that the deep waters became dry land,
Those who were redeemed gave praise with a new song.

Drowned in her deceit were the Anamite daughter's feet,
while the footsteps of the Shulamit were secured in their shoes.
Those who were redeemed gave praise with a new song.

Therefore will all who see Yeshurun give praise in My House of Glory,
declaring "There is none like Yeshurun's God" when our enemies will be judged.
Those who were redeemed gave praise with a new song.

Surely You will raise our banners over those who will remain,
when You will gather our dispersed as one who brings sheaves together.
Those who were redeemed gave praise with a new song.

Those who go with You bear Your seal of the covenant,
being circumcised they are dedicated to Your name from the womb.
Those who were redeemed gave praise with a new song.

Make known their sign of the covenant to all who will see them,
just as they in turn make fringes on the corners of their garments.
Those who were redeemed gave praise with a new song.

To whom is this one assigned, please recognize the truth,
whose is this seal, and whose these threads?
Those who were redeemed gave praise with a new song.

Return once more to betroth her, do not again send her away;
make the light of her sun arise once more, that the shadows flee away.
Those who were redeemed gave praise with a new song.

Your beloved ones raised You on high, greeted You with song, saying,
Who is like You, O Lord, among the mighty ones?
Those who were redeemed gave praise with a new song.

On account of the fathers please save the children
and bring redemption to their children's children.

פיוט לסעודת ברית מילה

Some say the following during the סעודת מצווה.

יוֹם לְיַבָּשָׁה נֶהֶפְכוּ מְצוּלִים
שִׁירָה חֲדָשָׁה שִׁבְּחוּ גְאוּלִים.

הִטְבַּעְתָּ בְּתַרְמִית / רַגְלֵי בַּת עֲנָמִית
וּפַעֲמֵי שׁוּלַמִּית / יָפוּ בַּנְּעָלִים. שִׁירָה חֲדָשָׁה שִׁבְּחוּ גְאוּלִים.

וְכָל רוֹאֵי יְשׁוּרוּן / בְּעֵת הוֹדְךָ יְשׁוֹרוּן
אֵין כָּאֵל יְשֻׁרוּן / וְאוֹיְבֵינוּ פְּלִילִים. שִׁירָה חֲדָשָׁה שִׁבְּחוּ גְאוּלִים.

דְּגָלַי כֵּן תָּרִים / עַל הַנִּשְׁאָרִים
וּתְלַקֵּט נְפוּרִים / כִּמְלַקֵּט שִׁבֳּלִים. שִׁירָה חֲדָשָׁה שִׁבְּחוּ גְאוּלִים.

הַבָּאִים עִמְּךָ / בִּבְרִית חוֹתָמְךָ
וּמִבֶּטֶן לְשִׁמְךָ / הֵמָּה נִמּוֹלִים. שִׁירָה חֲדָשָׁה שִׁבְּחוּ גְאוּלִים.

הַרְאוּ אוֹתוֹתָם / לְכָל רוֹאֶה אוֹתָם
וְעַל כַּנְפֵי כְסוּתָם / עֲשׂוּ גְּדִילִים. שִׁירָה חֲדָשָׁה שִׁבְּחוּ גְאוּלִים.

לְמִי זֹאת נִרְשֶׁמֶת / הַכֶּר נָא דְּבַר אֱמֶת
לְמִי הַחוֹתֶמֶת / וּלְמִי הַפְּתִילִים. שִׁירָה חֲדָשָׁה שִׁבְּחוּ גְאוּלִים.

וְשׁוּב שֵׁנִית לְקַדְּשָׁהּ / וְאַל תּוֹסֵף לְגָרְשָׁהּ
וְהַעֲלֵה אוֹר שִׁמְשָׁהּ / וְנָסוּ הַצְּלָלִים.
שִׁירָה חֲדָשָׁה שִׁבְּחוּ גְאוּלִים.

יְדִידִים רוֹמְמוּךָ / בְּשִׁירָה קִדְּמוּךָ
מִי כָמֹכָה / יהוה בָּאֵלִים. שִׁירָה חֲדָשָׁה שִׁבְּחוּ גְאוּלִים.

בִּגְלַל אָבוֹת תּוֹשִׁיעַ בָּנִים, וְתָבִיא גְאֻלָּה לִבְנֵי בְנֵיהֶם.

BIRKAT HAMAZON AT A BRIT MILA

שִׁיר הַמַּעֲלוֹת A song of ascents. When the LORD brought back the exiles of Zion, we were like dreamers – then were our mouths filled with laughter, our tongues with songs of joy; then was it said among the nations, "The LORD has done great things for them." The LORD has done great things for us, and we rejoiced. Bring back our exiles, LORD, like streams in the Negev. May those who sowed in tears reap in joy; may those who go out weeping, carrying a sack of seed, come back in glad song, carrying their sheaves. *Ps. 126*

Some say:

תְּהִלַּת My mouth shall speak the praise of the LORD, and all creatures shall bless His holy name for ever and all time. But we will bless the LORD now and forever. Halleluya! Thank the LORD for He is good – His loving-kindness is forever. Who can articulate the LORD's mighty acts; who can express all His praise? *Ps. 145* *Ps. 136*

The zimun when three or more men are present:

Leader: רַבּוֹתַי Esteemed companions, let us say grace.

Others: Blessed be the name of the LORD, now and for evermore. *Ps. 113*

Leader: Blessed be the name of the LORD, now and for evermore.

Leader: We give thanks to Your name among my faithful ones,
blessed are you to the LORD

Others: We give thanks to Your name among my faithful ones,
blessed are you to the LORD

Leader: With the permission of the God
Who is awesome and revered,
a fortress whenever there is trouble,
God Who is girded in might,
mighty is the LORD on high.

Others: We give thanks to Your name among my faithful ones,
blessed are you to the LORD

ברכת המזון לברית מילה

שִׁיר הַמַּעֲלוֹת, בְּשׁוּב יהוה אֶת־שִׁיבַת צִיּוֹן, הָיִינוּ כְּחֹלְמִים: תהלים קכו
אָז יִמָּלֵא שְׂחוֹק פִּינוּ וּלְשׁוֹנֵנוּ רִנָּה, אָז יֹאמְרוּ בַגּוֹיִם הִגְדִּיל
יהוה לַעֲשׂוֹת עִם־אֵלֶּה: הִגְדִּיל יהוה לַעֲשׂוֹת עִמָּנוּ, הָיִינוּ
שְׂמֵחִים: שׁוּבָה יהוה אֶת־שְׁבִיתֵנוּ, כַּאֲפִיקִים בַּנֶּגֶב: הַזֹּרְעִים
בְּדִמְעָה בְּרִנָּה יִקְצֹרוּ: הָלוֹךְ יֵלֵךְ וּבָכֹה נֹשֵׂא מֶשֶׁךְ־הַזָּרַע,
בֹּא־יָבֹא בְרִנָּה נֹשֵׂא אֲלֻמֹּתָיו:

Some say:

תְּהִלַּת יהוה יְדַבֶּר פִּי, וִיבָרֵךְ כָּל־בָּשָׂר שֵׁם קָדְשׁוֹ לְעוֹלָם תהלים קמה
וָעֶד: וַאֲנַחְנוּ נְבָרֵךְ יָהּ מֵעַתָּה וְעַד־עוֹלָם, הַלְלוּיָהּ: הוֹדוּ תהלים קטו תהלים קלו
לַיהוה כִּי־טוֹב, כִּי לְעוֹלָם חַסְדּוֹ: מִי יְמַלֵּל גְּבוּרוֹת יהוה, תהלים קו
יַשְׁמִיעַ כָּל־תְּהִלָּתוֹ:

The זימון *when three or more men are present:*

Leader רַבּוֹתַי, נְבָרֵךְ.

Others יְהִי שֵׁם יהוה מְבֹרָךְ מֵעַתָּה וְעַד־עוֹלָם: תהלים קיג

Leader יְהִי שֵׁם יהוה מְבֹרָךְ מֵעַתָּה וְעַד־עוֹלָם:

Leader נוֹדֶה לְשִׁמְךָ בְּתוֹךְ אֱמוּנַי, בְּרוּכִים אַתֶּם לַיהוה.

Others נוֹדֶה לְשִׁמְךָ בְּתוֹךְ אֱמוּנַי, בְּרוּכִים אַתֶּם לַיהוה.

Leader בִּרְשׁוּת אֵל אָיֹם וְנוֹרָא
מִשְׂגָּב לְעִתּוֹת בַּצָּרָה
אֵל נֶאְזָר בִּגְבוּרָה
אַדִּיר בַּמָּרוֹם יהוה.

Others נוֹדֶה לְשִׁמְךָ בְּתוֹךְ אֱמוּנַי, בְּרוּכִים אַתֶּם לַיהוה.

Leader: With the permission of the sacred Torah,
which is both pure and clear,
and which Moses, the servant of the LORD,
commanded us as our inheritance.

Others: We give thanks to Your name among my faithful ones,
blessed are you to the LORD

Leader: With the permission of the *Kohanim* and Levites,
I call upon the God of the Hebrews
to Whom I give thanks in every island,
and bless the LORD.

Others: We give thanks to Your name among my faithful ones,
blessed are you to the LORD

Leader: With your permission my masters,
teachers, and esteemed companions
I will open my mouth and my lips in song,
and my bones will declare
"Blessed is the one
who comes in the name of the LORD."

Others: We give thanks to Your name among my faithful ones,
blessed are you to the LORD

Leader: With your permission masters, teachers,
and esteemed companions
let us bless (*in a minyan:* our God) the One of Whose bounty
we have partaken.

Others: Blessed be (*in a minyan:* our God,) the One of Whose bounty
we have partaken and through Whose goodness we live.

Leader: Blessed be (*in a minyan:* our God,) the One of Whose bounty
we have partaken and through Whose goodness we live.
Blessed be He, and blessed be His name.

Leader בִּרְשׁוּת הַתּוֹרָה הַקְּדוֹשָׁה

טְהוֹרָה הִיא וְגַם פְּרוּשָׁה

צִוָּה לָנוּ מוֹרָשָׁה

מֹשֶׁה עֶבֶד יהוה.

Others נוֹדֶה לְשִׁמְךָ בְּתוֹךְ אֱמוּנַי, בְּרוּכִים אַתֶּם לַיהוה.

Leader בִּרְשׁוּת הַכֹּהֲנִים וְהַלְוִיִּם

אֶקְרָא לֵאלֹהֵי הָעִבְרִיִּים

אֲהוֹדֶנּוּ בְּכָל אִיִּים

אֲבָרְכָה אֶת יהוה.

Others נוֹדֶה לְשִׁמְךָ בְּתוֹךְ אֱמוּנַי, בְּרוּכִים אַתֶּם לַיהוה.

Leader בִּרְשׁוּת מָרָנָן וְרַבָּנָן וְרַבּוֹתַי

אֶפְתְּחָה בְּשִׁיר פִּי וּשְׂפָתַי

וְתֹאמַרְנָה עַצְמוֹתַי

בָּרוּךְ הַבָּא בְּשֵׁם יהוה.

Others נוֹדֶה לְשִׁמְךָ בְּתוֹךְ אֱמוּנַי, בְּרוּכִים אַתֶּם לַיהוה.

Leader בִּרְשׁוּת מָרָנָן וְרַבָּנָן וְרַבּוֹתַי

נְבָרֵךְ (במנין: אֱלֹהֵינוּ) שֶׁאָכַלְנוּ מִשֶּׁלּוֹ.

Others בָּרוּךְ (במנין: אֱלֹהֵינוּ) שֶׁאָכַלְנוּ מִשֶּׁלּוֹ וּבְטוּבוֹ חָיִינוּ.

Leader בָּרוּךְ (במנין: אֱלֹהֵינוּ) שֶׁאָכַלְנוּ מִשֶּׁלּוֹ וּבְטוּבוֹ חָיִינוּ.

בָּרוּךְ הוּא וּבָרוּךְ שְׁמוֹ.

BLESSING OF NOURISHMENT

בָּרוּךְ Blessed are You, Lord our God, King of the universe,
Who feeds the whole world in His goodness,
with grace, kindness, and mercy.
He gives food to all flesh,
for His mercy endures forever.
Thanks to His great goodness
we have never lacked what to eat.
For the sake of His great name
may we never be short of food,
for He is the God Who feeds and sustains all,
is good to all,
and provides food for all His creatures as created by Him.
Blessed are You, Lord,
Who provides food for all.

BLESSING FOR THE LAND

נוֹדֶה We thank You, Lord our God,
for the beloved, good, and spacious land
that You gave our fathers as an inheritance.
We thank You, Lord our God,
for bringing us out of the land of Egypt
and redeeming us from the house of bondage.
We thank You for Your covenant sealed in our flesh,
for Your Torah which You have taught us,
and for Your precepts that You made known to us.
We thank You also for the life, grace, and kindness
that You have graciously bestowed on us, and for the food we eat,
with which You nourish and sustain us continually,
every day, in every season, and at every hour.

ברכת הזן

בָּרוּךְ אַתָּה יהוה אֱלֹהֵינוּ מֶלֶךְ הָעוֹלָם
הַזָּן אֶת הָעוֹלָם כֻּלּוֹ בְּטוּבוֹ
בְּחֵן בְּחֶסֶד וּבְרַחֲמִים
הוּא נוֹתֵן לֶחֶם לְכָל בָּשָׂר, כִּי לְעוֹלָם חַסְדּוֹ.
וּבְטוּבוֹ הַגָּדוֹל, תָּמִיד לֹא חָסַר לָנוּ
וְאַל יֶחְסַר לָנוּ מָזוֹן לְעוֹלָם וָעֶד
בַּעֲבוּר שְׁמוֹ הַגָּדוֹל.
כִּי הוּא אֵל זָן וּמְפַרְנֵס לַכֹּל וּמֵטִיב לַכֹּל
וּמֵכִין מָזוֹן לְכָל בְּרִיּוֹתָיו אֲשֶׁר בָּרָא.
בָּרוּךְ אַתָּה יהוה, הַזָּן אֶת הַכֹּל.

ברכת הארץ

נוֹדֶה לְךָ, יהוה אֱלֹהֵינוּ
עַל שֶׁהִנְחַלְתָּ לַאֲבוֹתֵינוּ אֶרֶץ חֶמְדָּה טוֹבָה וּרְחָבָה
וְעַל שֶׁהוֹצֵאתָנוּ יהוה אֱלֹהֵינוּ מֵאֶרֶץ מִצְרַיִם
וּפְדִיתָנוּ מִבֵּית עֲבָדִים
וְעַל בְּרִיתְךָ שֶׁחָתַמְתָּ בִּבְשָׂרֵנוּ
וְעַל תּוֹרָתְךָ שֶׁלִּמַּדְתָּנוּ, וְעַל חֻקֶּיךָ שֶׁהוֹדַעְתָּנוּ
וְעַל חַיִּים חֵן וָחֶסֶד שֶׁחוֹנַנְתָּנוּ
וְעַל אֲכִילַת מָזוֹן שָׁאַתָּה זָן וּמְפַרְנֵס אוֹתָנוּ תָּמִיד
בְּכָל יוֹם וּבְכָל עֵת וּבְכָל שָׁעָה.

On Ḥanukka:

עַל הַנִּסִּים [We thank You] for the miracles, the deliverance, and the triumphant victories and salvation, as well as wars which You wrought for our ancestors in those days at this season.

בִּימֵי מַתִּתְיָהוּ It happened in the days of Mattathias son of Johanan, the Hasmonean high priest, and his sons. Then the cruel Hellenist power rose up to force Your people Israel to forget Your Torah and transgress the commands of Your will. In that hour of their distress, You in Your great mercy rose to take up their cause and defend their rights. Meting out retribution You delivered the strong into the hand of the weak, the many into the hand of the few, the impure into the hand of the pure, the evil ones into the hand of the righteous, and the wicked into the hand of devotees of Your Torah. You thereby made for Yourself a great and holy name throughout Your world, as well as bringing about great deliverance and salvation for Your people Israel (known) to this day. Then Your children came to the Holy of Holies in Your house, cleared Your Temple, purified Your holy place, kindled lights in Your holy courts, and instituted these eight days of Ḥanukka to give thanks and sing praise to Your great name.

Continue with "For all these."

On Purim:

עַל הַנִּסִּים [We thank You] for the miracles, the deliverance, and the triumphant victories and salvation, as well as wars which You wrought for our ancestors in those days at this season.

בִּימֵי מָרְדְּכַי In the days of Mordekhai and Esther, in Shushan the capital, when the wicked Haman rose up against them, he sought to kill, destroy, and annihilate all the Jews, young and old, children and *Esther 3* women alike, all in one day – the thirteenth day of the twelfth month, which is the month of Adar – and seize the plunder. In Your great mercy You nullified his counsel and subverted his designs, causing them to recoil on his own head so that he and his sons were hanged on the gallows.

Continue with "For all these."

בחנוכה:

עַל הַנִּסִּים וְעַל הַפֻּרְקָן וְעַל הַגְּבוּרוֹת וְעַל הַתְּשׁוּעוֹת וְעַל הַמִּלְחָמוֹת שֶׁעָשִׂיתָ לַאֲבוֹתֵינוּ בַּיָּמִים הָהֵם בַּזְּמַן הַזֶּה.

בִּימֵי מַתִּתְיָהוּ בֶּן יוֹחָנָן כֹּהֵן גָּדוֹל חַשְׁמוֹנַאי וּבָנָיו, כְּשֶׁעָמְדָה מַלְכוּת יָוָן הָרְשָׁעָה עַל עַמְּךָ יִשְׂרָאֵל לְהַשְׁכִּיחָם תּוֹרָתֶךָ וּלְהַעֲבִירָם מֵחֻקֵּי רְצוֹנֶךָ, וְאַתָּה בְּרַחֲמֶיךָ הָרַבִּים עָמַדְתָּ לָהֶם בְּעֵת צָרָתָם, רַבְתָּ אֶת רִיבָם, דַּנְתָּ אֶת דִּינָם, נָקַמְתָּ אֶת נִקְמָתָם, מָסַרְתָּ גִבּוֹרִים בְּיַד חַלָּשִׁים, וְרַבִּים בְּיַד מְעַטִּים, וּטְמֵאִים בְּיַד טְהוֹרִים, וּרְשָׁעִים בְּיַד צַדִּיקִים, וְזֵדִים בְּיַד עוֹסְקֵי תוֹרָתֶךָ, וּלְךָ עָשִׂיתָ שֵׁם גָּדוֹל וְקָדוֹשׁ בְּעוֹלָמֶךָ, וּלְעַמְּךָ יִשְׂרָאֵל עָשִׂיתָ תְּשׁוּעָה גְדוֹלָה וּפֻרְקָן כְּהַיּוֹם הַזֶּה. וְאַחַר כֵּן בָּאוּ בָנֶיךָ לִדְבִיר בֵּיתֶךָ, וּפִנּוּ אֶת הֵיכָלֶךָ, וְטִהֲרוּ אֶת מִקְדָּשֶׁךָ, וְהִדְלִיקוּ נֵרוֹת בְּחַצְרוֹת קָדְשֶׁךָ, וְקָבְעוּ שְׁמוֹנַת יְמֵי חֲנֻכָּה אֵלּוּ, לְהוֹדוֹת וּלְהַלֵּל לְשִׁמְךָ הַגָּדוֹל.

Continue with וְעַל הַכֹּל.

בפורים:

עַל הַנִּסִּים וְעַל הַפֻּרְקָן וְעַל הַגְּבוּרוֹת וְעַל הַתְּשׁוּעוֹת וְעַל הַמִּלְחָמוֹת שֶׁעָשִׂיתָ לַאֲבוֹתֵינוּ בַּיָּמִים הָהֵם בַּזְּמַן הַזֶּה.

בִּימֵי מָרְדְּכַי וְאֶסְתֵּר בְּשׁוּשַׁן הַבִּירָה, כְּשֶׁעָמַד עֲלֵיהֶם הָמָן
הָרָשָׁע, בִּקֵּשׁ לְהַשְׁמִיד לַהֲרֹג וּלְאַבֵּד אֶת־כָּל־הַיְּהוּדִים מִנַּעַר אסתר ג
וְעַד־זָקֵן טַף וְנָשִׁים בְּיוֹם אֶחָד, בִּשְׁלוֹשָׁה עָשָׂר לְחֹדֶשׁ שְׁנֵים־עָשָׂר, הוּא־חֹדֶשׁ אֲדָר, וּשְׁלָלָם לָבוֹז: וְאַתָּה בְּרַחֲמֶיךָ הָרַבִּים הֵפַרְתָּ אֶת עֲצָתוֹ, וְקִלְקַלְתָּ אֶת מַחֲשַׁבְתּוֹ, וַהֲשֵׁבוֹתָ לּוֹ גְּמוּלוֹ בְּרֹאשׁוֹ, וְתָלוּ אוֹתוֹ וְאֶת בָּנָיו עַל הָעֵץ.

Continue with וְעַל הַכֹּל.

וְעַל הַכֹּל For all these blessings, LORD our God,
we thank You and bless You.
May Your name be blessed, in the mouths of all living beings,
continually, forever and ever.
As it is written,
"And when you eat and are satisfied, *Deut. 8*
you shall bless the LORD your God
for the good land that He has given you."
Blessed are You, LORD,
for the land and for the sustenance.

BLESSING FOR JERUSALEM

רַחֵם (נָא) Have pity (please,) LORD our God,
on Israel Your people,
on Jerusalem Your city, and Zion
the dwelling place of Your glory,
on the royal house of David Your anointed,
and on the great and holy Temple
with which Your name is associated.
Our God, our Father,
shepherd us, sustain us, support us, provide for all our needs,
maintain us, and, LORD our God,
give us immediate relief from all our troubles.
LORD our God,
do not make us dependent
on the gifts of people of flesh and blood,
or in need of their loans.
Rather let us depend only
on Your full, open, sacred, and bountiful hand,
so that we need never be embarrassed or humiliated.

וְעַל הַכֹּל, יהוה אֱלֹהֵינוּ
אֲנַחְנוּ מוֹדִים לָךְ וּמְבָרְכִים אוֹתָךְ
יִתְבָּרַךְ שִׁמְךָ בְּפִי כָּל חַי תָּמִיד לְעוֹלָם וָעֶד
כַּכָּתוּב: וְאָכַלְתָּ וְשָׂבָעְתָּ, וּבֵרַכְתָּ אֶת־יהוה אֱלֹהֶיךָ דברים ח
עַל־הָאָרֶץ הַטֹּבָה אֲשֶׁר נָתַן־לָךְ:
בָּרוּךְ אַתָּה יהוה, עַל הָאָרֶץ וְעַל הַמָּזוֹן.

ברכת ירושלים

רַחֶם (נָא), יהוה אֱלֹהֵינוּ
עַל יִשְׂרָאֵל עַמֶּךָ, וְעַל יְרוּשָׁלַיִם עִירֶךָ
וְעַל צִיּוֹן מִשְׁכַּן כְּבוֹדֶךָ
וְעַל מַלְכוּת בֵּית דָּוִד מְשִׁיחֶךָ
וְעַל הַבַּיִת הַגָּדוֹל וְהַקָּדוֹשׁ שֶׁנִּקְרָא שִׁמְךָ עָלָיו.
אֱלֹהֵינוּ, אָבִינוּ
רְעֵנוּ, זוּנֵנוּ, פַּרְנְסֵנוּ וְכַלְכְּלֵנוּ
וְהַרְוִיחֵנוּ, וְהַרְוַח לָנוּ יהוה אֱלֹהֵינוּ מְהֵרָה מִכָּל צָרוֹתֵינוּ.
וְנָא אַל תַּצְרִיכֵנוּ, יהוה אֱלֹהֵינוּ
לֹא לִידֵי מַתְּנַת בָּשָׂר וָדָם
וְלֹא לִידֵי הַלְוָאָתָם
כִּי אִם לְיָדְךָ הַמְּלֵאָה, הַפְּתוּחָה, הַקְּדוֹשָׁה וְהָרְחָבָה
שֶׁלֹּא נֵבוֹשׁ וְלֹא נִכָּלֵם לְעוֹלָם וָעֶד.

On Shabbat, say:

רְצֵה Favor and invigorate us, LORD our God, with Your commandments,
and with the commandment of the seventh day,
this great and holy Sabbath.
For this day is great and holy before You,
for us to desist from work on it, and lovingly rest on it
in accordance with the commandment You have willed.
May it be Your will, LORD our God, to grant us a rest
during which there will be no sorrow, trouble, or sighing.
And, LORD our God, may You show us Zion Your city
comforted and the building of Jerusalem Your holy city,
for You are the Master of salvation, and the Master of consolation.

On Rosh Ḥodesh and Festivals, say:

אֱלֹהֵינוּ Our God and God of our fathers,
may there arise, arrive, reach, appear, be favored, heard,
considered and remembered, our remembrance and recollection,
Your remembrance of our fathers,
of the Messiah son of David Your servant,
of Jerusalem Your holy city
and of all Your people the house of Israel.
May they come before You for deliverance and benefit,
for grace, kindness, and mercy, for life and peace, on this day of:

On Rosh Ḥodesh:	Rosh Ḥodesh.
On Rosh HaShana:	the Day of Memorial.
On Pesaḥ:	the Festival of Matzot.
On Shavuot:	the Festival of Shavuot.
On Sukkot:	the Festival of Sukkot.
On Shemini Atzeret & Simḥat Torah:	the eighth day, this Festival of Atzeret.

LORD our God, remember us this day for good.
Be mindful of us this day for blessing, preserve us this day for life.
Regarding redemption and mercy show us compassion
and grace, and have pity on us and save us.
For our eyes are lifted toward You,
for You are a gracious and merciful God (*on Rosh HaShana:* King).

On שבת, *say:*

רְצֵה וְהַחֲלִיצֵנוּ, יהוה אֱלֹהֵינוּ, בְּמִצְוֹתֶיךָ
וּבְמִצְוַת יוֹם הַשְּׁבִיעִי הַשַּׁבָּת הַגָּדוֹל וְהַקָּדוֹשׁ הַזֶּה
כִּי יוֹם זֶה גָּדוֹל וְקָדוֹשׁ הוּא לְפָנֶיךָ
לִשְׁבָּת בּוֹ, וְלָנוּחַ בּוֹ בְּאַהֲבָה כְּמִצְוַת רְצוֹנֶךָ
וּבִרְצוֹנְךָ הָנִיחַ לָנוּ, יהוה אֱלֹהֵינוּ
שֶׁלֹּא תְהֵא צָרָה וְיָגוֹן וַאֲנָחָה בְּיוֹם מְנוּחָתֵנוּ
וְהַרְאֵנוּ, יהוה אֱלֹהֵינוּ, בְּנֶחָמַת צִיּוֹן עִירֶךָ
וּבְבִנְיַן יְרוּשָׁלַיִם עִיר קָדְשֶׁךָ
כִּי אַתָּה הוּא בַּעַל הַיְשׁוּעוֹת וּבַעַל הַנֶּחָמוֹת.

On ראש חודש *and* חגים, *say:*

אֱלֹהֵינוּ וֵאלֹהֵי אֲבוֹתֵינוּ
יַעֲלֶה וְיָבוֹא וְיַגִּיעַ, וְיֵרָאֶה וְיֵרָצֶה וְיִשָּׁמַע
וְיִפָּקֵד וְיִזָּכֵר זִכְרוֹנֵנוּ וּפִקְדוֹנֵנוּ, וְזִכְרוֹן אֲבוֹתֵינוּ
וְזִכְרוֹן מָשִׁיחַ בֶּן דָּוִד עַבְדֶּךָ, וְזִכְרוֹן יְרוּשָׁלַיִם עִיר קָדְשֶׁךָ
וְזִכְרוֹן כָּל עַמְּךָ בֵּית יִשְׂרָאֵל לְפָנֶיךָ
לִפְלֵיטָה לְטוֹבָה, לְחֵן וּלְחֶסֶד וּלְרַחֲמִים, לְחַיִּים וּלְשָׁלוֹם בְּיוֹם

בראש חודש: רֹאשׁ הַחֹדֶשׁ הַזֶּה.

בראש השנה: הַזִּכָּרוֹן הַזֶּה.

בפסח: חַג הַמַּצּוֹת הַזֶּה.

בשבועות: חַג הַשָּׁבוּעוֹת הַזֶּה.

בסוכות: חַג הַסֻּכּוֹת הַזֶּה.

בשמיני עצרת ושמחת תורה: הַשְּׁמִינִי חַג הָעֲצֶרֶת הַזֶּה.

זָכְרֵנוּ יהוה אֱלֹהֵינוּ בּוֹ לְטוֹבָה, וּפָקְדֵנוּ בוֹ לִבְרָכָה
וְהוֹשִׁיעֵנוּ בוֹ לְחַיִּים.
וּבִדְבַר יְשׁוּעָה וְרַחֲמִים, חוּס וְחָנֵּנוּ וְרַחֵם עָלֵינוּ, וְהוֹשִׁיעֵנוּ
כִּי אֵלֶיךָ עֵינֵינוּ, כִּי אֵל (בראש השנה: מֶלֶךְ) חַנּוּן וְרַחוּם אָתָּה.

וּבְנֵה Please rebuild Jerusalem the holy city soon in our own days. Blessed are You, Lord, Who in His mercy rebuilds Jerusalem. Amen.

BLESSING OF GOD'S GOODNESS

בָּרוּךְ Blessed are You, Lord our God, King of the universe,
God our Father, our King, our Sovereign,
our Creator, our Redeemer, our Maker, our Holy One,
Holy One of Jacob.
You are our Shepherd, Shepherd of Israel,
You are the King Who is good and Who does good to all.
For every single day He has done good, continues to do good,
and will do good for us.
Just as He has bestowed that upon us,
and continues to bestow it upon us,
so may He forever bestow upon us
grace, kindness, mercy, relief, salvation and success,
blessing and redemption, consolation, livelihood,
sustenance, compassion, life, peace,
and all manner of good things.
And may He never deprive us of any good thing.

ADDITIONAL REQUESTS

הָרַחֲמָן May the Compassionate One
reign over us forevermore.

May the Compassionate One be blessed
in the heavens and on earth.

May the Compassionate One be praised in every generation,
and glorified and honored among us
for all time, eternally.

וּבְנֵה יְרוּשָׁלַיִם עִיר הַקֹּדֶשׁ בִּמְהֵרָה בְיָמֵינוּ.
בָּרוּךְ אַתָּה יהוה, בּוֹנֵה בְרַחֲמָיו יְרוּשָׁלָיִם, אָמֵן.

ברכת הטוב והמטיב

בָּרוּךְ אַתָּה יהוה אֱלֹהֵינוּ מֶלֶךְ הָעוֹלָם
הָאֵל אָבִינוּ, מַלְכֵּנוּ, אַדִּירֵנוּ
בּוֹרְאֵנוּ, גּוֹאֲלֵנוּ, יוֹצְרֵנוּ, קְדוֹשֵׁנוּ, קְדוֹשׁ יַעֲקֹב
רוֹעֵנוּ, רוֹעֵה יִשְׂרָאֵל, הַמֶּלֶךְ הַטּוֹב וְהַמֵּטִיב לַכֹּל
שֶׁבְּכָל יוֹם וָיוֹם
הוּא הֵטִיב, הוּא מֵטִיב, הוּא יֵיטִיב לָנוּ
הוּא גְמָלָנוּ, הוּא גוֹמְלֵנוּ, הוּא יִגְמְלֵנוּ לָעַד
לְחֵן וּלְחֶסֶד וּלְרַחֲמִים, וּלְרֶוַח, הַצָּלָה וְהַצְלָחָה
בְּרָכָה וִישׁוּעָה, נֶחָמָה, פַּרְנָסָה וְכַלְכָּלָה
וְרַחֲמִים וְחַיִּים וְשָׁלוֹם וְכָל טוֹב
וּמִכָּל טוּב לְעוֹלָם אַל יְחַסְּרֵנוּ.

בקשות נוספות

הָרַחֲמָן הוּא יִמְלֹךְ עָלֵינוּ לְעוֹלָם וָעֶד.
הָרַחֲמָן הוּא יִתְבָּרַךְ בַּשָּׁמַיִם וּבָאָרֶץ.
הָרַחֲמָן הוּא יִשְׁתַּבַּח לְדוֹר דּוֹרִים
וְיִתְפָּאַר בָּנוּ לָעַד וּלְנֵצַח נְצָחִים
וְיִתְהַדַּר בָּנוּ לָעַד וּלְעוֹלְמֵי עוֹלָמִים.

May the Compassionate One maintain us
with honor.

May the Compassionate One break the yoke from our neck
and lead us upright to our land.

May the Compassionate One send us great blessing
on this household and on this table
at which we have eaten.

May the Compassionate One send us the prophet Elijah –
may he be remembered for good –
to herald good tidings of redemption and consolation.

הָרַחֲמָן May the Compassionate One bless –

When eating at one's own table, say
(include the words in parentheses that apply):
me, (my wife/husband, / my father, my teacher /
my mother, my teacher/ my children,)
and all that is mine,

A guest at someone else's table says
(include the words in parentheses that apply):
the head of this household, him (and his wife,
the head of this household / and his children,)
and all that is his,

Children at their parents' table say
(include the words in parentheses that apply):
my father, my teacher, (head of this household,)
and my mother, my teacher, (head of this household,)
them, their household, their children,
and all that is theirs.

For all other guests, add:
and all the diners here,

הָרַחֲמָן הוּא יְפַרְנְסֵנוּ בְּכָבוֹד.

הָרַחֲמָן הוּא יִשְׁבֹּר עֻלֵּנוּ מֵעַל צַוָּארֵנוּ
וְהוּא יוֹלִיכֵנוּ קוֹמְמִיּוּת לְאַרְצֵנוּ.

הָרַחֲמָן הוּא יִשְׁלַח לָנוּ בְּרָכָה מְרֻבָּה בַּבַּיִת הַזֶּה
וְעַל שֻׁלְחָן זֶה שֶׁאָכַלְנוּ עָלָיו.

הָרַחֲמָן הוּא יִשְׁלַח לָנוּ אֶת אֵלִיָּהוּ הַנָּבִיא זָכוּר לַטּוֹב
וִיבַשֶּׂר לָנוּ בְּשׂוֹרוֹת טוֹבוֹת יְשׁוּעוֹת וְנֶחָמוֹת.

הָרַחֲמָן הוּא יְבָרֵךְ

When eating at one's own table, say (include the words in parentheses that apply):

אוֹתִי (וְאֶת אִשְׁתִּי / וְאֶת בַּעֲלִי / וְאֶת אָבִי מוֹרִי / וְאֶת אִמִּי מוֹרָתִי / וְאֶת זַרְעִי) וְאֶת כָּל אֲשֶׁר לִי.

A guest at someone else's table says (include the words in parentheses that apply):

אֶת בַּעַל הַבַּיִת הַזֶּה, אוֹתוֹ (וְאֶת אִשְׁתּוֹ בַּעֲלַת הַבַּיִת הַזֶּה / וְאֶת זַרְעוֹ) וְאֶת כָּל אֲשֶׁר לוֹ.

Children at their parents' table say (include the words in parentheses that apply):

אֶת אָבִי מוֹרִי (בַּעַל הַבַּיִת הַזֶּה)
וְאֶת אִמִּי מוֹרָתִי (בַּעֲלַת הַבַּיִת הַזֶּה)
אוֹתָם וְאֶת בֵּיתָם וְאֶת זַרְעָם וְאֶת כָּל אֲשֶׁר לָהֶם

For all other guests, add:

וְאֶת כָּל הַמְסֻבִּין כָּאן

אוֹתָנוּ – together with us and all that is ours.
Just as our forefathers Abraham, Isaac, and Jacob were blessed
in all, from all, with all,
so may He bless all of us together with a complete blessing,
and let us say: Amen.

בַּמָּרוֹם In heaven may they invoke upon these people
and ourselves sufficient merit to ensure peace,
to bring blessing from the Lord,
and to have the God of our salvation treat us charitably.
May we find grace and good sense in the eyes of God and man.

The following six paragraphs are recited aloud by one or more men. Unlike sheva berakhot, the cup of wine is not passed between the participants.

Someone other than the baby's father says:

הָרַחֲמָן May the Compassionate One bless the father and mother
of the boy, to merit raising
and educating him to attain wisdom.
From this eighth day onward
may his (circumcision) blood be accepted,
so that the Lord his God be with him.

Someone other than the sandak says:

הָרַחֲמָן May the Compassionate One bless the *sandak*
who officiated during the *brit mila*,
while rejoicing in the performance
of a righteous deed with joy.
May He reward his deed in double measure,
raising him ever higher.

הָרַחֲמָן May the Compassionate One bless the tender boy
circumcised on the eighth day.
May his hands and heart be faithful to God,
and merit seeing the Divine Presence
three times a year.

אוֹתָֽנוּ וְאֶת כָּל אֲשֶׁר לָֽנוּ, כְּמוֹ שֶׁנִּתְבָּרְכוּ אֲבוֹתֵֽינוּ
אַבְרָהָם יִצְחָק וְיַעֲקֹב, בַּכֹּל, מִכֹּל, כֹּל
כֵּן יְבָרֵךְ אוֹתָֽנוּ כֻּלָּֽנוּ יַֽחַד בִּבְרָכָה שְׁלֵמָה, וְנֹאמַר אָמֵן.

בַּמָּרוֹם יְלַמְּדוּ עֲלֵיהֶם וְעָלֵֽינוּ זְכוּת שֶׁתְּהֵא לְמִשְׁמֶֽרֶת שָׁלוֹם
וְנִשָּׂא בְרָכָה מֵאֵת יהוה וּצְדָקָה מֵאֱלֹהֵי יִשְׁעֵֽנוּ
וְנִמְצָא חֵן וְשֵֽׂכֶל טוֹב בְּעֵינֵי אֱלֹהִים וְאָדָם.

The following six paragraphs are recited aloud by one or more men. Unlike שבע ברכות*, the cup of wine is not passed between the participants.*

Someone other than the baby's father says:

הָרַחֲמָן הוּא יְבָרֵךְ אֲבִי הַיֶּֽלֶד וְאִמּוֹ
וְיִזְכּוּ לְגַדְּלוֹ וּלְחַנְּכוֹ וּלְחַכְּמוֹ
מִיּוֹם הַשְּׁמִינִי וָהָֽלְאָה יֵרָצֶה דָמוֹ
וִיהִי יהוה אֱלֹהָיו עִמּוֹ.

Someone other than the סנדק *says:*

הָרַחֲמָן הוּא יְבָרֵךְ בַּֽעַל בְּרִית הַמִּילָה
אֲשֶׁר שָׂשׂ לַעֲשׂוֹת צֶֽדֶק בְּגִילָה
וִישַׁלֵּם פָּעֳלוֹ וּמַשְׂכֻּרְתּוֹ כְּפוּלָה
וְיִתְּנֵֽהוּ לְמַֽעְלָה לְמָֽעְלָה.

הָרַחֲמָן הוּא יְבָרֵךְ רַךְ הַנִּמּוֹל לִשְׁמוֹנָה
וְיִהְיוּ יָדָיו וְלִבּוֹ לָאֵל אֱמוּנָה
וְיִזְכֶּה לִרְאוֹת פְּנֵי הַשְּׁכִינָה
שָׁלֹשׁ פְּעָמִים בַּשָּׁנָה.

Someone other than the mohel says:

הָרַחֲמָן May the Compassionate One bless the one
who circumcised the flesh,
and also uncovered the membrane
and drew the blood of circumcision.
Had he been fearful and faint-hearted
and thus failed to perform
all three acts, his labors would have been disqualified.

הָרַחֲמָן May the Compassionate One send us
the anointed Messiah of perfect faith,
in the merit of the one
whose circumcision blood has initiated him.
May the Messiah be the herald of good news and consolation
for the singular nation scattered
and dispersed among the nations.

הָרַחֲמָן May the Compassionate One send us
(Elijah) the righteous *Kohen* who went into hiding
to reappear as bright as the sun and a diamond
whenever a chair would be prepared for him.
It was he who covered his face with his cloak
when he heard God say
"My covenant of life and peace will accompany him."

On Shabbat: May the Compassionate One cause us to inherit the time that is entirely Sabbath with repose in eternal life.

On Rosh Ḥodesh: May the Compassionate One renew for us this month for good and for blessing.

On Rosh HaShana: May the Compassionate One renew for us this year for good and for blessing.

On Yom Tov: May the Compassionate One cause us to inherit a day that is entirely good.

On Sukkot: May the Compassionate One reestablish for us the fallen Tabernacle of David.

Someone other than the מוהל *says:*

הָרַחֲמָן הוּא יְבָרֵךְ הַמָּל בְּשַׂר הָעָרְלָה
וּפָרַע וּמָצַץ דְּמֵי הַמִּילָה
אִישׁ הַיָּרֵא וְרַךְ הַלֵּבָב עֲבוֹדָתוֹ פְּסוּלָה
אִם שְׁלָשׁ אֵלֶּה לֹא יַעֲשֶׂה לָהּ.

הָרַחֲמָן הוּא יִשְׁלַח לָנוּ מְשִׁיחוֹ הוֹלֵךְ תָּמִים
בִּזְכוּת חֲתַן לַמּוּלוֹת דָּמִים
לְבַשֵּׂר בְּשׂוֹרוֹת טוֹבוֹת וְנִחוּמִים
לְעַם אֶחָד מְפֻזָּר וּמְפֹרָד בֵּין הָעַמִּים.

הָרַחֲמָן הוּא יִשְׁלַח לָנוּ כֹּהֵן צֶדֶק אֲשֶׁר לֻקַּח לְעֵילוֹם
עַד הוּכַן כִּסְאוֹ כַּשֶּׁמֶשׁ וְיַהֲלוֹם
וַיָּלֶט פָּנָיו בְּאַדַּרְתּוֹ וַיִּגְלֹם
בְּרִיתִי הָיְתָה אִתּוֹ הַחַיִּים וְהַשָּׁלוֹם.

בשבת: הָרַחֲמָן הוּא יַנְחִילֵנוּ
יוֹם שֶׁכֻּלּוֹ שַׁבָּת וּמְנוּחָה לְחַיֵּי הָעוֹלָמִים.

בראש חודש: הָרַחֲמָן הוּא יְחַדֵּשׁ עָלֵינוּ
אֶת הַחֹדֶשׁ הַזֶּה לְטוֹבָה וְלִבְרָכָה.

בראש השנה: הָרַחֲמָן הוּא יְחַדֵּשׁ עָלֵינוּ
אֶת הַשָּׁנָה הַזֹּאת לְטוֹבָה וְלִבְרָכָה.

ביום טוב: הָרַחֲמָן הוּא יַנְחִילֵנוּ יוֹם שֶׁכֻּלּוֹ טוֹב.

בסוכות: הָרַחֲמָן הוּא יָקִים לָנוּ אֶת סֻכַּת דָּוִד הַנּוֹפֶלֶת.

הָרַחֲמָן May the Compassionate One make us worthy
of the Messianic Age and the life of the World to Come.
On weekdays: He grants great victories *II Sam. 22*
/ *On Shabbat, Festivals, and Rosh Ḥodesh:* He is a Tower of victory /
for His king and shows loyalty to His anointed,
to David and his seed forever.
May He Who makes peace in the highest heaven
make peace for us and for all Israel,
and say, Amen.

יְראוּ Fear the Lord, you His holy ones, *Ps. 34*
for those who fear Him lack nothing.
Lions may grow weak and hungry,
but those who seek the Lord will never lack any good.
Thank the Lord for He is good; His loving-kindness is forever. *Ps. 118*
You open Your hand and satisfy the needs of every living thing. *Ps. 145*
Blessed is the person who trusts in the Lord. *Jer. 17*
The Lord will be his protector.
I was once young; now I am old, *Ps. 37*
yet I have never seen the righteous forsaken,
with their children begging for bread.
May the Lord give might to His people; *Ps. 29*
may the Lord bless His people with peace.

The Leader then recites the blessing over wine before drinking.

בָּרוּךְ Blessed are You, Lord, our God, King of the universe,
Who creates the fruit of the vine.

הָרַחֲמָן הוּא יְזַכֵּנוּ לִימוֹת הַמָּשִׁיחַ וּלְחַיֵּי הָעוֹלָם הַבָּא
מַגְדִּל/ *On* שבת, חגים, *and* ראש חודש מִגְדּוֹל/ יְשׁוּעוֹת מַלְכּוֹ שמואל ב׳ כב
וְעֹשֶׂה־חֶסֶד לִמְשִׁיחוֹ, לְדָוִד וּלְזַרְעוֹ עַד־עוֹלָם:
עֹשֶׂה שָׁלוֹם בִּמְרוֹמָיו
הוּא יַעֲשֶׂה שָׁלוֹם עָלֵינוּ וְעַל כָּל יִשְׂרָאֵל
וְאִמְרוּ אָמֵן.

יְראוּ אֶת־יהוה קְדֹשָׁיו, כִּי־אֵין מַחְסוֹר לִירֵאָיו: תהלים לד
כְּפִירִים רָשׁוּ וְרָעֵבוּ
וְדֹרְשֵׁי יהוה לֹא־יַחְסְרוּ כָל־טוֹב:
הוֹדוּ לַיהוה כִּי־טוֹב, כִּי לְעוֹלָם חַסְדּוֹ: תהלים קיח
פּוֹתֵחַ אֶת־יָדֶךָ, וּמַשְׂבִּיעַ לְכָל־חַי רָצוֹן: תהלים קמה
בָּרוּךְ הַגֶּבֶר אֲשֶׁר יִבְטַח בַּיהוה, וְהָיָה יהוה מִבְטַחוֹ: ירמיה יז
נַעַר הָיִיתִי גַּם־זָקַנְתִּי תהלים לז
וְלֹא־רָאִיתִי צַדִּיק נֶעֱזָב וְזַרְעוֹ מְבַקֶּשׁ־לָחֶם:
יהוה עֹז לְעַמּוֹ יִתֵּן, יהוה יְבָרֵךְ אֶת־עַמּוֹ בַשָּׁלוֹם: תהלים כט

The Leader then recites the blessing over wine before drinking.

בָּרוּךְ אַתָּה יהוה אֱלֹהֵינוּ מֶלֶךְ הָעוֹלָם, בּוֹרֵא פְּרִי הַגָּפֶן.

THE RABBINIC ROAD: CHALLENGES AND OPPORTUNITIES

NAMING A CHILD

The decisions surrounding the naming of a newborn or adopted child are often fraught with deep emotion. The desire to memorialize departed loved ones (within the Ashkenazic community) or to show abiding respect for living relatives (within the Sephardic community) often competes with parental preferences for other, more "socially acceptable" names. Tension can develop between husband and wife or between children and parents, marring a time of overwhelming joy. Coursing beneath the proceedings is the recognition of the permanence of the decision to be made, as parents wrestle with the first legacy to be bestowed by them upon their child.

The rabbi's role in the proceedings can be complex. As much as he would like to avoid being drawn into intra-family dynamics, he may be called upon to offer not only his advice, but his opinion. He should do so clearly, when warranted, but with sensitivity; offering his rabbinic expertise while clearly respecting the boundaries that demarcate the parents' domain.

- Beyond the well-known Ashkenazic practice of naming a child after departed relatives and the Sephardic practice of naming after living relatives, the rabbi should acquaint himself with other, less familiar, traditions and practices within both communities.

  For example, while there are no hard and fast rules, it is common practice for a Sephardic father to be given the right to choose the name of a firstborn child. In the Ashkenazic community, that right is traditionally granted to the mother.
- At times a family will possess a "mistaken" tradition concerning

a proposed name. The suggested name might be a diminutive of a proper Jewish name or simply a "name" with no clear basis, passed down in total error. In such cases, the rabbi should gently, but firmly, identify the error and suggest alternative possibilities that are as close to the proposed name as possible.

- Naming a child for a deceased relative is an emotionally charged decision and, according to tradition, a *zekhut* for the deceased. However, often there are pressures to add a name, whether because the deceased passed away at an early age (see *halakha* section), the parents have a preference for a different name, or they wish to honor more than one relative.

  It is the rabbi's role to guide the parents regarding traditional Jewish thought on these issues and then help them best balance that information with their own wishes and the wishes of grandparents and others.

- If the rabbi is unable to move the family toward the traditionally preferred decisions, he should reassure them that any decision they come to will be accepted in heaven and that, with God's help, their child will thrive and grow to be a wonderful member of Knesset Yisrael.

HALAKHOT CONCERNING NAMING A CHILD

WHEN TO NAME A CHILD: BOYS

1. Traditionally, boys are named at the time of the *brit mila*. If the *brit mila* is delayed, however, some authorities recommend that the child be named when the father receives an *aliya* to the Torah, so that prayers can be offered on behalf of the child with his given name (או נדברו יג:עג; הרב מאיר אייזיקואהן בשו"ת המאור ח"א עמ' קלה). Other authorities rule that in such a case the name should not be given until the *brit mila* (שו"ת המאור - שם).
2. If the *brit* of a *bekhor* was postponed due to illness of the baby, and the *pidyon haben* takes place before the *brit mila*, it is customary to name the baby at the *pidyon haben* (שערים מצויינים בהלכה ח"ד קסד:ג הערה 7).
3. If a boy is named prior to his *brit mila*, the *keriat hashem* is still recited at the *brit mila*. Some suggest that the wording be changed from *veyikareh shemo beYisrael* to *venikra shemo beYisrael*, though common practice is to retain the usual wording (או נדברו - שם; אוצר הברית ו:ב הערה ג).

WHEN TO NAME A CHILD: GIRLS

1. There is no definitive halakhic rule as to when a girl should be named (ציץ אליעזר ח"יג כ:ס). Many customs have developed, however, concerning the ideal time for the naming of a girl. Among the more common customs are:
   - A. The naming should occur at the father's first opportunity to receive an *aliya* (i.e., the first Monday, Thursday, or Shabbat after the child's birth) (מנחת יצחק ד:קז).
   - B. The naming should wait until the father receives an *aliya* on

the first Shabbat after the child's birth, in order to allow the occasion to be celebrated with a special meal. (שם).

C. The naming should wait until at least five days have passed after the child's birth (unless the third or fourth day is a Shabbat) (שם).

D. The naming should wait until the mother can come to the synagogue to recite *Birkat HaGomel* (but no longer than four weeks after the birth) (סידור בית יעקב כמנהג ספרד עמ׳ ריב).

2. If the father is out of town when his daughter is born, some maintain the custom of waiting until he returns to name the child (ספר הברית פירוטינסקי רסה:נה).

3. As all the above customs are legitimate, individuals should follow their family tradition without unnecessarily delaying the naming of the child. The key is to act for the sake of Heaven (מנחת יצחק – שם; משנה הלכות ח״ו רנד).

MI SHEBERAKH OF RABBI MOSHE FEINSTEIN

1. In a responsa, Rabbi Moshe Feinstein published his version of the *Mi Sheberakh* for naming a girl. Unlike the version printed in most *siddurim*, this version separates the prayer for the mother's health from the naming of the child (אגרות משה או״ח ד:סו).

   In addition, Rabbi Feinstein offered the option of inserting the words *legadla leTora uleven Tora* into the text of the *Mi Sheberakh*.

ZEVED HABAT

1. Among Sephardim there is a naming ceremony for girls called *zeved habat* – (lit. "the gift of a daughter" cf. Genesis 30:20) (בירת מגדל עז ליעב״ץ ברכות שמים שוקת ב׳ לנקבה). While this is not an Ashkenazic custom, many use this ceremony to celebrate the birth of a daughter (ויקרא שמו בישראל פרק ו הערה קט).

2. Some maintain the custom of serving a festive meal when naming

a daughter (טעמי המנהגים סימן תתקכט ד״ה ובספר המאור הגדול). This meal can be considered a *seudat mitzva* (ים של שלמה ב״ק ז:לז).

HALAKHIC ISSUES WITH CHOOSING A NAME

1. Some have a tradition to avoid naming a child for a person who died young (ים של שלמה גיטין ד:לא), unless an additional name is given as well (אגרות משה יו״ד ב:קכב). There are authorities, however, who permit using the name of one who died young (אגרות משה - שם, אוצר הידיעות חלק א (אייזנברגר) עמ׳ 640 בשם הרב יוסף אליהו הענקין).
2. While modern Hebrew names (those not found in *Tanakh*) are sometimes discouraged (איש וביתו פרק כג עמ׳ 301), many authorities find no issue with using such names (משנה הלכות ח״ט:שח; ספר ויקרא שמו בישראל פרק טו הערה א).
3. Using feminine versions of masculine names to name a girl for a man or vice versa is a longstanding practice and is not forbidden. Some authorities, however, discourage this practice. (ציץ אליעזר ח״ז סימן מ״ט פרק י״ג; שו״ת המאור - שם).
4. Naming a child for someone who passed away is considered a merit for the soul of the deceased. In addition, the Chazon Ish maintained that it is a merit for the child when a name is chosen in connection with the *parasha* of the Shabbat of the child's birth (אבני ישפה יורה דעה סימן קצו).
5. Often a child is named after multiple individuals. Some authorities object to the practice, ruling that the composite name is a different name (פאר הדור ח״ד עמ׳ ר). Others permit this only when the child will be called by both names (תשובות והנהגות ח״א תרח). Nevertheless, it is common custom to name a child after several individuals and to consider this a merit for all of their souls (ס׳ קוראי שמו עמ 148).

NAMING A CHILD

A special prayer for the mother and her newborn daughter, based on Rabbi Moshe Feinstein's ruling (Igrot Moshe OC 4:67).

מִי שֶׁבֵּרַךְ May He Who blessed our fathers
Abraham, Isaac, and Jacob,
Moses and Aaron, David and Solomon,
bless the mother (*mother's Hebrew name*)
daughter of (*her mother's mother's Hebrew name*)
who has given birth, together with her daughter
who has been born to her in good fortune
and for which her husband/father/father-in-law
has come up to the Torah.
In merit of this, may the Holy One, Blessed is God,
be filled with compassion for her to restore her health,
to heal her, to strengthen her, and to revitalize her.
May God send her a complete recovery from heaven
for all her organs and veins,
among the other sick people in Israel,
a recovery of the spirit and a recovery of the body –
(*On Shabbat or Yom Tov add:* though on the Sabbath/Yom Tov
it is forbidden to cry out),
yet may the recovery be speedily and in due time;
and (may God bless) her daughter who has been born to her
in good fortune for length of days and years;
let her name in Israel
be called (*child's Hebrew name*)
the daughter of (*father's name*). *(If the child has no halakhic father, mother's name is inserted)*
May her father (*omit "father" if the child has no halakhic father*) and mother
merit raising her to Torah, to marriage with a lover of Torah,
the marriage canopy, and good deeds, and let us say, Amen.

נתינת השם

A special prayer for the mother and her newborn daughter, based on Rabbi Moshe Feinstein's ruling (אגרות משה או״ח ח״ד ס״ז)*:*

מִי שֶׁבֵּרַךְ אֲבוֹתֵינוּ אַבְרָהָם יִצְחָק וְיַעֲקֹב
משֶׁה וְאַהֲרֹן דָּוִד וּשְׁלֹמֹה
הוּא יְבָרֵךְ אֶת הָאִשָּׁה הַיּוֹלֶדֶת (שם האם) **בַּת** (שם אמה)
עִם בִּתָּהּ שֶׁנּוֹלְדָה לָהּ לְמַזָּל טוֹב
בַּעֲבוּר שֶׁבַּעְלָהּ/אָבִיהָ/חָמִיהָ עָלָה לַתּוֹרָה.
בִּשְׂכַר זֶה הַקָּדוֹשׁ בָּרוּךְ הוּא יִמָּלֵא רַחֲמִים עָלֶיהָ
לְהַחֲלִימָהּ וּלְרַפְּאתָהּ וּלְהַחֲזִיקָהּ וּלְהַחֲיוֹתָהּ
וְיִשְׁלַח לָהּ מְהֵרָה רְפוּאָה שְׁלֵמָה מִן הַשָּׁמַיִם
לְכָל אֵבָרֶיהָ וּלְכָל גִּידֶיהָ
בְּתוֹךְ שְׁאָר חוֹלֵי יִשְׂרָאֵל
רְפוּאַת הַנֶּפֶשׁ וּרְפוּאַת הַגּוּף
(בשבת: **שַׁבָּת הִיא** / ביום טוב: **יוֹם טוֹב הוּא** /
מִלִּזְעֹק וּרְפוּאָה קְרוֹבָה לָבוֹא)
הַשְׁתָּא בַּעֲגָלָא וּבִזְמַן קָרִיב
וְאֶת בִּתָּהּ שֶׁנּוֹלְדָה לָהּ לְמַזָּל טוֹב, לְאֹרֶךְ יָמִים וְשָׁנִים;
וְיִקָּרֵא שְׁמָהּ בְּיִשְׂרָאֵל
(שם הילדה) **בַּת** (שם האב) (אם מבחינה הלכתית אין אב לבת, קוראים לה על שם אמה)**,**
וְיִזְכּוּ אָבִיהָ וְאִמָּהּ (אם מבחינה הלכתית אין אב לבת, אומרים: **וְתִזְכֶּה אִמָּהּ**)
לְגַדְּלָהּ לְתוֹרָה וּלְבֶן תּוֹרָה וּלְחֻפָּה וּלְמַעֲשִׂים טוֹבִים
וְנֹאמַר אָמֵן.

ZEVED HABAT

The leader says:

יוֹנָתִי O my dove, who is in the clefts of the rock, *Song. 2*
in the covert of the cliff, let me see your countenance,
let me hear your voice; for sweet is your voice,
and your countenance is comely.

If this is their first daughter, the mother or father adds:

אַחַת My dove, my undefiled, is but one; *Song. 6*
she is the only one of her mother;
she is the choice one of her that bore her.
The daughters saw her, and called her happy;
the queens and the concubines, and they praised her.

וַיְבָרְכוּ And they blessed Rebecca, *Gen. 24*
and said to her: "Our sister,
may you be the mother of thousands of ten thousands,
and may your seed possess the gate of those that hate them."

The leader says:

This prayer may be said even if the baby was already named in the Synagogue.

מִי שֶׁבֵּרַךְ May He Who blessed our mothers Sarah, Rebecca, Rachel, Leah, Miriam the prophetess, Avigail and Queen Esther daughter of Avihayil, bless this pleasant child, and she will be known among the Jewish people by the name *(child's name)* daughter of (*child's father's name*), at an auspicious time and in a time of blessing, and may she be raised to Torah and commandments in good health, peace and tranquility, and may her father and mother merit to witness her in joy and under the marriage canopy, with sons and daughters, wealth and honor. "They will still bring forth fruit in old age. They will be fat and *Ps. 92*
flourishing." And may it be His will, and let us say, Amen.

סדר זבד הבת

The leader says:

יוֹנָתִי בְּחַגְוֵי הַסֶּלַע, בְּסֵתֶר הַמַּדְרֵגָה שיר השירים ב
הַרְאִינִי אֶת־מַרְאַיִךְ, הַשְׁמִיעִנִי אֶת־קוֹלֵךְ
כִּי־קוֹלֵךְ עָרֵב וּמַרְאֵיךְ נָאוֶה:

If this is their first daughter, the mother or father adds:

אַחַת הִיא יוֹנָתִי תַמָּתִי שיר השירים ו
אַחַת הִיא לְאִמָּהּ, בָּרָה הִיא לְיוֹלַדְתָּהּ
רָאוּהָ בָנוֹת וַיְאַשְּׁרוּהָ, מְלָכוֹת וּפִילַגְשִׁים וַיְהַלְלוּהָ:

וַיְבָרְכוּ אֶת־רִבְקָה וַיֹּאמְרוּ לָהּ אֲחֹתֵנוּ אַתְּ בראשית כד
הֲיִי לְאַלְפֵי רְבָבָה
וְיִירַשׁ זַרְעֵךְ אֵת שַׁעַר שֹׂנְאָיו:

The leader says:
This prayer may be said even if the baby was already named in the בית הכנסת.

מִי שֶׁבֵּרַךְ אִמּוֹתֵינוּ שָׂרָה רִבְקָה, רָחֵל וְלֵאָה וּמִרְיָם הַנְּבִיאָה וַאֲבִיגַיִל וְאֶסְתֵּר הַמַּלְכָּה בַּת אֲבִיחַיִל, הוּא יְבָרֵךְ אֶת הַיַּלְדָּה הַנְּעִימָה הַזֹּאת, וְיִקָּרֵא שְׁמָהּ בְּיִשְׂרָאֵל (פלונית בַּת פלוני) בְּמַזָּל טוֹב וּבִשְׁעַת בְּרָכָה, וִיגַדְּלוּהָ לְתוֹרָה וּלְמִצְוֹת בִּבְרִיאוּת, שָׁלוֹם וּמְנוּחָה, וִיזַכֶּה אֶת אָבִיהָ וְאֶת אִמָּהּ לִרְאוֹת בְּשִׂמְחָתָהּ וּבְחֻפָּתָהּ, בְּבָנִים וּבְבָנוֹת, עֹשֶׁר וְכָבוֹד. עוֹד יְנוּבוּן בְּשֵׂיבָה, דְּשֵׁנִים וְרַעֲנַנִּים יִהְיוּ, וְכֵן יְהִי רָצוֹן תהלים צב
וְנֹאמַר, אָמֵן.

If the mother has not yet recited the HaGomel blessing, she recites it in the presence of a minyan of men.

בָּרוּךְ Blessed are You, Lord, our God, King of the universe,
Who bestows favors on the undeserving,
and Who has bestowed every good thing on me.

Those present respond:

Amen. May He Who has bestowed every good thing on you
continue to grant you every good thing, forever.

The parents place their hands on their newborn child's head and bless her:

יְשִׂימֵךְ May God make you
like Sarah, Rebecca, Rachel, and Leah. *Num. 6*
May the Lord bless you and keep you.
May the Lord make His countenance shine upon you
and be gracious to you.
May the Lord lift up His countenance to you
and give you peace.

יְפַת עַיִן You, of beautiful eye, have captured my heart,
Show me your glowing coutenance!
Sing your joyful song in the city of Zion,
Then will I return your captivity to there.

I have hoped for your redemption, / Your salvation is near,
My God, return to Your resting place,
Clothe me in garments of salvation.

Awaken, bride, beloved daughter,
Be strong and return through repentance,
You will be called Hefzibah, / Let me hear your voice facing me!

Build me my glorious house, God, / And restore my worship,
And I will sing my song there,
I will find favor, for You will have comforted me.

If the mother has not yet recited ברכת הגומל*,*
she recites it in the presence of a מנין *of men.*

בָּרוּךְ אַתָּה יהוה אֱלֹהֵינוּ מֶלֶךְ הָעוֹלָם
הַגּוֹמֵל לְחַיָּבִים טוֹבוֹת, שֶׁגְּמָלַנִי כָּל טוֹב.

Those present respond:

אָמֵן. מִי שֶׁגְּמָלֵךְ כָּל טוֹב
הוּא יִגְמְלֵךְ כָּל טוֹב, סֶלָה.

The parents place their hands on their newborn child's head and bless her:

יְשִׂמֵךְ אֱלֹהִים כְּשָׂרָה רִבְקָה רָחֵל וְלֵאָה.

יְבָרֶכְךָ יהוה וְיִשְׁמְרֶךָ: במדבר ו
יָאֵר יהוה פָּנָיו אֵלֶיךָ וִיחֻנֶּךָּ:
יִשָּׂא יהוה פָּנָיו אֵלֶיךָ, וְיָשֵׂם לְךָ שָׁלוֹם:

יְפַת עַיִן לְבַבְתִּינִי / זְהַר פָּנַיִךְ הַרְאִינִי
בְּעִיר צִיּוֹן שִׁיר הַרְנִינִי / וְאָז אָשִׁיב שְׁבוּתֵךְ שָׁם

שִׂבַּרְתִּי לִגְאֻלָּתֵךְ / קְרוֹבָה יְשׁוּעָתֵךְ
אֵלַי שׁוּבָה לִמְנוּחָתֵךְ / בִּגְדֵי יֶשַׁע הַלְבִּישִׁינִי

עוּרִי כַּלָּה בַּת אֲהוּבָה / חִזְקִי וְשׁוּבִי בִּתְשׁוּבָה
וְלָךְ יִקָּרֵא חֶפְצִי בָהּ / לְמוּל קוֹלֵךְ הַשְׁמִיעִינִי

יָהּ בְּנֵה לִי בֵּית תִּפְאַרְתִּי / וְהָשֵׁב אֶת עֲבוֹדָתִי
וְשָׁם אָשִׁיר אֶת שִׁירָתִי / אֶמְצָא חֵן כִּי נִחַמְתָּנִי

THE RABBINIC ROAD: CHALLENGES AND OPPORTUNITIES

PIDYON HABEN

While not a rarity, a *pidyon haben* occurs less frequently than other life cycle events. Its rules and regulations are, therefore, less familiar to the layman. In addition, because the *pidyon* is usually marked in a low-key fashion, the tension that often accompanies the preparation for other ritual occasions is singularly absent.

The rabbi, therefore, is granted the welcome opportunity to interact *benaḥat* with parents, as he guides them in the timing, execution, and meaning of the *pidyon*.

- The rabbi should familiarize himself with the (sometimes complex) rules that govern the necessity for and the timing of a pending *pidyon haben*. He should also be aware of the various *minhagim* associated with the ritual and, where there are choices, clearly delineate which path his community will follow.
- In addition to the halakhic guidance offered to the family, the rabbi should share practical information as well. What type of coinage can be used, where such coinage can be acquired, a list of *kohanim* in the community who are willing to participate in a *pidyon* in the absence of a family's preferred *Kohen*, are among the topics that can be covered by the rabbi in his advice to the family as he helps ease the process along.
- As with all events, the rabbi should take the time to discuss the significance and meaning of the *pidyon haben* ceremony with the family. If the mother of the child is reluctant to proceed with the *pidyon haben*, the rabbi should discuss this matter with her privately. There have been instances when the mother had a previous pregnancy of which her husband was unaware. (יביע אומר ח״ח יו״ד לב)

HALAKHOT CONCERNING PIDYON HABEN

WHO REQUIRES PIDYON

1. A male child, first born to his mother, whose father is neither a *Kohen* nor a *Levi,* and whose mother is neither the daughter of a *Kohen* nor a *Levi,* requires *pidyon haben.* If a man has had more than one wife, each woman's firstborn son is subject to *pidyon haben* (יו"ד שה:יז-יח).
2. A son delivered by Cesarean section is not subject to the obligation of *pidyon haben.* Following the birth of a child by Cesarean section, a son delivered vaginally is also exempt from the obligation of *pidyon haben* (יו"ד שה:כד).
3. Nowadays, a son delivered with forceps requires *pidyon haben* (נשמת אברהם ח"ב יו"ד שה ס"ק ה, אג"מ יו"ד ח"ג סימן קכה).
4. If a woman miscarried her first child:
   - A. If the miscarriage occured less than forty days after conception, a *pidyon haben* is required for the next child born, if it is a boy (יו"ד שה:כג).
   - B. If the miscarriage occured more than forty days after conception, but the fetus did not have the appearance of a child (*tzurat ha'vlad*), a subsequent son is required to have a *pidyon haben* (יו"ד שה:כג).
5. A woman's firstborn son, conceived with a non-Jewish man, is obligated in *pidyon haben.* This obligation applies even if the woman involved is the daughter of a *Kohen* (but not if the woman involved is the daughter of a *Levi*) (יו"ד שה:יט).
6. If a daughter of a *Kohen* had prior sexual relations with a non-Jew, and later gave birth to a firstborn son whose father is Jewish, that son requires a *pidyon haben* (באר היטב יו"ד שה ס"ק יט).
7. A woman's firstborn son conceived through in-vitro fertilization is subject to *pidyon haben* (שבט הלוי ח"ג סימן קעו).

WHO IS OBLIGATED TO PERFORM A PIDYON HABEN

1. The father of the firstborn son is obligated to perform the *pidyon haben* (יו״ד שה:א), even if he is not in the same location as the child when the *pidyon* takes place (יו״ד שה:י).
2. If the father dies before performing the *pidyon,* or did not perform the *pidyon* for some other reason, the son should redeem himself upon becoming a bar mitzva. In that situation, however, the *berakha* is changed to *asher kideshanu vetzivanu al pidyon bekhor.*
3. A *beit din* can perform a *pidyon haben* ceremony on behalf of a child under the age of bar mitzva whose father is not Jewish, is deceased, unavailable, or unknown (ש״ך יו״ד שה ס״ק יא וס״ק כ, באור הגר״א יו״ד שה ס״ק יג). Some scholars maintain that, in such a case, the *beit din*'s *pidyon* should be conditioned upon the boy's performance of a second *pidyon haben* ceremony for himself upon his becoming a bar mitzva; and that both the *beit din* and the child should perform their respective *pidyon* ceremonies without reciting a *berakha* (חתם סופר יו״ד קצה).
4. The mother is not obligated to perform the *pidyon haben,* even in the absence of the father. According to many authorities, the father can, however, appoint her to serve as his agent (ערוה״ש יו״ד שה:ה). A *pidyon haben* performed by the mother is, in any case, effective post facto (פדיון הבן כהלכתו א:ט).

WHEN IS PIDYON HABEN PERFORMED?

1. The *pidyon haben* takes place thirty days after birth, i.e., on the 31st day, counting the day of birth as "day one" (יו״ד שה:יא). Some authorities maintain, however, that the *pidyon haben* can only take place after the passage of 29 days, 12 hours, and 793 *ḥalakim* of an hour (there are 1080 *ḥalakim* in an hour) from the child's birth (ש״ך יו״ד שה ס״ק יב). Common Ashkenazic practice is to be stringent according to both opinions by waiting until the 31st day and 29 days, 12 hours, and 793 *ḥalakim* (פתחי תשובה יו״ד שה ס״ק יז) from the child's birth before conducting the *pidyon* ceremony. In cases of

need, however, one can rely upon the ruling of the majority of halakhic authorities, that a *pidyon haben* can be performed as soon as the child enters his 31st day (שו״ת רעק״א תנינא סימן כב).

2. If the boy is born *bein hashmashot*, the count of "day one" starts from the day that begins that evening (מנחת יצחק ח״ה סימן לג).
3. If the 31st day after the child's birth falls on Shabbat or Yom Tov, some authorities maintain that the *pidyon haben* should be held at night immediately following that Shabbat or Yom Tov (יו״ד שה:יא, יהודה יעלה – אסאד יו״ד רסב). Other authorities rule that the *pidyon haben* should wait until Sunday morning (חכמת אדם קנ:ח).
4. Ashkenazic custom mandates the performance of the *pidyon haben* ceremony during the day (ש״ך יו״ד שה ס״ק יב, ibid.) as soon as halakhically possible, without delay, even if more people can attend at a later time (פדיון הבן כהלכתו ח:ב).
5. Under extenuating circumstances (e.g., a *Kohen* may not be available during the day), the *pidyon haben* can even occur after nightfall (*tzet*) at the beginning of the 31st day (הרב שמואל וואזנר, בפדיון הבן כהלכתו מילואים ז).

WHAT CAN BE USED FOR PIDYON HABEN

1. Traditionally, five silver coins are used for *pidyon haben* (אג״מ יו״ד ח״א קפ״ט). Most authorities require that the coins weigh, in total, at least 96 grams of pure silver (חזו״א חו״מ טז:כב-כג, שיעורים דאורייתא – קניבסקי עמ׳ 35 מס׳ טז).
2. U.S. silver dollars that were minted through 1935 are 90 percent pure silver and weigh approximately 26.55 grams. Therefore, five such dollars can be used for *pidyon haben*. Similarly, the special *pidyon haben* coins minted in Israel are also 90 percent pure silver, weigh 26 grams and also be used for *pidyon haben.*
3. Items with intrinsic value can be used in place of the coins (but not land, promissory notes/checks, or paper money). The value of these items, however, must equal the value of 96 grams of silver on the day of the *pidyon haben*, i.e., the 31st day (יו״ד שה:ג, ערוה״ש יו״ד שה:יח).

4. The five silver coins must belong to the father and be given to the *Kohen* wholeheartedly, without an expectation of return. The *Kohen*, however, is permitted to return the coins to the father after the completion of the *pidyon haben*, should he choose to do so of his own accord (יו"ד שה:ח).

SEUDAT MITZVA

1. It is customary to serve a meal as part of the *pidyon haben* ceremony (יו"ד שה:י). This meal has the halakhic status of a *seudat mitzva* (משנה ברורה תקסח ס"ק טז), and, therefore, during the nine days meat and wine may be served (או"ח תקנא:י).
2. Ideally, the *pidyon haben* and *seudat mitzva* should include ten adult Jewish men to publicize the mitzva (יו"ד שה:י, פדיון הבן כהלכתו ח:לג).
3. Those participating should wash, eat bread and immediately begin the *pidyon haben* (באר הגולה יו"ד שה ס"ק י).
4. Following the *pidyon* ceremony, if wine is available, the *Kohen* recites the *berakha* of *Boreh Peri HaGafen* and drinks wine (יו"ד שה:י).
5. If wine is not available, the *pidyon haben* takes place before the *seuda* and beer or some other *ḥamar demedina* can be used by the *Kohen* (ט"ז יו"ד שה ס"ק י).
6. If the *pidyon haben* occurs on a fast day other than Yom Kippur but including Tisha B'Av, some authorities maintain that the *Kohen* recites the *berakha* for the wine, but then gives the wine to a child – who understands that a *berakha* has been recited over the wine (*katan shehigia leḥinukh*) – to drink (בצל החכמה ח"ד נו). Other authorities, however, recommend performing the *pidyon haben* on the night before minor fasts (the beginning of the 31st day), so that the *seuda* can be held in conjunction with the *pidyon haben*. If the 31st day coincides with Tisha B'Av, these authorities recommend postponing the *pidyon haben* ceremony until immediately after the fast (ערוה"ש יו"ד שה:מה).

PIDYON HABEN BY THE FATHER

The pidyon takes place after the assembled have washed their hands, recited HaMotzi and eaten some bread.

The father, presenting his child to the Kohen, declares:

זֶה This is my firstborn son,
the first to issue from his mother's womb.
The Holy One, blessed is He,
has commanded to redeem him,
as it says,

> "Their redemption price from the age of one month shall be set at five shekel of silver according to the Sanctuary weight: twenty gerah per shekel." *Num. 18*

And as it further says,

> "Consecrate every firstborn to Me. Man and beast, the first to emerge from every womb among the Israelites is Mine." *Ex. 13*

The Kohen then asks the father:

מַאי Which do you prefer:
to give your firstborn son,
who is the first issue of his mother's womb, to me,
or do you prefer to redeem him for five Selas,
as you are obligated by Torah law?

The father replies:

חָפֵץ I wish to keep my son,
and accordingly I give you the money
to effect his redemption
in accordance with my obligation by Torah law.

סדר פדיון הבן בידי האב

The פדיון *takes place after the assembled have washed their hands, recited* הַמּוֹצִיא *and eaten some bread.*

The father, presenting his child to the כהן*, declares:*

זֶה בְּנִי בְּכוֹרִי (בבכור לאם בלבד יאמר: **בְּנִי הַבְּכוֹר**)
הוּא פֶּטֶר רֶחֶם לְאִמּוֹ
וְהַקָּדוֹשׁ בָּרוּךְ הוּא צִוָּה לִפְדּוֹתוֹ
שֶׁנֶּאֱמַר
וּפְדוּיָו מִבֶּן־חֹדֶשׁ תִּפְדֶּה, בְּעֶרְכְּךָ כֶּסֶף חֲמֵשֶׁת שְׁקָלִים במדבר יח
בְּשֶׁקֶל הַקֹּדֶשׁ, עֶשְׂרִים גֵּרָה הוּא:
וְנֶאֱמַר
קַדֶּשׁ־לִי כָל־בְּכוֹר פֶּטֶר כָּל־רֶחֶם בִּבְנֵי יִשְׂרָאֵל בָּאָדָם שמות יג
וּבַבְּהֵמָה, לִי הוּא:

The כהן *then asks the father:*

מַאי בָּעֵית טְפֵי
לִתֵּן לִי בִּנְךָ בְּכוֹרְךָ (בבכור לאם בלבד יאמר: **בִּנְךָ הַבְּכוֹר**)
שֶׁהוּא פֶּטֶר רֶחֶם לְאִמּוֹ
אוֹ בָּעֵית לִפְדּוֹתוֹ בְּעַד חָמֵשׁ סְלָעִים
כְּדִמְחֻיַּבְתְּ מִדְּאוֹרַיְתָא.

The father replies:

חָפֵץ אֲנִי לִפְדּוֹת אֶת בְּנִי
וְהֵילָךְ דְּמֵי פִדְיוֹנוֹ כְּדִמְחֻיַּבְנָא מִדְּאוֹרַיְתָא.

Holding the redemption money, the father says:

בָּרוּךְ Blessed are You, Lord, our God, King of the universe,
Who has sanctified us with His commandments,
and has commanded us regarding the redemption of a son.

בָּרוּךְ Blessed are You, Lord, our God, King of the universe,
Who has given us life, sustained us, and brought us to this time.

The Kohen takes a cup of wine and says:

בָּרוּךְ Blessed are You, Lord, our God, King of the universe,
Who creates the fruit of the vine.

After sipping some wine, the Kohen waves the money in a circular motion over the child's head and says:

זֶה This (silver) is in place of this (child). This (silver) is in exchange for this (child). This (child) is desanctified because of this (silver). As a result of this exchange may this boy be initiated fully into life, Torah, and the fear of Heaven. May it be God's will that just as he has been initiated into being redeemed, so may he enter into Torah, the marriage canopy, and good deeds. And let us say, Amen.

Placing his right hand on the head of the child, the Kohen blesses him as follows:

יְשִׂמְךָ May God make you like Ephraim and Menashe. *Gen. 48*
May the Lord bless you and watch over you. *Num. 6*
May the Lord make His face shine upon you
and be gracious to you.
May the Lord raise His face toward you
and grant you peace.
For they will add longevity, years of vitality, *Prov. 3*
and bring peace to you.
The Lord will guard you from all harm; *Ps. 121*
He will guard your life.

The seudat mitzva in celebration of the pidyon continues, followed by Birkat HaMazon (see page 26).

Holding the redemption money, the father says:

בָּרוּךְ אַתָּה יהוה אֱלֹהֵינוּ מֶלֶךְ הָעוֹלָם
אֲשֶׁר קִדְּשָׁנוּ בְּמִצְוֹתָיו וְצִוָּנוּ עַל פִּדְיוֹן הַבֵּן.

בָּרוּךְ אַתָּה יהוה אֱלֹהֵינוּ מֶלֶךְ הָעוֹלָם
שֶׁהֶחֱיָנוּ וְקִיְּמָנוּ וְהִגִּיעָנוּ לַזְּמַן הַזֶּה.

The כהן *takes a cup of wine and says:*

בָּרוּךְ אַתָּה יהוה אֱלֹהֵינוּ מֶלֶךְ הָעוֹלָם
בּוֹרֵא פְּרִי הַגָּפֶן.

After sipping some wine, the כהן *waves the money in a circular motion over the child's head and says:*

זֶה תַּחַת זֶה. זֶה חִלּוּף זֶה. זֶה מָחוּל עַל זֶה. וְיִכָּנֵס זֶה הַבֵּן לְחַיִּים, לְתוֹרָה וּלְיִרְאַת שָׁמַיִם. יְהִי רָצוֹן שֶׁכְּשֵׁם שֶׁנִּכְנַס לְפִדְיוֹן, כֵּן יִכָּנֵס לְתוֹרָה וּלְחֻפָּה וּלְמַעֲשִׂים טוֹבִים. וְנֹאמַר אָמֵן.

Placing his right hand on the head of the child, the כהן *blesses him as follows:*

יְשִׂמְךָ אֱלֹהִים כְּאֶפְרַיִם וְכִמְנַשֶּׁה: בראשית מח
יְבָרֶכְךָ יהוה וְיִשְׁמְרֶךָ: במדבר ו
יָאֵר יהוה פָּנָיו אֵלֶיךָ וִיחֻנֶּךָּ:
יִשָּׂא יהוה פָּנָיו אֵלֶיךָ וְיָשֵׂם לְךָ שָׁלוֹם:
כִּי אֹרֶךְ יָמִים וּשְׁנוֹת חַיִּים וְשָׁלוֹם יוֹסִיפוּ לָךְ: משלי ג
יהוה יִשְׁמָרְךָ מִכָּל־רָע, יִשְׁמֹר אֶת־נַפְשֶׁךָ: תהלים קכא

The סעודת מצווה *in celebration of the* פדיון *continues, followed by* ברכת המזון *(see page 27).*

PIDYON HABEN IN ABSENCE OF THE SON

If the father of the firstborn is not in the same location as his son, a Pidyon Haben must still be performed on the 31st day.

The father approaches the Kohen and says:

יֵשׁ I have a firstborn son,
is the first to issue from his mother's womb.
The Holy One, blessed is He, has commanded to redeem him,
as it says,
"Their redemption price from the age of one month *Num. 18*
shall be set at five shekel of silver
according to the Sanctuary weight:
twenty gerah per shekel."

And as it further says,
"Consecrate every firstborn to Me. *Ex. 13*
Man and beast,
the first to emerge from every womb among the Israelites
is Mine."

The Kohen asks the father:

מַאי Which do you prefer:
to give your firstborn son,
or do you prefer to redeem him for five Selas?

The father replies:

חָפֵץ I wish to keep my son,
and accordingly I give you the money
to effect his redemption
in accordance with my obligation by Torah law.
Five Selas for the redemption
in accordance with my obligation by Torah law.

סדר פדיון הבן שלא במקום הבן

If the father of the firstborn is not in the same location as his son, a פדיון הבן *must still be performed on the 31st day.*

The father approaches the כהן *and says:*

יֵשׁ לִי בֵּן בְּכוֹר, וְהוּא פֶּטֶר רֶחֶם לְאִמּוֹ
וְהַקָּדוֹשׁ בָּרוּךְ הוּא צִוָּה לִפְדּוֹתוֹ
שֶׁנֶּאֱמַר
וּפְדוּיָו מִבֶּן־חֹדֶשׁ תִּפְדֶּה במדבר יח
בְּעֶרְכְּךָ כֶּסֶף חֲמֵשֶׁת שְׁקָלִים בְּשֶׁקֶל הַקֹּדֶשׁ
עֶשְׂרִים גֵּרָה הוּא:
וְנֶאֱמַר
קַדֶּשׁ־לִי כָל־בְּכוֹר שמות יג
פֶּטֶר כָּל־רֶחֶם בִּבְנֵי יִשְׂרָאֵל בָּאָדָם וּבַבְּהֵמָה
לִי הוּא:

The כהן *asks the father:*

מַאי בָּעֵית טְפֵי
בִּבְנָךְ בְּכוֹרָךְ (בבכור לאם בלבד יאמר: בִּבְנָךְ הַבְּכוֹר)
אוֹ בְּחָמֵשׁ סְלָעִים דְּמִחַיַּבְתְּ לִיתֵּן לִי בְּפִדְיוֹנוֹ.

The father replies:

חָפֵץ אֲנִי בִּבְנִי בְּכוֹרִי (בבכור לאם בלבד יאמר: בִּבְנִי הַבְּכוֹר)
וְהֵילָךְ דְּמֵי פִדְיוֹנוֹ כִּדְמִחַיַּבְנָא מִדְּאוֹרַיְתָא.
חֲמִשָּׁה סְלָעִים בְּפִדְיוֹן כִּדְמִחַיַּבְתְּ מִדְּאוֹרַיְתָא.

Holding the redemption money, the father says:

בָּרוּךְ Blessed are You, Lord, our God, King of the universe,
Who has sanctified us with His commandments,
and has commanded us regarding the redemption of a son.

בָּרוּךְ Blessed are You, Lord, our God, King of the universe,
Who has given us life, sustained us, and brought us to this time.

The redemption money is given to the Kohen who takes a cup of wine and says:

בָּרוּךְ Blessed are You, Lord, our God, King of the universe,
Who creates the fruit of the vine.

After drinking some wine, the Kohen says:

זֶה This (silver) is in place of your son. This (silver) is in exchange for your son. Your son is desanctified because of this (silver). This (silver) is for the *Kohen*, as a result of this exchange your son be initiated fully into life, Torah, and the fear of Heaven. May it be God's will that just as he has been initiated into being redeemed, so may he enter into Torah, the marriage canopy, and good deeds. And let us say, Amen.

Holding the redemption money, the father says:

בָּרוּךְ אַתָּה יהוה אֱלֹהֵינוּ מֶלֶךְ הָעוֹלָם
אֲשֶׁר קִדְּשָׁנוּ בְּמִצְוֹתָיו וְצִוָּנוּ עַל פִּדְיוֹן הַבֵּן.

בָּרוּךְ אַתָּה יהוה אֱלֹהֵינוּ מֶלֶךְ הָעוֹלָם
שֶׁהֶחֱיָנוּ וְקִיְּמָנוּ וְהִגִּיעָנוּ לַזְּמַן הַזֶּה.

The redemption money is given to the כהן *who takes a cup of wine and says:*

בָּרוּךְ אַתָּה יהוה אֱלֹהֵינוּ מֶלֶךְ הָעוֹלָם
בּוֹרֵא פְּרִי הַגָּפֶן.

After drinking some wine, the כהן *says:*

זֶה תַּחַת בִּנְךָ. זֶה חִלּוּף בִּנְךָ. זֶה מָחוּל עַל בִּנְךָ. יֵצֵא זֶה לַכֹּהֵן וְיִכָּנֵס בִּנְךָ לְחַיִּים, לְתוֹרָה וּלְיִרְאַת שָׁמַיִם. יְהִי רָצוֹן שֶׁכְּשֵׁם שֶׁנִּכְנַס לְפִדְיוֹן, כֵּן יִכָּנֵס לְתוֹרָה וּלְחֻפָּה וּלְמַעֲשִׂים טוֹבִים. וְנֹאמַר אָמֵן.

PIDYON HABEN BY A BEIT DIN

When a child is orphaned or has no halakhic father, the beit din may redeem the child on a conditional basis, using the court's money. The conditional redemption is made with the following stipulation: If the child, upon reaching maturity, will redeem himself, then this money is a gift to the Kohen, and if the child does not redeem himself upon reaching maturity, then the money is a gift to the firstborn, from now, for the purpose of redeeming himself (Responsa Ḥemdat Shelomo Y.D. siman. 32)

The pidyon takes place after the assembled have washed their hands, recited HaMotzi and eaten some bread.

The beit din says to the Kohen:

זֶה This firstborn son, is the first to issue from his mother's womb.
The Holy One, blessed is He, has commanded to redeem him,
as it says,
"Their redemption price from the age of one month shall be *Num. 18*
set at five shekel of silver according to the Sanctuary weight:
twenty gerah per shekel."
And as it further says,
"Consecrate every firstborn to Me. Man and beast, the first to *Ex. 13*
emerge from every womb among the Israelites is Mine."
We are prepared to redeem him,
since he has no father to redeem him,
and the time to redeem him has come.

The Kohen says:

מַאי Which do you prefer:
For you, beit din, to give away the firstborn son,
who is the first issue of his mother's womb,
or do you prefer to redeem him for five Selas,
as you are obligated by Torah law?

The beit din replies:

חֲפֵצִים We wish to redeem this firstborn,
and accordingly I give you the money of his redemption.

סדר פדיון הבן בידי בית דין

When a child is orphaned or has no halakhic father, the בית דין *may redeem the child on a conditional basis, using the court's money. The conditional redemption is made with the following stipulation:*
אִם הַבֵּן יִגְדַּל וְיִפְדֶּה עַצְמוֹ, הֲרֵי מָעוֹת הַלָּלוּ מַתָּנָה לַכֹּהֵן, וְאִם לֹא יִפְדֶּה עַצְמוֹ כְּשֶׁיִּגְדַּל, הֲרֵי הֵן מֵעַתָּה מַתָּנָה לִבְכוֹר זֶה עַל מְנַת שֶׁיִּפְדֶּה עַצְמוֹ (שו״ת חמדת שלמה, יורה דעה, סימן לב)

The פדיון *takes place after the assembled have washed their hands, recited* הַמּוֹצִיא *and eaten some bread.*

The בית דין *says to the* כהן:

זֶה הַבֵּן בְּכוֹר, הוּא פֶּטֶר רֶחֶם לְאִמּוֹ
וְהַקָּדוֹשׁ בָּרוּךְ הוּא צִוָּה לִפְדּוֹתוֹ
שֶׁנֶּאֱמַר, וּפְדוּיָו מִבֶּן־חֹדֶשׁ תִּפְדֶּה, בְּעֶרְכְּךָ כֶּסֶף חֲמֵשֶׁת שְׁקָלִים בְּשֶׁקֶל הַקֹּדֶשׁ, עֶשְׂרִים גֵּרָה הוּא: במדבר יח
וְנֶאֱמַר, קַדֶּשׁ־לִי כָל־בְּכוֹר פֶּטֶר כָּל־רֶחֶם בִּבְנֵי יִשְׂרָאֵל בָּאָדָם וּבַבְּהֵמָה, לִי הוּא: שמות יג
וַאֲנַחְנוּ מוּכָנִים לִפְדּוֹתוֹ, אַחֲרֵי שֶׁאֵין לוֹ אָב לִפְדּוֹתוֹ
וְהִגִּיעַ זְמַן הַפִּדְיוֹן.

The כהן *says:*

מַאי בָּעֵית טְפֵי
אַתֶּם בֵּית דִּין, לִתֵּן בֵּן הַבְּכוֹר שֶׁהוּא פֶּטֶר רֶחֶם לְאִמּוֹ
אוֹ בָּעֵית לִפְדּוֹתוֹ בְּעַד חָמֵשׁ סְלָעִים
כִּדְמִחַיַּבְתְּ מִדְּאוֹרָיְתָא.

The בית דין *replies:*

חֲפֵצִים אָנוּ לִפְדּוֹת הַבְּכוֹר הַזֶּה, וְהֵילָךְ דְּמֵי פִדְיוֹנוֹ.

Holding the redemption money,
a member of the beit din recites the following blessings:

בָּרוּךְ Blessed are You, LORD, our God, King of the universe,
Who has sanctified us with His commandments,
and has commanded us regarding the redemption of a son.

Preferably, the member of the beit din reciting the blessing should be wearing
a new piece of clothing, to which to apply the following blessing:

בָּרוּךְ Blessed are You, LORD, our God, King of the universe,
Who has given us life, sustained us, and brought us to this time.

The beit din gives the redemption money to the Kohen
who then takes a full cup of wine and recites:

בָּרוּךְ Blessed are You, LORD, our God, King of the universe,
Who creates the fruit of the vine.

After sipping some wine, the Kohen waves the money
in a circular motion over the child's head and says:

זֶה This (silver) is in place of this (child). This (silver) is in exchange for this (child). This (child) is desanctified because of this (silver). As a result of this exchange may this boy be initiated fully into life, Torah, and the fear of Heaven. May it be God's will that just as he has been initiated into being redeemed, so may he enter into Torah, the marriage canopy, and good deeds. And let us say, Amen.

Placing his right hand on the head of the child, the Kohen blesses him as follows:

יְשִׂמְךָ May God make you like Ephraim and Menashe. *Gen. 48*
'May the LORD bless you and watch over you. *Num. 6*
May the LORD make His face shine upon you
and be gracious to you.
May the LORD raise His face toward you and grant you peace.'
For they will add longevity, years of vitality, and bring peace to you. *Prov. 3*
The LORD will guard you from all harm; He will guard your life. *Ps. 121*

The seudat mitzva in celebration of the pidyon continues,
followed by Birkat HaMazon (see page 26).

Holding the redemption money,
a member of the בית דין *recites the following blessings:*

בָּרוּךְ אַתָּה יהוה אֱלֹהֵינוּ מֶלֶךְ הָעוֹלָם
אֲשֶׁר קִדְּשָׁנוּ בְּמִצְוֹתָיו וְצִוָּנוּ עַל פִּדְיוֹן הַבֵּן.

Preferably, the member of the בית דין *reciting the blessing should be wearing*
a new piece of clothing, to which to apply the following blessing:

בָּרוּךְ אַתָּה יהוה אֱלֹהֵינוּ מֶלֶךְ הָעוֹלָם
שֶׁהֶחֱיָנוּ וְקִיְּמָנוּ וְהִגִּיעָנוּ לַזְּמַן הַזֶּה.

The בית דין *gives the redemption money to the* כהן*,*
who then takes a full cup of wine and recites:

בָּרוּךְ אַתָּה יהוה אֱלֹהֵינוּ מֶלֶךְ הָעוֹלָם
בּוֹרֵא פְּרִי הַגָּפֶן.

After sipping some wine, the כהן *waves the money*
in a circular motion over the child's head and says:

זֶה תַּחַת זֶה. זֶה חִלּוּף זֶה. זֶה מָחוּל עַל זֶה. וְיִכָּנֵס זֶה הַבֵּן לְחַיִּים, לְתוֹרָה וּלְיִרְאַת שָׁמַיִם. יְהִי רָצוֹן שֶׁכְּשֵׁם שֶׁנִּכְנַס לְפִדְיוֹן, כֵּן יִכָּנֵס לְתוֹרָה וּלְחֻפָּה וּלְמַעֲשִׂים טוֹבִים. וְנֹאמַר אָמֵן.

Placing his right hand on the head of the child, the כהן *blesses him as follows:*

יְשִׂמְךָ אֱלֹהִים כְּאֶפְרַיִם וְכִמְנַשֶּׁה׃ בראשית מח
יְבָרֶכְךָ יהוה וְיִשְׁמְרֶךָ׃ במדבר ו
יָאֵר יהוה פָּנָיו אֵלֶיךָ וִיחֻנֶּךָּ׃
יִשָּׂא יהוה פָּנָיו אֵלֶיךָ וְיָשֵׂם לְךָ שָׁלוֹם׃
כִּי אֹרֶךְ יָמִים וּשְׁנוֹת חַיִּים וְשָׁלוֹם יוֹסִיפוּ לָךְ׃ משלי ג
יהוה יִשְׁמָרְךָ מִכָּל־רָע, יִשְׁמֹר אֶת־נַפְשֶׁךָ׃ תהלים קכא

The סעודת מצווה *in celebration of the* פדיון *continues,*
followed by ברכת המזון *(see page 27).*

PIDYON HABEN BY AN AGENT

On the rare occasion when the father cannot himself effect the pidyon, he may delegate an agent, including his wife, to act in his stead. This procedure should be employed only if there is no way that the father can be present or perform the pidyon without the child present (see pages 70–73 for that text).

The pidyon takes place after the assembled have washed their hands, recited HaMotzi and eaten some bread.

The father's agent says to the Kohen:

זֶה This firstborn son, is the first to issue from his mother's womb.
The Holy One, blessed is He, has commanded to redeem him,
as it says,

"Their redemption price from the age of one month shall be set at five shekel of silver according to the Sanctuary weight: twenty gerah per shekel." *Num. 18*

And as it further says,

"Consecrate every firstborn to Me. Man and beast, the first to emerge from every womb among the Israelites is Mine." *Ex. 13*

I am the agent of this firstborn son's father
and the time to redeem him has come.

The Kohen says:

מַאי Which do you prefer:
For you, the agent, to give away the firstborn son,
who is the first issue of his mother's womb,
or do you prefer to redeem him for five Selas,
as the agent of the firstborn's father for five Selas
as obligated of the one who delegated you by the Torah law?

The agent replies:

חָפֵץ We wish to redeem the firstborn
as the agent of this firstborn's father,
and accordingly I give you the money of his redemption
from the one who delegated me, as required by the Torah law.

סדר פדיון הבן על ידי שליח

On the rare occasion when the father cannot himself effect the פדיון*, he may delegate an agent, including his wife, to act in his stead. This procedure should be employed only if there is no way that the father can be present or perform the* פדיון *without the child present* (*see pages 70–73 for that text*).

The פדיון *takes place after the assembled have washed their hands, recited* הַמּוֹצִיא *and eaten some bread.*

The father's agent says to the כהן*:*

זֶה הַבֵּן בְּכוֹר, הוּא פֶּטֶר רֶחֶם לְאִמּוֹ
וְהַקָּדוֹשׁ בָּרוּךְ הוּא צִוָּה לִפְדּוֹתוֹ
שֶׁנֶּאֱמַר, וּפְדוּיָו מִבֶּן־חֹדֶשׁ תִּפְדֶּה, בְּעֶרְכְּךָ כֶּסֶף חֲמֵשֶׁת שְׁקָלִים בְּשֶׁקֶל הַקֹּדֶשׁ, עֶשְׂרִים גֵּרָה הוּא: במדבר יח
וְנֶאֱמַר, קַדֶּשׁ־לִי כָל־בְּכוֹר פֶּטֶר כָּל־רֶחֶם בִּבְנֵי יִשְׂרָאֵל בָּאָדָם וּבַבְּהֵמָה, לִי הוּא: שמות יג
וַאֲנִי הַשָּׁלִיחַ מֵאֲבִי הַיֶּלֶד הַבְּכוֹר הַזֶּה שֶׁהִגִּיעַ זְמַן הַפִּדְיוֹן.

The כהן *says:*

מַאי בָּעֵית טְפֵי
אַתָּה הַשָּׁלִיחַ בְּשֵׁם הַמְשַׁלֵּחֲךָ
לִתֵּן בֵּן הַבְּכוֹר שֶׁהוּא פֶּטֶר רֶחֶם לְאִמּוֹ
אוֹ בָּעֵית לִפְדּוֹתוֹ בִּשְׁלִיחוּת אֲבִי הַבְּכוֹר
בְּעַד חָמֵשׁ סְלָעִים כְּדִמְחֻיַּב הַמְשַׁלֵּחֲךָ מִדְּאוֹרַיְתָא.

The agent replies:

חָפֵץ אֲנִי לִפְדּוֹת הַבְּכוֹר בִּשְׁלִיחוּת אֲבִי הַבְּכוֹר הַזֶּה
וְהֵילָךְ דְּמֵי פִדְיוֹנוֹ מִן הַמְשַׁלֵּחַ כְּדִמְחֻיָּב מִדְּאוֹרַיְתָא.

Holding the redemption money,
the agent recites the following blessings:

בָּרוּךְ Blessed are You, Lord, our God, King of the universe,
Who has sanctified us with His commandments,
and has commanded us regarding the redemption of the firstborn.

It is preferable that the agent have on a new piece of clothing,
to which to apply the following blessing:

בָּרוּךְ Blessed are You, Lord, our God, King of the universe,
Who has given us life, sustained us,
and brought us to this time.

The agent gives the redemption money to the Kohen
who then takes a full cup of wine and recites:

בָּרוּךְ Blessed are You, Lord, our God, King of the universe,
Who creates the fruit of the vine.

After sipping some wine, the Kohen waves the money
in a circular motion over the child's head and says:

זֶה This (silver) is in place of this (child). This (silver) is in exchange for this (child). This (child) is desanctified because of this (silver). As a result of this exchange may this boy be initiated fully into life, Torah, and the fear of Heaven. May it be God's will that just as he has been initiated into being redeemed, so may he enter into Torah, the marriage canopy, and good deeds. And let us say, Amen.

Placing his right hand on the head of the child, the Kohen blesses him as follows:

יְשִׂמְךָ May God make you like Ephraim and Menashe. *Gen. 48*
'May the Lord bless you and watch over you. *Num. 6*
May the Lord make His face shine upon you
and be gracious to you.
May the Lord raise His face toward you and grant you peace.'
For they will add longevity, years of vitality, and bring peace to you. *Prov. 3*
The Lord will guard you from all harm; He will guard your life. *Ps. 121*

The seudat mitzva in celebration of the pidyon continues,
followed by Birkat HaMazon (see page 26).

Holding the redemption money,
the agent recites the following blessings:

בָּרוּךְ אַתָּה יהוה אֱלֹהֵינוּ מֶלֶךְ הָעוֹלָם
אֲשֶׁר קִדְּשָׁנוּ בְּמִצְוֹתָיו וְצִוָּנוּ עַל פִּדְיוֹן בְּכוֹר.

It is preferable that the agent have on a new piece of clothing,
to which to apply the following blessing:

בָּרוּךְ אַתָּה יהוה אֱלֹהֵינוּ מֶלֶךְ הָעוֹלָם
שֶׁהֶחֱיָנוּ וְקִיְּמָנוּ וְהִגִּיעָנוּ לַזְּמַן הַזֶּה.

The agent gives the redemption money to the כהן,
who then takes a full cup of wine and recites:

בָּרוּךְ אַתָּה יהוה אֱלֹהֵינוּ מֶלֶךְ הָעוֹלָם
בּוֹרֵא פְּרִי הַגָּפֶן.

After sipping some wine, the כהן *waves the money*
in a circular motion over the child's head and says:

זֶה תַּחַת זֶה. זֶה חִלּוּף זֶה. זֶה מָחוּל עַל זֶה. וְיִכָּנֵס זֶה הַבֵּן לְחַיִּים, לְתוֹרָה וּלְיִרְאַת שָׁמַיִם. יְהִי רָצוֹן שֶׁכְּשֵׁם שֶׁנִּכְנַס לְפִדְיוֹן, כֵּן יִכָּנֵס לְתוֹרָה וּלְחֻפָּה וּלְמַעֲשִׂים טוֹבִים. וְנֹאמַר אָמֵן.

Placing his right hand on the head of the child, the כהן *blesses him as follows:*

בראשית מח יְשִׂמְךָ אֱלֹהִים כְּאֶפְרַיִם וְכִמְנַשֶּׁה:
במדבר ו יְבָרֶכְךָ יהוה וְיִשְׁמְרֶךָ:
יָאֵר יהוה פָּנָיו אֵלֶיךָ וִיחֻנֶּךָּ:
יִשָּׂא יהוה פָּנָיו אֵלֶיךָ וְיָשֵׂם לְךָ שָׁלוֹם:
משלי ג כִּי אֹרֶךְ יָמִים וּשְׁנוֹת חַיִּים וְשָׁלוֹם יוֹסִיפוּ לָךְ:
תהלים קכא יהוה יִשְׁמָרְךָ מִכָּל־רָע, יִשְׁמֹר אֶת־נַפְשֶׁךָ:

The סעודת מצווה *in celebration of the* פדיון *continues,*
followed by ברכת המזון (*see page 27*).

PIDYON OF ONE WHO REDEEMS HIMSELF

When the father failed to redeem the son,
the firstborn son must redeem himself after he has attained the age of
thirteen years and one day (bar mitzva). The text of the pidyon is as follows.

The pidyon takes place after the assembled have washed their hands,
recited HaMotzi and eaten some bread.

The firstborn says to the Kohen:

זֶה I am a firstborn, first issue of the womb.
The Holy One, blessed is He,
has commanded to redeem the firstborn
(*if the father has passed away, the firstborn adds the following:*
unfortunately my father died before the time of my redemption)
and I was left with the obligation to redeem myself,
as it is written, 'your firstborn son you shall redeem...'
and we read 'shall be redeemed' to mean,
that I must redeem myself.
Behold I am ready and prepared to fulfill God's command,

The Kohen says:

מַאי Do you prefer yourself,
or the amount that you are required to pay
for your redemption:

The firstborn replies:

חָפֵץ I prefer myself,
and here is my redemption amount.

The firstborn recites the following blessings:

בָּרוּךְ Blessed are You, Lord, our God, King of the universe,
Who has sanctified us with His commandments,
and has commanded us regarding the redemption of the firstborn.

בָּרוּךְ Blessed are You, Lord, our God, King of the universe,
Who has given us life, sustained us, and brought us to this time.

סדר פדיון עצמי

When the father failed to redeem the son, the firstborn son must redeem himself after he has attained the age of thirteen years and one day (בר־מצוה). The text of the פדיון is as follows.

The פדיון takes place after the assembled have washed their hands, recited הַמּוֹצִיא and eaten some bread.

The firstborn says to the כהן:

אֲנִי בְּכוֹר פֶּטֶר רֶחֶם
וְהַקָּדוֹשׁ בָּרוּךְ הוּא צִוָּה לִפְדּוֹת אֶת הַבְּכוֹר
(אם מת אביו, מוסיף: וּבַעֲוֹנוֹתַי מֵת אָבִי קֹדֶם זְמַן פִּדְיוֹנִי)
וַאֲנִי נִשְׁאַרְתִּי בְּחִיּוּב לִפְדּוֹת עַצְמִי
דִּכְתִיב, בְּכוֹר בָּנֶיךָ תִּפְדֶּה, וְקָרֵינָן תִּפָּדֶה
רוֹצֶה לוֹמַר שֶׁאֶפְדֶּה אֶת עַצְמִי.
וַהֲרֵינִי מוּכָן וּמְזֻמָּן לְקַיֵּם מִצְוַת הַשֵּׁם.

The כהן says:

מַאי נִיחָא לָךְ
יַת גַּרְמָךְ אוֹ דְּמֵי פִּדְיוֹנָךְ, דְּמִחַיַּבְתְּ לִי בְּפוּרְקָנָךְ.

The firstborn replies:

יַת גַּרְמִי, וְהָא לָךְ דְּמֵי פִּדְיוֹנִי.

The firstborn recites the following blessings:

בָּרוּךְ אַתָּה יהוה אֱלֹהֵינוּ מֶלֶךְ הָעוֹלָם
אֲשֶׁר קִדְּשָׁנוּ בְּמִצְוֹתָיו וְצִוָּנוּ עַל פִּדְיוֹן בְּכוֹר.

בָּרוּךְ אַתָּה יהוה אֱלֹהֵינוּ מֶלֶךְ הָעוֹלָם
שֶׁהֶחֱיָנוּ וְקִיְּמָנוּ וְהִגִּיעָנוּ לַזְּמַן הַזֶּה.

The firstborn gives the redemption money to the Kohen who then takes a full cup of wine and recites:

בָּרוּךְ Blessed are You, LORD, our God, King of the universe, Who creates the fruit of the vine.

After sipping some wine, the Kohen waves the money or object in a circular motion over the firstborn's head and says:

זֶה This (silver) is in place of that (child). This (silver) is in exchange for that (child). This (silver) has gone to the Kohen and as a result you should enter into life, Torah, and the fear of Heaven. May it be God's will that just as you have entered into redemtion, so may you enter into Torah, the marriage canopy, and good deeds. And let us say, Amen.

Placing his right hand on the head of the firstborn, the Kohen blesses him as follows:

יְשִׂמְךָ May God make you like Ephraim and Menashe. *Gen. 48*
'May the LORD bless you and watch over you. *Num. 6*
May the LORD make His face shine upon you
and be gracious to you.
May the LORD raise His face toward you and grant you peace.'
For they will add longevity, years of vitality, *Prov. 3*
and bring peace to you.
The LORD will guard you from all harm; *Ps. 121*
He will guard your life.

The seudat mitzva in celebration of the pidyon continues, followed by Birkat HaMazon (see page 26).

The firstborn gives the redemption money to the כהן*,*
who then takes a full cup of wine and recites:

בָּרוּךְ אַתָּה יהוה אֱלֹהֵינוּ מֶלֶךְ הָעוֹלָם
בּוֹרֵא פְּרִי הַגָּפֶן.

After sipping some wine, the כהן *waves the money or object*
in a circular motion over the firstborn's head and says:

זֶה תַּחַת זֶה. זֶה חִלּוּף זֶה. זֶה מָחוּל עַל זֶה. יָצָא זֶה לַכֹּהֵן, וְאַתָּה תִּכָּנֵס לְחַיִּים, לְתוֹרָה וּלְיִרְאַת שָׁמַיִם. יְהִי רָצוֹן שֶׁכְּשֵׁם שֶׁנִּכְנַסְתָּ לְפִדְיוֹן, כֵּן תִּכָּנֵס לְתוֹרָה וּלְחֻפָּה וּלְמַעֲשִׂים טוֹבִים. וְנֹאמַר אָמֵן.

Placing his right hand on the head of the firstborn, the כהן *blesses him as follows:*

בראשית מח יְשִׂמְךָ אֱלֹהִים כְּאֶפְרַיִם וְכִמְנַשֶּׁה:
במדבר ו יְבָרֶכְךָ יהוה וְיִשְׁמְרֶךָ:
יָאֵר יהוה פָּנָיו אֵלֶיךָ וִיחֻנֶּךָּ:
יִשָּׂא יהוה פָּנָיו אֵלֶיךָ וְיָשֵׂם לְךָ שָׁלוֹם:
משלי ג כִּי אֹרֶךְ יָמִים וּשְׁנוֹת חַיִּים וְשָׁלוֹם יוֹסִיפוּ לָךְ:
תהלים קכא יהוה יִשְׁמָרְךָ מִכָּל־רָע, יִשְׁמֹר אֶת־נַפְשֶׁךָ:

The סעודת מצווה *in celebration of the* פדיון *continues,*
followed by ברכת המזון *(see page 27)*.

THE RABBINIC ROAD: CHALLENGES AND OPPORTUNITIES

WEDDINGS

The rabbi's potential role in advance of, and during, a wedding is multi-faceted and multi-layered. At any point he may be called upon to serve as halakhic arbiter, personal counselor, family advisor, diplomatic mediator, director of proceedings etc.

If the rabbi will be honored with *siddur kiddushin*:

- The rabbi should immediately determine whether there are any halakhic impediments to, or complications concerning, the proposed union (i.e., questionable *yiḥus*, or issues related to the marriage of a *Kohen*, see the *Halakha* section). The questioning of the couple, while thorough, should be conducted with great sensitivity, allowing the couple to feel as though they are partners in the process.
- Any halakhic problems that do arise should be fully explained to the couple, and potential solutions, if any, should be immediately explored.

  In the rare instance that a problem emerges for which there is no apparent solution, and the rabbi must recuse himself from further involvement, the situation should be fully discussed with the couple and, if appropriate, with their respective families.
- Once the above halakhic issues have been addressed, the rabbi should guide the couple (at this or subsequent meetings) step-by-step through the marriage ceremony, explaining the significance of each stage and allowing for questions to be raised by the couple.

  Included in this discussion should be the halakhic requirements for the *edut* required at various junctures of the proceedings, and general advice concerning the hierarchy of the honors available for distribution. Raised, as well, should be the option of a short speech by the rabbi beneath the *ḥuppa* and any other optional elements that may be of concern to the *ḥatan* and *kalla.*

- The rabbi should ensure that both the *ḥatan* and the *kalla* make arrangements to study the laws of *taharat hamishpaḥa.* When appropriate, the rabbi and rebbetzin should offer to study these *halakhot* with the *ḥatan* and *kalla,* respectively.
- The rabbi should also introduce and explain the prenuptial agreement of the Rabbinical Council of America and arrange for its signing prior to the wedding.
- If the couple plans to use a calligraphed/artistic *ketuba,* the rabbi should connect with the calligrapher/artist before the wedding to review the rabbi's requirements for the *ketuba.* He should also arrange to review the prepared text prior to the wedding, in order to avoid any issues that might arise.
- The rabbi should also encourage premarital counseling for every couple.
- If the rabbi will be speaking beneath the *ḥuppa,* he should, prior to the wedding day, gather information from the *ḥatan* and *kalla* concerning: their families, each other, their hopes, etc., to ensure that his remarks will be as personal and appropriate as possible.

  A good technique is to ask the *ḥatan* and *kalla* to write down what they might want their loved ones (and each other) to hear beneath the *ḥuppa.* The rabbi can use that information to help fashion his message, perhaps including a quote or two from the *ḥatan* and *kalla* themselves.

  The speech itself should be short, personal, and to the point.
- During the wedding, the rabbi should ensure the smooth running of the proceedings, directing the couple, their families, the *edim,* and others, as they move from step to step.

  He should, if possible, remain at the event through the *sheva berakhot* following the meal, or, if that is not possible, ensure that someone will be present to direct the proceedings at that point.

HALAKHOT CONCERNING TENA'IM, THE KETUBA, AND THE WEDDING CEREMONY

IN PREPARATION FOR A WEDDING

Yiḥus

1. The *Shulḥan Arukh* maintains that "all families are considered fit and it is permitted to marry with them" (אבה״ע ב:ב). This principle only applies, however, to families who are known members of the Jewish community. In preparation for the wedding, therefore, the *mesader kiddushin* must ascertain the Jewish status of both the *ḥatan* and *kalla* and identify any potential impediments to the marriage (e.g., *mamzerut*, a divorcée to a *Kohen*, etc.) (בית שמואל אבה״ע ב ס״ק ג, באר היטב אבה״ע ב:ד, שו״ת ריב״ש תקד).
2. A *Kohen* may not marry a divorcée (or *ḥalutza*), a convert, or someone classified as a *zona* (i.e., a woman who had sexual relations with a person she would be forbidden to marry, e.g., a non-Jew, or a prohibited relative) (אבה״ע ו:א, טו:ח).

Ḥuppat Nidda

1. As part of the preparations for marriage, a *kalla* should determine her monthly cycle and ensure that the wedding is properly scheduled to allow for her immersion in a *mikva* prior to the wedding day.
2. It is common for *kallot* to take medications to regulate their cycles to ensure the proper scheduling of the wedding (ציץ אליעזר ח״יג סימן קג).
3. In the event of a *ḥuppat nidda* (the *kalla* was unable to immerse prior to the wedding), some changes must be made to the wedding ceremony (see pages 98–99).

Halakhic Prenuptial Agreement

1. The halakhic prenuptial agreement of the Beit Din of America/ Rabbinical Council of America is an important vehicle toward averting the problem of *agunot*. It is critical for rabbis to encourage prospective couples to sign the agreement. To view a copy of the pre-nuptial agreement, visit www.theprenup.org .
2. The signing of the prenuptial agreement should be done in advance of the wedding day. Postponing the signing until the wedding day may expose the agreement to unnecessary legal challenges.

DAY OF THE WEDDING

Marriage is one of the most significant events in a person's life. To this end, various customs have become an integral part of the wedding day:

Fasting

A. The *ḥatan* and *kalla* should fast on the day of their wedding (רמ״א אבה״ע סא:א). This fast begins from *alot hashaḥar* (approximately seventy-two minutes before sunrise) and continues until the time of the *ḥuppa*.

B. When the *ḥuppa* takes place at night, most authorities maintain that the fast should continue until the *ḥuppa*. If fasting beyond the end of the day proves difficult for either the *ḥatan* or *kalla*, however, he or she may eat before the *ḥuppa* (פתחי תשובה אבה״ע סא ס״ק ט).

C. On days when *Taḥanun* is not recited, the *ḥatan* and *kalla* do not fast (משנה ברורה או״ח תקעג ס״ק ז).

D. If fasting is difficult for the *ḥatan* or *kalla*, he or she is exempted from fasting (ערוה״ש אבה״ע סא:כא).

Viduy

E. The *ḥatan* and *kalla* should recite *Viduy* at the end of the

Minḥa Amida recited prior to the wedding (פתחי תשובה אבה"ע סא ס"ק ט).

F. If the wedding takes place before it is time to recite *Minḥa*, *Viduy* is added to the end of the *Shaḥarit Amida* (שלחן העזר ח"ב ו:ה ס"ק א).

Mikva

In some communities it is customary for the *ḥatan* to immerse in a *mikva* on his wedding day, mirroring the immersion on Erev Yom Kippur (חופת חתנים ו:א, מעם לועז דברים כב:יב).

TENA'IM

1. While *tena'im* were traditionally written at the time of a couple's engagement, it was also common practice to prepare another, more public document closer to the time of the wedding (נחלת שבעה ט:ב). Nowadays, the *tena'im* are generally signed immediately before the wedding ceremony (נטעי גבריאל נשואין ח"א יב:ח).
2. While it is common practice to prepare only one copy of the *tena'im* for the witnesses to sign, Rabbi Hershel Schachter maintains that a copy should be prepared for each family. If only one document is signed, it should be given to someone who will safeguard it for both parties.
3. Two individuals are appointed to represent the families of the *ḥatan* and *kalla* for the signing of the *tena'im*.
4. Typically, the fathers of the *ḥatan* and *kalla* serve as these representatives. If either father is not available, however, the family may designate the mother or another individual to serve as their appointed representative (נטעי גבריאל נשואין ח"א כו:ט).
5. A *kinyan ḥalifin*, witnessed by two halachically valid witnesses, is performed with each family representative prior to the document's signing as follows: The *mesader kiddushin* takes an item that belongs to him (handkerchief, pen, cellphone, etc.) and asks each

representative to lift that item at least three *tefaḥim* as a sign of acceptance of the terms of the *tena'im* (חו"מ קצח:ב, משפט הכתובה ח"ה מא:יג, נטעי גבריאל נשואין ח"א כו:ד).Some suggest that the item used for the *kinyan* should belong to one of the witnesses (הנשואין כהלכתה ג:לד).

6. Prior to the *kinyan,* the representatives and the witnesses must be given the opportunity to read and understand the terms of the *tena'im*. When necessary, those terms should be explained to them by the *mesader kiddushin.*
7. After the completion of the *kinyan,* the *tena'im* document is signed by the two witnesses.
8. Following the signing of the *tena'im,* the document is read and a plate is broken, typically by the two mothers (שלחן העזר ח"א סימן ב ס"ק כ). The breaking of the plate serves either as a commemoration of the destruction of the *Beit HaMikdash,* or to symbolize the irrevocable nature of the *tena'im* agreement (משנה ברורה תקס ס"ק ט, ערוה"ש אבה"ע נ:כו).

KETUBA

1. The *ketuba* is a legal document and must conform to the *halakhot* of *shtarot*. There should be clear margins, letters should be spaced properly, and there should be no extra spaces in the body of the text that could be filled in after its signing (נחלת שבעה ג:ב).
2. The spelling of names and the location of the wedding are halakhically mandated, and should follow the same spelling used for *gittin* (נחלת שבעה יב:טו).
3. As with the *tena'im* (see above), the *ḥatan* and two valid witnesses must know and understand the contents of the *ketuba* (אבה"ע נה:יג, נחלת שבעה ב:ח).
4. Prior to the signing of the *ketuba,* a *kinyan ḥalifin* should be performed between the *mesader kiddushin* (serving as the representative of the *kalla*) and the *ḥatan,* as follows: The *mesader kiddushin* takes an item that belongs to him (handkerchief, pen, cellphone, etc.) and asks the *ḥatan* to lift that item at least three

tefaḥim as a sign of acceptance of the terms of the *ketuba* (חו״מ קצח:ב, משפט הכתובה ח״ה מא:יג, נטעי גבריאל נשואין ח״א כו:ד) The witnesses must witness this *kinyan* (אבה״ע סו:א).

5. It is customary in some communities for a letter or part of a letter (such as the *regel ha'kuf*) to be omitted from the *ketuba* until after the *kinyan* has been performed. If this has been done, care should be taken to ensure that the omitted portion is completed before the witnesses sign the document (לבוש אבה״ע סו:י). Many view this entire procedure as an unnecessary stringency, however, and complete the *ketuba* well before it is signed (שבט הלוי ח״ח סימן רפו:ד).
6. Following the *kinyan*, the witnesses must sign the *ketuba* one signature above the other (אבה״ע קל:ב). If the signatures are on the same line, however, the *ketuba* is valid (חו״מ מה:יא, רמ״א אבה״ע קל:א).
7. The signing of the *ketuba* and the *ḥuppa* should take place on the same day (i.e., both before sunset or both after *tzet hakokhavim*). If a scheduling mistake was made, or a delay occurs, and the *ḥuppa* takes place after sunset – but the *kinyan* and signing of the *ketuba* will be performed before sunset – the *ketuba* should be dated according to the date of the signing (נפש הרב עמ׳ רס, בית שמואל אבה״ע סו:ז). If the signing takes place during *bein hashmashot*, the date of the following day should be used.
8. An adopted child may include the name of the adoptive father in place of a biological father, but the word שגידלו/שגידלה should be inserted after the name of the adoptive father (i.e., Yaakov ben Shlomo *shegidelo*). When reading the *ketuba* under the *ḥuppa*, this added word can be skipped (אג״מ אבה״ע ח״א סימן צט). (A similar approach can be followed when reading the *ketuba* of a convert or in other sensitive situations.)
9. Some authorities rule that if the father of either the *ḥatan* or *kalla* is not Jewish, the mother's name should be included in the *ketuba* in place of the father's name (i.e., Yaakov ben Rachel) (גט פשוט קכט:נא, חתם סופר ח״ד סימן מא). Other authorities maintain that, in such a case, the parents' names should be entirely omitted

(קנין תורה ח״א סימן נו). Under all circumstances, a non-Jewish parent's name should not be included in the *ketuba*.

10. In situations of a first marriage where the *kalla* is not a *betula*, the husband, if he so chooses, can grant her the financial rights of a *betula*, i.e., the two hundred zuz of *mohar betulaikhi*. This option is based upon the principle of *hodaat baal din* (אגרות משה אבה״ע א:קא). To avoid embarrassment, some authorities permit the *ketuba* text to refer to her as a *betula* (משפט הכתובה ח״ג כא:כג בשם הרב אבא שאול; ע״ע אגרות משה שם). Many authorities, however, require some modification to the text to indicate that, if widowed, further investigation would be necessary before permitting her to marry a *kohen* (i.e., if she had relations with a non-Jew, a *mamzer* or a *halal*). Therefore, while permitting the text to refer to a *mohar betulaikhi*, the term of *itita* [איתתא] is used in place of *betulta* [בתולתא]. (בשם הרב צבי שכטר)
11. If the *ḥatan* is a *kohen* or *levi*, his name should include that designation every time it is written in the *ketuba* (נחלת שבעה סימן י״ב). If the title is accidently omitted, the *ketuba* is valid and need not be rewritten (אגרות משה או״ח ה:כ:כט).
12. If a mistake is found in the *ketuba* and it was corrected, the document must be "upheld" through the application of a *kiyum* – the inclusion of additional text acknowledging the mistake(s) and confirming the continued validity of the *ketuba*.

    Corrections that require *kiyum* include: words that are noticeably erased, words that are missing or written between the lines, words that extend beyond the margins of the text.
13. When dealing with a completed *ketuba* that already contains the concluding phrase *hakol sharir vekayam*, the text of the *kiyum* is written in the document below the signatures of the witnesses. The *kiyum* opens with an acknowledgement of the mistake(s) as follows:

    A. If words were erased:

    תיבות אלו (list the words) בשורה (list the line number) נמחקו.

B. If words were inserted between the lines:

תיבות אלו (list the words) בין השיטין.

C. If words were written outside the margin:

תיבות אלו (list the words) מחוץ לשיטה.

The *kiyum* concludes with a repetition of the formula *vehakol sharir vekayam*, followed on the next two lines by the signatures of the two witnesses.

14. When dealing with a *ketuba* that has not yet been completed (i.e., the words *vehakol sharir vekayam* were not yet written), the *kiyum* is included at the end of the text, followed by the signatures of the witnesses.

15. If mistakes were made concerning the date or the full names of the *ḥatan* or *kalla*, a new *ketuba* should preferably be written (נחלת שבעה ג:יז).

WITNESSES

1. Two witnesses are required at the following points of the wedding ceremony: as signatories to the *tena'im* and *ketuba* (see above), beneath the *ḥuppa* to witness the *kiddushin*, outside the *yiḥud* room to ensure the privacy of the *ḥatan* and *kalla* (see below).
2. All witnesses participating at any point of the wedding ceremony must be Torah-observant Jewish men, above the age of bar mitzva (חו״מ לד), who are not related to each other or to either the *ḥatan* or *kalla* (חו״מ לג:א,יז).
3. While distant relatives (e.g., third cousins/*revi'i sheberivi'i*) may serve as witnesses, it is customary not to select witnesses who are even distantly related (נשואין כהלכתה ח:כד).
4. A witness from one set of witnesses can be related to a witness from a different set (e.g., a witness for the *ketuba* can be related to a witness for the *kiddushin*, etc.).
5. Witnesses signing either the *ketuba* or *tena'im* should sign their names as they would be called to the Torah (e.g., Yitzḥak ben

Avraham). Some authorities recommend that the witnesses should also add their last names as an additional identifier (אג״מ אבה״ע ח״א סימן קעח, אג״מ או״ח ח״ד סימן ד:כ).

6. The witnesses' signatures must be legible and written without abbreviations (נטעי גבריאל נשואין ח״א לא:יג-יד).

PRIOR TO THE ḤUPPA

Bedeken

A. There are various explanations of the origins and reasons for the custom of veiling the *kalla*, and several opinions as to who should perform the veiling. Common custom is for the *ḥatan* to be escorted to the *kalla* prior to the *ḥuppa* ceremony, so that he may personally perform the veiling (ערוה״ש אבה״ע נה:טז).

B. Some authorities require witnesses for the *bedeken* (based on רמ״א אבה״ע נה:א, נפש הרב עמק רנח).

C. At the time of the veiling, the parents, grandparents, and often the rabbis present bless the *kalla* with the words "*aḥoteinu at heyii le'alfei revava*" (Bereishit 24:60) followed by the parents' usual blessing for their children (קשו״ע קמז:ג).

Preparations for the Ḥuppa

A. Many authorities maintain the custom of placing ashes on the *ḥatan*'s head where the *tefillin* are worn, to commemorate the *ḥurban* (או״ח תקס:ב). Rabbi Yosef Dov Soloveitchik held that the ashes should be placed after the *kiddushin* ceremony (נפש הרב עמ׳ רנו).

B. Other authorities, however, maintain that the breaking of a glass beneath the *ḥuppa* following the *nissu'in* ceremony serves as sufficient commemoration of the *ḥurban* and, therefore, do not place ashes on the *ḥatan's* head (ערוה״ש תקס:ו, כף החיים תקס:כא).

C. While some ḥasidic communities maintain the custom of untying shoelaces and other knots in the *ḥatan* and *kalla*'s clothing, Rabbi Yosef Dov Soloveitchik ruled that this a mistaken practice.

D. It is customary in some communities for the *ḥatan* and *kalla* to remove all jewelry before the *ḥuppa* (נפש הרב עמ' רנו) This practice, however, is not halakhically mandated.

THE ḤUPPA

1. While the precise nature of the term *ḥuppa* is subject to debate, colloquially the *ḥuppa* refers to a canopy that is supported by four poles that extend down to the ground.
2. If stationary poles are not available, the canopy can be held aloft by four individuals (אג"מ או"ח ח"ד סימן ע:ז).
3. Some authorities rule that the canopy must be above the poles, so that a halakhic space [*reshut*] is created, while others rule that the canopy can be attached at the sides of the poles (נטעי גבריאל נשואין ח"א טז:א).

THE MARRIAGE CEREMONY

1. There are various customs concerning escorting the *ḥatan* and *kalla* to the *ḥuppa*. In some communities, both fathers escort the *ḥatan* and both mothers escort the *kalla*, while in other communities parents escort their own children. At his own children's weddings, Rabbi Yaakov Kamenetsky reportedly followed "whatever was the other side's custom."
2. Following the *ḥatan*'s arrival beneath the *ḥuppa*, the *kalla* is escorted to the *ḥuppa* and circles the *ḥatan* seven times, counter-clockwise (קשו"ע קמז:ה). In some communities the *kalla* only circles him three times (מטה משה החלק השלישי הכנסת כלה ד). In many communities both mothers accompany the *kalla* as she circles the *ḥatan*.

3. The prevalent custom is that the *kalla* stands to the *ḥatan*'s right beneath the *ḥuppa* (ערוה״ש אבה״ע סב:ט). A kabbalistic tradition maintains, however, that the *ḥatan* should stand to the *kalla*'s right (עדות לישראל – ורדיגר סדר נשואין ט:ג).
4. While some authorities maintain that the *ḥatan* and *kalla* should face eastward while standing beneath the *ḥuppa*, many others do not insist on any specific direction (כנסת הגדולה הגהות בית יוסף אבה״ע סא:ד).

Birkat Erusin

1. The *mesader kiddushin* recites *Boreh Peri HaGafen* and the *Birkat Erusin* on behalf of the *ḥatan* and *kalla* (נודע ביהודה תנינא אבה״ע סימן א). The *mesader kiddushin* must therefore have intent on their behalf as he recites the blessings, while they must have intent as they listen to them (שלחן העזר ח״א ח:א ס״ק ט).
2. Following the *Birkat Erusin*, the *ḥatan* and then the *kalla are* given to drink from the cup of wine.
3. According to the common custom, the *mesader kiddushin* does not drink from the cup of wine (ערוה״ש אבה״ע סב:ח). Some authorities maintain, however, that the *mesader kiddushin* should sip from the cup or spill a few drops onto his hand and sip from his hand before offering the cup to the *ḥatan* and *kalla* (מאזנים למשפט א:יב).

The Ring

1. The ring used for the *kiddushin* ceremony must belong to the *ḥatan* (אבה״ע כח:א).
2. Ideally, the *ḥatan* should personally buy the ring. If, however, it is discovered at the *ḥuppa* that the ring was given to him as a present, he should be instructed to affect a *kinyan* on the ring by holding it in his hand (*kinyan yad*) and lifting it at least three *tefaḥim* (*kinyan hagbaha*) (אוצר הפוסקים אבה״ע כח:א ס״ק יג).
3. The ring should not have any semi-precious or precious stones (אבה״ע לא:ב).

4. Some authorities maintain that there should be no engravings on the ring's surface (תשובות והנהגות ח״ב סימן תרל).
5. Two eligible witnesses are called to the *ḥuppa* to witness the transference of the ring. Many hold that the *mesader kiddushin* should instruct the *ḥatan* to officially designate these witnesses as witnesses, to the exclusion of all others present (ערוה״ש מב:לא).
6. In the presence of the two witnesses, the *mesader kiddushin* then asks the *ḥatan* to attest to his ownership of the ring (בית שמואל אבה״ע כח:מט). The *mesader kiddushin* then asks the witnesses to attest to the fact that the ring has at least minimal value (*shaveh peruta*) (רמ״א אבה״ע לא:ב). Ideally, these attestations should be made before the *Birkat Erusin* (בשם הרב צבי שכטר).
7. Prior to the giving of the ring, the *ḥatan* recites *harei at* loud enough to be heard by the *kalla* and the witnesses (אבה״ע כו:א).
8. Using his dominant hand (בצל החכמה ח״ה סימן לו), the *ḥatan* then places the ring on the *kalla*'s index finger (באר היטב אבה״ע כו ס״ק א). The ring is placed on the *kalla*'s right hand, even if she is left-handed. If the *ḥatan* placed the ring on the *kalla*'s left hand, the *kiddushin* does not need to be repeated (חיים ושלום ח״ב סימן י״ט). There are authorities who rule that if the *kalla* is left-handed, and typically wears her rings on her left-hand, the *ḥatan* should place the ring on her left hand (באר משה ח״ב סימן ב).

The Ketuba

1. The reading of the *ketuba* serves to separate the *Birkat Erusin* from the *Birkat Nisu'in* (רמ״א אבה״ע סב:ט).
2. Following the reading of the *ketuba,* the *ḥatan* hands the *ketuba* to the *kalla.*
3. After receiving the *ketuba* from the *ḥatan,* the *kalla* may hand it to someone else (usually her mother) for safekeeping.

Birkat Nisu'in (Sheva Berakhot)

1. A second cup of wine is filled (or the first cup is refilled) and the *Sheva Berakhot* are recited.

2. A different man may be selected for the recitation of each blessing (אג״מ אבה״ע ח״א סימן צד).
3. A blessing that is accidentally omitted can be inserted out of order (באר היטב אבה״ע סב ס״ק א). If the third blessing, *Yotzer HaAdam*, was omitted, however, and the final blessing of *Asher Yatzar* has already been recited, *Yotzer HaAdam* should not then be said (רבבות אפרים ח״ג סימן קנו).

Breaking the Glass

1. It is customary to break a glass under the *ḥuppa* in commemoration of the *ḥurban* (או״ח תקס:ב).
2. The *ḥatan* breaks the glass with his right foot (שלחן העזר ח״ב סימן ח ס״ק כד).
3. Outside of Israel, the glass is broken following the *Birkat Nisu'in* (Rema EH 65:3). Some authorities maintain, however, that the glass should be broken before the *ketuba* is read (מטה משה חלק השלישי הכנסת כלה א:ט). This is *minhag Yerushalayim*.

Yiḥud

1. Immediately after the ceremony, the *ḥatan* and *kalla* are led to a private room for *yiḥud*. According to some authorities, *yiḥud* marks the completion of the marriage ceremony (אבה״ע נא:א).
2. While some authorities maintain that the *ḥatan* should specifically rent the *yiḥud* room for the purpose of *yiḥud* (מועדים וזמנים ח״ד סימן רפו), others deem this unnecessary (בעקבי הצאן לט:ב).
3. The witnesses must establish that no one else is in the *yiḥud* room, before the *kalla* and *ḥatan* enter (בית שמואל אבה״ע נה ס״ק ה).
4. The witnesses must remain outside the *yiḥud* room for a period of time after the *ḥatan* and *kalla* enter. There are various opinions regarding the amount of time necessary for *yiḥud*, ranging from just a few moments (המקנה אבה״ע סד ס״ק ה) to five minutes (מנחת יצחק ד:צה), to eight minutes (מפניני הרב עמ רעו).

Birkat HaMazon and Sheva Berakhot

1. Two cups of wine are poured before the recitation of *Birkat HaMazon* (ט"ז אבה"ע סב ס"ק ז). The first of these cups serves as the *kos shel berakha* for *Birkat HaMazon*; while the second cup is designated for the *sheva berakhot* (ערוה"ש אבה"ע סב:יח) and is passed to each individual reciting a blessing.
2. According to common practice, the short *piyut Devai Haser* is added to the *Birkat HaZimun* (ט"ז אבה"ע סב ס"ק ז).
3. Following the *sheva berakhot*, the person leading *Birkat HaMazon* recites the final blessing of *Boreh Peri HaGafen*. If by mistake the blessing for the wine was said at the beginning of *sheva berakhot*, it need not be repeated (שלחן העזר ח"ב סימן ט ס"ק ה).
4. The two cups of wine are mixed and the *ḥatan* and *kalla* are given to drink of the mixture (ערוה"ש אבה"ע סב:יח).

ḤUPPAT NIDDA

In a case when the *kalla* was unable to immerse in a *mikva* prior to the wedding, the following halakhic guidelines apply:

1. The *ḥatan* and *kalla* may not have physical contact until she has immersed in a *mikva*. Most authorities, however, permit him to place the ring on her finger during the *kiddushin* ceremony (באר היטב אבה"ע סא ס"ק ח).
2. Following the reading of the *ketuba* someone other than the *ḥatan* should hand the *ketuba* to the *kalla*.
3. Witnesses should still be placed outside the *yiḥud* room. Because the couple may not be alone until after her immersion, however, most authorities maintain that a private arrangement is necessary, such as having a child or close friend discreetly enter the room before the couple so that they are not left alone during this time (אג"מ אבה"ע ח"ד סימן פו). Rabbi Yosef Dov Soloveitchik, however, did not require an additional person in the *yiḥud* room (נפש הרב עמ' רנט).

4. Following the wedding and until the *kalla* can immerse in the mikva, the *ḥatan* and *kalla* may not be alone. At night there should be at least two children staying with them, and at least one child during the day (יו״ד קצב:ד). Rabbi Soloveitchik allowed *yiḥud* during the day (נפש הרב עמ׳ רנט).

SECOND MARRIAGES

1. In the case of a *kalla*'s second marriage:
   A. The primary effectuation of the marriage is *yiḥud*. Every effort should be made, therefore, to ensure that the *kalla* is not a *nidda* at the time of the wedding and can enter *yiḥud* with the *ḥatan* (אבה״ע סד:ה). Nevertheless, if the *kalla* is a *nidda*, the wedding can proceed.
   B. There are various opinions regarding *bedeken* in the case of a woman's second marriage. Some authorities maintain that the *kalla* is not veiled at all (ערוה״ש נה:כד). Others rule that someone other than the *ḥatan* veils the *kalla* before the *ḥuppa* ceremony (שלחן העזר ח״ב ז:ה), while yet others maintain that the *kalla* is veiled by someone other than the *ḥatan* beneath the *ḥuppa* (שו״ת מהריי״ץ סימן ח).
2. If both the *ḥatan* and *kalla* were previously married:
   A. *Sheva berakhot* are added to *Birkat HaMazon* only at the first meal following the ceremony.
   B. If the wedding takes place during the day and the first meal is held the following night, most authorities maintain that *sheva berakhot* can be recited at the meal (ט״ז אבה״ע סב ס״ק ג), but others say they should not (חכמת אדם קכט:ד).
3. If either the *ḥatan* or *kalla* were never married before, the full week of *sheva berakhot* is observed (אבה״ע סב:ו).
4. If the *ḥatan* was previously married, but the *kalla* was not, all customs of a first marriage are retained.

THE TENA'IM

To good fortune

May it sprout and flourish like a lush garden.
He who finds a wife has found good,
and obtains favor of God Who is good,
Who endorses this union

May He who can foretell the last from the first bestow a good name and permanence to the obligations and conditions that were agreed upon by the following two parties; that is, the party of the first part, (*groom's father's name, or whoever is representing the groom*) ______________ who represents (*his son*), the groom (*groom's name*) ______________ and as party of the second part, (*bride's father's name, or whoever is representing the bride*) ______________, who represents (*his daughter*), the bride (*bride's name*) ______________, that all the obligations of the groom toward the bride have been fulfilled, and likewise the obligations of the bride toward the groom have been fulfilled. Neither has any claims or demands on the other, but there remains yet to fulfill that the aforementioned groom marries the aforementioned bride, through ḥupah and betrothal, in accordance with the Law of Moses and Israel, on the ________ day of ________ in the year __________. They shall not keep nor conceal from each other anything with regard to their possessions; rather, they should have equal ownership over their possessions, sharing peacefully and calmly as befits those who love the Torah and fear God, blessed be He. All this was done in full knowledge and agreement. We have effected the legal formality of a binding agreement from both parties on all that is written and elaborated above, through an object that legally binds a transaction, this was done here __________ on the day __________ and everything is valid and confirmed.

Attested to ____________________________ witness

Attested to ____________________________ witness

התנאים

מַזָּל טוב

יַעֲלֶה וְיִצְמַח כְּגַן רָטוֹב   מָצָא אִשָּׁה מָצָא טוב
וְיָפֵק רָצוֹן מֵהַשֵּׁם הַטּוֹב   הָאוֹמֵר לַדֶּבֶק טוב

הַמַּגִּיד מֵרֵאשִׁית אַחֲרִית הוּא יִתֵּן שֵׁם טוֹב וּשְׁאֵרִית לְדִבְרֵי הַתְּנָאִים וְהַבְּרִית שֶׁנִּדְבְּרוּ וְהֻתְנוּ בֵּין הָנֵי שְׁנֵי הַצְּדָדִים, הַיְנוּ מִצַּד הָאֶחָד הר' (שם אבי החתן או מי שעומד מצד החתן) __________ הָעוֹמֵד מִצַּד (בְּנוֹ) הֶחָתָן (שם החתן) __________ וּמִצַּד הַשֵּׁנִי הר' (שם אבי הכלה או מי שעומד מצד הכלה) __________ הָעוֹמֵד מִצַּד (בִּתּוֹ) הַכַּלָּה הַבְּתוּלָה מָרַת __________ (שם הכלה), אֲשֶׁר כְּבָר נִתְקַיְּמוּ כָּל הַחִיּוּבִים מִצַּד הֶחָתָן לַכַּלָּה וְכֵן נִתְקַיְּמוּ כָּל הַחִיּוּבִים מִצַּד הַכַּלָּה לֶחָתָן. וְאֵין לָהֶם זֶה עַל זֶה שׁוּם טְעָנוֹת וּתְבִיעוֹת, אֲבָל נִשְׁאַר עוֹד לְהִתְקַיֵּם מַה שֶּׁהֶחָתָן הַנַּ"ל יִשָּׂא אֶת הַכַּלָּה הַנַּ"ל בְּחֻפָּה וְקִדּוּשִׁין כְּדַת מֹשֶׁה וְיִשְׂרָאֵל, בְּיוֹם __________ לְחֹדֶשׁ __________ שְׁנַת __________ וְאַל יַבְרִיחוּ וְאַל יַעֲלִימוּ לֹא זֶה מִזּוֹ וְלֹא זוֹ מִזֶּה שׁוּם הַבְרָחַת מָמוֹן בָּעוֹלָם; אֶלָּא יִשְׁלְטוּ בִּנְכְסֵיהוֹן שָׁוֶה בְּשָׁוֶה וּבְשָׁלוֹם וְשַׁלְוָה כְּדֶרֶךְ בְּנֵי תוֹרָה וְיִרְאֵי הַשֵּׁם יִתְבָּרַךְ. כָּל זֶה נַעֲשָׂה בְּדֵעָה שְׁלֵמָה וּמְיֻשֶּׁבֶת. וְקָנִינָא מִן שְׁנֵי הַצְּדָדִים עַל כָּל מַה דִּכְתוּב וּמְפֹרָשׁ לְעֵיל, בְּמָנָא דְּכָשֵׁר לְמִקְנְיָא בֵּיהּ, נַעֲשָׂה פֹּה __________ יוֹם __________ וְהַכֹּל שָׁרִיר וְקַיָּם.

נְאוּם __________ עֵד

נְאוּם __________ עֵד

THE KETUBA

The numbers in this Ketuba refer to the charts on pages 108–109.

On the (1) day of the week, the (2) day of the month (3) in the year five thousand (4) hundred and (5) since the Creation of the world, according to the reckoning customarily used here in *(city, state/privince and country)*, how *(bridegroom's name)* son of *(father's name)* of the family *(surname)* said to (6) *(bride's name)* daughter of *(father's name)* of the family *(surname)*. "Be my wife according to the law of Moses and Israel. I will sustain, honor, support and keep you in accordance with the custom of Jewish husbands who honestly sustain, honor, support, and keep their wives. I hereby set aside for you the portion of (7) (8), silver zuzim, which accrues to you according to (9) law, together with your food, clothing, and necessities, and undertake to live with you as husband and wife according to universal custom." And *(bride's name)* (6) consented and became his wife. Her belongings that she brought to him *(from her* (10) *house)*, in silver, gold, valuables, apparel, house furnishings, and linens, all the *(bridegroom's name)*, the said bridegroom, accepted in the sum of (11) silver pieces, with *(bridegroom's name)*, the bridegroom adding from his own property the sum of (12) silver pieces, making in all (13) silver pieces. And thus said *(bridegroom's name)* the bridegroom: "The responsibility of this marriage contract, this wedding dowry, and this additional sum, I take upon myself and my heirs after me, so that they shall be paid from the best part of all the property and possessions that I have below the heavens, that which I now possess or may hereafter acquire. All my property, real and personal, down to the shirt on my back, shall be mortgaged to secure the payment of this marriage contract, the wedding dowry, and the addition made thereto, during my lifetime and after my lifetime, from the present day and forever." *(Bridegroom's name)*, the bridegroom, has taken upon himself the responsibility of this marriage contract, of the wedding dowry and the addition made thereto according to the restrictive usages of all marriage contracts and the additions thereto made for the daughters of Israel, in accordance with the institution of our Sages of blessing memory. It is not to be regarded as an indecisive contractual obligation or as a stereotyped form. We have effected the legal formality of binding agreement *(kinyan)* (14) between *(bridegroom's name)* the son of *(father's name*)*, the bridegroom, and *(bride's name)* the daughter of *(father's name*)*, this (6), through an object that legally binds a transaction, and everything is valid and confirmed.

Attested to *(full name and parent's name of the first witness)* witness;

Attested to *(full name and parent's name of the second witness)* witness.

---

*When there is no halakhic father, refer to pages 93–94.

הכתובה

The numbers in this כתובה *refer to the charts on pages 108–109.*

בְּ (1) בְּשַׁבָּת (2) לְחֹדֶשׁ (3) שְׁנַת חֲמֵשֶׁת אֲלָפִים (4) מֵאוֹת (5) לִבְרִיאַת עוֹלָם
לְמִנְיָן שֶׁאָנוּ מוֹנִין כָּאן (שם המקום). אֵיךְ הֶחָתָן (שם החתן) בֶּן (שם אביו) לְמִשְׁפַּחַת
(פלוני) אָמַר לַהֲדָא (6) (שם הכלה) בַּת (שם אביה) לְמִשְׁפַּחַת (פלוני) הֲוִי לִי לְאִנְתּוּ
כְּדַת מֹשֶׁה וְיִשְׂרָאֵל וַאֲנָא אֶפְלַח וְאוֹקִיר וְאָזוּן וַאֲפַרְנֵס יָתִיכִי לִיכִי כְּהִלְכוֹת
גּוּבְרִין יְהוּדָאִין דְּפָלְחִין וּמוֹקְרִין וְזָנִין וּמְפַרְנְסִין לִנְשֵׁיהוֹן בְּקוּשְׁטָא. וְיָהֵיבְנָא
לִיכִי מֹהַר (7) כֶּסֶף זוּזֵי (8) דְּחָזֵי לִיכִי (9) וּמְזוֹנַיְכִי וּכְסוּתַיְכִי וְסִפּוּקַיְכִי וּמֵיעַל
לְוָתַיְכִי כְּאוֹרַח כָּל אַרְעָא. וּצְבִיאַת מָרַת (שם הכלה) (6) דָא וַהֲוָת לֵיהּ לְאִנְתּוּ.
וְדֵין נְדוּנְיָא דְהַנְעֵלַת לֵיהּ מִבֵּי (10) בֵּין בְּכֶסֶף בֵּין בְּזָהָב בֵּין בְּתַכְשִׁיטִין
בְּמָאנֵי דִלְבוּשָׁא בְּשִׁמּוּשֵׁי דִירָה וּבְשִׁמּוּשָׁא דְעַרְסָא. הַכֹּל קִבֵּל עָלָיו
(שם החתן) חֲתַן דְּנָן (11) זְקוּקִים כֶּסֶף צָרוּף וְצָבִי (שם החתן) חֲתַן דְּנָן וְהוֹסִיף לָהּ
מִן דִּילֵיהּ עוֹד (12) זְקוּקִים כֶּסֶף צָרוּף אֲחֵרִים כְּנֶגְדָּן, סַךְ הַכֹּל (13) זְקוּקִים
כֶּסֶף צָרוּף. וְכָךְ אָמַר (שם החתן), חֲתַן דְּנָן, אַחֲרָיוּת שְׁטַר כְּתוּבְּתָא דָא וּנְדוּנְיָא
דֵין וְתוֹסֶפְתָּא דָא קַבָּלִית עָלַי וְעַל יַרְתַאי בַּתְרַאי לְהִתְפָּרַע מִכָּל שְׁפַר אֲרַג
נִכְסִין וְקִנְיָנִין דְּאִית לִי תְּחוֹת כָּל שְׁמַיָּא, דִּקְנָאִי וּדְעָתִיד אֲנָא לְמִקְנֵא, נִכְסִין
דְּאִית לְהוֹן אַחֲרָיוּת וּדְלֵית לְהוֹן אַחֲרָיוּת כֻּלְּהוֹן יְהוֹן אַחֲרָאִין וְעַרְבָאִין
לִפְרֹעַ מִנְהוֹן שְׁטַר כְּתוּבְּתָא דָא וּנְדוּנְיָא דֵין וְתוֹסֶפְתָּא דָא מִנַּאי וַאֲפִילּוּ
מִן גְּלִימָא דְעַל כַּתְפַּאי, בְּחַיֵּי וּבָתַר חַיֵּי מִן יוֹמָא דְנָן וּלְעָלַם וְאַחֲרָיוּת שְׁטַר
כְּתוּבְּתָא דָא וּנְדוּנְיָא דֵין וְתוֹסֶפְתָּא דָא, קִבֵּל עָלָיו (שם החתן) חֲתַן דְּנָן כְּחֹמֶר
כָּל שִׁטְרֵי כְתֻבּוֹת וְתוֹסֶפְתּוֹת דְּנָהֲגִין בִּבְנוֹת יִשְׂרָאֵל הָעֲשׂוּיִן כְּתִקּוּן חֲכָמֵינוּ
זִכְרוֹנָם לִבְרָכָה דְּלָא כְּאַסְמַכְתָּא וְלָא כְּטוֹפְסֵי דִשְׁטָרֵי (14) מִן (שם החתן)
בֶּן (שם אביו*) לְמִשְׁפַּחַת (פלוני) חֲתַן דְּנָן, (שם הכלה) בַּת (שם אביה*) לְמִשְׁפַּחַת
(פלוני) (6) דָא, עַל כֹּל מַה דִּכְתוּב וּמְפֹרָשׁ לְעֵיל בְּמָנָא דְכָשֵׁר לְמִקְנְיָא בֵיהּ.

וְהַכֹּל שָׁרִיר וְקַיָּם.

נְאוּם (שמו המלא של העד הראשון ושם אביו) **עֵד;**

נְאוּם (שמו המלא של העד השני ושם אביו) **עֵד.**

(1)

DAY OF THE WEEK					
חֲמִישִׁי	*Thursday*	שְׁלִישִׁי	*Tuesday*	אֶחָד	*Sunday*
שִׁשִּׁי	*Friday*	רְבִיעִי	*Wednesday*	שֵׁנִי	*Monday*

Note: the days refer, of course, to the halakhic day of the week (i.e., Sunday night is considered as Monday).

(2)

DAY OF THE MONTH					
אֶחָד וְעֶשְׂרִים יוֹם	21	אַחַד עָשָׂר יוֹם	11	יוֹם אֶחָד	1
שְׁנַיִם וְעֶשְׂרִים יוֹם	22	שְׁנֵים עָשָׂר יוֹם	12	שְׁנֵי יָמִים	2
שְׁלֹשָׁה וְעֶשְׂרִים יוֹם	23	שְׁלֹשָׁה עָשָׂר יוֹם	13	שְׁלֹשָׁה יָמִים	3
אַרְבָּעָה וְעֶשְׂרִים יוֹם	24	אַרְבָּעָה עָשָׂר יוֹם	14	אַרְבָּעָה יָמִים	4
חֲמִשָּׁה וְעֶשְׂרִים יוֹם	25	חֲמִשָּׁה עָשָׂר יוֹם	15	חֲמִשָּׁה יָמִים	5
שִׁשָּׁה וְעֶשְׂרִים יוֹם	26	שִׁשָּׁה עָשָׂר יוֹם	16	שִׁשָּׁה יָמִים	6
שִׁבְעָה וְעֶשְׂרִים יוֹם	27	שִׁבְעָה עָשָׂר יוֹם	17	שִׁבְעָה יָמִים	7
שְׁמֹנָה וְעֶשְׂרִים יוֹם	28	שְׁמֹנָה עָשָׂר יוֹם	18	שְׁמֹנָה יָמִים	8
תִּשְׁעָה וְעֶשְׂרִים יוֹם	29	תִּשְׁעָה עָשָׂר יוֹם	19	תִּשְׁעָה יָמִים	9
		עֶשְׂרִים יוֹם	20	עֲשָׂרָה יָמִים	10
				יוֹם שְׁלֹשִׁים לְחֹדֶשׁ (3) שֶׁהוּא רֹאשׁ חֹדֶשׁ (3).	30

(3)

NAMES OF THE MONTHS						
אֲדָר הָרִאשׁוֹן	שְׁבָט	כִּסְלֵו	תִּשְׁרֵי	אָב	סִיוָן	נִיסָן
אֲדָר הַשֵּׁנִי	אֲדָר	טֵבֵת	מַרְחֶשְׁוָן	אֱלוּל	תַּמּוּז	אִיָּר

(4)

CENTURIES		
וְתֵשַׁע	וּשְׁמֹנֶה	וְשֶׁבַע

(5)

YEARS			
וְאַחַת	וְעֶשֶׂר	וּתְשַׁע עֶשְׂרֵה	וְעֶשְׂרִים וּשְׁמֹנֶה
וּשְׁתַּיִם	וְאַחַת עֶשְׂרֵה	וְעֶשְׂרִים	וְעֶשְׂרִים וָתֵשַׁע
וְשָׁלֹשׁ	וּשְׁתֵּים עֶשְׂרֵה	וְעֶשְׂרִים וְאַחַת	וּשְׁלֹשִׁים
וְאַרְבַּע	וּשְׁלֹשׁ עֶשְׂרֵה	וְעֶשְׂרִים וּשְׁתַּיִם	וְאַרְבָּעִים
וְחָמֵשׁ	וְאַרְבַּע עֶשְׂרֵה	וְעֶשְׂרִים וְשָׁלֹשׁ	וַחֲמִשִּׁים
וָשֵׁשׁ	וַחֲמֵשׁ עֶשְׂרֵה	וְעֶשְׂרִים וְאַרְבַּע	וְשִׁשִּׁים
וָשֶׁבַע	וְשֵׁשׁ עֶשְׂרֵה	וְעֶשְׂרִים וְחָמֵשׁ	וְשִׁבְעִים
וּשְׁמֹנֶה	וּשְׁבַע עֶשְׂרֵה	וְעֶשְׂרִים וָשֵׁשׁ	וּשְׁמֹנִים
וָתֵשַׁע	וּשְׁמֹנֶה עֶשְׂרֵה	וְעֶשְׂרִים וָשֶׁבַע	וְתִשְׁעִים

	לבתולה	לאלמנה	לגרושה	לגיורת
(6)	בְּתוּלְתָא	אַרְמַלְתָּא	מְתַרְכְתָא	גִּיּוֹרְתָּא
(7)	בְּתוּלַיְכִי	אַרְמְלוּתַיְכִי	מְתַרְכוּתַיְכִי	גִּיּוֹרוּתַיְכִי
(8)	מָאתַן	מְאָה	מְאָה	מְאָה
(9)	מִדְּאוֹרָיְיתָא	מִדְּרַבָּנָן	מִדְּרַבָּנָן	מִדְּרַבָּנָן

(10) (בתולה שיש לה אב) **אֲבוּהָ** / (ליתומה, אלמנה ולגרושה) **נשא** / (לגיורת) **"דְּהַנְעָלַת לֵיהּ בֵּין..."**

	לבתולה	לאלמנה	לגרושה	לגיורת
(11)	בְּמֵאָה	בַּחֲמִשִּׁים	בַּחֲמִשִּׁים	בַּחֲמִשִּׁים
(12)	מֵאָה	חֲמִשִּׁים	חֲמִשִּׁים	חֲמִשִּׁים
(13)	מָאתַיִם	מֵאָה	מֵאָה	מֵאָה

(14) **וְקָנֵינָא** *is filled in – see intructions on page 92–93*

MARRIAGE SERVICE

BEDEKEN

Before the wedding ceremony, the ḥatan is escorted to the kalla, where he covers the kalla with her veil, amidst joy and dancing. At the time of the veiling, the parents, grandparents, and often the rabbis present bless the kalla with the following:

Our sister, may you grow into thousands of myriads. *Gen. 24*

יְשִׂימֵךְ May God make you like Sarah, Rebecca, Rachel and Leah.
May the Lord bless you and protect you. *Num. 6*
May the Lord make His face shine on you
and be gracious to you.
May the Lord turn His face toward you
and grant you peace.

ERUSIN – BETROTHAL

The ḥatan is escorted to the ḥuppa.
Upon his arrival, the following welcome is recited or sung:

בָּרוּךְ הַבָּא Blessed is he who has come!
May He Who is supreme in power,
as well as blessed above all,
greater than all, and exalted above all –
bless the groom and the bride.

The kalla is escorted to the ḥuppa.
Upon her arrival, the following welcome is recited or sung. While the kalla circles the ḥatan counterclockwise three or seven times, according to custom:

בְּרוּכָה הַבָּאָה Blessed is she who has come!
May the one, who understands the deeper meaning
of the phrase "the rose among the thorns,"
as well as the love of a bride
who is celebrated by those who cherish her –
bless the groom and the bride.

סדר קידושין ונישואין

כיסוי ההינומה

Before the wedding ceremony, the חתן *is escorted to the* כלה*, where he covers the* כלה *with her veil, amidst joy and dancing. At the time of the veiling, the parents, grandparents, and often the rabbis present bless the* כלה *with the following:*

בראשית כד אֲחֹתֵנוּ, אַתְּ הֲיִי לְאַלְפֵי רְבָבָה:

יְשִׂימֵךְ אֱלֹהִים כְּשָׂרָה רִבְקָה רָחֵל וְלֵאָה.

במדבר ו יְבָרֶכְךָ יהוה וְיִשְׁמְרֶךָ:

יָאֵר יהוה פָּנָיו אֵלֶיךָ וִיחֻנֶּךָּ:

יִשָּׂא יהוה פָּנָיו אֵלֶיךָ וְיָשֵׂם לְךָ שָׁלוֹם:

אירוסין

The חתן *is escorted to the* חופה*.*
Upon his arrival, the following welcome is recited or sung:

בָּרוּךְ הַבָּא.
מִי אַדִּיר עַל הַכֹּל, מִי בָּרוּךְ עַל הַכֹּל
מִי גָּדוֹל עַל הַכֹּל, מִי דָּגוּל עַל הַכֹּל
הוּא יְבָרֵךְ אֶת הֶחָתָן וְאֶת הַכַּלָּה.

The כלה *is escorted to the* חופה*.*
Upon her arrival, the following welcome is recited or sung. While the כלה *circles the* חתן *counterclockwise three or seven times, according to custom:*

בְּרוּכָה הַבָּאָה.
מִי בָּן שִׂיחַ שׁוֹשַׁן חוֹחִים
אַהֲבַת כַּלָּה מְשׂוֹשׂ דּוֹדִים
הוּא יְבָרֵךְ אֶת הֶחָתָן וְאֶת הַכַּלָּה.

The kalla stands to the ḥatan's right. The witnesses to the kiddushin are called to the ḥuppa and the ring is produced.
The mesader kiddushin asks the ḥatan to attest to his ownership of the ring in the presence of the witnesses. The mesader kiddushin then shows the ring to the witnesses that they may confirm that it is of at least minimal value (shaveh peruta).

BLESSINGS OF BETROTHAL

The mesader kiddushin raises a full cup of wine and recites the following:

בָּרוּךְ Blessed are You, LORD, our God, King of the universe,
Who creates the fruit of the vine.

בָּרוּךְ Blessed are You, LORD, our God, King of the universe,
Who has sanctified us with His commandments,
and has commanded us regarding forbidden unions;
Who has forbidden us from betrothed women
while permitting us to those whom we have married
by means of *Ḥuppa* and *Kiddushin*/consecration.
Blessed are You, LORD,
Who sanctifies His people Israel
by means of *Ḥuppa* and *Kiddushin*/consecration.

The ḥatan and then the kalla drink from the cup of wine.

The ḥatan holds the ring in his dominant hand, turns to the kalla, and, in the presence of the witnesses, says:

הֲרֵי אַתְּ You are consecrated to me by means of this ring,
in accordance with the laws of Moses and Israel.

The ḥatan places the ring on the kalla's right index finger, in full view of the witnesses.

INTERLUDE: READING OF THE KETUBA

To mark the separation between the kiddushin and nisu'in ceremonies, the ketuba is read. The ketuba is then given to the ḥatan, who hands it to the kalla.

The כלה *stands to the* חתן *right. The witnesses to the* קידושין
are called to the חופה *and the ring is produced.*
The מסדר קידושין *asks the* חתן *to attest to his ownership of the ring in the presence of the witnesses. The* מסדר קידושין *then shows the ring to the witnesses that they may confirm that it is of at least minimal value (*שווה פרוטה*).*

ברכות האירוסין

The מסדר קידושין *raises a full cup of wine and recites the following:*

בָּרוּךְ אַתָּה יהוה אֱלֹהֵינוּ מֶלֶךְ הָעוֹלָם
בּוֹרֵא פְּרִי הַגָּפֶן.

בָּרוּךְ אַתָּה יהוה אֱלֹהֵינוּ מֶלֶךְ הָעוֹלָם
אֲשֶׁר קִדְּשָׁנוּ בְּמִצְוֹתָיו וְצִוָּנוּ עַל הָעֲרָיוֹת
וְאָסַר לָנוּ אֶת הָאֲרוּסוֹת
וְהִתִּיר לָנוּ אֶת הַנְּשׂוּאוֹת לָנוּ עַל יְדֵי חֻפָּה וְקִדּוּשִׁין.
בָּרוּךְ אַתָּה יהוה
מְקַדֵּשׁ עַמּוֹ יִשְׂרָאֵל עַל יְדֵי חֻפָּה וְקִדּוּשִׁין.

The חתן *and then the* כלה *drink from the cup of wine.*

The חתן *holds the ring in his dominant hand,*
turns to the כלה*, and, in the presence of the witnesses, says:*

הֲרֵי אַתְּ מְקֻדֶּשֶׁת לִי בְּטַבַּעַת זוֹ כְּדָת מֹשֶׁה וְיִשְׂרָאֵל.

The חתן *places the ring on the* כלה*'s right index finger, in full view of the witnesses.*

קריאת הכתובה

To mark the separation between the קידושין *and* נישואין *ceremonies, the* כתובה *is read. The* כתובה *is then given to the* חתן*, who hands it to the* כלה*.*

MARRIAGE

A second cup of wine is poured and the sheva berakhot are recited.

בָּרוּךְ Blessed are You, Lord, our God, King of the universe, Who creates the fruit of the vine.

בָּרוּךְ Blessed are You, Lord, our God, King of the universe, in that He created all that exists for His glory.

בָּרוּךְ Blessed are You, Lord, our God, King of the universe, Who forms all of humanity.

בָּרוּךְ Blessed are You, Lord, our God, King of the universe, Who formed man in His image, in the image of His likeness, and Who for his sake and from him made an everlasting being. Blessed are You, Lord, Who forms all of humanity.

שׂוֹשׂ Bring great rejoicing and exultation to the desolate land by gathering in its children in celebration. Blessed are You, Lord, Who gladdens Zion through her children.

שַׂמֵּחַ Bring great happiness to this couple who are so beloved of each other, just as You brought happiness to those whom You formed in the Garden of Eden of old. Blessed are You, Lord, Who causes both groom and bride to rejoice.

בָּרוּךְ Blessed are You, Lord, our God, King of the universe, Who created joy and happiness, groom and bride, rejoicing and song, joy and delight, love and brotherhood, peace and fellowship. Lord our God, may there soon be heard in the cities of Judah and the streets of Jerusalem the sounds of jubilation and rejoicing, celebratory noises of grooms and brides, echoes of grooms exalting under their marriage canopy, and youths feasting in song. Blessed are You, Lord, Who causes groom and bride to rejoice together.

The ḥatan and then the kalla drink from the cup of wine.

נישואין

A second cup of wine is poured and the שבע ברכות *are recited.*

בָּרוּךְ אַתָּה יהוה אֱלֹהֵֽינוּ מֶֽלֶךְ הָעוֹלָם, בּוֹרֵא פְּרִי הַגָּֽפֶן.

בָּרוּךְ אַתָּה יהוה אֱלֹהֵֽינוּ מֶֽלֶךְ הָעוֹלָם, שֶׁהַכֹּל בָּרָא לִכְבוֹדוֹ.

בָּרוּךְ אַתָּה יהוה אֱלֹהֵֽינוּ מֶֽלֶךְ הָעוֹלָם, יוֹצֵר הָאָדָם.

בָּרוּךְ אַתָּה יהוה אֱלֹהֵֽינוּ מֶֽלֶךְ הָעוֹלָם, אֲשֶׁר יָצַר אֶת הָאָדָם בְּצַלְמוֹ, בְּצֶֽלֶם דְּמוּת תַּבְנִיתוֹ, וְהִתְקִין לוֹ מִמֶּֽנּוּ בִּנְיַן עֲדֵי עַד. בָּרוּךְ אַתָּה יהוה, יוֹצֵר הָאָדָם.

שׂוֹשׂ תָּשִׂישׂ וְתָגֵל הָעֲקָרָה בְּקִבּוּץ בָּנֶֽיהָ לְתוֹכָהּ בְּשִׂמְחָה. בָּרוּךְ אַתָּה יהוה, מְשַׂמֵּֽחַ צִיּוֹן בְּבָנֶֽיהָ.

שַׂמֵּֽחַ תְּשַׂמַּח רֵעִים הָאֲהוּבִים כְּשַׂמֵּֽחֲךָ יְצִירְךָ בְּגַן עֵֽדֶן מִקֶּֽדֶם. בָּרוּךְ אַתָּה יהוה, מְשַׂמֵּֽחַ חָתָן וְכַלָּה.

בָּרוּךְ אַתָּה יהוה אֱלֹהֵֽינוּ מֶֽלֶךְ הָעוֹלָם, אֲשֶׁר בָּרָא שָׂשׂוֹן וְשִׂמְחָה, חָתָן וְכַלָּה, גִּילָה, רִנָּה, דִּיצָה וְחֶדְוָה, אַהֲבָה וְאַחֲוָה וְשָׁלוֹם וְרֵעוּת. מְהֵרָה יהוה אֱלֹהֵֽינוּ, יִשָּׁמַע בְּעָרֵי יְהוּדָה וּבְחוּצוֹת יְרוּשָׁלָֽיִם, קוֹל שָׂשׂוֹן וְקוֹל שִׂמְחָה, קוֹל חָתָן וְקוֹל כַּלָּה, קוֹל מִצְהֲלוֹת חֲתָנִים מֵחֻפָּתָם וּנְעָרִים מִמִּשְׁתֵּה נְגִינָתָם. בָּרוּךְ אַתָּה יהוה, מְשַׂמֵּֽחַ הֶחָתָן עִם הַכַּלָּה.

The חתן *and then the* כלה *drink from the cup of wine.*

The glass that will be broken in remembrance of the destruction of the Temple is placed on the floor near the ḥatan. In many communities the passage 'Im Eshkakhekh' is pronounced or sung.

אִם־אֶשְׁכָּחֵךְ If I forget you, O Jerusalem, *Ps. 137*
may my right hand forget its skill.
May my tongue cling to the roof of my mouth,
if I do not remember you,
if I do not set Jerusalem above my highest joy.

The ḥatan breaks the glass with his right foot. This marks the end of the marriage ceremony under the ḥuppa.

The glass that will be broken in remembrance of the destruction of the בית המקדש *is placed on the floor near the* חתן*. In many communities the passage* אִם־אֶשְׁכָּחֵךְ *is pronounced or sung.*

תהלים קלז

אִם־אֶשְׁכָּחֵךְ יְרוּשָׁלָֽםִ, תִּשְׁכַּח יְמִינִי:
תִּדְבַּק לְשׁוֹנִי לְחִכִּי אִם־לֹא אֶזְכְּרֵכִי
אִם־לֹא אַעֲלֶה אֶת־יְרוּשָׁלַֽםִ
עַל רֹאשׁ שִׂמְחָתִי:

The חתן *breaks the glass with his right foot. This marks the end of the marriage ceremony under the* חופה*.*

HALAKHOT FOR SHEVA BERAKHOT

SHEVA BERKHOT

1. *Sheva berakhot* are recited at all meals following the week of the wedding when
   A. both the *ḥatan* and *kalla* are present (מסורת הרב חלק ב׳ עמ׳ שלח) and at least one of them has not been married before
   B. bread is served
   C. a *minyan* (including the *ḥatan*) is present (אה״ע סב:ד)
   D. at least one man who was not at the wedding meal or a previous *sheva berakhot* is present (*panim ḥadashot*). A man who attended the *ḥuppa* and heard the *sheva berakhot* at the ceremony, but did not attend the meal can serve as *panim ḥadashot* (אה״ע סב:ז). *Panim ḥadashot* are not required on Shabbat or Yom Tov (אה״ע סב:ח).
2. If both *ḥatan* and *kalla* were previously married, *sheva berakhot* are recited only at the meal following the *ḥuppa*. Some authorities, however, only allow for the recitation of *sheva berakhot* at the wedding meal if the *ḥuppa* and meal were on the same halakhic day (פתחי תשובה אה״ע סב). If a *minyan* is present at a meal during the first three days following the *ḥuppa*, the final blessing of *Asher Bara* is recited (אה״ע סב:ו, חלקת מחוקק אבה״ע סב:ו).
3. Some authorities hold that at least three of the men comprising the *minyan* must partake in the meal in order for *sheva berakhot* to be recited (האלף לך שלמה או״ח צג). Other authorities require ten participants in the meal (seven who ate bread and three who ate fruit or cake; שובע שמחות - דבליצקי פרק א׳ הערה כו). The latter opinion is widely accepted (הנשואין כהלכתה יד:מא).
4. Someone who has not eaten at the meal may recite one or more of the *sheva berakhot* (נפש הרב עמ׳ רנו).

5. If a *minyan* is not present, only the final *berakha* of *Asher Bara* is recited (אבה"ע סב:ד).
6. On days when *panim ḥadashot* are required, if there are none present, only the final blessing of *Asher Bara* is recited (אבה"ע סב:ו).
7. The authorities debate whether *sheva berakhot* should be recited at *seuda shelishit* on Shabbat, and if so, whether *panim ḥadashot* are required (אבה"ע סב:ח). Common practice is to recite *sheva berakhot* and not require *panim ḥadashot*. Ideally, however, in such circumstances the *ḥatan* should offer *divrei Torah* at the meal, thereby adding to the *simḥa* (פתחי תשובה אבה"ע סב ס"ק טז, שובע שמחות – דבליצקי פרק א' הערה סו).
8. The week of *sheva berakhot* is counted from the day of the *ḥuppa* even when the *ḥuppa* occurred at the end of the day (כנסת יחזקאל ס).
9. If the *ḥuppa* occurred during *bein hashmashot*, but the meal did not begin until the night (*tzeit hakokhavim*), the week of *sheva berakhot* begins from the day of the meal (אהלי ישורון עמ' לב הערות 9–10).
10. When the final day of *sheva berakhot* coincides with Shabbat, some authorities rule that *sheva berakhot* should be concluded before sunset, even when Shabbat is extended later into the night (רעק"א אבה"ע סב:ב). Other authorities, however, permit the recitation of *sheva berakhot* if the meal began before sunset and *Havdala* has not yet been recited (אהלי ישורון עמ' לב הערה 10 בשם הגרמ"פ, שבט הלוי ח"א סימן לט).
11. There are various opinions regarding drinking the *sheva berakhot* wine at *seuda shelishit*. Some authorities maintain that only the *ḥatan* and *kallah* should drink of the wine (אג"מ או"ח ח"ד סימן סט:א); others argue that the wine should be saved for *Havdala*; yet others hold that the individual leading *Birkat Hamazon* should drink (משיב הלכה ח"א סימן צב); finally, others maintain that the *ḥatan, kalla,* and *mevarekh* should all drink of the wine (יסודי ישורון ח"ה עמ' 455). All of these are valid halakhic customs (רבבות אפרים ח"א סימן רסה).
12. *Sheva berakhot* are only recited when the meal is in honor of the

ḥatan and *kalla*. If a *ḥatan* and *kalla* attend a celebratory meal for someone else (a wedding, a *brit mila*, etc,) *sheva berakhot* are not recited for them (ארחות חיים סא). If food is added specifically for the *sheva berakhot*, however, or if an announcement concerning the presence of the *ḥatan* and *kalla* is made before the meal begins, *sheva berakhot* may be recited (אהלי ישורון ב:ב:ג).

13. The introductory *piyut* of "*Devai Haser*" precedes the *zimun*. Some omit this on Shabbat or Yom Tov (שובע שמחות ד:י), while others recite it (אהלי ישורון עמ׳ לו הערה 88).
14. If necessary, a mourner may participate to complete the *minyan* for *sheva berakhot* (חידושי רעק״א יו״ד שצא).

BIRKAT HAMAZON
FOLLOWED BY SHEVA BERAKHOT

שִׁיר הַמַּעֲלוֹת A song of ascents. *Ps. 126*
When the Lord brought back the exiles of Zion,
we were like dreamers –
then were our mouths filled with laughter,
our tongues with songs of joy;
then was it said among the nations,
"The Lord has done great things for them."
The Lord has done great things for us,
and we rejoiced.
Bring back our exiles, Lord, like streams in the Negev.
May those who sowed in tears reap in joy;
may those who go out weeping,
carrying a sack of seed,
come back in glad song,
carrying their sheaves.

Some say:

תְּהִלַּת My mouth shall speak the praise of the Lord, *Ps. 145*
and all creatures shall bless His holy name
for ever and all time.
But we will bless the Lord
now and forever. Halleluya!
Thank the Lord for He is good – *Ps. 136*
His loving-kindness is forever.
Who can articulate the Lord's mighty acts;
who can express all His praise?

ברכת המזון לסעודת שבע ברכות

שִׁיר הַמַּעֲלוֹת תהלים קכו
בְּשׁוּב יהוה אֶת־שִׁיבַת צִיּוֹן
הָיִינוּ כְּחֹלְמִים:
אָז יִמָּלֵא שְׂחוֹק פִּינוּ וּלְשׁוֹנֵנוּ רִנָּה
אָז יֹאמְרוּ בַגּוֹיִם
הִגְדִּיל יהוה לַעֲשׂוֹת עִם־אֵלֶּה:
הִגְדִּיל יהוה לַעֲשׂוֹת עִמָּנוּ, הָיִינוּ שְׂמֵחִים:
שׁוּבָה יהוה אֶת־שְׁבִיתֵנוּ, כַּאֲפִיקִים בַּנֶּגֶב:
הַזֹּרְעִים בְּדִמְעָה בְּרִנָּה יִקְצֹרוּ:
הָלוֹךְ יֵלֵךְ וּבָכֹה נֹשֵׂא מֶשֶׁךְ־הַזָּרַע
בֹּא־יָבֹא בְרִנָּה נֹשֵׂא אֲלֻמֹּתָיו:

Some say:

תְּהִלַּת יהוה יְדַבֶּר פִּי תהלים קמה
וִיבָרֵךְ כָּל־בָּשָׂר שֵׁם קָדְשׁוֹ לְעוֹלָם וָעֶד:
וַאֲנַחְנוּ נְבָרֵךְ יָהּ מֵעַתָּה וְעַד־עוֹלָם, הַלְלוּיָהּ: תהלים קטו
הוֹדוּ לַיהוה כִּי־טוֹב, כִּי לְעוֹלָם חַסְדּוֹ: תהלים קלו
מִי יְמַלֵּל גְּבוּרוֹת יהוה, יַשְׁמִיעַ כָּל־תְּהִלָּתוֹ: תהלים קו

ZIMUN FOR THE SHEVA BRAKHOT FEAST

The zimun when three or more men are present:

Leader: רַבּוֹתַי Esteemed companions, let us say grace.

Others: Blessed be the name of the Lord, *Ps. 113*
now and for evermore.

Leader: Blessed be the name of the Lord,
now and for evermore.

דְּוַי הָסֵר Remove all sorrow and anger,
so that all – even the mute – will rejoice in song;
Lead us in the ways of righteousness,
so as to merit the blessing
of the descendants of Aaron.

Leader: With your permission
masters, teachers, and esteemed companions
let us bless (*in a minyan:* our God) the One of Whose bounty
we have partaken.

Others: Blessed be (*in a minyan:* our God,) the One of Whose bounty
we have partaken and through Whose goodness we live.

Leader: Blessed be (*in a minyan:* our God,) the One of Whose bounty
we have partaken and through Whose goodness we live.
Blessed be He, and blessed be His name.

זימון לסעודת שבע ברכות

The זימון *when three or more men are present:*

Leader רַבּוֹתַי, נְבָרֵךְ.

Others יְהִי שֵׁם יהוה מְבֹרָךְ מֵעַתָּה וְעַד־עוֹלָם: תהלים קיג

Leader יְהִי שֵׁם יהוה מְבֹרָךְ מֵעַתָּה וְעַד־עוֹלָם:

דְּוַי הָסֵר וְגַם חָרוֹן
וְאָז אִלֵּם בְּשִׁיר יָרֹן.
נְחֵנוּ בְּמַעְגְּלֵי צֶדֶק
שְׁעֵה בִּרְכַּת בְּנֵי אַהֲרֹן.

Leader בִּרְשׁוּת מָרָנָן וְרַבָּנָן וְרַבּוֹתַי
נְבָרֵךְ (במנין: אֱלֹהֵינוּ) שֶׁאָכַלְנוּ מִשֶּׁלּוֹ.

Others בָּרוּךְ (במנין: אֱלֹהֵינוּ) שֶׁאָכַלְנוּ מִשֶּׁלּוֹ וּבְטוּבוֹ חָיִינוּ.

Leader בָּרוּךְ (במנין: אֱלֹהֵינוּ) שֶׁאָכַלְנוּ מִשֶּׁלּוֹ וּבְטוּבוֹ חָיִינוּ.
בָּרוּךְ הוּא וּבָרוּךְ שְׁמוֹ.

BLESSING OF NOURISHMENT

בָּרוּךְ Blessed are You, Lord our God, King of the universe,
Who feeds the whole world in His goodness,
with grace, kindness, and mercy.
He gives food to all flesh,
for His mercy endures forever.
Thanks to His great goodness
we have never lacked what to eat.
For the sake of His great name
may we never be short of food,
for He is the God Who feeds and sustains all,
is good to all,
and provides food for all His creatures as created by Him.
Blessed are You, Lord,
Who provides food for all.

BLESSING FOR THE LAND

נוֹדֶה We thank You, Lord our God,
for the beloved, good, and spacious land
that You gave our fathers as an inheritance.
We thank You, Lord our God,
for bringing us out of the land of Egypt
and redeeming us from the house of bondage.
We thank You for Your covenant sealed in our flesh,
for Your Torah which You have taught us,
and for Your precepts that You made known to us.
We thank You also for the life, grace, and kindness
that You have graciously bestowed on us, and for the food we eat,
with which You nourish and sustain us continually,
every day, in every season, and at every hour.

ברכת הזן

בָּרוּךְ אַתָּה יהוה אֱלֹהֵינוּ מֶלֶךְ הָעוֹלָם
הַזָּן אֶת הָעוֹלָם כֻּלּוֹ בְּטוּבוֹ
בְּחֵן בְּחֶסֶד וּבְרַחֲמִים
הוּא נוֹתֵן לֶחֶם לְכָל בָּשָׂר, כִּי לְעוֹלָם חַסְדּוֹ.
וּבְטוּבוֹ הַגָּדוֹל, תָּמִיד לֹא חָסַר לָנוּ
וְאַל יֶחְסַר לָנוּ מָזוֹן לְעוֹלָם וָעֶד
בַּעֲבוּר שְׁמוֹ הַגָּדוֹל.
כִּי הוּא אֵל זָן וּמְפַרְנֵס לַכֹּל וּמֵטִיב לַכֹּל
וּמֵכִין מָזוֹן לְכָל בְּרִיּוֹתָיו אֲשֶׁר בָּרָא.
בָּרוּךְ אַתָּה יהוה, הַזָּן אֶת הַכֹּל.

ברכת הארץ

נוֹדֶה לְךָ, יהוה אֱלֹהֵינוּ
עַל שֶׁהִנְחַלְתָּ לַאֲבוֹתֵינוּ אֶרֶץ חֶמְדָּה טוֹבָה וּרְחָבָה
וְעַל שֶׁהוֹצֵאתָנוּ יהוה אֱלֹהֵינוּ מֵאֶרֶץ מִצְרַיִם
וּפְדִיתָנוּ מִבֵּית עֲבָדִים
וְעַל בְּרִיתְךָ שֶׁחָתַמְתָּ בִּבְשָׂרֵנוּ
וְעַל תּוֹרָתְךָ שֶׁלִּמַּדְתָּנוּ, וְעַל חֻקֶּיךָ שֶׁהוֹדַעְתָּנוּ
וְעַל חַיִּים חֵן וָחֶסֶד שֶׁחוֹנַנְתָּנוּ
וְעַל אֲכִילַת מָזוֹן שָׁאַתָּה זָן וּמְפַרְנֵס אוֹתָנוּ תָּמִיד
בְּכָל יוֹם וּבְכָל עֵת וּבְכָל שָׁעָה.

On Ḥanukka:

עַל הַנִּסִּים [We thank You] for the miracles, the deliverance, and the triumphant victories and salvation, as well as wars which You wrought for our ancestors in those days at this season.

בִּימֵי מַתִּתְיָהוּ It happened in the days of Mattathias son of Johanan, the Hasmonean high priest, and his sons. Then the cruel Hellenist power rose up to force Your people Israel to forget Your Torah and transgress the commands of Your will. In that hour of their distress, You in Your great mercy rose to take up their cause and defend their rights. Meting out retribution You delivered the strong into the hand of the weak, the many into the hand of the few, the impure into the hand of the pure, the evil ones into the hand of the righteous, and the wicked into the hand of devotees of Your Torah. You thereby made for Yourself a great and holy name throughout Your world, as well as bringing about great deliverance and salvation for Your people Israel (known) to this day. Then Your children came to the Holy of Holies in Your house, cleared Your Temple, purified Your holy place, kindled lights in Your holy courts, and instituted these eight days of Ḥanukka to give thanks and sing praise to Your great name.

Continue with "For all these."

On Purim:

עַל הַנִּסִּים [We thank You] for the miracles, the deliverance, and the triumphant victories and salvation, as well as wars which You wrought for our ancestors in those days at this season.

בִּימֵי מָרְדְּכַי In the days of Mordekhai and Esther, in Shushan the capital, when the wicked Haman rose up against them, he sought to
kill, destroy, and annihilate all the Jews, young and old, children and *Esther 3*
women alike, all in one day – the thirteenth day of the twelfth month, which is the month of Adar – and seize the plunder. In Your great mercy You nullified his counsel and subverted his designs, causing them to recoil on his own head so that he and his sons were hanged on the gallows.

Continue with "For all these."

בחנוכה:

עַל הַנִּסִּים וְעַל הַפֻּרְקָן וְעַל הַגְּבוּרוֹת וְעַל הַתְּשׁוּעוֹת וְעַל הַמִּלְחָמוֹת שֶׁעָשִׂיתָ לַאֲבוֹתֵינוּ בַּיָּמִים הָהֵם בַּזְּמַן הַזֶּה.

בִּימֵי מַתִּתְיָהוּ בֶּן יוֹחָנָן כֹּהֵן גָּדוֹל חַשְׁמוֹנַאי וּבָנָיו, כְּשֶׁעָמְדָה מַלְכוּת יָוָן הָרְשָׁעָה עַל עַמְּךָ יִשְׂרָאֵל לְהַשְׁכִּיחָם תּוֹרָתֶךָ וּלְהַעֲבִירָם מֵחֻקֵּי רְצוֹנֶךָ, וְאַתָּה בְּרַחֲמֶיךָ הָרַבִּים עָמַדְתָּ לָהֶם בְּעֵת צָרָתָם, רַבְתָּ אֶת רִיבָם, דַּנְתָּ אֶת דִּינָם, נָקַמְתָּ אֶת נִקְמָתָם, מָסַרְתָּ גִבּוֹרִים בְּיַד חַלָּשִׁים, וְרַבִּים בְּיַד מְעַטִּים, וּטְמֵאִים בְּיַד טְהוֹרִים, וּרְשָׁעִים בְּיַד צַדִּיקִים, וְזֵדִים בְּיַד עוֹסְקֵי תוֹרָתֶךָ, וּלְךָ עָשִׂיתָ שֵׁם גָּדוֹל וְקָדוֹשׁ בְּעוֹלָמֶךָ, וּלְעַמְּךָ יִשְׂרָאֵל עָשִׂיתָ תְּשׁוּעָה גְדוֹלָה וּפֻרְקָן כְּהַיּוֹם הַזֶּה. וְאַחַר כֵּן בָּאוּ בָנֶיךָ לִדְבִיר בֵּיתֶךָ, וּפִנּוּ אֶת הֵיכָלֶךָ, וְטִהֲרוּ אֶת מִקְדָּשֶׁךָ, וְהִדְלִיקוּ נֵרוֹת בְּחַצְרוֹת קָדְשֶׁךָ, וְקָבְעוּ שְׁמוֹנַת יְמֵי חֲנֻכָּה אֵלּוּ, לְהוֹדוֹת וּלְהַלֵּל לְשִׁמְךָ הַגָּדוֹל.

Continue with וְעַל הַכֹּל.

בפורים:

עַל הַנִּסִּים וְעַל הַפֻּרְקָן וְעַל הַגְּבוּרוֹת וְעַל הַתְּשׁוּעוֹת וְעַל הַמִּלְחָמוֹת שֶׁעָשִׂיתָ לַאֲבוֹתֵינוּ בַּיָּמִים הָהֵם בַּזְּמַן הַזֶּה.

בִּימֵי מָרְדְּכַי וְאֶסְתֵּר בְּשׁוּשַׁן הַבִּירָה, כְּשֶׁעָמַד עֲלֵיהֶם הָמָן הָרָשָׁע, בִּקֵּשׁ לְהַשְׁמִיד לַהֲרֹג וּלְאַבֵּד אֶת־כָּל־הַיְּהוּדִים מִנַּעַר אסתר ג
וְעַד־זָקֵן טַף וְנָשִׁים בְּיוֹם אֶחָד, בִּשְׁלוֹשָׁה עָשָׂר לְחֹדֶשׁ שְׁנֵים־עָשָׂר, הוּא־חֹדֶשׁ אֲדָר, וּשְׁלָלָם לָבוֹז: וְאַתָּה בְּרַחֲמֶיךָ הָרַבִּים הֵפַרְתָּ אֶת עֲצָתוֹ, וְקִלְקַלְתָּ אֶת מַחֲשַׁבְתּוֹ, וַהֲשֵׁבוֹתָ לּוֹ גְּמוּלוֹ בְּרֹאשׁוֹ, וְתָלוּ אוֹתוֹ וְאֶת בָּנָיו עַל הָעֵץ.

Continue with וְעַל הַכֹּל.

וְעַל הַכֹּל For all these blessings, LORD our God,
we thank You and bless You.
May Your name be blessed, in the mouths of all living beings,
continually, forever and ever.
As it is written,
"And when you eat and are satisfied, *Deut. 8*
you shall bless the LORD your God
for the good land that He has given you."
Blessed are You, LORD,
for the land and for the sustenance.

BLESSING FOR JERUSALEM

רַחֵם (נָא) Have pity (please,) LORD our God,
on Israel Your people,
on Jerusalem Your city, and Zion
the dwelling place of Your glory,
on the royal house of David Your anointed,
and on the great and holy Temple
with which Your name is associated.
Our God, our Father,
shepherd us, sustain us, support us, provide for all our needs,
maintain us, and, LORD our God,
give us immediate relief from all our troubles.
LORD our God,
do not make us dependent
on the gifts of people of flesh and blood,
or in need of their loans.
Rather let us depend only
on Your full, open, sacred, and bountiful hand,
so that we need never be embarrassed or humiliated.

וְעַל הַכֹּל, יהוה אֱלֹהֵינוּ
אֲנַחְנוּ מוֹדִים לָךְ וּמְבָרְכִים אוֹתָךְ
יִתְבָּרַךְ שִׁמְךָ בְּפִי כָּל חַי תָּמִיד לְעוֹלָם וָעֶד
כַּכָּתוּב: וְאָכַלְתָּ וְשָׂבָעְתָּ, וּבֵרַכְתָּ אֶת־יהוה אֱלֹהֶיךָ דברים ח
עַל־הָאָרֶץ הַטֹּבָה אֲשֶׁר נָתַן־לָךְ:
בָּרוּךְ אַתָּה יהוה, עַל הָאָרֶץ וְעַל הַמָּזוֹן.

ברכת ירושלים

רַחֵם (נָא), יהוה אֱלֹהֵינוּ
עַל יִשְׂרָאֵל עַמֶּךָ, וְעַל יְרוּשָׁלַיִם עִירֶךָ
וְעַל צִיּוֹן מִשְׁכַּן כְּבוֹדֶךָ
וְעַל מַלְכוּת בֵּית דָּוִד מְשִׁיחֶךָ
וְעַל הַבַּיִת הַגָּדוֹל וְהַקָּדוֹשׁ שֶׁנִּקְרָא שִׁמְךָ עָלָיו.
אֱלֹהֵינוּ, אָבִינוּ
רְעֵנוּ, זוּנֵנוּ, פַּרְנְסֵנוּ וְכַלְכְּלֵנוּ
וְהַרְוִיחֵנוּ, וְהַרְוַח לָנוּ יהוה אֱלֹהֵינוּ מְהֵרָה מִכָּל צָרוֹתֵינוּ.
וְנָא אַל תַּצְרִיכֵנוּ, יהוה אֱלֹהֵינוּ
לֹא לִידֵי מַתְּנַת בָּשָׂר וָדָם
וְלֹא לִידֵי הַלְוָאָתָם
כִּי אִם לְיָדְךָ הַמְּלֵאָה, הַפְּתוּחָה, הַקְּדוֹשָׁה וְהָרְחָבָה
שֶׁלֹּא נֵבוֹשׁ וְלֹא נִכָּלֵם לְעוֹלָם וָעֶד.

On Shabbat, say:

רְצֵה Favor and invigorate us, LORD our God, with Your commandments,
and with the commandment of the seventh day,
this great and holy Sabbath.
For this day is great and holy before You,
for us to desist from work on it, and lovingly rest on it
in accordance with the commandment You have willed.
May it be Your will, LORD our God, to grant us a rest
during which there will be no sorrow, trouble, or sighing.
And, LORD our God, may You show us Zion Your city
comforted and the building of Jerusalem Your holy city,
for You are the Master of salvation, and the Master of consolation.

On Rosh Ḥodesh and Festivals, say:

אֱלֹהֵינוּ Our God and God of our fathers,
may there arise, arrive, reach, appear, be favored, heard,
considered and remembered, our remembrance and recollection,
Your remembrance of our fathers,
of the Messiah son of David Your servant,
of Jerusalem Your holy city
and of all Your people the house of Israel.
May they come before You for deliverance and benefit,
for grace, kindness, and mercy, for life and peace, on this day of:

On Rosh Ḥodesh:	Rosh Ḥodesh.
On Rosh HaShana:	the Day of Memorial.
On Pesaḥ:	the Festival of Matzot.
On Shavuot:	the Festival of Shavuot.
On Sukkot:	the Festival of Sukkot.
On Shemini Atzeret & Simḥat Torah:	the eighth day, this Festival of Atzeret.

LORD our God, remember us this day for good.
Be mindful of us this day for blessing, preserve us this day for life.
Regarding redemption and mercy show us compassion
and grace, and have pity on us and save us.
For our eyes are lifted toward You,
for You are a gracious and merciful God (*on Rosh HaShana:* King).

On שבת*, say:*

רְצֵה וְהַחֲלִיצֵנוּ, יהוה אֱלֹהֵינוּ, בְּמִצְוֹתֶיךָ
וּבְמִצְוַת יוֹם הַשְּׁבִיעִי הַשַּׁבָּת הַגָּדוֹל וְהַקָּדוֹשׁ הַזֶּה
כִּי יוֹם זֶה גָּדוֹל וְקָדוֹשׁ הוּא לְפָנֶיךָ
לִשְׁבָּת בּוֹ, וְלָנוּחַ בּוֹ בְּאַהֲבָה כְּמִצְוַת רְצוֹנֶךָ
וּבִרְצוֹנְךָ הָנִיחַ לָנוּ, יהוה אֱלֹהֵינוּ
שֶׁלֹּא תְהֵא צָרָה וְיָגוֹן וַאֲנָחָה בְּיוֹם מְנוּחָתֵנוּ
וְהַרְאֵנוּ, יהוה אֱלֹהֵינוּ, בְּנֶחָמַת צִיּוֹן עִירֶךָ
וּבְבִנְיַן יְרוּשָׁלַיִם עִיר קָדְשֶׁךָ
כִּי אַתָּה הוּא בַּעַל הַיְשׁוּעוֹת וּבַעַל הַנֶּחָמוֹת.

On ראש חודש *and* חגים*, say:*

אֱלֹהֵינוּ וֵאלֹהֵי אֲבוֹתֵינוּ
יַעֲלֶה וְיָבוֹא וְיַגִּיעַ, וְיֵרָאֶה וְיֵרָצֶה וְיִשָּׁמַע
וְיִפָּקֵד וְיִזָּכֵר זִכְרוֹנֵנוּ וּפִקְדוֹנֵנוּ, וְזִכְרוֹן אֲבוֹתֵינוּ
וְזִכְרוֹן מָשִׁיחַ בֶּן דָּוִד עַבְדֶּךָ, וְזִכְרוֹן יְרוּשָׁלַיִם עִיר קָדְשֶׁךָ
וְזִכְרוֹן כָּל עַמְּךָ בֵּית יִשְׂרָאֵל לְפָנֶיךָ
לִפְלֵיטָה לְטוֹבָה, לְחֵן וּלְחֶסֶד וּלְרַחֲמִים, לְחַיִּים וּלְשָׁלוֹם בְּיוֹם

בראש חודש: רֹאשׁ הַחֹדֶשׁ הַזֶּה.
בראש השנה: הַזִּכָּרוֹן הַזֶּה.
בפסח: חַג הַמַּצּוֹת הַזֶּה.
בשבועות: חַג הַשָּׁבוּעוֹת הַזֶּה.
בסוכות: חַג הַסֻּכּוֹת הַזֶּה.
בשמיני עצרת ושמחת תורה: הַשְּׁמִינִי חַג הָעֲצֶרֶת הַזֶּה.

זָכְרֵנוּ יהוה אֱלֹהֵינוּ בּוֹ לְטוֹבָה, וּפָקְדֵנוּ בוֹ לִבְרָכָה
וְהוֹשִׁיעֵנוּ בוֹ לְחַיִּים.
וּבִדְבַר יְשׁוּעָה וְרַחֲמִים, חוּס וְחָנֵּנוּ וְרַחֵם עָלֵינוּ, וְהוֹשִׁיעֵנוּ
כִּי אֵלֶיךָ עֵינֵינוּ, כִּי אֵל (בראש השנה: מֶלֶךְ) חַנּוּן וְרַחוּם אָתָּה.

וּבְנֵה Please rebuild Jerusalem the holy city soon in our own days.
Blessed are You, LORD, Who in His mercy rebuilds Jerusalem.
Amen.

BLESSING OF GOD'S GOODNESS

בָּרוּךְ Blessed are You, LORD our God, King of the universe,
God our Father, our King, our Sovereign,
our Creator, our Redeemer, our Maker, our Holy One,
Holy One of Jacob.
You are our Shepherd, Shepherd of Israel,
You are the King Who is good and Who does good to all.
For every single day He has done good, continues to do good,
and will do good for us.
Just as He has bestowed that upon us,
and continues to bestow it upon us,
so may He forever bestow upon us
grace, kindness, mercy, relief, salvation and success,
blessing and redemption, consolation, livelihood,
sustenance, compassion, life, peace,
and all manner of good things.
And may He never deprive us of any good thing.

ADDITIONAL REQUESTS

הָרַחֲמָן May the Compassionate One
reign over us forevermore.

May the Compassionate One be blessed
in the heavens and on earth.

May the Compassionate One be praised in every generation,
and glorified and honored among us
for all time, eternally.

וּבְנֵה יְרוּשָׁלַיִם עִיר הַקֹּדֶשׁ בִּמְהֵרָה בְיָמֵינוּ.
בָּרוּךְ אַתָּה יהוה, בּוֹנֵה בְרַחֲמָיו יְרוּשָׁלָיִם, אָמֵן.

ברכת הטוב והמטיב

בָּרוּךְ אַתָּה יהוה אֱלֹהֵינוּ מֶלֶךְ הָעוֹלָם
הָאֵל אָבִינוּ, מַלְכֵּנוּ, אַדִּירֵנוּ
בּוֹרְאֵנוּ, גּוֹאֲלֵנוּ, יוֹצְרֵנוּ, קְדוֹשֵׁנוּ, קְדוֹשׁ יַעֲקֹב
רוֹעֵנוּ, רוֹעֵה יִשְׂרָאֵל, הַמֶּלֶךְ הַטּוֹב וְהַמֵּטִיב לַכֹּל
שֶׁבְּכָל יוֹם וָיוֹם
הוּא הֵיטִיב, הוּא מֵטִיב, הוּא יֵיטִיב לָנוּ
הוּא גְמָלָנוּ, הוּא גוֹמְלֵנוּ, הוּא יִגְמְלֵנוּ לָעַד
לְחֵן וּלְחֶסֶד וּלְרַחֲמִים, וּלְרֶוַח, הַצָּלָה וְהַצְלָחָה
בְּרָכָה וִישׁוּעָה, נֶחָמָה, פַּרְנָסָה וְכַלְכָּלָה
וְרַחֲמִים וְחַיִּים וְשָׁלוֹם וְכָל טוֹב
וּמִכָּל טוּב לְעוֹלָם אַל יְחַסְּרֵנוּ.

בקשות נוספות

הָרַחֲמָן הוּא יִמְלֹךְ עָלֵינוּ לְעוֹלָם וָעֶד.
הָרַחֲמָן הוּא יִתְבָּרַךְ בַּשָּׁמַיִם וּבָאָרֶץ.
הָרַחֲמָן הוּא יִשְׁתַּבַּח לְדוֹר דּוֹרִים
וְיִתְפָּאַר בָּנוּ לָעַד וּלְנֵצַח נְצָחִים
וְיִתְהַדַּר בָּנוּ לָעַד וּלְעוֹלְמֵי עוֹלָמִים.

May the Compassionate One maintain us
with honor.

May the Compassionate One break the yoke from our neck
and lead us upright to our land.

May the Compassionate One send us great blessing
on this household and on this table
at which we have eaten.

May the Compassionate One send us the prophet Elijah –
may he be remembered for good –
to herald good tidings of redemption and consolation.

הָרַחֲמָן May the Compassionate One bless –

When eating at one's own table, say
(include the words in parentheses that apply):
me, (my wife/husband, / my father, my teacher /
my mother, my teacher/ my children,)
and all that is mine,

A guest at someone else's table says
(include the words in parentheses that apply):
the head of this household, him (and his wife,
the head of this household / and his children,)
and all that is his,

Children at their parents' table say
(include the words in parentheses that apply):
my father, my teacher, (head of this household,)
and my mother, my teacher, (head of this household,)
them, their household, their children,
and all that is theirs.

For all other guests, add:
and all the diners here,

הָרַחֲמָן הוּא יְפַרְנְסֵנוּ בְּכָבוֹד.

הָרַחֲמָן הוּא יִשְׁבֹּר עֻלֵּנוּ מֵעַל צַוָּארֵנוּ
וְהוּא יוֹלִיכֵנוּ קוֹמְמִיּוּת לְאַרְצֵנוּ.

הָרַחֲמָן הוּא יִשְׁלַח לָנוּ בְּרָכָה מְרֻבָּה בַּבַּיִת הַזֶּה
וְעַל שֻׁלְחָן זֶה שֶׁאָכַלְנוּ עָלָיו.

הָרַחֲמָן הוּא יִשְׁלַח לָנוּ אֶת אֵלִיָּהוּ הַנָּבִיא זָכוּר לַטּוֹב
וִיבַשֶּׂר לָנוּ בְּשׂוֹרוֹת טוֹבוֹת יְשׁוּעוֹת וְנֶחָמוֹת.

הָרַחֲמָן הוּא יְבָרֵךְ

When eating at one's own table, say
(include the words in parentheses that apply):

אוֹתִי (וְאֶת אִשְׁתִּי / וְאֶת בַּעְלִי / וְאֶת אָבִי מוֹרִי / וְאֶת אִמִּי מוֹרָתִי / וְאֶת זַרְעִי) וְאֶת כָּל אֲשֶׁר לִי.

A guest at someone else's table says
(include the words in parentheses that apply):

אֶת בַּעַל הַבַּיִת הַזֶּה, אוֹתוֹ (וְאֶת אִשְׁתּוֹ בַּעֲלַת הַבַּיִת הַזֶּה / וְאֶת זַרְעוֹ) וְאֶת כָּל אֲשֶׁר לוֹ.

Children at their parents' table say
(include the words in parentheses that apply):

אֶת אָבִי מוֹרִי (בַּעַל הַבַּיִת הַזֶּה)
וְאֶת אִמִּי מוֹרָתִי (בַּעֲלַת הַבַּיִת הַזֶּה)
אוֹתָם וְאֶת בֵּיתָם וְאֶת זַרְעָם וְאֶת כָּל אֲשֶׁר לָהֶם

For all other guests, add:

וְאֶת כָּל הַמְסֻבִּין כָּאן

אוֹתָֽנוּ – together with us and all that is ours.
Just as our forefathers
Abraham, Isaac, and Jacob were blessed
in all, from all, with all,
so may He bless all of us together with a complete blessing,
and let us say: Amen.

בַּמָּרוֹם In heaven may they invoke upon these people
and ourselves sufficient merit to ensure peace,
to bring blessing from the Lord,
and to have the God of our salvation treat us charitably.
May we find grace and good sense in the eyes of God and man.

On Shabbat: May the Compassionate One
cause us to inherit the time that is entirely Sabbath
with repose in eternal life.

On Rosh Ḥodesh: May the Compassionate One
renew for us this month for good and for blessing.

On Rosh HaShana: May the Compassionate One
renew for us this year for good and for blessing.

On Yom Tov: May the Compassionate One
cause us to inherit a day that is entirely good.

On Sukkot: May the Compassionate One
reestablish for us the fallen Tabernacle of David.

הָרַחֲמָן May the Compassionate One make us worthy
of the messianic age and the life of the World to Come.
On weekdays: He grants great victories *II Sam. 22*
/ *On Shabbat, Festivals, and Rosh Ḥodesh:* He is a tower of victory /
for His king and shows loyalty to His anointed,
to David and his seed forever.
May He Who makes peace in the highest heaven
make peace for us and for all Israel,
and say, Amen.

אוֹתָֽנוּ וְאֶת כָּל אֲשֶׁר לָֽנוּ, כְּמוֹ שֶׁנִּתְבָּֽרְכוּ אֲבוֹתֵֽינוּ
אַבְרָהָם יִצְחָק וְיַֽעֲקֹב, בַּכֹּל, מִכֹּל, כֹּל
כֵּן יְבָרֵךְ אוֹתָֽנוּ כֻּלָּֽנוּ יַֽחַד בִּבְרָכָה שְׁלֵמָה
וְנֹאמַר אָמֵן.

בַּמָּרוֹם יְלַמְּדוּ עֲלֵיהֶם וְעָלֵֽינוּ זְכוּת שֶׁתְּהֵא לְמִשְׁמֶֽרֶת שָׁלוֹם
וְנִשָּׂא בְרָכָה מֵאֵת יהוה וּצְדָקָה מֵאֱלֹהֵי יִשְׁעֵֽנוּ
וְנִמְצָא חֵן וְשֵֽׂכֶל טוֹב בְּעֵינֵי אֱלֹהִים וְאָדָם.

בשבת: הָֽרַחֲמָן הוּא יַנְחִילֵֽנוּ
יוֹם שֶׁכֻּלּוֹ שַׁבָּת וּמְנוּחָה לְחַיֵּי הָעוֹלָמִים.

בראש חודש: הָֽרַחֲמָן הוּא יְחַדֵּשׁ עָלֵֽינוּ
אֶת הַחֹֽדֶשׁ הַזֶּה לְטוֹבָה וְלִבְרָכָה.

בראש השנה: הָֽרַחֲמָן הוּא יְחַדֵּשׁ עָלֵֽינוּ
אֶת הַשָּׁנָה הַזֹּאת לְטוֹבָה וְלִבְרָכָה.

ביום טוב: הָֽרַחֲמָן הוּא יַנְחִילֵֽנוּ יוֹם שֶׁכֻּלּוֹ טוֹב.

בסוכות: הָֽרַחֲמָן הוּא יָקִים לָֽנוּ אֶת סֻכַּת דָּוִד הַנּוֹפֶֽלֶת.

הָֽרַחֲמָן הוּא יְזַכֵּֽנוּ לִימוֹת הַמָּשִֽׁיחַ וּלְחַיֵּי הָעוֹלָם הַבָּא
מַגְדִּל/ *On* שבת, חגים, *and* ראש חודש מִגְדּוֹל/ יְשׁוּעוֹת מַלְכּוֹ שמואל ב׳ כב
וְעֹֽשֶׂה־חֶֽסֶד לִמְשִׁיחוֹ, לְדָוִד וּלְזַרְעוֹ עַד־עוֹלָם:
עֹשֶׂה שָׁלוֹם בִּמְרוֹמָיו
הוּא יַעֲשֶׂה שָׁלוֹם עָלֵֽינוּ וְעַל כָּל יִשְׂרָאֵל
וְאִמְרוּ אָמֵן.

יְראוּ Fear the LORD, you His holy ones, *Ps. 34*
for those who fear Him lack nothing.
Lions may grow weak and hungry,
but those who seek the LORD will never lack any good.
Thank the LORD for He is good; His loving-kindness is forever. *Ps. 118*
You open Your hand and satisfy the needs of every living thing. *Ps. 145*
Blessed is the person who trusts in the LORD. *Jer. 17*
The LORD will be his protector.
I was once young; now I am old, *Ps. 37*
yet I have never seen the righteous forsaken,
with their children begging for bread.
May the LORD give might to His people; *Ps. 29*
may the LORD bless His people with peace.

The sheva berakhot are now recited (see *the next page*).

יְראוּ אֶת־יהוה קְדֹשָׁיו, כִּי־אֵין מַחְסוֹר לִירֵאָיו: תהלים לד
כְּפִירִים רָשׁוּ וְרָעֵבוּ
וְדֹרְשֵׁי יהוה לֹא־יַחְסְרוּ כָל־טוֹב:
הוֹדוּ לַיהוה כִּי־טוֹב, כִּי לְעוֹלָם חַסְדּוֹ: תהלים קיח
פּוֹתֵחַ אֶת־יָדֶךָ, וּמַשְׂבִּיעַ לְכָל־חַי רָצוֹן: תהלים קמה
בָּרוּךְ הַגֶּבֶר אֲשֶׁר יִבְטַח בַּיהוה, וְהָיָה יהוה מִבְטַחוֹ: ירמיה יז
נַעַר הָיִיתִי גַּם־זָקַנְתִּי תהלים לז
וְלֹא־רָאִיתִי צַדִּיק נֶעֱזָב וְזַרְעוֹ מְבַקֶּשׁ־לָחֶם:
יהוה עֹז לְעַמּוֹ יִתֵּן, יהוה יְבָרֵךְ אֶת־עַמּוֹ בַשָּׁלוֹם: תהלים כט

The שבע ברכות *are now recited* (see *the next page*).

SHEVA BERAKHOT BLESSINGS

The second cup of wine is now used for the sheva berakhot.

בָּרוּךְ Blessed are You, Lord, our God, King of the universe, in that He created all that exists for His glory.

בָּרוּךְ Blessed are You, Lord, our God, King of the universe, Who forms all of humanity.

בָּרוּךְ Blessed are You, Lord, our God, King of the universe, Who formed man in His image, in the image of His likeness, and Who for his sake and from him made an everlasting being. Blessed are You, Lord, Who forms all of humanity.

שׂוֹשׂ Bring great rejoicing and exultation to the desolate land by gathering in its children in celebration. Blessed are You, Lord, Who gladdens Zion through her children.

שַׂמֵּחַ Bring great happiness to this couple who are so beloved of each other, just as You brought happiness to those whom You formed in the Garden of Eden of old. Blessed are You, Lord, Who causes both groom and bride to rejoice.

בָּרוּךְ Blessed are You, Lord, our God, King of the universe, Who created joy and happiness, groom and bride, rejoicing and song, joy and delight, love and brotherhood, peace and fellowship. Lord our God, may there soon be heard in the cities of Judah and the streets of Jerusalem the sounds of jubilation and rejoicing, celebratory noises of grooms and brides, echoes of grooms exalting under their marriage canopy, and youths feasting in song. Blessed are You, Lord, Who causes groom and bride to rejoice together.

The two cups of wine are now mixed
and the leader drinks from the cup used for Birkat HaMazon,
and the ḥatan and kalla are each handed a cup of wine.

בָּרוּךְ Blessed are You, Lord, our God, King of the universe, Who creates the fruit of the vine.

שבע ברכות

The second cup of wine is now used for the שבע ברכות.

בָּרוּךְ אַתָּה יהוה אֱלֹהֵינוּ מֶלֶךְ הָעוֹלָם, שֶׁהַכֹּל בָּרָא לִכְבוֹדוֹ.

בָּרוּךְ אַתָּה יהוה אֱלֹהֵינוּ מֶלֶךְ הָעוֹלָם, יוֹצֵר הָאָדָם.

בָּרוּךְ אַתָּה יהוה אֱלֹהֵינוּ מֶלֶךְ הָעוֹלָם, אֲשֶׁר יָצַר אֶת הָאָדָם בְּצַלְמוֹ, בְּצֶלֶם דְּמוּת תַּבְנִיתוֹ, וְהִתְקִין לוֹ מִמֶּנּוּ בִּנְיַן עֲדֵי עַד. בָּרוּךְ אַתָּה יהוה, יוֹצֵר הָאָדָם.

שׂוֹשׂ תָּשִׂישׂ וְתָגֵל הָעֲקָרָה בְּקִבּוּץ בָּנֶיהָ לְתוֹכָהּ בְּשִׂמְחָה. בָּרוּךְ אַתָּה יהוה, מְשַׂמֵּחַ צִיּוֹן בְּבָנֶיהָ.

שַׂמֵּחַ תְּשַׂמַּח רֵעִים הָאֲהוּבִים כְּשַׂמֵּחֲךָ יְצִירְךָ בְּגַן עֵדֶן מִקֶּדֶם. בָּרוּךְ אַתָּה יהוה, מְשַׂמֵּחַ חָתָן וְכַלָּה.

בָּרוּךְ אַתָּה יהוה אֱלֹהֵינוּ מֶלֶךְ הָעוֹלָם, אֲשֶׁר בָּרָא שָׂשׂוֹן וְשִׂמְחָה, חָתָן וְכַלָּה, גִּילָה, רִנָּה, דִּיצָה וְחֶדְוָה, אַהֲבָה וְאַחֲוָה וְשָׁלוֹם וְרֵעוּת. מְהֵרָה יהוה אֱלֹהֵינוּ, יִשָּׁמַע בְּעָרֵי יְהוּדָה וּבְחוּצוֹת יְרוּשָׁלָיִם, קוֹל שָׂשׂוֹן וְקוֹל שִׂמְחָה, קוֹל חָתָן וְקוֹל כַּלָּה, קוֹל מִצְהֲלוֹת חֲתָנִים מֵחֻפָּתָם וּנְעָרִים מִמִּשְׁתֵּה נְגִינָתָם. בָּרוּךְ אַתָּה יהוה, מְשַׂמֵּחַ הֶחָתָן עִם הַכַּלָּה.

The two cups of wine are now mixed and the מברך *drinks from the cup used for* ברכת המזון, *and the* חתן *and* כלה *are each handed a cup of wine.*

בָּרוּךְ אַתָּה יהוה אֱלֹהֵינוּ מֶלֶךְ הָעוֹלָם, בּוֹרֵא פְּרִי הַגָּפֶן.

THE RABBINIC ROAD: CHALLENGES AND OPPORTUNITIES ḤANUKAT HABAYIT

A *ḥanukat habayit* presents the rabbi with a unique opportunity to focus upon the most important institution in Jewish life: the Jewish home and family. So significant is a *ḥanukat habayit,* the Midrash maintains, that upon finishing the Creation, God celebrated a *ḥanukat habayit,* blessing His new world with Shabbat (שאילתות דרב אחאי פרשת בראשית שאילתא א).

Through a variety of concrete actions, the rabbi can direct his congregants to consider the spiritual aspects of "home-building," as they take their first steps into their new home.

- The rabbi should advise the family concerning the character of the celebratory meal that marks the *ḥanukat habayit* (see halakhic section). Rather than a "party," this meal should be a religious event, replete with learning and *divrei Torah,* setting the tone for the family's beginning in their new home.
- The rabbi should sensitize the new homeowners to the synergy between the synagogue and the home, which is essential to the realization of a full Jewish life. It is the home that sets the tone for, and transmits, the values of daily living; while the synagogue serves as the gathering place for the public expression and the sharing of those values with the community.
- In addition to advising the family concerning the placement of *mezuzot* in the home, the rabbi might offer to be present (perhaps with other friends, as well) during the affixing of the *mezuzot.* The rabbi's personal involvement in this mitzva will highlight the significance of the moment and will provide an opportunity for the sharing of important thoughts and *berakhot.*

- Finally, the entry of a family into a new home often coincides with their entry into the community as a whole. In such circumstances, the rabbi's involvement in a *ḥanukat habayit* ceremony can be a meaningful first step in the ongoing journey that he will share with this new congregational family.

HALAKHOT CONCERNING ḤANUKAT HABAYIT

1. Upon building or buying a new home, one should recite the *berakha* of *HaTov VeHaMeitiv*. If the home was purchased by an indiviudal for a his or her exclusive use (i.e., a single person) the *berakha* recited is *Sheheḥeyanu* (או"ח רכג:ג ומשנה ברורה שם ס"ק יא, אג"מ או"ח ח"ג סימן פ).
2. According to some authorities, it is a mitzva to dedicate a new home in Israel with a *seudat mitzva* (מג"א או"ח תקסח ס"ק ה) known as a *ḥanukat habayit* (ספר השרשים לרד"ק - שורש חנך). Most authorities maintain, however, that this celebratory meal is optional even in Israel. If the meal is accompanied by *divrei Torah*, it is considered a *seudat mitzva* (ים של שלמה ב"ק פרק ז' סימן ל"ז, שו"ת באר שבע סימן ע).
3. A *ḥanukat habayit* meal demonstrates gratitude to God for His goodness and expresses the hope that all experiences and accomplishments in this new home will be infused with Torah, joy, and continuing gratitude (תורה לשמה תפ"ד).
4. Some maintain the custom of conducting a *ḥanukat habayit* even upon renting or borrowing a home, by gathering people to learn Torah in their new residence (סדר יחיאלי בית האדם ה עמוד א).
5. According to some authorities, a person who is in mourning for a close relative, should not attend a *ḥanukat habayit*, even though it is a *seudat mitzva* and *divrei Torah* are recited. This applies even during the twelve months of mourning for a parent (אג"מ יו"ד ח"ג סימן קסא). Other authorities, however, permit a mourner to attend (כל בו על אבילות ח"א ה:א:ל).

ḤANUKAT HABAYIT

This liturgy is suggested in the Siddur Minḥat Yerushalayim.

Before affixing the first mezuza, the following verses are recited responsively, led by the homeowner:

וּבַמָּה What then can I offer the Lord when I bow low to the God Most High? *Micha 6*
Now the Lord has given us space, and we will flourish in the land. *Gen. 26*
Whoever comes forward to take him on – I will reward him! Everything under heaven is Mine. *Gen. 22*
Accept our goodness – instead of calves we offer You our words of prayer. *Hosh. 14*
Let us come before Him with thanksgiving, let us raise our voice in song. *Ps. 95*
You have welcomed him with rich blessing
The Lord was with Yosef, and he became a successful man. *Gen. 39*
with rich blessing David was successful in every way, and the Lord was with him. *1 Shmuel 1, 14*
Whoever comes forward to take him on – I will reward him! *Ps. 90*
Everything under heaven is Mine.
and let the pleasantness of the Lord our God be upon us, and establish the work of our hands upon us, and establish it, the work of our hands.

All continue:

יֹשֵׁב He who lives in the shelter of the Most High dwells in the shadow of Shaddai. I say of the Lord, "My refuge and stronghold, my God in whom I trust," for He will save you from the fowler's snare, from deadly plague. With His pinions He will cover you; beneath His wings you will find shelter; His loyalty is an encircling shield. You need not fear terror by night, nor the arrow that flies by day, nor the plague that stalks in darkness, nor disease that ravages at noon. A thousand may fall beside you, ten thousand at your *Ps. 91*

סדר חנוכת הבית

This liturgy is suggested in the סידור מנחת ירושלים.

Before affixing the first מזוזה*, the following verses are recited responsively, led by the homeowner:*

בַּמָּה אֲקַדֵּם יהוה אִכַּף לֵאלֹהֵי מָרוֹם: מיכה ו

כִּי־עַתָּה הִרְחִיב יהוה לָנוּ וּפָרִינוּ בָאָרֶץ: בראשית כו

מִי הִקְדִּימַנִי וַאֲשַׁלֵּם תַּחַת כָּל־הַשָּׁמַיִם לִי־הוּא: בראשית כב

וְקַח־טוֹב וּנְשַׁלְּמָה פָרִים שְׂפָתֵינוּ: הושע יד

נְקַדְּמָה פָנָיו בְּתוֹדָה, בִּזְמִרוֹת נָרִיעַ לוֹ: תהלים צה

כִּי־תְקַדְּמֶנּוּ בִּרְכוֹת טוֹב: תהלים כא

וַיְהִי יהוה אֶת־יוֹסֵף וַיְהִי אִישׁ מַצְלִיחַ: בראשית לט

וַיְהִי דָוִד לְכָל־דְּרָכָו מַשְׂכִּיל וַיהוה עִמּוֹ: שמואל א׳ יד

וִיהִי נֹעַם אֲדֹנָי אֱלֹהֵינוּ עָלֵינוּ וּמַעֲשֵׂה יָדֵינוּ כּוֹנְנָה עָלֵינוּ וּמַעֲשֵׂה יָדֵינוּ כּוֹנְנֵהוּ: תהלים צ

All continue:

יֹשֵׁב בְּסֵתֶר עֶלְיוֹן, בְּצֵל שַׁדַּי יִתְלוֹנָן: אֹמַר לַיהוה מַחְסִי וּמְצוּדָתִי, אֱלֹהַי אֶבְטַח־בּוֹ: כִּי הוּא יַצִּילְךָ מִפַּח יָקוּשׁ, מִדֶּבֶר הַוּוֹת: בְּאֶבְרָתוֹ יָסֶךְ לָךְ, וְתַחַת־כְּנָפָיו תֶּחְסֶה, צִנָּה וְסֹחֵרָה אֲמִתּוֹ: לֹא־תִירָא מִפַּחַד לָיְלָה, מֵחֵץ יָעוּף יוֹמָם: מִדֶּבֶר בָּאֹפֶל יַהֲלֹךְ, מִקֶּטֶב יָשׁוּד צָהֳרָיִם: יִפֹּל מִצִּדְּךָ אֶלֶף, וּרְבָבָה מִימִינֶךָ, אֵלֶיךָ לֹא יִגָּשׁ: רַק בְּעֵינֶיךָ תַבִּיט, וְשִׁלֻּמַת רְשָׁעִים תִּרְאֶה: כִּי־אַתָּה יהוה תהלים צא

right hand, but it will not come near you. You will only look with your eyes and see the punishment of the wicked. For you – "the Lord is my Refuge" – you have made the Most High your abode. No harm will befall you; no sickness will come near your home, for He will command His angels about you to guard you in all your ways. They will lift you in their hands lest your foot stumble on a stone. You will tread over lions and vipers; you will trample on young lions and serpents. "Because he loves Me, I will rescue him; I will protect him because he acknowledges My name. When he calls on Me, I will answer him; I will be with him in distress; I will rescue him and bring him honor. With long life I will satisfy him and show him My salvation."

מִזְמוֹר לְתוֹדָה *A psalm of thanksgiving.* Shout out to the Lord, all the earth! Serve the Lord with joy; come before Him in glad song. Know that the Lord is God; He made us, and we are His; we are His people, the flock He tends. Enter His gates with thanksgiving, His courts with praise; thank Him and bless His name, for the Lord is good; His loving-kindness is forever, His faithfulness for all generations. *Ps. 100*

The following brakha is recited and the mezuza is affixed.

בָּרוּךְ Blessed are You, LORD, our God, King of the universe,
Who has sanctified us with His commandments,
and has commanded us to affix the *mezuza*.

If the home is owned by a number of people,
each homeonwer recites (MB 223:11):

בָּרוּךְ Blessed are You, LORD, our God, King of the universe,
Who is good and does good.

If the home is owned by only one person, the homeowner recites:

בָּרוּךְ Blessed are You, LORD, our God, King of the universe,
Who has given us life, sustained us, and brought us to this time.

מַחְסִי, עֶלְיוֹן שַׂמְתָּ מְעוֹנֶךָ: לֹא־תְאֻנֶּה אֵלֶיךָ רָעָה, וְנֶגַע לֹא־יִקְרַב בְּאָהֳלֶךָ: כִּי מַלְאָכָיו יְצַוֶּה־לָּךְ, לִשְׁמָרְךָ בְּכָל־דְּרָכֶיךָ: עַל־כַּפַּיִם יִשָּׂאוּנְךָ, פֶּן־תִּגֹּף בָּאֶבֶן רַגְלֶךָ: עַל־שַׁחַל וָפֶתֶן תִּדְרֹךְ, תִּרְמֹס כְּפִיר וְתַנִּין: כִּי בִי חָשַׁק וַאֲפַלְּטֵהוּ, אֲשַׂגְּבֵהוּ כִּי־יָדַע שְׁמִי: יִקְרָאֵנִי וְאֶעֱנֵהוּ, עִמּוֹ אָנֹכִי בְצָרָה, אֲחַלְּצֵהוּ וַאֲכַבְּדֵהוּ: אֹרֶךְ יָמִים אַשְׂבִּיעֵהוּ, וְאַרְאֵהוּ בִּישׁוּעָתִי:

מִזְמוֹר לְתוֹדָה, הָרִיעוּ לַיהוה כָּל־הָאָרֶץ: עִבְדוּ אֶת־יהוה בְּשִׂמְחָה, בֹּאוּ לְפָנָיו בִּרְנָנָה: דְּעוּ כִּי־יהוה הוּא אֱלֹהִים, הוּא עָשָׂנוּ וְלוֹ אֲנַחְנוּ, עַמּוֹ וְצֹאן מַרְעִיתוֹ: בֹּאוּ שְׁעָרָיו בְּתוֹדָה, חֲצֵרֹתָיו בִּתְהִלָּה, הוֹדוּ לוֹ, בָּרְכוּ שְׁמוֹ: כִּי־טוֹב יהוה, לְעוֹלָם חַסְדּוֹ, וְעַד־דֹּר וָדֹר אֱמוּנָתוֹ: תהלים ק

The following ברכה *is recited and the* מזוזה *is affixed.*

בָּרוּךְ אַתָּה יהוה אֱלֹהֵינוּ מֶלֶךְ הָעוֹלָם
אֲשֶׁר קִדְּשָׁנוּ בְּמִצְוֹתָיו וְצִוָּנוּ לִקְבֹּעַ מְזוּזָה.

If the home is owned by a number of people,
each homeonwer recites (מ״ב רכג:יא)

בָּרוּךְ אַתָּה יהוה אֱלֹהֵינוּ מֶלֶךְ הָעוֹלָם
הַטּוֹב וְהַמֵּיטִיב.

If the home is owned by only one person, the homeowner recites:

בָּרוּךְ אַתָּה יהוה אֱלֹהֵינוּ מֶלֶךְ הָעוֹלָם
שֶׁהֶחֱיָנוּ וְקִיְּמָנוּ וְהִגִּיעָנוּ לַזְּמַן הַזֶּה.

Torah passages are traditionally studied and recited at the seudat mitzvah. Some maintain the custom of studying three mishnayot whose first letters together form the word בית *"home," for example, Avot 5:1 and 1:4. This is followed by studying Berakhot 4:1. The following psalms appropriate to the occasion, can also be recited: Ps. 111, 30, 67, 16, 127, 150.*

The program concludes with the following prayer:

יְהִי May it be Your will, Lord, our God and the God of our fathers, the God of Abraham, the God of Isaac, and the God of Jacob; God, compassionate and gracious, merciful Father, that our study of Your holy Torah be as satisfactory to You as a sweet fragrance. And in Your great compassion have mercy upon (*name*) the son/daughter of (*father's name*), the owners of this house, who, upon coming to live in this house, followed the promptings of their souls and dedicated their home with words of Your holy Torah, in order to establish and inaugurate it with words of Torah. Therefore, in the merit of Your holy Torah, bless (*name*) the son/daughter of (*father's name*), the owners of this house, with eternal blessings, and fulfill all their hearts' desires for good. May this house be blessed with everything, and may there be heard in this home – and in the homes of all of Israel – the sound of joy and the sound of gladness.

Please, in Your abundant compassion, be a protection for them, nullify all decrees, sickness, and all evil things from upon them. By decree of the heavenly King, may they be protected against every evil eye. Send blessing and success to all of their handiwork, and let them have long days and years of vigor and abundance, for You are the One Who hears the prayers of Your nation, Israel, with compassion.

May the words of my mouth and the my heart's reflections *Ps. 19*
please You, Lord, my Rock and Redeemer.

Torah passages are traditionally studied and recited at the סעודת מצווה*. Some maintain the custom of studying three* משניות *whose first letters together form the word* בית *"home," for example,* אבות ה, א; א, ד*. This is followed by studying* ברכות ד, א*. The following* תהלים *appropriate to the occasion, can also be recited:* תהלים קיא, ל, סו, טו, קכו, קנ*.*

The program concludes with the following prayer:

יְהִי רָצוֹן מִלְּפָנֶיךָ אֲדֹנָי אֱלֹהֵינוּ וֵאלֹהֵי אֲבוֹתֵינוּ, אֱלֹהֵי אַבְרָהָם, אֱלֹהֵי יִצְחָק, וֵאלֹהֵי יַעֲקֹב, אֵל רַחוּם וְחַנּוּן, אַב הָרַחֲמִים, שֶׁיְּהֵא חָשׁוּב וּמְרֻצֶּה לְפָנֶיךָ הַלִּמּוּד שֶׁלָּמַדְנוּ בְּתוֹרָתְךָ הַקְּדוֹשָׁה כְּרֵיחַ נִיחוֹחַ. וּבְרֹב רַחֲמֶיךָ תְּרַחֵם עַל (פלוני/ת בֶּן/בַּת פלוני), בַּעֲלֵי הַבַּיִת הַזֶּה, אֲשֶׁר בְּבוֹאָם לִשְׁכֹּן בַּבַּיִת הַזֶּה, נַפְשָׁם אִוּוּ וְעָשׂוּ חֲנֻכַּת הַבַּיִת בְּדִבְרֵי תוֹרָתְךָ הַקְּדוֹשָׁה, לְיַסֵּד אֶת הַבַּיִת וּלְחָנְכוֹ בְּדִבְרֵי תוֹרָה. וּבְכֵן בִּזְכוּת תּוֹרָתְךָ הַקְּדוֹשָׁה תְּבָרֵךְ אֶת (פלוני/ת בֶּן/בַּת פלוני), בַּעֲלֵי הַבַּיִת הַזֶּה, בְּרָכוֹת לָעַד, וּתְמַלֵּא כָּל מִשְׁאֲלוֹת לִבָּם לְטוֹבָה, וִיהְיֶה לָהֶם הַבַּיִת הַזֶּה מֻצְלָח וּמְבֹרָךְ בַּכֹּל מִכֹּל כֹּל, וְיִשָּׁמַע בַּבַּיִת הַזֶּה וּבְבָתֵּי כָּל יִשְׂרָאֵל קוֹל שָׂשׂוֹן וְקוֹל שִׂמְחָה.

אָנָּא בְּרַחֲמֶיךָ הָרַבִּים, הֱיֵה עֲלֵיהֶם סִתְרָה, צִנָּה וְסֹחֵרָה, וּתְבַטֵּל מֵהֶם כָּל גְּזֵרוֹת וְנֶגַע וּמַחֲלָה וְכָל רָעוֹת, וּבְהַרְמָנָא מַלְכָּא עִלָּאָה, תִּשָּׁמֵר מִכָּל עַיִן רָע, וְתִשְׁלַח בְּרָכָה וְהַצְלָחָה בְּכָל מַעֲשֵׂי יְדֵיהֶם, וְיַאֲרִיכוּ יָמִים וְשָׁנִים דְּשֵׁנִים וְרַעֲנַנִּים, כִּי אַתָּה שׁוֹמֵעַ תְּפִלּוֹת כָּל פֶּה עַמְּךָ יִשְׂרָאֵל בְּרַחֲמִים.

יִהְיוּ לְרָצוֹן אִמְרֵי־פִי וְהֶגְיוֹן לִבִּי לְפָנֶיךָ, יהוה צוּרִי וְגֹאֲלִי: תהלים יט

THE RABBINIC ROAD: CHALLENGES AND OPPORTUNITIES HAKHNASAT SEFER TORAH

One of the most meaningful events in Jewish life is the dedication of a new *sefer Torah.* Such a dedication can mark a personal milestone, or can serve as a tribute to a person or institution. In times past, the dedication of a *sefer Torah* was a rare event. Today it has become more common, but still treasured.

A *hakhnasat sefer Torah* provides the rabbi with a unique opportunity to create an event focusing on the *kavod haTorah* that is central to our *mesora*. As the Ḥatam Sofer wrote: "The completion of a Torah creates a lasting keepsake for generations. The children and grandchildren of those involved will speak of the day when their parents/grandparents performed this mitzva, and their awe of Hashem will be increased" (דרשות חתם סופר דף רעג׳ ד״ה ראשית - באה״ד).

- The rabbi should help the donor plan the event, making sure to extend the honor of completing letters to both family, friends, and community leaders.
- Schoolchildren should be invited to attend this special event, for it is their learning of Torah (הבל פיהם של תינוקות של בית רבן) that ensures the continued existence of our world.
- Celebrating a new *sefer Torah* must be accomplished with an appropriate balance of joy and awe. The rabbi should work with the donors to ensure that there is a proper spirit of Torah throughout the event.
- The rabbi should remind the celebrants to focus on the Torah, rather than the menu, the decor, or the music. How this event is celebrated reflects the community's commitment to its Torah values.

HALAKHOT CONCERNING HAKHNASAT SEFER TORAH

1. The authorities debate whether or not the positive commandment to write a *sefer Torah* still applies in our day when the Torah is only used for public reading in the synagogue and books serve as the primary resource for the study of *Torah shebikhtav* and *Torah shebe'al peh* (יו"ד ע"ר:ב, ט"ז וש"ך שם). Nevertheless, writing a new *sefer Torah* remains a moment of great celebration.
2. Toward the completion of the writing of the Torah, some letters are left incomplete, and various individuals are each given the honor of completing one of these remaining letters (משנת אברהם א:כח). Originally, these participants wrote the letters themselves. Out of concern for the beauty of the Torah, however, and to assure that all who participate are halakhically permitted to do so, it is recommended that the *sofer* write the letters (שו"ת תירוש ויצהר סימן ריג).
3. Often, the *sofer* who wrote the Torah is not available to participate in the final celebration. In such a case, the letters of the last several lines of the Torah are written in outline form, and the participants, or a different *sofer*, fill in those letters (שו"ת קנאת סופרים סימן פו, שו"ת שואל ומשיב ח"ג סימן קב).
4. If a *sofer* completes the remaining letters, those who are invited to participate appoint the *sofer* to serve as their *shaliaḥ*. Women, who according to some authorities also have an obligation to write a *sefer Torah*, may also be invited to participate in this manner (ע"ע שאגת אריה סימן ל"ה).
5. Some maintain the custom of specifically completing a letter that corresponds to their name (סידור מנחת ירושלים עמ' 1053 סעיף ב').
6. While there is no *berakha* mandated for the writing of a *sefer Torah*, ceremonies have evolved that include the recitation of various *tefillot* at the time of a Torah's completion (see pages 158–65).

7. Some authorities suggest that the *berakha* of *Sheheḥeyanu* should be recited at the completion of the writing (ערוה״ש או״ח רכג:ח). Others maintain that the proper time for the *berakha* is when the Torah is first placed in the *aron hakodesh* (שו״ת בית יהודה יו״ד סימן כג), while yet others indicate that the *berakha* should be recited by the person who receives the first *aliya* read from the Torah (שערי אפרים שער ד׳ סע׳ לד). If this latter approach is followed, many authorities recommend that the individual receiving the aliyah should also wear a new article of clothing, similar to our practice when reciting *Sheheḥeyanu* on the second day of Rosh Hashana (שערי אפרים שער ד׳ סעיף לד).
8. Once the writing of the Torah is complete, the Torah is carried under a *ḥuppa*, escorted with music, dancing, flags for the children, and, when safe, torches and candles (נוהג כצאן יוסף הלכות קריאת ספר תורה עמ׳ קלה-קלו; קונטרס ויצבר יוסף אות ה). Some invite *Kohanim* and *Leviim* to carry the Torah, reminiscent of when David HaMelekh brought the *Aron* to Yerushalayim (שו״ת מהר״י אסאד יו״ד סימן רפג). Others honor community leaders with carrying the Torah.
9. When the procession arrives at the final destination, the other Torahs in the *aron hakodesh* are brought out to "greet" the new Torah (שערי אפרים שער ט סע׳ מו). It was even customary in some communities, when the procession passed another synagogue, for the *sifrei Torah* of that other synagogue to be removed from the *aron hakodesh* and brought to the doorway to honor the new Torah (שו״ת לב חיים חלק ב סימן כא).
10. Following the *hakhnasat sefer Torah* it is appropriate to make a *seudat mitzva* (חוות יאיר ס׳ ע; שו״ת דברי יציב יו״ד סימן קע). Authorities, however, discourage extravagant celebrations, recommending that the money be applied toward *tzedaka* instead (חיי אדם כלל לא סע׳ נ).

HAKHNASAT SEFER TORAH

The following ceremony is based upon the text found in Siddur Minḥat Yerushalayim.

As the procession gathers to escort the Sefer Torah, the Leader announces:

הָבוּ Render to the Lord glory and might. Ps. 29
Render to the Lord the glory due His name;
in the splendor of holiness.
Render and deliver honor to the Torah.

As the Sefer Torah enters the procession the Leader says:

וַיְהִי בִּנְסֹעַ When the Ark moved forward, Moses would say, Num. 10
"Arise, O Lord, and may Your enemies be dispersed,
and they who hate You flee from You."

The Leader and the congregation:

אַתָּה Rise up and have mercy on Zion; Ps. 102
Build the walls of Jerusalem.

כִּי מִצִּיּוֹן For from Zion shall go forth Torah, Is. 2
and the word of the Lord from Jerusalem.

Community leaders, family and friends
are honored with the carrying of the Sefer Torah.
As each one takes hold of the Torah, he kisses it and says:

יהוה "The Lord came from Sinai, Deut. 33
He shone upon them from Se'ir,
He appeared over the crest of Paran
and came among myriads of holy ones:

Songs are sung in honor of the Sefer Torah.

When the Sefer Torah arrives at its new home all sing:

וַיְהִי He became king in Yeshurun, Deut. 33
when the heads of the people gathered –
the tribes of Israel together.

סדר הכנסת ספר תורה

The following ceremony is based upon the text found in the סידור מנחת ירושלים.

As the procession gathers to escort the ספר תורה*, the* חזן *announces*

תהלים כט הָבוּ לַיהוה כָּבוֹד וָעֹז:
הָבוּ לַיהוה כְּבוֹד שְׁמוֹ בְּהַדְרַת־קֹדֶשׁ.
הָבוּ וּנְחַלֵּק כָּבוֹד לַתּוֹרָה.

As the ספר תורה *enters the procession the* חזן *says:*

במדבר י וַיְהִי בִּנְסֹעַ הָאָרֹן וַיֹּאמֶר מֹשֶׁה
קוּמָה יהוה וְיָפֻצוּ אֹיְבֶיךָ וְיָנֻסוּ מְשַׂנְאֶיךָ מִפָּנֶיךָ:

The חזן *and the* קהל*:*

תהלים קב אַתָּה תָקוּם תְּרַחֵם צִיּוֹן, תִּבְנֶה חוֹמוֹת יְרוּשָׁלָיִם:
ישעיה ב כִּי מִצִּיּוֹן תֵּצֵא תוֹרָה וּדְבַר־יהוה, מִירוּשָׁלָיִם:

Community leaders, family and friends
are honored with the carrying of the ספר תורה.
As each one takes hold of the תורה*, he kisses it and says:*

דברים לג יהוה מִסִּינַי בָּא וְזָרַח מִשֵּׂעִיר לָמוֹ, הוֹפִיעַ מֵהַר פָּארָן
וְאָתָה מֵרִבְבֹת קֹדֶשׁ, מִימִינוֹ אֵשׁ דָּת לָמוֹ:

Songs are sung in honor of the ספר תורה.

When the ספר תורה *arrives at its new home all sing:*

דברים לג וַיְהִי בִישֻׁרוּן מֶלֶךְ, בְּהִתְאַסֵּף רָאשֵׁי עָם
יַחַד שִׁבְטֵי יִשְׂרָאֵל:

The Leader and the congregation say these verses responsively.

לְדָוִד מִזְמוֹר Of David. A psalm. *Ps. 24*
The Lord owns the earth and all it contains,
the world and all who live in it,
for He founded it on the seas, set it on the streams.
Who may ascend the Lord's mountain?
Who may stand in His holy place?
Those who have clean hands and pure hearts,
who do not take false oaths by My life,
who have not sworn deceitfully,
they shall receive blessing from the Lord,
due reward from the God of their salvation.
Such is the generation who seek Him –
Jacob who seek Your presence, Selah.

When the Torah arrives at the Ark.
The Leader and the congregation say these verses responsively.

Lift up your heads, O gates, and be lifted up, O everlasting doors,
so that the King of glory may come in.
Who is this King of glory?
The Lord strong and mighty, the Lord mighty in battle.
Lift up your heads, O gates, and lift them up, O everlasting doors,
so that the King of glory may come in.
Who is He, this King of glory?
The Lord of hosts, He is the King of glory. Selah.

The Ark is opened and all sing:

וַיְהִי בִּנְסֹעַ When the Ark moved forward, Moses would say, *Num. 10*
"Arise, O Lord, and may Your enemies be dispersed,
and they who hate You flee from You."
For from Zion shall go forth Torah, *Is. 2*
and the word of the Lord from Jerusalem.
Blessed is He Who, in His holiness,
has given the Torah to His people Israel.

The חזן *and the* קהל *say these verses responsively.*

לְדָוִד מִזְמוֹר, לַיהוה הָאָרֶץ וּמְלוֹאָהּ, תֵּבֵל וְיֹשְׁבֵי בָהּ: תהלים כד
כִּי־הוּא עַל־יַמִּים יְסָדָהּ, וְעַל־נְהָרוֹת יְכוֹנְנֶהָ:
מִי־יַעֲלֶה בְהַר־יהוה, וּמִי־יָקוּם בִּמְקוֹם קָדְשׁוֹ:
נְקִי כַפַּיִם וּבַר־לֵבָב
אֲשֶׁר לֹא־נָשָׂא לַשָּׁוְא נַפְשִׁי וְלֹא נִשְׁבַּע לְמִרְמָה:
יִשָּׂא בְרָכָה מֵאֵת יהוה, וּצְדָקָה מֵאֱלֹהֵי יִשְׁעוֹ:
זֶה דּוֹר דֹּרְשָׁו, מְבַקְשֵׁי פָנֶיךָ, יַעֲקֹב, סֶלָה:

When the Torah arrives at the ארון קודש.
The חזן *and the* קהל *say these verses responsively.*

שְׂאוּ שְׁעָרִים רָאשֵׁיכֶם, וְהִנָּשְׂאוּ פִּתְחֵי עוֹלָם
וְיָבוֹא מֶלֶךְ הַכָּבוֹד:
מִי זֶה מֶלֶךְ הַכָּבוֹד
יהוה עִזּוּז וְגִבּוֹר, יהוה גִּבּוֹר מִלְחָמָה:
שְׂאוּ שְׁעָרִים רָאשֵׁיכֶם, וּשְׂאוּ פִּתְחֵי עוֹלָם
וְיָבֹא מֶלֶךְ הַכָּבוֹד:
מִי הוּא זֶה מֶלֶךְ הַכָּבוֹד
יהוה צְבָאוֹת הוּא מֶלֶךְ הַכָּבוֹד, סֶלָה:

The ארון קודש *is opened and all sing:*

וַיְהִי בִּנְסֹעַ הָאָרֹן וַיֹּאמֶר מֹשֶׁה במדבר י
קוּמָה יהוה וְיָפֻצוּ אֹיְבֶיךָ וְיָנֻסוּ מְשַׂנְאֶיךָ מִפָּנֶיךָ:
כִּי מִצִּיּוֹן תֵּצֵא תוֹרָה וּדְבַר־יהוה מִירוּשָׁלָיִם: ישעיה ב
בָּרוּךְ שֶׁנָּתַן תּוֹרָה לְעַמּוֹ יִשְׂרָאֵל בִּקְדֻשָּׁתוֹ.

The Leader takes the Torah and faces the congregation, and the following two verses are recited responsively.

שְׁמַע Hear, O Israel, the LORD is our God, the LORD is One. Deut. 6

אֶחָד One is our GOD, great is our Master,
holy is His name.

The Leader turns to face the Ark, bows and says:

גַּדְּלוּ Glorify the LORD with me; Ps. 34
let us exalt His name together.

The Leader says:

יְהַלְלוּ Let them praise the name of the LORD, Ps. 148
that His name alone is exalted.

The congregation responds:

His glory is over the earth and the heavens.
And He has raised the horn of His people,
praise for all His pious ones, for the children of Israel,
the people near to Him. Praise the Lord.

As the Torah scroll is placed into the Ark, all say:

וּבְנֻחֹה And when the Ark rested, Moses would say: "Return, Num. 10
O LORD, to the myriad thousands of Israel." Arise, O LORD, Ps. 132
to Your resting place, You and the Ark of Your strength. May Your priests be clothed in righteousness, and may Your pious ones shout for joy. For the sake of David Your servant, do not
turn away the face of Your anointed. I have given you a good Prov. 4
doctrine, My Torah, do not forsake it. It is a tree of life for Prov. 3
those who grasp it, and they who uphold it are made happy. Its ways are ways of pleasantness, and all its paths are peace.
▸ LORD, turn us to You once again, for we wish to return; renew Lam. 5
our days as of old.

The Ark is closed.

The חזן *takes the* ספר תורה *and faces the* קהל*,*
and the following two verses are recited responsively.

שְׁמַע יִשְׂרָאֵל, יהוה אֱלֹהֵינוּ, יהוה אֶחָד׃ דברים ו

אֶחָד אֱלֹהֵינוּ, גָּדוֹל אֲדוֹנֵינוּ, קָדוֹשׁ שְׁמוֹ.

The חזן *turns to face the* ארון קודש*, bows and says:*

גַּדְּלוּ לַיהוה אִתִּי וּנְרוֹמְמָה שְׁמוֹ יַחְדָּו׃ תהלים לד

The חזן *says:*

יְהַלְלוּ אֶת־שֵׁם יהוה, כִּי־נִשְׂגָּב שְׁמוֹ, לְבַדּוֹ תהלים קמח

The קהל *responds:*

הוֹדוֹ עַל־אֶרֶץ וְשָׁמָיִם׃
וַיָּרֶם קֶרֶן לְעַמּוֹ, תְּהִלָּה לְכָל־חֲסִידָיו
לִבְנֵי יִשְׂרָאֵל עַם קְרֹבוֹ, הַלְלוּיָהּ׃

As the ספר תורה *is placed into the* ארון קודש*, all say:*

וּבְנֻחֹה יֹאמַר, שׁוּבָה יהוה רִבְבוֹת אַלְפֵי יִשְׂרָאֵל׃ קוּמָה במדבר י תהלים קלב
יהוה לִמְנוּחָתֶךָ, אַתָּה וַאֲרוֹן עֻזֶּךָ׃ כֹּהֲנֶיךָ יִלְבְּשׁוּ־צֶדֶק,
וַחֲסִידֶיךָ יְרַנֵּנוּ׃ בַּעֲבוּר דָּוִד עַבְדֶּךָ אַל־תָּשֵׁב פְּנֵי מְשִׁיחֶךָ׃
כִּי לֶקַח טוֹב נָתַתִּי לָכֶם, תּוֹרָתִי אַל־תַּעֲזֹבוּ׃ עֵץ־חַיִּים משלי ד משלי ג
הִיא לַמַּחֲזִיקִים בָּהּ, וְתֹמְכֶיהָ מְאֻשָּׁר׃ דְּרָכֶיהָ דַרְכֵי־נֹעַם
וְכָל־נְתִיבוֹתֶיהָ שָׁלוֹם׃ ‹ הֲשִׁיבֵנוּ יהוה אֵלֶיךָ וְנָשׁוּבָה, חַדֵּשׁ איכה ה
יָמֵינוּ כְּקֶדֶם׃

The ארון קודש *is closed.*

The service concludes with Aleinu.

עָלֵינוּ We must, all of us, praise the Master of all, and ascribe greatness to He Who formed creation, for He did not make us like the nations of the world, nor render us like the families of the earth. He did not make our portion to be as theirs, nor our destiny like that of their masses. (For idolaters bow to vanity and emptiness and pray to a god who cannot save.) ▾We, however, bend our knees, bow, and give thanks before the King of the most exalted of kings, the Holy One, blessed is He. He is the One Who spreads out the heavens and establishes the earth. The seat of His glory is in the heavens above, and His Presence in all its strength is found in its highest abode. He is our God – there is no other. In truth He is our King; there is none but Him; as is written in His Torah: "On this day you should know, and take to heart, that *Deut. 4*
the LORD is God in the heavens above and on the earth below – there is no other."

We therefore hope in You, LORD our God, that we may soon see the glory of Your might when You will remove abominations from the earth and the idols shall be utterly destroyed, when the world shall be perfected under the rule of the Almighty. Then all mankind shall invoke Your name, to turn all the wicked on earth toward You. All dwellers on earth will perceive and understand that to You every knee must bend, every tongue vow fealty. Before You, LORD our God, all will kneel and bow down, and give honor to Your glorious name. They will all accept the rule of Your dominion, and You will speedily rule over them forevermore. For the kingdom is Yours, and to all eternity You shall reign in glory, as it is written in Your Torah, "The LORD shall *Ex. 15*
reign forever and ever." ▸ And it is said, "And the LORD shall be *Zech. 14*
King over all the earth; in that day shall the LORD be One, and His name One."

The service concludes with עָלֵינוּ.

עָלֵינוּ לְשַׁבֵּחַ לַאֲדוֹן הַכֹּל, לָתֵת גְּדֻלָּה לְיוֹצֵר בְּרֵאשִׁית, שֶׁלֹּא עָשָׂנוּ כְּגוֹיֵי הָאֲרָצוֹת, וְלֹא שָׂמָנוּ כְּמִשְׁפְּחוֹת הָאֲדָמָה, שֶׁלֹּא שָׂם חֶלְקֵנוּ כָּהֶם וְגוֹרָלֵנוּ כְּכָל הֲמוֹנָם. (שֶׁהֵם מִשְׁתַּחֲוִים לְהֶבֶל וָרִיק וּמִתְפַּלְלִים אֶל אֵל לֹא יוֹשִׁיעַ.) ׳וַאֲנַחְנוּ כּוֹרְעִים וּמִשְׁתַּחֲוִים וּמוֹדִים, לִפְנֵי מֶלֶךְ מַלְכֵי הַמְּלָכִים, הַקָּדוֹשׁ בָּרוּךְ הוּא, שֶׁהוּא נוֹטֶה שָׁמַיִם וְיוֹסֵד אָרֶץ, וּמוֹשַׁב יְקָרוֹ בַּשָּׁמַיִם מִמַּעַל, וּשְׁכִינַת עֻזּוֹ בְּגָבְהֵי מְרוֹמִים. הוּא אֱלֹהֵינוּ, אֵין עוֹד.
אֱמֶת מַלְכֵּנוּ, אֶפֶס זוּלָתוֹ, כַּכָּתוּב בְּתוֹרָתוֹ, וְיָדַעְתָּ הַיּוֹם וַהֲשֵׁבֹתָ אֶל־לְבָבֶךָ, כִּי יהוה הוּא הָאֱלֹהִים בַּשָּׁמַיִם מִמַּעַל וְעַל־הָאָרֶץ מִתָּחַת, אֵין עוֹד: דברים ד

עַל כֵּן נְקַוֶּה לְּךָ יהוה אֱלֹהֵינוּ, לִרְאוֹת מְהֵרָה בְּתִפְאֶרֶת עֻזֶּךָ, לְהַעֲבִיר גִּלּוּלִים מִן הָאָרֶץ, וְהָאֱלִילִים כָּרוֹת יִכָּרֵתוּן, לְתַקֵּן עוֹלָם בְּמַלְכוּת שַׁדַּי. וְכָל בְּנֵי בָשָׂר יִקְרְאוּ בִשְׁמֶךָ לְהַפְנוֹת אֵלֶיךָ כָּל רִשְׁעֵי אָרֶץ. יַכִּירוּ וְיֵדְעוּ כָּל יוֹשְׁבֵי תֵבֵל, כִּי לְךָ תִּכְרַע כָּל בֶּרֶךְ, תִּשָּׁבַע כָּל לָשׁוֹן. לְפָנֶיךָ יהוה אֱלֹהֵינוּ יִכְרְעוּ וְיִפֹּלוּ, וְלִכְבוֹד שִׁמְךָ יְקָר יִתֵּנוּ, וִיקַבְּלוּ כֻלָּם אֶת עֹל מַלְכוּתֶךָ, וְתִמְלֹךְ עֲלֵיהֶם מְהֵרָה לְעוֹלָם וָעֶד. כִּי הַמַּלְכוּת שֶׁלְּךָ הִיא וּלְעוֹלְמֵי עַד תִּמְלֹךְ בְּכָבוֹד, כַּכָּתוּב בְּתוֹרָתֶךָ,
יהוה יִמְלֹךְ לְעֹלָם וָעֶד: · וְנֶאֱמַר, וְהָיָה יהוה לְמֶלֶךְ עַל־כָּל־ שמות טו / זכריה יד
הָאָרֶץ, בַּיּוֹם הַהוּא יִהְיֶה יהוה אֶחָד וּשְׁמוֹ אֶחָד:

THE RABBINIC ROAD: CHALLENGES AND OPPORTUNITIES *BIKUR ḤOLIM*

The sense of aloneness that often accompanies serious illness presents the rabbi with a unique opportunity for *ḥesed*. The rabbi can serve as a trusted confidant and advisor to ill individuals who are unwilling or unable to unburden their honest fears and concerns to others. Sensitivity toward the individual and those around him/her is essential if the rabbi is to successfully play this important role.

- The rabbi should develop a network through which he is informed of any congregant who is ill, whether hospitalized or homebound. Congregants should be encouraged to share such information with the rabbi, and requests should be made to local hospital chaplain for notification of any congregant's hospitalization.
- While regular rabbinic *bikur ḥolim* visits to hospitalized and homebound congregants can be emotionally draining and time-consuming, their importance cannot be overstated. The individuals and their families will always remember rabbinic kindness shown to them at this critical time.
- Common sense should guide the timing and length of any *bikur ḥolim* visit. The rabbi should remain acutely aware of the condition of the patient and adjust his visit accordingly.
- Conversation during the visit should be shaped, by the condition and emotional state of the patient. While platitudes and unrealistic assessments of the patient's situation should be scrupulously avoided, realistic encouragement and positivity should be offered. In some cases, other topics should be focused on entirely, in order to provide the patient with needed respite from concentration on his/her illness.

HALAKHOT CONCERNING BIKUR ḤOLIM

BIKUR ḤOLIM

1. There are three aspects to the mitzva of *bikur ḥolim*:
   - A. To care for the needs of the *ḥoleh* (נדרים מ.);
   - B. To pray for the *ḥoleh* (פרישה יו״ד שלה:ד);
   - C. To encourage the *ḥoleh* and raise his spirits (רמב״ן תורת האדם שער המיחוש).
2. It is a mitzva to visit a *ḥoleh* as often as possible as long as it is not a burden on the *ḥoleh* (יו״ד שלה:ב).
3. One who visits a *ḥoleh* and does not offer a prayer on behalf of the *ḥoleh* has not fulfilled the *mitzva* of *bikur ḥolim* (רמ״א יו״ד שלה:ד).
4. If a *ḥoleh* is terminally ill and the doctors have no hope for his recovery, the prayers offered can be changed to *sheyitav laḥoleh veyitav lemishpaḥto, veHashem hatov be'einav yaaseh* – may the outcome be best for the *ḥoleh* and for the family, may God do what is best in His eyes. (הליכות שלמה תפילה פרק ח הערה נו, רב עקיבא איגר או״ח רל). If the *ḥoleh* is suffering greatly and there is no further hope of recovery, it is permitted to pray that the *ḥoleh* pass away without pain (ערוך השלחן יו״ד שלה:ג).
5. When speaking with a *ḥoleh* one must be judicious and careful with one's words. One should neither offer false hope nor say things that may depress the *ḥoleh* (קצור שלחן ערוך קצג:ה, הלכה ורפואה כרך ג דף קג, קשו״ע קצג:ה).
6. When speaking with a *ḥoleh* one should refrain from asking questions which might upset the *ḥoleh* (פני ברוך כרך א פרק א הערה מד).
7. If visiting a *ḥoleh* in person is not possible, the *mitzva* of *bikur ḥolim* can be fulfilled by calling the *ḥoleh* on the phone (אג״מ יו״ד ח״א סימן רכב).

TEFILLAH IN THE HOSPITAL ROOM

1. If non-Jewish religious symbols (such as a crucifix) are present in a *ḥoleh*'s hospital room, and it is unreasonable to ask that they be removed, the *ḥoleh* may pray in the room, but should turn away from those symbols (משנה ברורה צד ס"ק ל).
2. A *ḥoleh* who desires to recite daily prayers, but finds it too difficult to recite the entire service, may say an abbreviated *tefilla* (e.g., omitting *Pesukei DeZimra*). If necessary, the abbreviated *tefilla* of *Havineinu* may also be substituted for the full *Amida*.
3. A *ḥoleh* who has an indwelling catheter is permitted to recite the daily prayer. Ideally however, both the catheter and the bag should be covered (אגרות משה או"ח א כו).

PRAYER FOR THE SICK

FOR A SICK MAN

מִי שֶׁבֵּרַךְ May He Who blessed our fathers Abraham, Isaac, and Jacob, Moses and Aaron, David and Solomon, bless and heal the sick person (*name*) son of (*mother's names*), on whose behalf (*name of supplicant*) vows to make a charitable gift. As a reward for this, may the Holy One, blessed is He, show him the fullness of compassion by restoring his health, healing him, strengthening him, and granting him life. May He speedily send him a complete healing from heaven, to all his two hundred and forty-eight organs and three hundred and sixty-five sinews, among the other sick people of Israel, a healing of the spirit and a healing of the body (*On Shabbat:* though on the Sabbath / *On Yom Tov:* though on Yom Tov / it is forbidden to cry out, may his healing be quick to come), now, swiftly and soon. And let us say, Amen.

FOR A SICK WOMAN

מִי שֶׁבֵּרַךְ May He Who blessed our fathers Abraham, Isaac, and Jacob, Moses and Aaron, David, and Solomon, bless and heal the sick person (*name*) daughter of (*mother's names*), on whose behalf (*name of supplicant*) will make a charitable gift. As a reward for this, may the Holy One, blessed is He, show her the fullness of compassion by restoring her health, healing her, strengthening her, and granting her life. May He speedily send her a complete healing from heaven, to all her organs and sinews, among the other sick people of Israel, a healing of the spirit and a healing of the body (*On Shabbat:* though on the Sabbath / *On Yom Tov:* though on Yom Tov / it is forbidden to cry out, may her healing be quick to come), now, swiftly and soon. And let us say, Amen.

תפילה לחולה

לחולֶה

מִי שֶׁבֵּרַךְ אֲבוֹתֵינוּ אַבְרָהָם יִצְחָק וְיַעֲקֹב, מֹשֶׁה וְאַהֲרֹן דָּוִד וּשְׁלֹמֹה הוּא יְבָרֵךְ וִירַפֵּא אֶת הַחוֹלֶה (פלוני בֶּן פלונית) בַּעֲבוּר שֶׁנּוֹדְרִים צְדָקָה בַּעֲבוּרוֹ. בִּשְׂכַר זֶה הַקָּדוֹשׁ בָּרוּךְ הוּא יִמָּלֵא רַחֲמִים עָלָיו לְהַחֲלִימוֹ וּלְרַפְּאתוֹ וּלְהַחֲזִיקוֹ וּלְהַחֲיוֹתוֹ וְיִשְׁלַח לוֹ מְהֵרָה רְפוּאָה שְׁלֵמָה מִן הַשָּׁמַיִם לְרַמַ"ח אֵבָרָיו וּשְׁסָ"ה גִּידָיו בְּתוֹךְ שְׁאָר חוֹלֵי יִשְׂרָאֵל, רְפוּאַת הַנֶּפֶשׁ וּרְפוּאַת הַגּוּף (בשבת: שַׁבָּת הִיא / ביום טוב: יוֹם טוֹב הוּא / מִלִּזְעֹק וּרְפוּאָה קְרוֹבָה לָבוֹא), הַשְׁתָּא בַּעֲגָלָא וּבִזְמַן קָרִיב, וְנֹאמַר אָמֵן.

לחולָה

מִי שֶׁבֵּרַךְ אֲבוֹתֵינוּ אַבְרָהָם יִצְחָק וְיַעֲקֹב, מֹשֶׁה וְאַהֲרֹן דָּוִד וּשְׁלֹמֹה, הוּא יְבָרֵךְ וִירַפֵּא אֶת הַחוֹלָה (פלונית בַּת פלונית) בַּעֲבוּר שֶׁנּוֹדְרִים צְדָקָה בַּעֲבוּרָהּ. בִּשְׂכַר זֶה הַקָּדוֹשׁ בָּרוּךְ הוּא יִמָּלֵא רַחֲמִים עָלֶיהָ לְהַחֲלִימָהּ וּלְרַפְּאתָהּ וּלְהַחֲזִיקָהּ וּלְהַחֲיוֹתָהּ וְיִשְׁלַח לָהּ מְהֵרָה רְפוּאָה שְׁלֵמָה מִן הַשָּׁמַיִם לְכָל אֵבָרֶיהָ וּלְכָל גִּידֶיהָ בְּתוֹךְ שְׁאָר חוֹלֵי יִשְׂרָאֵל, רְפוּאַת הַנֶּפֶשׁ וּרְפוּאַת הַגּוּף (בשבת: שַׁבָּת הִיא / ביום טוב: יוֹם טוֹב הוּא / מִלִּזְעֹק וּרְפוּאָה קְרוֹבָה לָבוֹא), הַשְׁתָּא בַּעֲגָלָא וּבִזְמַן קָרִיב, וְנֹאמַר אָמֵן.

FOR A CRITICALLY SICK MAN

מִי שֶׁבֵּרַךְ May He Who blessed our fathers Abraham, Isaac, and Jacob, Moses and Aaron, David and Solomon, have mercy on the sick person (*name*) son of (*mother's name*), on whose behalf I/we vow to give charity. As a reward for this, may the Holy One, blessed is He, bring blessing on him and his family and may God do what is best for him (*On Shabbat:* though on the Sabbath / *On Yom Tov:* though on Yom Tov / it is forbidden to cry out), and deliverance, swiftly and soon. And let us say, Amen.

FOR A CRITICALLY SICK WOMAN

מִי שֶׁבֵּרַךְ May He Who blessed our fathers Abraham, Isaac, and Jacob, Moses and Aaron, David, and Solomon, have mercy on the sick person (*name*) daughter of (*mother's name*), on whose behalf I/we vow to give charity. As a reward for this, may the Holy One, blessed is He, bring blessing on her and her family and may God do what is best for her (*On Shabbat:* though on the Sabbath / *On Yom Tov:* though on Yom Tov / it is forbidden to cry out), and deliverance, swiftly and soon. And let us say, Amen.

לחולֶה אנוש

מִי שֶׁבֵּרַךְ אֲבוֹתֵינוּ אַבְרָהָם יִצְחָק וְיַעֲקֹב, מֹשֶׁה וְאַהֲרֹן דָּוִד וּשְׁלֹמֹה הוּא יְרַחֵם עַל הַחוֹלֶה (פלוני בֶּן פלונית) בַּעֲבוּר שֶׁאֲנִי נוֹדֵר / שֶׁאָנוּ נוֹדְרִים / צְדָקָה בַּעֲבוּרוֹ. בִּשְׂכַר זֶה הַקָּדוֹשׁ בָּרוּךְ הוּא יֵיטִיב לוֹ וְלִבְנֵי מִשְׁפַּחְתּוֹ וְהַטּוֹב בְּעֵינָיו יַעֲשֶׂה, (בשבת: שַׁבָּת הִיא / ביום טוב: יוֹם טוֹב הוּא / מִלִּזְעֹק) וִישׁוּעָה קְרוֹבָה לָבוֹא, הַשְׁתָּא בַּעֲגָלָא וּבִזְמַן קָרִיב, וְנֹאמַר אָמֵן.

לחולָה אנושה

מִי שֶׁבֵּרַךְ אֲבוֹתֵינוּ אַבְרָהָם יִצְחָק וְיַעֲקֹב, מֹשֶׁה וְאַהֲרֹן דָּוִד וּשְׁלֹמֹה, הוּא יְרַחֵם עַל הַחוֹלָה (פלונית בַּת פלונית) בַּעֲבוּר שֶׁאֲנִי נוֹדֵר / שֶׁאָנוּ נוֹדְרִים / צְדָקָה בַּעֲבוּרָהּ. בִּשְׂכַר זֶה הַקָּדוֹשׁ בָּרוּךְ הוּא יֵיטִיב לָהּ וְלִבְנֵי מִשְׁפַּחְתָּהּ וְהַטּוֹב בְּעֵינָיו יַעֲשֶׂה, (בשבת: שַׁבָּת הִיא / ביום טוב: יוֹם טוֹב הוּא / מִלִּזְעֹק) וִישׁוּעָה קְרוֹבָה לָבוֹא, הַשְׁתָּא בַּעֲגָלָא וּבִזְמַן קָרִיב, וְנֹאמַר אָמֵן.

HALAKHOT CONCERNING SHINUI SHEM AND VIDUY

CHANGING THE NAME – SHINUI SHEM

1. When a person is seriously ill, and there remains hope for recovery, some maintain the custom of adding a name to the *ḥoleh*'s existing name (רמ״א יו״ד שלה:י).
2. Often, the additional name chosen reflects a prayer for life or for divine intervention (e.g., for men: Alter, Azriel, Eliezer, Hayyim, Yeraḥmiel, Paltiel, or Refael; and for women: Hava, Haya, Sarah, or Yocheved). Alternatively, some consult with a *talmid hakham* to use a *goral haGr"a* – opening a *Tanakh* and selecting the first appropriate name that appears.
3. While some add the name at the time of Torah reading, others gather a minyan for the recitation of Psalms, the prayer for the changing of the name, and a closing *mi sheberakh*.
4. The added name should be used as the first name of the *ḥoleh*. If the *ḥoleh* recovers (for at least thirty days), the new name becomes a permanent part of the person's name. If however, the *ḥoleh* does not recover, the added name is no longer used (גשר החיים א:ג:ה).

VIDUY

1. When a *ḥoleh* becomes critically ill, it is appropriate for the *ḥoleh* to recite the *Viduy*. At the time of recitation, the *ḥoleh* should be reminded that many have recited *Viduy* and ultimately recovered (יו״ד שלח:א, ש״ך יו״ד שלח:א).
2. There are different forms of *Viduy*; a brief one-sentence confession, or full paragraph confession (known as the *Viduy HaKatzar*). In addition, there are those who add the *Ashamnu* of Yom Kippur followed by Psalms 16, 23, 25, 51, 91, 102, 121, 139, and 142. The selection of the appropriate *Viduy* for recitation should be determined

on a case-by-case basis, depending on the physical condition of the *ḥoleh* (גשר החיים א:ה:א-ב,ה).

3. If the *ḥoleh* cannot speak, but is conscious, the *Viduy* may be recited by another, while the *ḥoleh* "recites" the *Vidui Belibo* in his thoughts (טור יו"ד שלח).
4. If the *ḥoleh* is no longer conscious, someone present may recite the *Viduy* on his behalf (מפנקסו של רופא עמ' קנב-קנג, מסורת משה ח"ב רע"ח).

CHANGING THE NAME

If the sick person is a male:

וְאַף If it has been decreed upon him in Your court of Justice that he must die of this illness, our holy rabbis have said: Three things annul a decree against a person. One of those is changing the name; that is, that they should change the name of the person who is sick. We have fulfilled their words and have changed his name, and it is therefore different. And if on (*sick person's original name*) there is a decree, on (*sick person's new name*) there is no decree, for he is different and is no longer the one called by that previous name. And just as his name has been changed so may the decree be changed from strict justice to mercy, from death to life, from sickness to complete recovery, for (*new name*) son of (*mother's name*). In the name of all the names written in this Torah Scroll, and in the name of all the angels appointed over all healing and salvation, swiftly send a complete recovery to (*new name*) son of (*mother's name*). Lengthen his days and years in pleasantness, let him spend his days well, with abundant strength and peace, from now and through eternity. Amen, Selah.

If the sick person is a female:

וְאַף If it has been decreed upon her in Your court of Justice that she must die of this illness, our holy rabbis have said: Three things annul a decree against a person. One of those is changing the name; that is, that they should change the name of the person who is sick. We have fulfilled their words and have changed her name, and it is therefore different. And if on (*sick person's original name*) there is a decree, on (*sick person's new name*)

שינוי שם

If the sick person is a male:

וְאַף אִם נִגְזַר עָלָיו בְּבֵית דִּינְךָ הַצֶּדֶק שֶׁיָּמוּת מֵחָלְיִ זֶה, הִנֵּה רַבּוֹתֵינוּ הַקְּדוֹשִׁים אָמְרוּ: שְׁלֹשָׁה דְּבָרִים קוֹרְעִים גְּזַר דִּינוֹ שֶׁל אָדָם. וְאֶחָד מֵהֶם שִׁנּוּי הַשֵּׁם, שֶׁיְּשַׁנּוּ הַשֵּׁם שֶׁל הַחוֹלֶה. וְקִיַּמְנוּ דִּבְרֵיהֶם וְנִשְׁתַּנָּה שְׁמוֹ וְלָכֵן אַחֶרֶת הִיא וְאִם עַל (שם הישן בן שם אמו) נִגְזַר גְּזַר הַדִּין, עַל (שם החדש בן שם אמו) לֹא נִגְזַר כִּי אַחֵר הוּא וְאֵינוֹ הוּא הַנִּקְרָא בַּשֵּׁם הָרִאשׁוֹן. וּכְשֵׁם שֶׁנִּשְׁתַּנָּה שְׁמוֹ כֵּן יִשְׁתַּנֶּה גְּזַר הַדִּין מֵעָלָיו מִדִּין לְרַחֲמִים וּמִמִּיתָה לְחַיִּים וּמִמַּחֲלָה לִרְפוּאָה שְׁלֵמָה לְ(שם החדש בן שם אמו) בְּשֵׁם כָּל הַשֵּׁמוֹת הַכְּתוּבִים בְּסֵפֶר תּוֹרָה זֶה וּבְשֵׁם כָּל הַמַּלְאָכִים הַמְּמוּנִים עַל כָּל הָרְפוּאוֹת וְהַהַצָּלוֹת, וְתִשְׁלַח מְהֵרָה רְפוּאָה שְׁלֵמָה לְ(שם החדש בן שם אמושם אמו) וְתַאֲרִיךְ יָמָיו וּשְׁנוֹתָיו בַּנְּעִימִים, וִיבַלֶּה בְּטוֹב יָמָיו בְּרֹב עֹז וְשָׁלוֹם מֵעַתָּה וְעַד עוֹלָם, אָמֵן סֶלָה.

If the sick person is a female:

וְאַף אִם נִגְזַר עָלֶיהָ בְּבֵית דִּינְךָ הַצֶּדֶק שֶׁתָּמוּת מֵחָלְיִ זֶה, הִנֵּה רַבּוֹתֵינוּ הַקְּדוֹשִׁים אָמְרוּ: שְׁלֹשָׁה דְּבָרִים קוֹרְעִים גְּזַר דִּינוֹ שֶׁל אָדָם. וְאֶחָד מֵהֶם שִׁנּוּי הַשֵּׁם, שֶׁיְּשַׁנּוּ הַשֵּׁם שֶׁל הַחוֹלֶה. וְקִיַּמְנוּ דִּבְרֵיהֶם וְנִשְׁתַּנָּה שְׁמָהּ וְלָכֵן אַחֶרֶת הִיא וְאִם עַל (שם הישן בת שם אמה) נִגְזַר גְּזַר הַדִּין, עַל (שם החדש בת

there is no decree, for she is different and is no longer the one called by that previous name. And just as her name has been changed so may the decree be changed from strict justice to mercy, from death to life, from sickness to complete recovery, for (*new name*) daughter of (*mother's name*). In the name of all the names written in this Torah Scroll, and in the name of all the angels appointed over all healing and salvation, swiftly send a complete recovery to (*new name*) daughter of (*mother's name*). Lengthen her days and years in pleasantness, let her spend her days well, with abundant strength and peace, from now and through eternity. Amen, Selah.

שם אמה) לֹא נִגְזַר כִּי אַחֶרֶת הִיא וְאֵינָהּ הִיא הַנִּקְרֵאת בַּשֵּׁם הָרִאשׁוֹן. וּכְשֵׁם שֶׁנִּשְׁתַּנָּה שְׁמָהּ כֵּן יִשְׁתַּנֶּה גְּזַר הַדִּין מֵעָלֶיהָ מִדִּין לְרַחֲמִים וּמִמִּיתָה לְחַיִּים וּמִמַּחֲלָה לִרְפוּאָה שְׁלֵמָה לְ(שם החדש בת שם אמה) בְּשֵׁם כָּל הַשֵּׁמוֹת הַכְּתוּבִים בְּסֵפֶר תּוֹרָה זֶה וּבְשֵׁם כָּל הַמַּלְאָכִים הַמְּמוּנִים עַל כָּל הָרְפוּאוֹת וְהַהַצָּלוֹת, וְתִשְׁלַח מְהֵרָה רְפוּאָה שְׁלֵמָה לְ(שם החדש בת שם אמה) וְתַאֲרִיךְ יָמֶיהָ וּשְׁנוֹתֶיהָ בַּנְּעִימִים, וּתְבַלֶּה בְּטוֹב יָמֶיהָ בְּרֹב עֹז וְשָׁלוֹם מֵעַתָּה וְעַד עוֹלָם, אָמֵן סֶלָה.

CONFESSION BEFORE DEATH

ONE-SENTENCE *VIDUY*

If one is unable to recite the entire Viduy, this abbreviated phrase should be said. If even that is not possible, this phrase should be contemplated in one's thoughts

אִם If heaven forfend I will die, may my death be an atonement for all my sins.

THE SHORT *VIDUY*

If one is able to recite a longer Viduy, the following two paragraphs should be recited. If the person can recite even more, the additions to Viduy found on the following pages should be added.

מוֹדֶה I give thanks to You, LORD my God and the God of my fathers, in Whose hands is my recovery and my death, for all the life and the necessities of life that You have provided for me. May it be Your will that You grant me a full recovery, and if heaven forfend I die, may my death be an atonement for all my sins, iniquities, and transgressions that I have perpetrated before You. Grant that my portion will be in the Garden of Eden and allow me to merit the World to Come that is reserved for the righteous. Please God, please heal me.

אֲנִי מַאֲמִין I believe with complete faith that God is true, that His name is true, [I believe in] the thirteen principles of faith. I hereby forgive every person, and request that they all will forgive me.

וידוי לפני המוות

וידוי במשפט אחד

If one is unable to recite the entire וידוי*, this abbreviated phrase should be said. If even that is not possible, this phrase should be contemplated in one's thoughts*

אִם חַס וְשָׁלוֹם אָמוּת, תְּהֵא מִיתָתִי כַּפָּרָה עַל כָּל עֲוֹנוֹתָי.

וידוי הקצר

If one is able to recite a longer וידוי*, the following two paragraphs should be recited. If the person can recite even more, the additions to* וידוי *found on the following pages should be added.*

man מוֹדֶה / *woman* מוֹדָה/ אֲנִי לְפָנֶיךָ, יהוה אֱלֹהַי וֵאלֹהֵי אֲבוֹתַי שֶׁרְפוּאָתִי וּמִיתָתִי בְּיָדֶךָ עַל כָּל הַחַיִּים וְצָרְכֵי הַחַיִּים שֶׁנָּתַתָּ לִי. יְהִי רָצוֹן מִלְּפָנֶיךָ, שֶׁתִּרְפָּאֵנִי רְפוּאָה שְׁלֵמָה, וְאִם חַס וְשָׁלוֹם אָמוּת, תְּהֵא מִיתָתִי כַּפָּרָה עַל כָּל הַחֲטָאִים וַעֲוֹנוֹת וְהַפְּשָׁעִים שֶׁחָטָאתִי וְשֶׁעָוִיתִי וְשֶׁפָּשַׁעְתִּי לְפָנֶיךָ. וְתֵן חֶלְקִי בְּגַן עֵדֶן, וְזַכֵּנִי לָעוֹלָם הַבָּא הַצָּפוּן לַצַּדִּיקִים. אֵל נָא רְפָא נָא לִי.

אֲנִי מַאֲמִין/מַאֲמִינָה בֶּאֱמוּנָה שְׁלֵמָה, שֶׁאֱלֹהִים אֱמֶת וּשְׁמוֹ אֱמֶת, וּבִשְׁלֹשָׁה עָשָׂר הָעִקָּרִים. וְהִנְנִי מוֹחֵל/מוֹחֶלֶת לְכָל אָדָם וּמְבַקֵּשׁ/וּמְבַקֶּשֶׁת שֶׁכֻּלָּם יִמְחֲלוּ לִי.

THE LONG *VIDUY*/ADDITIONS TO *VIDUY*

After saying the viduy one may add any or all of the following prayers:

אָשַׁמְנוּ We have sinned, we have acted treacherously, we have robbed, we have spoken slander.
We have acted perversely, we have acted wickedly, we have acted presumptuously, we have been violent, we have framed lies.
We have given bad advice, we have deceived, we have scorned, we have rebelled, we have provoked, we have turned away,
we have committed iniquity, we have transgressed, we have persecuted, we have been obstinate.
We have acted wickedly, we have corrupted, we have acted abominably, we have strayed, we have led others astray.

לַמְנַצֵּחַ *To the lead singer – a psalm of David.* The heavens tell of God's glory; the skies proclaim His handiwork. Day to day pours forth speech; night to night expresses knowledge. There is no speech; there are no words; their voice is not heard, yet their music carries across the land, their words to the end of the earth. In them21 He has set a tent for the sun, which emerges like a groom from his marriage chamber, glowing like a champion about to run his course. It rises at one end of the heaven and circuits to the other; nothing can hide from its heat. The Lord's teaching is perfect, reviving the spirit; the Lord's decree is steadfast, making the simple wise. The Lord's precepts are just, cheering the heart; the Lord's commandment is radiant, lighting up the eyes. Fear of the Lord is pure, enduring forever; the Lord's judgments are true and righteous without exception – more precious than gold, than boundless fine gold, sweeter than honey, than nectar from the honeycomb. Your servant, too, is careful of them; in keeping them there is great reward. Yet who can discern his errors? Cleanse me of hidden faults. Spare Your servant from the insolent; let them rule me not. Then shall I be blameless, cleansed of grave sin. May the words of my mouth and my heart's reflections please You, Lord, my Rock and redeemer. *Ps. 19*

וידוי הארוך/הוספות לוידוי

After saying the וידוי *one may add any or all of the following prayers:*

**אָשַׁמְנוּ, בָּגַדְנוּ, גָּזַלְנוּ, דִּבַּרְנוּ דֹפִי
הֶעֱוִינוּ, וְהִרְשַׁעְנוּ, זַדְנוּ, חָמַסְנוּ, טָפַלְנוּ שֶׁקֶר
יָעַצְנוּ רָע, כִּזַּבְנוּ, לַצְנוּ, מָרַדְנוּ, נִאַצְנוּ, סָרַרְנוּ
עָוִינוּ, פָּשַׁעְנוּ, צָרַרְנוּ, קִשִּׁינוּ עֹרֶף
רָשַׁעְנוּ, שִׁחַתְנוּ, תִּעַבְנוּ, תָּעִינוּ, תִּעְתָּעְנוּ.**

לַמְנַצֵּחַ מִזְמוֹר לְדָוִד: הַשָּׁמַיִם מְסַפְּרִים כְּבוֹד־אֵל, וּמַעֲשֵׂה תהלים יט
יָדָיו מַגִּיד הָרָקִיעַ: יוֹם לְיוֹם יַבִּיעַ אֹמֶר, וְלַיְלָה לְּלַיְלָה יְחַוֶּה־
דָּעַת: אֵין־אֹמֶר וְאֵין דְּבָרִים, בְּלִי נִשְׁמָע קוֹלָם: בְּכָל־הָאָרֶץ
יָצָא קַוָּם, וּבִקְצֵה תֵבֵל מִלֵּיהֶם, לַשֶּׁמֶשׁ שָׂם־אֹהֶל בָּהֶם: וְהוּא
כְּחָתָן יֹצֵא מֵחֻפָּתוֹ, יָשִׂישׂ כְּגִבּוֹר לָרוּץ אֹרַח: מִקְצֵה הַשָּׁמַיִם
מוֹצָאוֹ, וּתְקוּפָתוֹ עַל־קְצוֹתָם, וְאֵין נִסְתָּר מֵחַמָּתוֹ: תּוֹרַת
יהוה תְּמִימָה, מְשִׁיבַת נָפֶשׁ, עֵדוּת יהוה נֶאֱמָנָה, מַחְכִּימַת
פֶּתִי: פִּקּוּדֵי יהוה יְשָׁרִים, מְשַׂמְּחֵי־לֵב, מִצְוַת יהוה בָּרָה,
מְאִירַת עֵינָיִם: יִרְאַת יהוה טְהוֹרָה, עוֹמֶדֶת לָעַד, מִשְׁפְּטֵי־
יהוה אֱמֶת, צָדְקוּ יַחְדָּו: הַנֶּחֱמָדִים מִזָּהָב וּמִפַּז רָב, וּמְתוּקִים
מִדְּבַשׁ וְנֹפֶת צוּפִים: גַּם־עַבְדְּךָ נִזְהָר בָּהֶם, בְּשָׁמְרָם עֵקֶב רָב:
שְׁגִיאוֹת מִי־יָבִין, מִנִּסְתָּרוֹת נַקֵּנִי: גַּם מִזֵּדִים חֲשֹׂךְ עַבְדֶּךָ,
אַל־יִמְשְׁלוּ־בִי אָז אֵיתָם, וְנִקֵּיתִי מִפֶּשַׁע רָב: יִהְיוּ לְרָצוֹן
אִמְרֵי־פִי וְהֶגְיוֹן לִבִּי לְפָנֶיךָ, יהוה, צוּרִי וְגֹאֲלִי:

מִזְמוֹר לְדָוִד A psalm of David. The Lord is my Shepherd; I lack nothing. He lets me lie down in green pastures; He leads me beside still waters. He refreshes my soul, guiding me along the right paths for the sake of His name. Though I walk through the valley of the shadow of death, I fear no evil, for You are with me; Your rod and Your staff encourage me. You set a table before me in the face of my foes; You anoint my head with oil; my cup brims over. May only goodness and kindness follow me all the days of my life; let me live in the Lord's House for evermore. *Ps. 23*

לְדָוִד Of David. To You, O Lord, I lift up my soul; in You, my God, I place my trust. Do not let me be put to shame; do not let my enemies gloat over me. Let none who hope for You be put to shame, but let traitors, empty-handed, be ashamed. Show me Your ways, Lord; teach me Your paths. Guide me in Your truth; teach me, for You are the God of my salvation; I constantly look to You in hope. Remember Your compassion, Lord, Your loyalty, for they have always been. Do not remember the sins of my youth or my offenses, but remember me in keeping with Your loyalty, in keeping with Your goodness, Lord. Good and upright is the Lord; therefore He shows sinners the way; He guides the lowly along the right path and teaches the lowly His way. All the ways of the Lord are loyal and true to those who keep His covenant, His rules. For the sake of Your name, Lord, forgive my sin though it is great. Who, then, is one who fears the Lord? He will show them which path to choose. They will live good lives, and their children will inherit the earth. The Lord confides in those who fear Him; to them He reveals His covenant. My eyes are ever on the Lord, for only He can free my feet from the net. Turn to me and show me favor, for I am lonely and suffering; my heart swells with grief; relieve me from *Ps. 25*

תהלים כג

מִזְמוֹר לְדָוִד, יהוה רֹעִי לֹא אֶחְסָר: בִּנְאוֹת דֶּשֶׁא יַרְבִּיצֵנִי,
עַל־מֵי מְנֻחוֹת יְנַהֲלֵנִי: נַפְשִׁי יְשׁוֹבֵב, יַנְחֵנִי בְמַעְגְּלֵי־צֶדֶק
לְמַעַן שְׁמוֹ: גַּם כִּי־אֵלֵךְ בְּגֵיא צַלְמָוֶת לֹא־אִירָא רָע, כִּי־אַתָּה
עִמָּדִי, שִׁבְטְךָ וּמִשְׁעַנְתֶּךָ הֵמָּה יְנַחֲמֻנִי: תַּעֲרֹךְ לְפָנַי שֻׁלְחָן
נֶגֶד צֹרְרָי, דִּשַּׁנְתָּ בַשֶּׁמֶן רֹאשִׁי, כּוֹסִי רְוָיָה: אַךְ טוֹב וָחֶסֶד
יִרְדְּפוּנִי כָּל־יְמֵי חַיָּי, וְשַׁבְתִּי בְּבֵית־יהוה לְאֹרֶךְ יָמִים:

תהלים כה

לְדָוִד אֵלֶיךָ יהוה, נַפְשִׁי אֶשָּׂא: אֱלֹהַי בְּךָ בָטַחְתִּי אַל־
אֵבוֹשָׁה, אַל־יַעַלְצוּ אוֹיְבַי לִי: גַּם כָּל־קֹוֶיךָ לֹא יֵבֹשׁוּ, יֵבֹשׁוּ
הַבּוֹגְדִים רֵיקָם: דְּרָכֶיךָ יהוה הוֹדִיעֵנִי, אֹרְחוֹתֶיךָ לַמְּדֵנִי:
הַדְרִיכֵנִי בַאֲמִתֶּךָ וְלַמְּדֵנִי כִּי־אַתָּה אֱלֹהֵי יִשְׁעִי, אוֹתְךָ קִוִּיתִי
כָּל־הַיּוֹם: זְכֹר־רַחֲמֶיךָ יהוה וַחֲסָדֶיךָ, כִּי מֵעוֹלָם הֵמָּה:
חַטֹּאות נְעוּרַי וּפְשָׁעַי אַל־תִּזְכֹּר, כְּחַסְדְּךָ זְכָר־לִי־אַתָּה,
לְמַעַן טוּבְךָ יהוה: טוֹב־וְיָשָׁר יהוה, עַל־כֵּן יוֹרֶה חַטָּאִים
בַּדָּרֶךְ: יַדְרֵךְ עֲנָוִים בַּמִּשְׁפָּט, וִילַמֵּד עֲנָוִים דַּרְכּוֹ: כָּל־אָרְחוֹת
יהוה חֶסֶד וֶאֱמֶת, לְנֹצְרֵי בְרִיתוֹ וְעֵדֹתָיו: לְמַעַן־שִׁמְךָ יהוה,
וְסָלַחְתָּ לַעֲוֹנִי כִּי רַב־הוּא: מִי־זֶה הָאִישׁ יְרֵא יהוה, יוֹרֶנּוּ
בְּדֶרֶךְ יִבְחָר: נַפְשׁוֹ בְּטוֹב תָּלִין, וְזַרְעוֹ יִירַשׁ אָרֶץ: סוֹד
יהוה לִירֵאָיו, וּבְרִיתוֹ לְהוֹדִיעָם: עֵינַי תָּמִיד אֶל־יהוה, כִּי
הוּא־יוֹצִיא מֵרֶשֶׁת רַגְלָי: פְּנֵה־אֵלַי וְחָנֵּנִי, כִּי־יָחִיד וְעָנִי
אָנִי: צָרוֹת לְבָבִי הִרְחִיבוּ, מִמְּצוּקוֹתַי הוֹצִיאֵנִי: רְאֵה עָנְיִי
וַעֲמָלִי, וְשָׂא לְכָל־חַטֹּאותָי: רְאֵה־אוֹיְבַי כִּי־רָבּוּ, וְשִׂנְאַת

my agony; see my suffering and my pain, and forgive all my sins. See how many enemies I have and their violent hatred toward me. Protect me and save me; let me not be put to shame, for in You I take refuge. Let integrity and decency keep me, for I look to You in hope. May God free Israel from all its grief.

לַמְנַצֵּחַ To the lead singer – a psalm of David, when the prophet Natan came to him after he came to Batsheva. Show me grace, God, in Your loyalty; in Your great mercy, erase my offense; wash me well of my guilt; purify me of my sin, for I am aware of my transgression, and my sin is ever before me. I sinned against You alone; I committed what is evil in Your eyes, so Your sentence is just, and Your judgment is fair. Yes, with guilt I came to be; in sin did my mother conceive me. Yes, You desire truth to course deep within me – to teach wisdom to my innermost self. Purge me with hyssop, and I will be pure; wash me, and I will be whiter than snow. Let me hear gladness and joy; let the bones You have crushed rejoice. Hide Your face from my sins; erase all my guilt. Create a pure heart for me, God; renew a firm spirit within me. Do not cast me away from Your presence or take Your holy spirit away from me. Restore your glad salvation to me; let a willing spirit sustain me. I will teach offenders Your ways, and sinners will come back to You. Save me from bloodshed, God, God of my salvation; my tongue will sing of Your justice. O Lord, open my lips, and my mouth will declare Your praise. You have no desire for me to bring sacrifice; You do not want burnt offerings. To God, a broken spirit is an offering; a crushed and broken heart, God, You will not spurn. Favor Zion with Your goodness; rebuild the walls of Jerusalem. Then You will delight in sincere sacrifices, burnt offerings and whole offerings; then bulls will be offered up on Your altar. *Ps. 51*

חֲמַס שְׂנֵאוּנִי: שָׁמְרָה נַפְשִׁי וְהַצִּילֵנִי, אַל־אֵבוֹשׁ כִּי־חָסִיתִי
בָךְ: תֹּם־וָיֹשֶׁר יִצְּרוּנִי, כִּי קִוִּיתִיךָ: פְּדֵה אֱלֹהִים אֶת־יִשְׂרָאֵל
מִכֹּל צָרוֹתָיו:

תהלים נא
לַמְנַצֵּחַ מִזְמוֹר לְדָוִד: בְּבוֹא־אֵלָיו נָתָן הַנָּבִיא, כַּאֲשֶׁר־בָּא
אֶל־בַּת־שָׁבַע: חָנֵּנִי אֱלֹהִים כְּחַסְדֶּךָ, כְּרֹב רַחֲמֶיךָ מְחֵה
פְשָׁעָי: הֶרֶב כַּבְּסֵנִי מֵעֲוֹנִי, וּמֵחַטָּאתִי טַהֲרֵנִי: כִּי־פְשָׁעַי
אֲנִי אֵדָע, וְחַטָּאתִי נֶגְדִּי תָמִיד: לְךָ לְבַדְּךָ חָטָאתִי וְהָרַע
בְּעֵינֶיךָ עָשִׂיתִי, לְמַעַן תִּצְדַּק בְּדָבְרֶךָ תִּזְכֶּה בְשָׁפְטֶךָ: הֵן־
בְּעָווֹן חוֹלָלְתִּי, וּבְחֵטְא יֶחֱמַתְנִי אִמִּי: הֵן־אֱמֶת חָפַצְתָּ
בַטֻּחוֹת, וּבְסָתֻם חָכְמָה תוֹדִיעֵנִי: תְּחַטְּאֵנִי בְאֵזוֹב וְאֶטְהָר,
תְּכַבְּסֵנִי וּמִשֶּׁלֶג אַלְבִּין: תַּשְׁמִיעֵנִי שָׂשׂוֹן וְשִׂמְחָה, תָּגֵלְנָה
עֲצָמוֹת דִּכִּיתָ: הַסְתֵּר פָּנֶיךָ מֵחֲטָאָי, וְכָל־עֲוֹנֹתַי מְחֵה:
לֵב טָהוֹר בְּרָא־לִי אֱלֹהִים, וְרוּחַ נָכוֹן חַדֵּשׁ בְּקִרְבִּי: אַל־
תַּשְׁלִיכֵנִי מִלְּפָנֶיךָ, וְרוּחַ קָדְשְׁךָ אַל־תִּקַּח מִמֶּנִּי: הָשִׁיבָה
לִּי שְׂשׂוֹן יִשְׁעֶךָ, וְרוּחַ נְדִיבָה תִסְמְכֵנִי: אֲלַמְּדָה פֹשְׁעִים
דְּרָכֶיךָ, וְחַטָּאִים אֵלֶיךָ יָשׁוּבוּ: הַצִּילֵנִי מִדָּמִים אֱלֹהִים אֱלֹהֵי
תְּשׁוּעָתִי, תְּרַנֵּן לְשׁוֹנִי צִדְקָתֶךָ: אֲדֹנָי שְׂפָתַי תִּפְתָּח, וּפִי יַגִּיד
תְּהִלָּתֶךָ: כִּי לֹא־תַחְפֹּץ זֶבַח וְאֶתֵּנָה, עוֹלָה לֹא תִרְצֶה: זִבְחֵי
אֱלֹהִים רוּחַ נִשְׁבָּרָה, לֵב־נִשְׁבָּר וְנִדְכֶּה, אֱלֹהִים לֹא תִבְזֶה:
הֵיטִיבָה בִרְצוֹנְךָ אֶת־צִיּוֹן, תִּבְנֶה חוֹמוֹת יְרוּשָׁלָםִ: אָז תַּחְפֹּץ
זִבְחֵי־צֶדֶק עוֹלָה וְכָלִיל, אָז יַעֲלוּ עַל־מִזְבַּחֲךָ פָרִים:

יֹשֵׁב He who lives in the shelter of the Most High dwells in the shadow of Shaddai. I say of the Lord, "My refuge and stronghold, my God in whom I trust," for He will save you from the fowler's snare, from deadly plague. With His pinions He will cover you; beneath His wings you will find shelter; His loyalty is an encircling shield. You need not fear terror by night, nor the arrow that flies by day, nor the plague that stalks in darkness, nor disease that ravages at noon. A thousand may fall beside you, ten thousand at your right hand, but it will not come near you. You will only look with your eyes and see the punishment of the wicked. For you – "the Lord is my Refuge" – you have made the Most High your abode. No harm will befall you; no sickness will come near your home, for He will command His angels about you to guard you in all your ways. They will lift you in their hands lest your foot stumble on a stone. You will tread over lions and vipers; you will trample on young lions and serpents. "Because he loves Me, I will rescue him; I will protect him because he acknowledges My name. When he calls on Me, I will answer him; I will be with him in distress; I will rescue him and bring him honor. With long life I will satisfy him and show him My salvation." *Ps. 91*

תְּפִלָּה לְעָנִי A prayer for the lowly when they grow overwhelmed and pour out their lament before the Lord. O Lord, listen to my prayer; let my cry reach You. Do not hide Your face from me on the day of my distress; lend Your ear to me on the day that I call – hurry, answer me! – for my days dissipate like smoke; my bones are scorched as in a furnace; my heart is trampled and withered like grass; I neglect to eat my food. From the noise of my groans, my bones cleave to my flesh. I have become like a desert owl, like an owl among ruins; I lie awake; I have become like a lonely bird upon a rooftop. All day long my enemies taunt me; my revilers use my name as a curse, for I eat ashes for bread and mingle my drink with tears because of Your fury and wrath, because You raised me up and flung me down. My days *Ps. 102*

תהלים צא

יֹשֵׁב בְּסֵתֶר עֶלְיוֹן, בְּצֵל שַׁדַּי יִתְלוֹנָן: אֹמַר לַיהוה מַחְסִי וּמְצוּדָתִי, אֱלֹהַי אֶבְטַח־בּוֹ: כִּי הוּא יַצִּילְךָ מִפַּח יָקוּשׁ, מִדֶּבֶר הַוּוֹת: בְּאֶבְרָתוֹ יָסֶךְ לָךְ, וְתַחַת־כְּנָפָיו תֶּחְסֶה, צִנָּה וְסֹחֵרָה אֲמִתּוֹ: לֹא־תִירָא מִפַּחַד לָיְלָה, מֵחֵץ יָעוּף יוֹמָם: מִדֶּבֶר בָּאֹפֶל יַהֲלֹךְ, מִקֶּטֶב יָשׁוּד צָהֳרָיִם: יִפֹּל מִצִּדְּךָ אֶלֶף, וּרְבָבָה מִימִינֶךָ, אֵלֶיךָ לֹא יִגָּשׁ: רַק בְּעֵינֶיךָ תַבִּיט, וְשִׁלֻּמַת רְשָׁעִים תִּרְאֶה: כִּי־אַתָּה יהוה מַחְסִי, עֶלְיוֹן שַׂמְתָּ מְעוֹנֶךָ: לֹא־תְאֻנֶּה אֵלֶיךָ רָעָה, וְנֶגַע לֹא־יִקְרַב בְּאָהֳלֶךָ: כִּי מַלְאָכָיו יְצַוֶּה־לָּךְ, לִשְׁמָרְךָ בְּכָל־דְּרָכֶיךָ: עַל־כַּפַּיִם יִשָּׂאוּנְךָ, פֶּן־תִּגֹּף בָּאֶבֶן רַגְלֶךָ: עַל־שַׁחַל וָפֶתֶן תִּדְרֹךְ, תִּרְמֹס כְּפִיר וְתַנִּין: כִּי בִי חָשַׁק וַאֲפַלְּטֵהוּ, אֲשַׂגְּבֵהוּ כִּי־יָדַע שְׁמִי: יִקְרָאֵנִי וְאֶעֱנֵהוּ, עִמּוֹ אָנֹכִי בְצָרָה, אֲחַלְּצֵהוּ וַאֲכַבְּדֵהוּ: אֹרֶךְ יָמִים אַשְׂבִּיעֵהוּ, וְאַרְאֵהוּ בִּישׁוּעָתִי:

תהלים קב

תְּפִלָּה לְעָנִי כִי־יַעֲטֹף, וְלִפְנֵי יהוה יִשְׁפֹּךְ שִׂיחוֹ: יהוה שִׁמְעָה תְפִלָּתִי, וְשַׁוְעָתִי אֵלֶיךָ תָבוֹא: אַל־תַּסְתֵּר פָּנֶיךָ מִמֶּנִּי בְּיוֹם צַר לִי, הַטֵּה־אֵלַי אָזְנֶךָ בְּיוֹם אֶקְרָא מַהֵר עֲנֵנִי: כִּי־כָלוּ בְעָשָׁן יָמָי, וְעַצְמוֹתַי כְּמוֹקֵד נִחָרוּ: הוּכָּה כָעֵשֶׂב וַיִּבַשׁ לִבִּי, כִּי־שָׁכַחְתִּי מֵאֲכֹל לַחְמִי: מִקּוֹל אַנְחָתִי, דָּבְקָה עַצְמִי לִבְשָׂרִי: דָּמִיתִי לִקְאַת מִדְבָּר, הָיִיתִי כְּכוֹס חֳרָבוֹת: שָׁקַדְתִּי וָאֶהְיֶה, כְּצִפּוֹר בּוֹדֵד עַל־גָּג: כָּל־הַיּוֹם חֵרְפוּנִי אוֹיְבָי, מְהוֹלָלַי בִּי נִשְׁבָּעוּ: כִּי־אֵפֶר כַּלֶּחֶם אָכָלְתִּי, וְשִׁקֻּוַי בִּבְכִי מָסָכְתִּי: מִפְּנֵי־

are like lengthening shadows, and I wither away like grass, but You, Lord, are enthroned forever; Your name endures for all generations. Rise up and have mercy on Zion; the time has come to grant her grace; the hour has arrived, for Your servants love her very stones; they even cherish her dust. Then the nations will fear the name of the Lord, all the kings of the earth Your glory – when the Lord rebuilds Zion and appears in His glory. He turns to the prayer of the destitute and does not show contempt for their prayers. May this be inscribed for a generation to come, that people yet unborn will praise the Lord. For the Lord gazes down from His holy heights; He looks down from heaven to earth to hear the groans of captives, to free those doomed to death; so that the Lord's name may be proclaimed in Zion and in Jerusalem His praise when peoples gather together, as well as kingdoms, to serve the Lord. He has sapped my strength in midcourse and shortened my days. I say, "O my God, do not take me away when only half my days are done – You whose years span the generations." You founded the earth long ago; the heavens are Your handiwork. When they are long gone, You will still stand; they will all wear out like a garment; You change them like clothing, and they fade away, but You are always the same – Your years never end. May Your servants' children dwell in peace and their own seed be established in Your presence.

שִׁיר לַמַּעֲלוֹת *A song of ascents.* I lift my eyes up to the hills; where *Ps. 121*
will my help come from? My help comes from the Lord, Maker of heaven and earth. He will not let your foot slip; He who guards you does not slumber. Behold – the Guardian of Israel neither slumbers nor sleeps. The Lord is your guardian; the Lord is your shade at your right hand. The sun will not strike you by day, nor the moon by night. The Lord will guard you from all harm; He will guard your life. The Lord will guard your going and coming, now and for evermore.

זַעַמְךָ וְקִצְפֶּךָ, כִּי נְשָׂאתַנִי וַתַּשְׁלִיכֵנִי: יָמַי כְּצֵל נָטוּי, וַאֲנִי כָּעֵשֶׂב אִיבָשׁ: וְאַתָּה יהוה לְעוֹלָם תֵּשֵׁב, וְזִכְרְךָ לְדֹר וָדֹר: אַתָּה תָקוּם תְּרַחֵם צִיּוֹן, כִּי־עֵת לְחֶנְנָהּ כִּי־בָא מוֹעֵד: כִּי־רָצוּ עֲבָדֶיךָ אֶת־אֲבָנֶיהָ, וְאֶת־עֲפָרָהּ יְחֹנֵנוּ: וְיִירְאוּ גוֹיִם אֶת־שֵׁם יהוה, וְכָל־מַלְכֵי הָאָרֶץ אֶת־כְּבוֹדֶךָ: כִּי־בָנָה יהוה צִיּוֹן, נִרְאָה בִּכְבוֹדוֹ: פָּנָה אֶל־תְּפִלַּת הָעַרְעָר, וְלֹא־בָזָה אֶת־תְּפִלָּתָם: תִּכָּתֶב זֹאת לְדוֹר אַחֲרוֹן, וְעַם נִבְרָא יְהַלֶּל־יָהּ: כִּי־הִשְׁקִיף מִמְּרוֹם קָדְשׁוֹ, יהוה מִשָּׁמַיִם אֶל־אֶרֶץ הִבִּיט: לִשְׁמֹעַ אֶנְקַת אָסִיר, לְפַתֵּחַ בְּנֵי תְמוּתָה: לְסַפֵּר בְּצִיּוֹן שֵׁם יהוה, וּתְהִלָּתוֹ בִּירוּשָׁלָםִ: בְּהִקָּבֵץ עַמִּים יַחְדָּו, וּמַמְלָכוֹת לַעֲבֹד אֶת־יהוה: עִנָּה בַדֶּרֶךְ כֹּחִי קִצַּר יָמָי: אֹמַר אֵלִי אַל־תַּעֲלֵנִי בַּחֲצִי יָמָי, בְּדוֹר דּוֹרִים שְׁנוֹתֶיךָ: לְפָנִים הָאָרֶץ יָסַדְתָּ, וּמַעֲשֵׂה יָדֶיךָ שָׁמָיִם: הֵמָּה יֹאבֵדוּ וְאַתָּה תַעֲמֹד, וְכֻלָּם כַּבֶּגֶד יִבְלוּ, כַּלְּבוּשׁ תַּחֲלִיפֵם וְיַחֲלֹפוּ: וְאַתָּה־הוּא, וּשְׁנוֹתֶיךָ לֹא יִתָּמּוּ: בְּנֵי־עֲבָדֶיךָ יִשְׁכּוֹנוּ, וְזַרְעָם לְפָנֶיךָ יִכּוֹן:

תהלים קכא

שִׁיר לַמַּעֲלוֹת, אֶשָּׂא עֵינַי אֶל־הֶהָרִים, מֵאַיִן יָבֹא עֶזְרִי: עֶזְרִי מֵעִם יהוה, עֹשֵׂה שָׁמַיִם וָאָרֶץ: אַל־יִתֵּן לַמּוֹט רַגְלֶךָ, אַל־יָנוּם שֹׁמְרֶךָ: הִנֵּה לֹא־יָנוּם וְלֹא יִישָׁן שׁוֹמֵר יִשְׂרָאֵל: יהוה שֹׁמְרֶךָ, יהוה צִלְּךָ עַל־יַד יְמִינֶךָ: יוֹמָם הַשֶּׁמֶשׁ לֹא־יַכֶּכָּה, וְיָרֵחַ בַּלָּיְלָה: יהוה יִשְׁמָרְךָ מִכָּל־רָע, יִשְׁמֹר אֶת־נַפְשֶׁךָ: יהוה יִשְׁמָר־צֵאתְךָ וּבוֹאֶךָ, מֵעַתָּה וְעַד־עוֹלָם:

לַמְנַצֵּחַ לְדָוִד To the lead singer, of David – a psalm. O LORD, You have searched me, and You know – You know when I sit and when I rise; You understand my thoughts from afar. You trace my going out and lying down; You are familiar with all my ways. Even before a word is on my tongue, You, LORD, know it all. You keep close guard behind and before me; You have laid Your hand upon me. Knowledge so wonderful is beyond me, so high that it is above my reach. Where can I escape from Your spirit? Where can I flee from Your presence? If I climb to heaven, You are there; if I make my bed in the underworld, there You are. If I rise on the wings of the dawn, if I settle on the far side of the sea, even there Your hand will guide me; Your right hand will hold me fast. Were I to say, "Surely the darkness will hide me and light become night around me," to You the darkness would not be dark; night is light as day; to You dark and light are one, for You created my innermost being; You knit me together in my mother's womb. I praise You because I am awesomely, wondrously made; wonderful are Your works; I know that full well. My frame was not hidden from You when I was formed in a secret place, woven in the depths of the earth. Your eyes saw my unformed substance; in Your book it was all inscribed when each part would be formed before any of them came to be. How precious to me are Your thoughts, God; how vast in number they are. Were I to count them, they would outnumber the grains of the sand, and when I wake again, I am still with You! God, if only You would slay the wicked – away from me, you men of blood! They speak of You with evil intent; Your adversaries misuse Your name. Do I not hate those who hate You, LORD, and loathe those who rise up against You? I have nothing but hatred for them; I count them my enemies. Search me, God, and know my heart; test me and know my innermost thoughts. See if there is any grievous way within me, and lead me in the everlasting way. *Ps. 139*

תהלים קלט

לַמְנַצֵּחַ לְדָוִד מִזְמוֹר, יהוה חֲקַרְתַּנִי וַתֵּדָע: אַתָּה יָדַעְתָּ שִׁבְתִּי וְקוּמִי, בַּנְתָּה לְרֵעִי מֵרָחוֹק: אָרְחִי וְרִבְעִי זֵרִיתָ, וְכָל־דְּרָכַי הִסְכַּנְתָּה: כִּי אֵין מִלָּה בִּלְשׁוֹנִי, הֵן יהוה יָדַעְתָּ כֻלָּהּ: אָחוֹר וָקֶדֶם צַרְתָּנִי, וַתָּשֶׁת עָלַי כַּפֶּכָה: פְּלִיאָה דַעַת מִמֶּנִּי, נִשְׂגְּבָה לֹא־אוּכַל לָהּ: אָנָה אֵלֵךְ מֵרוּחֶךָ, וְאָנָה מִפָּנֶיךָ אֶבְרָח: אִם־אֶסַּק שָׁמַיִם שָׁם אָתָּה, וְאַצִּיעָה שְּׁאוֹל הִנֶּךָּ: אֶשָּׂא כַנְפֵי־שָׁחַר, אֶשְׁכְּנָה בְּאַחֲרִית יָם: גַּם־שָׁם יָדְךָ תַנְחֵנִי, וְתֹאחֲזֵנִי יְמִינֶךָ: וָאֹמַר אַךְ־חֹשֶׁךְ יְשׁוּפֵנִי, וְלַיְלָה אוֹר בַּעֲדֵנִי: גַּם־חֹשֶׁךְ לֹא־יַחְשִׁיךְ מִמֶּךָ, וְלַיְלָה כַּיּוֹם יָאִיר, כַּחֲשֵׁיכָה כָּאוֹרָה: כִּי־אַתָּה קָנִיתָ כִלְיֹתָי, תְּסֻכֵּנִי בְּבֶטֶן אִמִּי: אוֹדְךָ עַל כִּי נוֹרָאוֹת נִפְלֵיתִי, נִפְלָאִים מַעֲשֶׂיךָ, וְנַפְשִׁי יֹדַעַת מְאֹד: לֹא־נִכְחַד עָצְמִי מִמֶּךָּ, אֲשֶׁר־עֻשֵּׂיתִי בַסֵּתֶר, רֻקַּמְתִּי בְּתַחְתִּיּוֹת אָרֶץ: גָּלְמִי רָאוּ עֵינֶיךָ וְעַל־סִפְרְךָ כֻּלָּם יִכָּתֵבוּ, יָמִים יֻצָּרוּ וְלוֹ אֶחָד בָּהֶם: וְלִי מַה־יָּקְרוּ רֵעֶיךָ אֵל, מֶה עָצְמוּ רָאשֵׁיהֶם: אֶסְפְּרֵם מֵחוֹל יִרְבּוּן, הֱקִיצֹתִי וְעוֹדִי עִמָּךְ: אִם־תִּקְטֹל אֱלוֹהַּ רָשָׁע, וְאַנְשֵׁי דָמִים סוּרוּ מֶנִּי: אֲשֶׁר יֹמְרוּךָ לִמְזִמָּה, נָשֻׂא לַשָּׁוְא עָרֶיךָ: הֲלוֹא־מְשַׂנְאֶיךָ יהוה אֶשְׂנָא, וּבִתְקוֹמְמֶיךָ אֶתְקוֹטָט: תַּכְלִית שִׂנְאָה שְׂנֵאתִים, לְאוֹיְבִים הָיוּ לִי: חָקְרֵנִי אֵל וְדַע לְבָבִי, בְּחָנֵנִי וְדַע שַׂרְעַפָּי: וּרְאֵה אִם־דֶּרֶךְ־עֹצֶב בִּי, וּנְחֵנִי בְּדֶרֶךְ עוֹלָם:

מַשְׂכִּיל לְדָוִד A maskil of David while he was in the cave – a prayer. *Ps. 142*
My voice cries to the LORD; my voice pleads with the LORD. I will pour out my lament before Him, tell my troubles to Him when my spirit grows faint within me. You know my path – along the way I walk they have laid a trap for me. Look to the right and witness – I have not one friend; I have nowhere to flee; no one cares for me. I cry out to You, LORD – I say, "You are my refuge, my share in the land of the living." Listen to my plea, for I have sunk so low; save me from my pursuers, for they are too strong for me. Set me free from this confinement so that I may give thanks to Your name; the righteous will gather around me when You are good to me.

מַשְׂכִּיל לְדָוִד, בִּהְיוֹתוֹ בַמְּעָרָה תְפִלָּה: קוֹלִי אֶל־יהוה אֶזְעָק, תהלים קמב
קוֹלִי אֶל־יהוה אֶתְחַנָּן: אֶשְׁפֹּךְ לְפָנָיו שִׂיחִי, צָרָתִי לְפָנָיו אַגִּיד:
בְּהִתְעַטֵּף עָלַי רוּחִי וְאַתָּה יָדַעְתָּ נְתִיבָתִי, בְּאֹרַח־זוּ אֲהַלֵּךְ,
טָמְנוּ פַח לִי: הַבֵּיט יָמִין וּרְאֵה וְאֵין־לִי מַכִּיר, אָבַד מָנוֹס
מִמֶּנִּי, אֵין דּוֹרֵשׁ לְנַפְשִׁי: זָעַקְתִּי אֵלֶיךָ יהוה, אָמַרְתִּי אַתָּה
מַחְסִי, חֶלְקִי בְּאֶרֶץ הַחַיִּים: הַקְשִׁיבָה אֶל־רִנָּתִי כִּי־דַלּוֹתִי
מְאֹד, הַצִּילֵנִי מֵרֹדְפַי, כִּי אָמְצוּ מִמֶּנִּי: הוֹצִיאָה מִמַּסְגֵּר נַפְשִׁי
לְהוֹדוֹת אֶת־שְׁמֶךָ, בִּי יַכְתִּרוּ צַדִּיקִים, כִּי תִגְמֹל עָלָי:

HALAKHOT CONCERNING A *GOSESS* AND THE MOMENT OF PASSING

A *GOSESS* AND THE MOMENT OF PASSING

1. Halakhically, when the process of death begins, a person is deemed a *gosess*. Due to advances in modern medicine, however, a clear definition of the moment a person becomes a *gosess* has become difficult to determine (רמב"ם פירוש המשניות אהלות א:ו).
2. As a rule, a *gosess* may not be moved or "handled" in any way. Necessary medical and nursing care, however, is permitted. This includes washing and cleaning the patient (נשמת אברהם יו"ד שלט:א ס"ק ג).
3. Someone should always be at the bedside of a *gosess* so that the *gosess* is not left alone (יו"ד שלט:ד).
4. Prior to a person's passing, no preparations should be made for the funeral (יו"ד שלט:א). Preparations of which a *ḥoleh* is unaware, however, may be made (ב"ח יו"ד שלט).

AT THE MOMENT OF AN INDIVIDUAL'S PASSING

1. In the final moments of a person's life, the *ḥoleh* should, if possible, recite the following verses: Micha 7:18–19, Psalms 31:6, Numbers 6: 24–26, *lishuatkha kiviti, Hashem Kel emet, Shema Yisrael,* and *Baruch Shem*. If the *ḥoleh* is unable to recite these texts, others present may recite them on the *ḥoleh*'s behalf (גשר החיים ב:א:א).
2. If there is time, all who are present immediately prior to an individual's passing should recite Psalms 121, 130, and 91, followed by *Yigdal, Adon Olam, Ana BeKoaḥ,* and *Al Kein*. If there is not enough time for this full recitation before the *ḥoleh*'s passing, the chapters of Psalms are omitted (גשר החיים ב:א:א).

3. At the moment of an individual's passing, all present should recite the *Shema,* followed by *Barukh shem kevod malkhuto* (three times), *Hashem hu haElokim* (seven times), *Hashem melekh Hashem malakh Hashem yimlokh leolam va'ed* (גשר החיים ב:ג:א).
4. Immediately following an individual's passing, all present should recite the phrase *Hashem natan…* and the blessing *Dayan HaEmet* (*Gesher HaHayyim* 2:1:4–5).
5. While in the past it was customary for anyone present at the time of death to tear *keria,* common practice today is for the relatives to wait until the funeral, and for others not to tear (ציץ אליעזר ח״יג לה:ד, גשר החיים ג:א:ב).
6. Following a person's death, his/her limbs should be straightened, hands opened palms upward, mouth and eyes closed (when possible, by members of the family) (גשר החיים טו:ב:ו), (יו״ד שנב:ד).
7. When possible, the custom is to lay the deceased on the floor, feet facing the doorway (גשר החיים ג:ב:א).
8. A candle should be lit near the deceased's head, at which point the following verses should be recited three times (גשר החיים ג:ב:ב):

בית יעקב לכו ונלכה באור ה׳ - ישעיהו ב:ה.

אלקים דיבר ויקרא ארץ ארץ ממזרח שמש עד מבואו - תהלים נ:א.

יבוא שלום ינוחו על משכבותם הולך נכוחו - ישעיהו נו:ב.

כי עפר אתה ואל עפר תשוב - בראשית ג:יט.

9. Any standing water in the room where the person passed away should be poured out (ט״ז יו״ד שלט:ד).
10. On Shabbat and Yom Tov, the body of the deceased is *muktza.* The eyes and mouth should, therefore, not be shut, nor should the limbs be straightened. If the body is clothed, it may be moved as necessary (as the clothing is not considered *muktza*). If the body is unclothed, a non-*muktza* item must be placed on the body before it is moved (שמירת שבת כהלכתה סד:ח:יג).

AT THE MOMENT OF PASSING

In the last hours, if it is at all possible, the sick person should recite or think the following:

מִי־אֵל כָּמוֹךָ Who is like you, God, Mic. 7
pardoning iniquity and overlooking transgression
for the remnant of God's people,
Who has not retained wrath forever
for God desires mercifulness.
God will return us in compassion,
God will suppress our iniquities,
and will cast all their sins into the sea-depths.

בְּיָדְךָ Into Your hand I entrust my spirit. Ps. 31
Redeem me, O Lord, God of truth.

יְבָרֶכְךָ May the Lord bless you and keep you. Num. 6
May the Lord make His countenance shine upon you
and be gracious to you.
May the Lord lift up His countenance toward you
and grant you peace.

לִישׁוּעָתְךָ For Your salvation I hope, Lord. Gen. 49
I hope, Lord, for Your salvation.
Lord, for Your salvation, I hope.

יהוה The Lord is the true God,
Moses is true, as is His Torah.

שְׁמַע יִשְׂרָאֵל Hear, O Israel, the Lord is our God, Deut. 6
the Lord is One.

בָּרוּךְ Blessed is the name of His glorious kingdom
forever and ever.

בשעת מות

In the last hours, if it is at all possible, the sick person should recite or think the following:

מיכה ז מִי־אֵל כָּמוֹךָ נֹשֵׂא עָוֹן וְעֹבֵר עַל־פֶּשַׁע לִשְׁאֵרִית נַחֲלָתוֹ
לֹא־הֶחֱזִיק לָעַד אַפּוֹ
כִּי־חָפֵץ חֶסֶד הוּא:
יָשׁוּב יְרַחֲמֵנוּ, יִכְבֹּשׁ עֲוֹנֹתֵינוּ
וְתַשְׁלִיךְ בִּמְצֻלוֹת יָם כָּל־חַטֹּאתָם:

תהלים לא בְּיָדְךָ אַפְקִיד רוּחִי
פָּדִיתָה אוֹתִי יהוה אֵל אֱמֶת:

במדבר ו יְבָרֶכְךָ יהוה וְיִשְׁמְרֶךָ:
יָאֵר יהוה פָּנָיו אֵלֶיךָ וִיחֻנֶּךָּ:
יִשָּׂא יהוה פָּנָיו אֵלֶיךָ וְיָשֵׂם לְךָ שָׁלוֹם:

בראשית מט לִישׁוּעָתְךָ קִוִּיתִי יהוה:
קִוִּיתִי יהוה לִישׁוּעָתְךָ
יהוה לִישׁוּעָתְךָ קִוִּיתִי.

יהוה אֵל אֱמֶת
מֹשֶׁה אֱמֶת וְתוֹרָתוֹ אֱמֶת.

דברים ו שְׁמַע יִשְׂרָאֵל, יהוה אֱלֹהֵינוּ, יהוה אֶחָד:

בָּרוּךְ שֵׁם כְּבוֹד מַלְכוּתוֹ לְעוֹלָם וָעֶד.

Immediately prior to a person's death, those present should recite.

שִׁיר לַמַּעֲלוֹת *A song of ascents.* I lift my eyes up to the hills; where will Ps. 121
my help come from? My help comes from the Lord, Maker of heaven and earth. He will not let your foot slip; He who guards you does not slumber. Behold – the Guardian of Israel neither slumbers nor sleeps. The Lord is your guardian; the Lord is your shade at your right hand. The sun will not strike you by day, nor the moon by night. The Lord will guard you from all harm; He will guard your life. The Lord will guard your going and coming, now and for evermore.

שִׁיר הַמַּעֲלוֹת *A song of ascents.* From the depths I have called out to You, Ps. 130
O Lord. Lord, hear my voice; let Your ears be attuned to the sound of my plea. If You, Lord, keep account of sins, O Lord, who could stand? But with You there is forgiveness; therefore You may be revered. I wait for the Lord – my soul waits – in His word I put my hope. My soul waits for the Lord more than watchmen for the morning, more than watchmen for the morning. Israel, put your hope in the Lord, for loving-kindness is the Lord's, and great is His power to redeem. It is He who will redeem Israel from all their sins.

יֹשֵׁב He who lives in the shelter of the Most High dwells in the shadow Ps. 91
of Shaddai. I say of the Lord, "My refuge and stronghold, my God in whom I trust," for He will save you from the fowler's snare, from deadly plague. With His pinions He will cover you; beneath His wings you will find shelter; His loyalty is an encircling shield. You need not fear terror by night, nor the arrow that flies by day, nor the plague that stalks in darkness, nor disease that ravages at noon. A thousand may fall beside you, ten thousand at your right hand, but it will not come near you. You will only look with your eyes and see the punishment of the wicked. For you – "the Lord is my Refuge" – you have made the Most High your abode. No harm will befall you; no sickness will come near your home, for He will command His angels about you to guard you in all your ways. They will lift you in their hands lest your foot stumble on a stone. You will tread over lions and vipers; you will trample on young lions and serpents. "Because he loves Me, I will rescue him; I

Immediately prior to a person's death, those present should recite.

שִׁיר לַמַּעֲלוֹת, אֶשָּׂא עֵינַי אֶל־הֶהָרִים, מֵאַיִן יָבֹא עֶזְרִי: עֶזְרִי מֵעִם יהוה, עֹשֵׂה שָׁמַיִם וָאָרֶץ: אַל־יִתֵּן לַמּוֹט רַגְלֶךָ, אַל־יָנוּם שֹׁמְרֶךָ: הִנֵּה לֹא־יָנוּם וְלֹא יִישָׁן שׁוֹמֵר יִשְׂרָאֵל: יהוה שֹׁמְרֶךָ, יהוה צִלְּךָ עַל־יַד יְמִינֶךָ: יוֹמָם הַשֶּׁמֶשׁ לֹא־יַכֶּכָּה, וְיָרֵחַ בַּלָּיְלָה: יהוה יִשְׁמָרְךָ מִכָּל־רָע, יִשְׁמֹר אֶת־נַפְשֶׁךָ: יהוה יִשְׁמָר־צֵאתְךָ וּבוֹאֶךָ, מֵעַתָּה וְעַד־עוֹלָם: תהלים קכא

שִׁיר הַמַּעֲלוֹת, מִמַּעֲמַקִּים קְרָאתִיךָ יהוה: אֲדֹנָי שִׁמְעָה בְקוֹלִי, תִּהְיֶינָה אָזְנֶיךָ קַשֻּׁבוֹת לְקוֹל תַּחֲנוּנָי: אִם־עֲוֹנוֹת תִּשְׁמָר־יָהּ, אֲדֹנָי מִי יַעֲמֹד: כִּי־עִמְּךָ הַסְּלִיחָה, לְמַעַן תִּוָּרֵא: קִוִּיתִי יהוה קִוְּתָה נַפְשִׁי, וְלִדְבָרוֹ הוֹחָלְתִּי: נַפְשִׁי לַאדֹנָי, מִשֹּׁמְרִים לַבֹּקֶר, שֹׁמְרִים לַבֹּקֶר: יַחֵל יִשְׂרָאֵל אֶל־יהוה, כִּי־עִם־יהוה הַחֶסֶד, וְהַרְבֵּה עִמּוֹ פְדוּת: וְהוּא יִפְדֶּה אֶת־יִשְׂרָאֵל, מִכֹּל עֲוֹנֹתָיו: תהלים קל

יֹשֵׁב בְּסֵתֶר עֶלְיוֹן, בְּצֵל שַׁדַּי יִתְלוֹנָן: אֹמַר לַיהוה מַחְסִי וּמְצוּדָתִי, אֱלֹהַי אֶבְטַח־בּוֹ: כִּי הוּא יַצִּילְךָ מִפַּח יָקוּשׁ, מִדֶּבֶר הַוּוֹת: בְּאֶבְרָתוֹ יָסֶךְ לָךְ, וְתַחַת־כְּנָפָיו תֶּחְסֶה, צִנָּה וְסֹחֵרָה אֲמִתּוֹ: לֹא־תִירָא מִפַּחַד לָיְלָה, מֵחֵץ יָעוּף יוֹמָם: מִדֶּבֶר בָּאֹפֶל יַהֲלֹךְ, מִקֶּטֶב יָשׁוּד צָהֳרָיִם: יִפֹּל מִצִּדְּךָ אֶלֶף, וּרְבָבָה מִימִינֶךָ, אֵלֶיךָ לֹא יִגָּשׁ: רַק בְּעֵינֶיךָ תַבִּיט, וְשִׁלֻּמַת רְשָׁעִים תִּרְאֶה: כִּי־אַתָּה יהוה מַחְסִי, עֶלְיוֹן שַׂמְתָּ מְעוֹנֶךָ: תהלים צא

will protect him because he acknowledges My name. When he calls on Me, I will answer him; I will be with him in distress; I will rescue him and bring him honor. With long life I will satisfy him and show him My salvation."

יִגְדַּל The living God will be exalted and praised;
He exists, and His existence endures beyond time.

He is One and His oneness is like that of no other;
He is beyond our comprehension, for His unity is infinite.

He has no physical image, neither does He have a body;
nothing can be compared to Him in His Holiness.

He preceded everything that was created;
He was the first, and His primordial existence had no beginning.

Behold He is the eternal Master,
and every creature shall make His greatness and sovereignty known.

He bestowed His prophetic overflow
upon those individuals who were His treasured and glorious ones.

Never did there arise in Israel another prophet like Moses,
who alone was able to view God's image.

God gave His people the Torah of truth
by the hand of His prophet who was the most trusted in all His house.

God will not exchange or replace His law;
never will He alter it to become something else.

He sees and knows all that we conceal;
He discerns the end result of all that happens before it.

He rewards the compassionate person in accordance with his deeds;
He imposes punishment on the wicked person
in accordance with his evil.

He will send our Messiah at the end of days
to redeem with His salvation those who await the end of days.

God in His great kindness will resurrect the dead;
blessed is His illustrious name for ever and ever.

לֹא־תְאֻנֶּה אֵלֶיךָ רָעָה, וְנֶגַע לֹא־יִקְרַב בְּאָהֳלֶךָ: כִּי מַלְאָכָיו יְצַוֶּה־לָּךְ, לִשְׁמָרְךָ בְּכָל־דְּרָכֶיךָ: עַל־כַּפַּיִם יִשָּׂאוּנְךָ, פֶּן־תִּגֹּף בָּאֶבֶן רַגְלֶךָ: עַל־שַׁחַל וָפֶתֶן תִּדְרֹךְ, תִּרְמֹס כְּפִיר וְתַנִּין: כִּי בִי חָשַׁק וַאֲפַלְּטֵהוּ, אֲשַׂגְּבֵהוּ כִּי־יָדַע שְׁמִי: יִקְרָאֵנִי וְאֶעֱנֵהוּ, עִמּוֹ אָנֹכִי בְצָרָה, אֲחַלְּצֵהוּ וַאֲכַבְּדֵהוּ: אֹרֶךְ יָמִים אַשְׂבִּיעֵהוּ, וְאַרְאֵהוּ בִּישׁוּעָתִי:

יִגְדַּל אֱלֹהִים חַי וְיִשְׁתַּבַּח, נִמְצָא וְאֵין עֵת אֶל מְצִיאוּתוֹ.
אֶחָד וְאֵין יָחִיד כְּיִחוּדוֹ, נֶעְלָם וְגַם אֵין סוֹף לְאַחְדוּתוֹ.
אֵין לוֹ דְּמוּת הַגּוּף וְאֵינוֹ גוּף, לֹא נַעֲרֹךְ אֵלָיו קְדֻשָּׁתוֹ.
קַדְמוֹן לְכָל דָּבָר אֲשֶׁר נִבְרָא, רִאשׁוֹן וְאֵין רֵאשִׁית לְרֵאשִׁיתוֹ.
הִנּוֹ אֲדוֹן עוֹלָם, וְכָל נוֹצָר יוֹרֶה גְדֻלָּתוֹ וּמַלְכוּתוֹ.
שֶׁפַע נְבוּאָתוֹ נְתָנוֹ אֶל־אַנְשֵׁי סְגֻלָּתוֹ וְתִפְאַרְתּוֹ.
לֹא קָם בְּיִשְׂרָאֵל כְּמֹשֶׁה עוֹד נָבִיא וּמַבִּיט אֶת תְּמוּנָתוֹ.
תּוֹרַת אֱמֶת נָתַן לְעַמּוֹ אֵל עַל יַד נְבִיאוֹ נֶאֱמַן בֵּיתוֹ.
לֹא יַחֲלִיף הָאֵל וְלֹא יָמִיר דָּתוֹ לְעוֹלָמִים לְזוּלָתוֹ.
צוֹפֶה וְיוֹדֵעַ סְתָרֵינוּ, מַבִּיט לְסוֹף דָּבָר בְּקַדְמָתוֹ.
גּוֹמֵל לְאִישׁ חֶסֶד כְּמִפְעָלוֹ, נוֹתֵן לְרָשָׁע רָע כְּרִשְׁעָתוֹ.
יִשְׁלַח לְקֵץ יָמִין מְשִׁיחֵנוּ לִפְדּוֹת מְחַכֵּי קֵץ יְשׁוּעָתוֹ.
מֵתִים יְחַיֶּה אֵל בְּרֹב חַסְדּוֹ, בָּרוּךְ עֲדֵי עַד שֵׁם תְּהִלָּתוֹ.

אֲדוֹן עוֹלָם Eternal Master, Who reigned before anything was created –
when by His will all things were brought into being,
then as King was His name proclaimed.

After all things have ceased to be,
He will reign alone in awesome majesty.

He was. He is. He will always be; His eternal glory can never fade.

He is One. There is no other; beyond compare, or any metaphor.

He had no beginning, will have no end.
He above all others has strength and power.

He is my God, my living Redeemer,
a Rock when I am in pain in troubled times.

My banner and my refuge,
to Whom I will raise a cup on the day I proclaim my salvation.

I entrust my spirit to His hand, when sleeping and when awake.

With my body my soul will stay; the Lord is with me, I need not fear.

אָנָּא We pray, through the awesome power of Your right hand,
that You set captive Israel free.

Receive Your people's prayer; uplift us, make us pure, God of awe.

Almighty God, we pray You guard as the apple of Your eye
those who seek Your unity.

Bless us, cleanse us, and please,
mitigate Your justice for us with Your mercy.

Almighty Holy One, lead us, Your flock, in Your bountiful goodness.

Supreme and Only God, turn to Your people
who are mindful of Your holiness.

Accept our prayer, give ear to our cry,
You Who know our most private thoughts.

Blessed is the name of His glorious kingdom forever and ever.

אֲדוֹן עוֹלָם אֲשֶׁר מָלַךְ בְּטֶרֶם כָּל־יְצִיר נִבְרָא.
לְעֵת נַעֲשָׂה בְחֶפְצוֹ כֹּל אֲזַי מֶלֶךְ שְׁמוֹ נִקְרָא.
וְאַחֲרֵי כִּכְלוֹת הַכֹּל לְבַדּוֹ יִמְלֹךְ נוֹרָא.
וְהוּא הָיָה וְהוּא הֹוֶה וְהוּא יִהְיֶה בְּתִפְאָרָה.
וְהוּא אֶחָד וְאֵין שֵׁנִי לְהַמְשִׁיל לוֹ לְהַחְבִּירָה.
בְּלִי רֵאשִׁית בְּלִי תַכְלִית וְלוֹ הָעֹז וְהַמִּשְׂרָה.
וְהוּא אֵלִי וְחַי גּוֹאֲלִי וְצוּר חֶבְלִי בְּעֵת צָרָה.
וְהוּא נִסִּי וּמָנוֹס לִי מְנָת כּוֹסִי בְּיוֹם אֶקְרָא.
בְּיָדוֹ אַפְקִיד רוּחִי בְּעֵת אִישַׁן וְאָעִירָה.
וְעִם רוּחִי גְּוִיָּתִי יהוה לִי וְלֹא אִירָא.

אָנָּא, בְּכֹחַ גְּדֻלַּת יְמִינְךָ, תַּתִּיר צְרוּרָה.
קַבֵּל רִנַּת עַמְּךָ, שַׂגְּבֵנוּ, טַהֲרֵנוּ, נוֹרָא.
נָא גִבּוֹר, דּוֹרְשֵׁי יִחוּדְךָ כְּבָבַת שָׁמְרֵם.
בָּרְכֵם, טַהֲרֵם, רַחֲמֵם, צִדְקָתְךָ תָּמִיד גָּמְלֵם.
חֲסִין קָדוֹשׁ, בְּרֹב טוּבְךָ נַהֵל עֲדָתֶךָ.
יָחִיד גֵּאֶה, לְעַמְּךָ פְּנֵה, זוֹכְרֵי קְדֻשָּׁתֶךָ.
שַׁוְעָתֵנוּ קַבֵּל וּשְׁמַע צַעֲקָתֵנוּ, יוֹדֵעַ תַּעֲלוּמוֹת.
בָּרוּךְ שֵׁם כְּבוֹד מַלְכוּתוֹ לְעוֹלָם וָעֶד.

עַל כֵּן We therefore hope in You, LORD our God, that we may soon see the glory of Your might when You will remove abominations from the earth and the idols shall be utterly destroyed, when the world shall be perfected under the rule of the Almighty. Then all mankind shall invoke Your name, to turn all the wicked on earth toward You. All dwellers on earth will perceive and understand that to You every knee must bend, every tongue vow fealty. Before You, LORD our God, all will kneel and bow down, and give honor to Your glorious name. They will all accept the rule of Your dominion, and You will speedily rule over them forevermore. For the kingdom is Yours, and to all eternity
You shall reign in glory, as it is written in Your Torah, "The LORD shall *Ex. 15*
reign forever and ever." And it is said, "And the LORD shall be King over *Zech. 14*
all the earth; in that day shall the LORD be One, and His name One."

At the moment of death those present should recite:

שְׁמַע יִשְׂרָאֵל Hear, O Israel, the LORD our God, the LORD is One. *Deut. 6*

Recite three times:

בָּרוּךְ Blessed is the name of His glorious kingdom forever and ever.

Recite seven times:

יהוה The LORD, He is God.

Once:

יהוה מֶלֶךְ The LORD is King, the LORD was King, and the LORD will be King for ever and ever.

Immediately after a person's death, those present should recite:

יהוה The LORD has given and the LORD has taken away: blessed *Job 1*
be the name of the LORD.

בָּרוּךְ Blessed are You, LORD, our God, King of the universe, the true Judge.

עַל כֵּן נְקַוֶּה לְּךָ יהוה אֱלֹהֵינוּ, לִרְאוֹת מְהֵרָה בְּתִפְאֶרֶת עֻזֶּךָ,
לְהַעֲבִיר גִּלּוּלִים מִן הָאָרֶץ, וְהָאֱלִילִים כָּרוֹת יִכָּרֵתוּן, לְתַקֵּן
עוֹלָם בְּמַלְכוּת שַׁדַּי. וְכָל בְּנֵי בָשָׂר יִקְרְאוּ בִשְׁמֶךָ לְהַפְנוֹת
אֵלֶיךָ כָּל רִשְׁעֵי אָרֶץ. יַכִּירוּ וְיֵדְעוּ כָּל יוֹשְׁבֵי תֵבֵל, כִּי לְךָ
תִּכְרַע כָּל בֶּרֶךְ, תִּשָּׁבַע כָּל לָשׁוֹן. לְפָנֶיךָ יהוה אֱלֹהֵינוּ יִכְרְעוּ
וְיִפֹּלוּ, וְלִכְבוֹד שִׁמְךָ יְקָר יִתֵּנוּ, וִיקַבְּלוּ כֻלָּם אֶת עֹל מַלְכוּתֶךָ,
וְתִמְלֹךְ עֲלֵיהֶם מְהֵרָה לְעוֹלָם וָעֶד. כִּי הַמַּלְכוּת שֶׁלְּךָ הִיא
וּלְעוֹלְמֵי עַד תִּמְלֹךְ בְּכָבוֹד, כַּכָּתוּב בְּתוֹרָתֶךָ, יהוה יִמְלֹךְ שמות טו
לְעֹלָם וָעֶד: וְנֶאֱמַר, וְהָיָה יהוה לְמֶלֶךְ עַל־כָּל־הָאָרֶץ, בַּיּוֹם זכריה יד
הַהוּא יִהְיֶה יהוה אֶחָד וּשְׁמוֹ אֶחָד:

At the moment of death those present should recite:

שְׁמַע יִשְׂרָאֵל, יהוה אֱלֹהֵינוּ, יהוה אֶחָד: דברים ו

Recite three times:

בָּרוּךְ שֵׁם כְּבוֹד מַלְכוּתוֹ לְעוֹלָם וָעֶד.

Recite seven times:

יהוה הוּא הָאֱלֹהִים.

Once:

יהוה מֶלֶךְ, יהוה מָלָךְ, יהוה יִמְלֹךְ לְעוֹלָם וָעֶד.

Immediately after a person's death, those present should recite:

יהוה נָתַן וַיהוה לָקָח, יְהִי שֵׁם יהוה מְבֹרָךְ: איוב א

בָּרוּךְ אַתָּה יהוה אֱלֹהֵינוּ מֶלֶךְ הָעוֹלָם, דַּיַּן הָאֱמֶת.

THE RABBINIC ROAD: CHALLENGES AND OPPORTUNITIES

BEREAVEMENT

Interacting with a family at a time of loss presents some of the most challenging moments for a rabbi. At the same time, the opportunity to offer assistance is never greater. This is when congregants need their rabbi most and look to him as a guide.

- Every rabbi should maintain ready access to updated contact information of the communal *ḥevra kaddisha,* local funeral homes, burial in Israel, etc.
- Beyond offering halakhic guidance, the rabbi should serve as guide and enabler, helping the family along an unfamiliar path.

  Often the "clearest head" in the room, the rabbi should assist the family in: addressing immediate needs (e.g., care for the *niftar, shemira*); determining next steps (e.g., communication with other family members, friends, etc.); considering factors the family may not be aware of in the planning and scheduling of the funeral, burial, *shiva,* etc.
- Even in non-halakhic matters, the rabbi should not shy away from rendering his experienced opinion as he deems necessary. He should allow space, however, for final decisions on critical matters to be determined by the family members.
- A subsequent meeting should be held with the family, preferably at their home, to clearly discuss the funeral ceremony, *shiva,* etc. As many members of the immediate family as possible should be present at this meeting. Family members who are unable to attend should subsequently be contacted individually by the rabbi to ensure their personal involvement.

It is often helpful to open this meeting with a review of the halakhot of *aninut, shiva,* and beyond. This approach serves to begin the encounter in a structured, emotionally neutral way before moving into the sensitive memories and recollections of the family. It also clearly defines the rabbi's role as a guide through this difficult time.

HALAKHOT CONCERNING KERIA, DAYAN HA'EMET AND THE FUNERAL SERVICE

THE TIMING OF THE FUNERAL

It is a mitzva to bury the deceased as soon as possible, and it is prohibited to wait even one night (*halanat hameit*) (יו"ד שנז:א). For this reason, in Jerusalem, funerals are held even at night (גשר החיים ז:ג:א-ב).

1. The funeral may be delayed, however, in order to bring about greater honor for the deceased (e.g., to acquire a casket or shrouds, so that mourners can attend, or to inform the public) (יו"ד שנז:א).
2. Undue delay, even to await the arrival of immediate relatives, should be avoided (כל בו על אבילות א:ט:א הערה 9).
3. Postponing the burial because of a secular holiday and increased cost is forbidden (אגרות משה יו"ד ח"ג קל"ט).
4. It is technically permissible to bury the deceased on the first day of Yom Tov with non-Jewish labor (או"ח תקכ"ו:א), and in the Diaspora on the second day of Yom Tov even with Jewish participation (או"ח תקכ"ו:ד). Due to a concern for the violation of Yom Tov, however, most communities no longer follow this approach (אגרות משה או"ח ח"ג עו). It is therefore appropriate to delay burial until after the conclusion of the second day of Yom Tov.

KERIA

1. *Keria* is performed upon the death of a parent, spouse, child, or sibling, i.e., anyone for whom there is an obligation to mourn (יו"ד שמ:א).
2. The garment of a small child is rent only slightly, while the garment of a child who has reached the age of *ḥinukh* is rent in accordance with the laws of *keria*. (גשר החיים ד:ב).

3. Traditionally, individuals who were present at the time of death of a close relative would perform *keria,* immediately preceded by the blessing of *Dayan HaEmet*. Because many are unfamiliar with the relevant halakhot, it has become customary to wait until the funeral service both for the rending of the garment and the recitation of the *berakha*. If *keria* was not performed on either of those occasions, the garment(s) should be torn during the *shiva*. (גשר החיים ד:ו).

4. *Keria* is performed while standing. It is customary for a person other than the mourner to begin cutting the garment, and for the mourner to complete the *keria* (יו״ד שמ:א). It is appropriate for a man to help the male mourners and a woman to help the female mourners tear *keria*.

   A. A mourner for one's parents tears all garments "until he reveals his heart," except for: an overcoat and undergarments (i.e., any garment worn for perspiration). While a knife may be used to begin the *keria,* after the initial tear the mourner must rend the garments by hand on the left side, over the heart, reflecting particularly intense grief.

   B. For other relatives, only an outer garment is torn, on the right side, with either a knife or by hand. A male mourner generally tears a garment such as a jacket or shirt that will be worn during shiva. A female mourner generally tears a garment such as a blouse or jacket.

5. The *keria* tear should begin at the upper edge of the garment, at the neck, and continue along the length of the garment vertically, not horizontally, for at least one handbreadth [*tefaḥ,* 3–4 inches] (מועד קטן כב:). A woman should perform *keria* in a modest manner, and should either close the tear with a safety pin or wear a shirt under the outer garment.

6. It is permitted to change garments (i.e., from a more expensive

suit or shirt to a less expensive one) before tearing *keria* (גליון מהרש"א יו"ד שמ:ט).

7. During the week of *shiva,* individuals mourning the death of a parent should not change their upper garments. If those garments are changed, the replacement garments must be torn. Individuals mourning other relatives may change into a different shirt if necessary and need not tear that garment, although it is customary to wear a torn shirt for the entire week of mourning (יו"ד שמ:יד).
8. Unfortunately, in modern times some have opted to tear a small black ribbon instead of performing the mitzva of *keria* on a garment. This custom originates in secular culture and has no basis in Jewish tradition.

HESPED

The purpose of a *hesped* (eulogy) is to grant honor to the deceased (סנהדרין מו:). Therefore, if the deceased left instructions that a eulogy not be said, those wishes should be honored (יו"ד שמד:ט-י).

1. The delivery of a proper eulogy, designed to evoke mourning and "break the heart" of the listeners, is considered a great mitzva. The eulogy may not, however, overly exaggerate the accomplishments and deeds of the deceased (יו"ד שמד:א). In all ways, the eulogy must mirror reality, as "it is an act of appraisal, and an attempt to evaluate the repercussions of what has transpired" (Rabbi Joseph B. Soloveitchik, "Man of Faith in the Modern World," p. 87).
2. Traditionally, a funeral service is not conducted in a synagogue. When necessary, however, eulogies may be delivered in a synagogue sanctuary, dependent upon communal custom. As a rule, the deceased is not brought into the sanctuary. Exception may be made upon the passing of a great *talmid ḥakham* or the rabbi of the synagogue (יו"ד שמד:כ, יביע אומר יו"ד ח"ז לא, ציץ אליעזר ח"ה רמת רחל נד).

KEL MALEH

1. *Kel Maleh* is customarily recited both at the conclusion of the funeral service and upon the interment, except on days when *Taḥanun* is not recited (או״ח ת״כ:ב and חק יעקב תכט:וחק יעקב תכט:ז). On those days, Psalm 16 is said instead.
2. Some authorities, however, permit the recitation of *Kel Maleh* even on days when *Taḥanun* is not recited, since it is considered a prayer and not a "lament" (קינה) (מג״א או״ח תרצו:ה, הלכות אבילות רי״צ רימון עמ׳ 197).

ORDER OF KERIA

Keria is performed by the seven immediate relatives who observe mourning following the death of a loved one. (See pages 211–13 for the halakhot.)

Before the *keria* is performed, the following *berakha* is recited by the mourners.

בָּרוּךְ אַתָּה יהוה אֱלֹהֵינוּ מֶלֶךְ הָעוֹלָם, דַּיַּן הָאֱמֶת.

Blessed are You, Lord, our God, King of the universe,
the true Judge.

Others present say:

בָּרוּךְ דַּיַּן הָאֱמֶת

Blessed is the true Judge.

THE FUNERAL SERVICE

The funeral service opens with a selection of readings from Tanakh. The following are some of the readings frequently used:

אַשְׁרֵי־הָאִישׁ Happy is the one who does not walk in the counsel of *Ps. 1* the wicked, who does not stand on the path of sinners, who does not sit among the jeering cynics – instead, the Lord's teaching is all his desire, and he contemplates that teaching day and night. He is like a tree planted on streams of water yielding fruit in its season, its leaves never withering – all it produces thrives. Not so the wicked – they are like chaff blown away by the wind. Therefore, the wicked will not endure judgment, nor the sinners among the righteous crowd. For the Lord cares for the way of the righteous, while the way of the wicked will be lost forever.

מִזְמוֹר לְדָוִד* A psalm of David. The Lord is my Shepherd; I lack *Ps. 23* nothing. He lets me lie down in green pastures; He leads me beside still waters. He refreshes my soul, guiding me along the right paths for the sake of His name. Though I walk through the valley of the shadow of death, I fear no evil, for You are with me; Your rod and Your staff encourage me. You set a table before me in the face of my foes; You anoint my head with oil; my cup brims over. May only goodness and kindness follow me all the days of my life; let me live in the Lord's House for evermore.

---

the valley of the shadow of death, I will fear no evil: for thou art with me; thy rod and thy staff they comfort me. Thou preparest a table before me in the presence of mine enemies: thou anointest my head with oil; my cup runneth over. Surely goodness and mercy shall follow me all the days of my life: and I will dwell in the house of the Lord for ever.

לוויית המת

The funeral service opens with a selection of readings from Tanakh. The following are some of the readings frequently used:

אַשְׁרֵי־הָאִישׁ אֲשֶׁר לֹא הָלַךְ בַּעֲצַת רְשָׁעִים, וּבְדֶרֶךְ חַטָּאִים תהלים א
לֹא עָמָד, וּבְמוֹשַׁב לֵצִים לֹא יָשָׁב: כִּי אִם בְּתוֹרַת יהוה חֶפְצוֹ,
וּבְתוֹרָתוֹ יֶהְגֶּה יוֹמָם וָלָיְלָה: וְהָיָה כְּעֵץ שָׁתוּל עַל־פַּלְגֵי מָיִם,
אֲשֶׁר פִּרְיוֹ יִתֵּן בְּעִתּוֹ וְעָלֵהוּ לֹא־יִבּוֹל, וְכֹל אֲשֶׁר־יַעֲשֶׂה
יַצְלִיחַ: לֹא־כֵן הָרְשָׁעִים, כִּי אִם־כַּמֹּץ אֲשֶׁר־תִּדְּפֶנּוּ רוּחַ:
עַל־כֵּן לֹא־יָקֻמוּ רְשָׁעִים בַּמִּשְׁפָּט, וְחַטָּאִים בַּעֲדַת צַדִּיקִים:
כִּי־יוֹדֵעַ יהוה דֶּרֶךְ צַדִּיקִים, וְדֶרֶךְ רְשָׁעִים תֹּאבֵד:

מִזְמוֹר לְדָוִד, יהוה רֹעִי לֹא אֶחְסָר: בִּנְאוֹת דֶּשֶׁא יַרְבִּיצֵנִי, תהלים כג
עַל־מֵי מְנֻחוֹת יְנַהֲלֵנִי: נַפְשִׁי יְשׁוֹבֵב, יַנְחֵנִי בְמַעְגְּלֵי־צֶדֶק
לְמַעַן שְׁמוֹ: גַּם כִּי־אֵלֵךְ בְּגֵיא צַלְמָוֶת לֹא־אִירָא רָע, כִּי־
אַתָּה עִמָּדִי, שִׁבְטְךָ וּמִשְׁעַנְתֶּךָ הֵמָּה יְנַחֲמֻנִי: תַּעֲרֹךְ לְפָנַי
שֻׁלְחָן נֶגֶד צֹרְרָי, דִּשַּׁנְתָּ בַשֶּׁמֶן רֹאשִׁי, כּוֹסִי רְוָיָה: אַךְ
טוֹב וָחֶסֶד יִרְדְּפוּנִי כָּל־יְמֵי חַיָּי, וְשַׁבְתִּי בְּבֵית־יהוה לְאֹרֶךְ
יָמִים:

מִזְמוֹר לְדָוִד PSALM 23 – *CLASSIC TRANSLATION*

A Psalm of David. The Lord is my shepherd; I shall not want. He maketh me to lie down in green pastures: He leadeth me beside the still waters. He restoreth my soul: He leadeth me in the paths of righteousness for his name's sake. Yea, though I walk through

מִזְמוֹר לְדָוִד A psalm of David. LORD, who may dwell in Your tent? Ps. 15
Who may live on Your holy mountain? The one whose ways are blameless, who does what is right, who speaks truth from the heart; the one who has no malice on his tongue, who does no wrong to his fellow, who does not cast a slur against his neighbor; the one who scorns those who are vile, who honors those who fear the LORD, who keeps an oath even when it hurts; the one who does not loan money for interest, who does not take a bribe against the innocent – anyone who acts thus will never be shaken.

שִׁיר לַמַּעֲלוֹת A song of ascents. I lift my eyes up to the hills; where Ps. 121
will my help come from? My help comes from the LORD, Maker of heaven and earth. He will not let your foot slip; He who guards you does not slumber. Behold – the Guardian of Israel neither slumbers nor sleeps. The LORD is your guardian; the LORD is your shade at your right hand. The sun will not strike you by day, nor the moon by night. The LORD will guard you from all harm; He will guard your life. The LORD will guard your going and coming, now and for evermore.

שִׁיר הַמַּעֲלוֹת A song of ascents. From the depths I have called out Ps. 130
to You, O LORD. Lord, hear my voice; let Your ears be attuned to the sound of my plea. If You, LORD, keep account of sins, O Lord, who could stand? But with You there is forgiveness; therefore You may be revered. I wait for the LORD – my soul waits – in His word I put my hope. My soul waits for the Lord more than watchmen for the morning, more than watchmen for the morning. Israel, put your hope in the LORD, for loving-kindness is the LORD's, and great is His power to redeem. It is He who will redeem Israel from all their sins.

מִזְמוֹר לְדָוִד, יהוה מִי־יָגוּר בְּאָהֳלֶךָ, מִי־יִשְׁכֹּן בְּהַר קָדְשֶׁךָ: תהלים טו
הוֹלֵךְ תָּמִים וּפֹעֵל צֶדֶק, וְדֹבֵר אֱמֶת בִּלְבָבוֹ: לֹא־רָגַל עַל־
לְשֹׁנוֹ לֹא־עָשָׂה לְרֵעֵהוּ רָעָה, וְחֶרְפָּה לֹא־נָשָׂא עַל־קְרֹבוֹ:
נִבְזֶה בְּעֵינָיו נִמְאָס וְאֶת־יִרְאֵי יהוה יְכַבֵּד, נִשְׁבַּע לְהָרַע וְלֹא
יָמִר: כַּסְפּוֹ לֹא־נָתַן בְּנֶשֶׁךְ וְשֹׁחַד עַל־נָקִי לֹא־לָקָח, עֹשֵׂה
אֵלֶּה לֹא יִמּוֹט לְעוֹלָם:

שִׁיר לַמַּעֲלוֹת, אֶשָּׂא עֵינַי אֶל־הֶהָרִים, מֵאַיִן יָבֹא עֶזְרִי: עֶזְרִי תהלים קכא
מֵעִם יהוה, עֹשֵׂה שָׁמַיִם וָאָרֶץ: אַל־יִתֵּן לַמּוֹט רַגְלֶךָ, אַל־
יָנוּם שֹׁמְרֶךָ: הִנֵּה לֹא־יָנוּם וְלֹא יִישָׁן, שׁוֹמֵר יִשְׂרָאֵל: יהוה
שֹׁמְרֶךָ, יהוה צִלְּךָ עַל־יַד יְמִינֶךָ: יוֹמָם הַשֶּׁמֶשׁ לֹא־יַכֶּכָּה,
וְיָרֵחַ בַּלָּיְלָה: יהוה יִשְׁמָרְךָ מִכָּל־רָע, יִשְׁמֹר אֶת־נַפְשֶׁךָ:
יהוה יִשְׁמָר־צֵאתְךָ וּבוֹאֶךָ, מֵעַתָּה וְעַד־עוֹלָם:

שִׁיר הַמַּעֲלוֹת, מִמַּעֲמַקִּים קְרָאתִיךָ יהוה: אֲדֹנָי שִׁמְעָה תהלים קל
בְקוֹלִי, תִּהְיֶינָה אָזְנֶיךָ קַשֻּׁבוֹת לְקוֹל תַּחֲנוּנָי: אִם־עֲוֹנוֹת
תִּשְׁמָר־יָהּ, אֲדֹנָי מִי יַעֲמֹד: כִּי־עִמְּךָ הַסְּלִיחָה, לְמַעַן תִּוָּרֵא:
קִוִּיתִי יהוה קִוְּתָה נַפְשִׁי, וְלִדְבָרוֹ הוֹחָלְתִּי: נַפְשִׁי לַאדֹנָי,
מִשֹּׁמְרִים לַבֹּקֶר, שֹׁמְרִים לַבֹּקֶר: יַחֵל יִשְׂרָאֵל אֶל־יהוה,
כִּי־עִם־יהוה הַחֶסֶד, וְהַרְבֵּה עִמּוֹ פְדוּת: וְהוּא יִפְדֶּה אֶת־
יִשְׂרָאֵל, מִכֹּל עֲוֹנוֹתָיו:

אֵשֶׁת־חַיִל An exemplary woman who can find? She is more valuable than pearls. *Prov. 31*
Her husband's heart trusts in her; he will lack no benefit.
She will repay his favors, not his insults, in all of her life's circumstances.
She searches for wool and flax, and her hands work adroitly.
She becomes like the merchant ships; she brings her bread from afar.
She rises while it is yet night; she gives sustenance to her household and portions to her maidservants.
When she sets her mind upon a field she buys it; with the fruits of her labor she plants a vineyard.
She girds herself with strength and vigorously exerts her limbs.
When she discerns that her wares are good, her lamp is not extinguished by night.
She sets her hands to the distaff, and her palms grasp the spinning rod.
She stretches out her palm to the poor and extends her hands to the needy.
She need not fear for her household because of snow, for her entire household is clothed in scarlet.
She makes bedcoverings for herself; linen and purple is her garment.
Her husband is well known in the city gates as he sits among the elders of the land.
She makes clothing and sells it and offers belts to the merchant.
Strength and beauty are her garment; she smiles as she faces the future.
She opens her mouth with wisdom, and the teaching of kindness is upon her tongue.
She watches over the conduct of her household, and she does not eat the bread of indolence.
Her children rise up and extol her; so does her husband praise her:
"Many women have excelled, but you have surpassed them all."
Charm is false and beauty – empty breath; a woman who fears the Lord, she is praiseworthy.
Commend her for the fruit of her hands, and let her deeds praise her in the city gates.

משלי לא

אֵשֶׁת־חַיִל מִי יִמְצָא, וְרָחֹק מִפְּנִינִים מִכְרָהּ:
בָּטַח בָּהּ לֵב בַּעְלָהּ, וְשָׁלָל לֹא יֶחְסָר:
גְּמָלַתְהוּ טוֹב וְלֹא־רָע, כֹּל יְמֵי חַיֶּיהָ:
דָּרְשָׁה צֶמֶר וּפִשְׁתִּים, וַתַּעַשׂ בְּחֵפֶץ כַּפֶּיהָ:
הָיְתָה כָּאֳנִיּוֹת סוֹחֵר, מִמֶּרְחָק תָּבִיא לַחְמָהּ:
וַתָּקָם בְּעוֹד לַיְלָה, וַתִּתֵּן טֶרֶף לְבֵיתָהּ, וְחֹק לְנַעֲרֹתֶיהָ:
זָמְמָה שָׂדֶה וַתִּקָּחֵהוּ, מִפְּרִי כַפֶּיהָ נָטְעָ כָּרֶם:
חָגְרָה בְעוֹז מָתְנֶיהָ, וַתְּאַמֵּץ זְרוֹעֹתֶיהָ:
טָעֲמָה כִּי־טוֹב סַחְרָהּ, לֹא־יִכְבֶּה בַלַּיְל נֵרָהּ:
יָדֶיהָ שִׁלְּחָה בַכִּישׁוֹר, וְכַפֶּיהָ תָּמְכוּ פָלֶךְ:
כַּפָּהּ פָּרְשָׂה לֶעָנִי, וְיָדֶיהָ שִׁלְּחָה לָאֶבְיוֹן:
לֹא־תִירָא לְבֵיתָהּ מִשָּׁלֶג, כִּי כָל־בֵּיתָהּ לָבֻשׁ שָׁנִים:
מַרְבַדִּים עָשְׂתָה־לָּהּ, שֵׁשׁ וְאַרְגָּמָן לְבוּשָׁהּ:
נוֹדָע בַּשְּׁעָרִים בַּעְלָהּ, בְּשִׁבְתּוֹ עִם־זִקְנֵי־אָרֶץ:
סָדִין עָשְׂתָה וַתִּמְכֹּר, וַחֲגוֹר נָתְנָה לַכְּנַעֲנִי:
עוֹז־וְהָדָר לְבוּשָׁהּ, וַתִּשְׂחַק לְיוֹם אַחֲרוֹן:
פִּיהָ פָּתְחָה בְחָכְמָה, וְתוֹרַת־חֶסֶד עַל־לְשׁוֹנָהּ:
צוֹפִיָּה הֲלִיכוֹת בֵּיתָהּ, וְלֶחֶם עַצְלוּת לֹא תֹאכֵל:
קָמוּ בָנֶיהָ וַיְאַשְּׁרוּהָ, בַּעְלָהּ וַיְהַלְלָהּ:
רַבּוֹת בָּנוֹת עָשׂוּ חָיִל, וְאַתְּ עָלִית עַל־כֻּלָּנָה:
שֶׁקֶר הַחֵן וְהֶבֶל הַיֹּפִי, אִשָּׁה יִרְאַת־יהוה הִיא תִתְהַלָּל:
תְּנוּ־לָהּ מִפְּרִי יָדֶיהָ, וִיהַלְלוּהָ בַשְּׁעָרִים מַעֲשֶׂיהָ:

Following the introductory readings, eulogies are delivered by the officiating rabbi and, when appropriate, representatives of the family and friends.

The funeral service closes with the recitation of Kel Maleh. On days when Taḥanun is not recited, Psalm 16 is read in place of Kel Maleh.

For a male:

אֵל מָלֵא רַחֲמִים God, full of mercy, Who dwells on high, grant fitting rest beneath (*some say:* above) the protective wings of the Divine Presence, where the souls of the holy and pure ones – whose radiance is like that of the heavens – reside, to the soul of (*name of the deceased*) the son of (*father of the deceased*), who has gone to his eternal reward, insofar as I will make a charitable gift in memory of his soul, may the Garden of Eden be his resting place. For this reason may the ever-merciful One shelter the deceased under His protective wings forever, and may He bind his soul in lasting life. For the Lord will surely be his benefactor, so that he can rest in peace in his allotted place. And let us say, Amen.

For a female:

אֵל מָלֵא רַחֲמִים God, full of mercy, Who dwells on high, grant fitting rest beneath (*some say:* above) the protective wings of the Divine Presence, where the souls of the holy and pure ones – whose radiance is like that of the heavens – reside, to the soul of (*name of the deceased*) the daughter of (*father of the deceased*), who has gone to her eternal reward, insofar as I will make a charitable gift in memory of her soul, may the Garden of Eden be her resting place. For this reason may the ever-merciful One shelter the deceased under His protective wings forever, and may He bind her soul in lasting life. For the Lord will surely be her benefactor, so that she can rest in peace in her allotted place. And let us say, Amen.

On days when Taḥanun is not recited, Psalm 16 is read.

מִכְתָּם לְדָוִד A mikhtam of David. Protect me, God, for in You I take *Ps. 16*
refuge. I said to the Lord, "You are my Lord; My favor comes from none but You." As for the holy ones in the land, the mighty who

Following the introductory readings, eulogies are delivered by the officiating rabbi and, when appropriate, representatives of the family and friends.

The funeral service closes with the recitation of אֵל מָלֵא רַחֲמִים.
On days when תחנון *is not recited, Psalm 16 is read in place of* אֵל מָלֵא רַחֲמִים.

For a male:

אֵל מָלֵא רַחֲמִים, שׁוֹכֵן בַּמְּרוֹמִים, הַמְצֵא מְנוּחָה נְכוֹנָה תַּחַת (נ״א עַל) כַּנְפֵי הַשְּׁכִינָה, בְּמַעֲלוֹת קְדוֹשִׁים וּטְהוֹרִים, כְּזֹהַר הָרָקִיעַ מַזְהִירִים, לְנִשְׁמַת (פלוני בֶּן פלוני) שֶׁהָלַךְ לְעוֹלָמוֹ, בַּעֲבוּר שֶׁאֶתֵּן צְדָקָה בְּעַד הַזְכָּרַת נִשְׁמָתוֹ, בְּגַן עֵדֶן תְּהֵא מְנוּחָתוֹ. לָכֵן, בַּעַל הָרַחֲמִים יַסְתִּירֵהוּ בְּסֵתֶר כְּנָפָיו לְעוֹלָמִים, וְיִצְרֹר בִּצְרוֹר הַחַיִּים אֶת נִשְׁמָתוֹ, יהוה הוּא נַחֲלָתוֹ, וְיָנוּחַ בְּשָׁלוֹם עַל מִשְׁכָּבוֹ, וְנֹאמַר אָמֵן.

For a female:

אֵל מָלֵא רַחֲמִים, שׁוֹכֵן בַּמְּרוֹמִים, הַמְצֵא מְנוּחָה נְכוֹנָה תַּחַת (נ״א עַל) כַּנְפֵי הַשְּׁכִינָה, בְּמַעֲלוֹת קְדוֹשִׁים וּטְהוֹרִים, כְּזֹהַר הָרָקִיעַ מַזְהִירִים, לְנִשְׁמַת (פלונית בַּת פלוני) שֶׁהָלְכָה לְעוֹלָמָהּ, בַּעֲבוּר שֶׁאֶתֵּן צְדָקָה בְּעַד הַזְכָּרַת נִשְׁמָתָהּ, בְּגַן עֵדֶן תְּהֵא מְנוּחָתָהּ. לָכֵן, בַּעַל הָרַחֲמִים יַסְתִּירֶהָ בְּסֵתֶר כְּנָפָיו לְעוֹלָמִים, וְיִצְרֹר בִּצְרוֹר הַחַיִּים אֶת נִשְׁמָתָהּ, יהוה הוּא נַחֲלָתָהּ, וְתָנוּחַ בְּשָׁלוֹם עַל מִשְׁכָּבָהּ, וְנֹאמַר אָמֵן.

On days when תחנון *is not recited, Psalm 16 is read.*

מִכְתָּם לְדָוִד, שָׁמְרֵנִי אֵל כִּי־חָסִיתִי בָךְ: אָמַרְתְּ לַיהוה, אֲדֹנָי תהלים טז
אָתָּה, טוֹבָתִי בַּל־עָלֶיךָ: לִקְדוֹשִׁים אֲשֶׁר־בָּאָרֶץ הֵמָּה, וְאַדִּירֵי
כָּל־חֶפְצִי־בָם: יִרְבּוּ עַצְּבוֹתָם אַחֵר מָהָרוּ, בַּל־אַסִּיךְ נִסְכֵּיהֶם

were all my delight, may those who court other gods suffer many sorrows – I will not pour out their libations of blood; I will not bear their names on my lips. The LORD is my chosen portion and my cup. You direct my fate. A sweet heritage has fallen to my lot; my share is delightful to me. I will bless the LORD who has guided me; even at night, my conscience stirs me. I have set the LORD before me always; He is at my right hand; I shall not be shaken. Therefore my heart is glad, my spirit rejoices, and my body rests secure, for You will not abandon me to Sheol nor let Your devoted one see the Pit. You will teach me the path of life. In Your presence is fullness of joy; at Your right hand, bliss for evermore.

While escorting the deceased from the funeral chapel, Psalm 91 is recited

יֹשֵׁב בְּסֵתֶר He who lives in the shelter of the Most High dwells in the shadow of Shaddai. I say of the LORD, "My refuge and stronghold, my God in whom I trust," for He will save you from the fowler's snare, from deadly plague. With His pinions He will cover you; beneath His wings you will find shelter; His loyalty is an encircling shield. You need not fear terror by night, nor the arrow that flies by day, nor the plague that stalks in darkness, nor disease that ravages at noon. A thousand may fall beside you, ten thousand at your right hand, but it will not come near you. You will only look with your eyes and see the punishment of the wicked. For you – "the LORD is my Refuge" – you have made the Most High your abode. No harm will befall you; no sickness will come near your home, for He will command His angels about you to guard you in all your ways. They will lift you in their hands lest your foot stumble on a stone. You will tread over lions and vipers; you will trample on young lions and snakes. "Because he loves Me, I will rescue him; I will protect him because he acknowledges My name. When he calls on Me, I will answer him; I will be with him in distress; I will rescue him and bring him honor. With long life I will satisfy him and show him My salvation." *Ps. 91*

With long life I will satisfy him and show him My salvation.

מִדָּם, וּבַל־אֶשָּׂא אֶת־שְׁמוֹתָם עַל־שְׂפָתָי: יהוה, מְנָת־חֶלְקִי וְכוֹסִי, אַתָּה תּוֹמִיךְ גּוֹרָלִי: חֲבָלִים נָפְלוּ־לִי בַּנְּעִמִים, אַף־נַחֲלָת שָׁפְרָה עָלָי: אֲבָרֵךְ אֶת־יהוה אֲשֶׁר יְעָצָנִי, אַף־לֵילוֹת יִסְּרוּנִי כִלְיוֹתָי: שִׁוִּיתִי יהוה לְנֶגְדִּי תָמִיד, כִּי מִימִינִי בַּל־אֶמּוֹט: לָכֵן שָׂמַח לִבִּי וַיָּגֶל כְּבוֹדִי, אַף־בְּשָׂרִי יִשְׁכֹּן לָבֶטַח: כִּי לֹא־תַעֲזֹב נַפְשִׁי לִשְׁאוֹל, לֹא־תִתֵּן חֲסִידְךָ לִרְאוֹת שָׁחַת: תּוֹדִיעֵנִי אֹרַח חַיִּים, שֹׂבַע שְׂמָחוֹת אֶת־פָּנֶיךָ, נְעִמוֹת בִּימִינְךָ נֶצַח:

While escorting the deceased from the funeral chapel, Psalm 91 is recited

תהלים צא

יֹשֵׁב בְּסֵתֶר עֶלְיוֹן, בְּצֵל שַׁדַּי יִתְלוֹנָן: אֹמַר לַיהוה מַחְסִי וּמְצוּדָתִי, אֱלֹהַי אֶבְטַח־בּוֹ: כִּי הוּא יַצִּילְךָ מִפַּח יָקוּשׁ, מִדֶּבֶר הַוּוֹת: בְּאֶבְרָתוֹ יָסֶךְ לָךְ, וְתַחַת־כְּנָפָיו תֶּחְסֶה, צִנָּה וְסֹחֵרָה אֲמִתּוֹ: לֹא־תִירָא מִפַּחַד לָיְלָה, מֵחֵץ יָעוּף יוֹמָם: מִדֶּבֶר בָּאֹפֶל יַהֲלֹךְ, מִקֶּטֶב יָשׁוּד צָהֳרָיִם: יִפֹּל מִצִּדְּךָ אֶלֶף, וּרְבָבָה מִימִינֶךָ, אֵלֶיךָ לֹא יִגָּשׁ: רַק בְּעֵינֶיךָ תַבִּיט, וְשִׁלֻּמַת רְשָׁעִים תִּרְאֶה: כִּי־אַתָּה יהוה מַחְסִי, עֶלְיוֹן שַׂמְתָּ מְעוֹנֶךָ: לֹא־תְאֻנֶּה אֵלֶיךָ רָעָה, וְנֶגַע לֹא־יִקְרַב בְּאָהֳלֶךָ: כִּי מַלְאָכָיו יְצַוֶּה־לָּךְ, לִשְׁמָרְךָ בְּכָל־דְּרָכֶיךָ: עַל־כַּפַּיִם יִשָּׂאוּנְךָ, פֶּן־תִּגֹּף בָּאֶבֶן רַגְלֶךָ: עַל־שַׁחַל וָפֶתֶן תִּדְרֹךְ, תִּרְמֹס כְּפִיר וְתַנִּין: כִּי בִי חָשַׁק וַאֲפַלְּטֵהוּ, אֲשַׂגְּבֵהוּ כִּי־יָדַע שְׁמִי: יִקְרָאֵנִי וְאֶעֱנֵהוּ, עִמּוֹ אָנֹכִי בְצָרָה, אֲחַלְּצֵהוּ וַאֲכַבְּדֵהוּ:

אֹרֶךְ יָמִים אַשְׂבִּיעֵהוּ, וְאַרְאֵהוּ בִּישׁוּעָתִי:

אֹרֶךְ יָמִים אַשְׂבִּיעֵהוּ, וְאַרְאֵהוּ בִּישׁוּעָתִי:

HALAKHOT CONCERNING MAAMADOT, BURIAL, TZIDDUK HADIN, KADDISH, THE SHURA, AND LEAVING THE CEMETERY

MAAMADOT

At the cemetery, it is customary for the pallbearers to pause several times as they escort the deceased to the grave. Different communities maintain different customs regarding the number of stops and the ritual formula recited with each stop. Common custom is to begin the *maamadot* thirty *amot* (45–60 feet) from the grave and pause seven times (every three to four *amot*) upon approaching the grave (מעבר יבוק מג:יז, קשו״ע קצח:יב). Another custom mandates pausing only two to three times (every four *amot*) upon approaching the grave (רמ״א יו״ד שנח:ג), while others pause once or twice before even entering the cemetery (גשר החיים יד:ג:א).

1. According to the common practice of seven stops, *Yoshev BeSeter* (Psalms 91:1–11) is recited as the grave is approached, in the following manner: With the first stop, the recitation ends after the first word of verse 11; with the second stop, the first and second words of verse 11 are recited. This pattern continues until all seven words of verse 11 are recited, corresponding with the seventh stop, at which point the psalm is concluded.
2. In Yerushalayim, the custom is to stop only two to three times and to recite the mishna of *Akavia ben Mehalalel* (Avot 3:1), an abbreviated *Tzidduk HaDin*, and the Mourner's Kaddish with each stop.

BURIAL

It is a biblical commandment to bury the deceased in the ground (*kevura bekarka*). The mourners and heirs are responsible to fulfill this commandment. If the family of the deceased is unable to fulfill this obligation, however, the responsibility for burial shifts to the community (יו״ד שסב:א, גשר החיים טו:א-ב).

1. Out of respect for the deceased, the entire grave should be filled in by those attending the funeral (גשר החיים טז:א:ה). In difficult situations (e.g., inclement weather or a very small funeral), however, once three *tefaḥim* of earth cover the grave, machinery may be used to complete the process.
2. Customs vary regarding the participation of women in funerals. While mystical traditions prohibit women from entering cemeteries (יו״ד שנט:א), most communities allow women to attend and many allow them to participate fully in the funeral service.
3. While the origin of the custom that pregnant women do not enter a cemetery is unknown (מנחת יצחק ח״י בסימן מב), their participation is dependent on family and community traditions.
4. Many communities in the Diaspora bury the deceased in a casket which is then placed into the ground. In order for this to be considered *kevura bekarka* the casket should have either holes in the bottom or a section of the casket removed. (ש״ך יו״ד שסב ס״ק א, באר היטב יו״ד שסב ס״ק א).
5. A single grave may contain the remains of a married couple, or a parent and child (*kevura zugit*). When burying more than one person in the same grave, six *tefaḥim* (18–24 inches) of earth must separate them (יו״ד שסב:ד).
6. In Israel it is not unusual to find multi-storied cemeteries (*kevurat rama*) or other burial structures (e.g., *kevurat Sanhedrin*). Such cemeteries and structures are permitted if properly constructed (יו״ד שסד:א, יביע אומר יו״ד ח״ט סימן לד, אג״מ יו״ד ח״ג סימן קמד, הל׳ אבילות - רי״צ רימון עמ׳ נה-נו).

7. The use of a concrete burial vault that is placed into the grave to hold the casket is permitted (אג״מ יו״ד ח״ג סימן קמד).
8. When filling the grave with earth, it is customary not to hand the shovel from one person to the next. The shovel should be placed in the ground at the side of the grave, enabling the next participant to lift it independently (בית לחם יהודה יו״ד שע״ו, חכמת אדם קנח:ל).
9. Some communities maintain the custom of placing the initial 1–3 shovelfuls of earth in the grave with the backside of the shovel while reciting the verse from Psalms (78:38) of *vehu raḥum* (מעבר יבוק, סדר הקפות, הדרת קודש ליקוטים ד׳ עמ׳ מד).
10. In some communities it is customary to forbid family members from participating in the filling in of the grave.
11. The grave should be filled until there is a mound of earth rising above the ground (אג״מ יו״ד ח״ג סימן קמד:ב).

TZIDDUK HADIN

While there are various customs regarding when to recite *Tzidduk HaDin*, the predominant custom is to recite it after the grave has been filled with earth (גשר החיים טז:ו:א, כל בו על אבילות ח״א ג:ד:ג).

1. *Tzidduk HaDin* is recited by the mourners and others who are involved in the burial (the rabbi, members of the *ḥevra kaddisha*, etc.) (גשר החיים טז:ו:א).
2. Some maintain the custom to stand at least four *amot* (6–8 feet) from the grave during the recitation of *Tzidduk HaDin*. Common practice, however, is to allow its recitation even next to the grave (גשר החיים טז:ו:ד).
3. In situations of need (e.g., severe weather, a burial close to sunset, etc.) *Tzidduk HaDin* (and Kaddish) may be recited after three *tefaḥim* of earth cover the grave (אג״מ או״ח ח״ג סימן כג). According to some authorities, *Tzidduk HaDin* may be recited before the grave is covered (כל בו על אבילות ג:ד:טו הערה 12), while others maintain that *Tzidduk HaDin* may even be recited prior to the actual burial (קשו״ע קצח:יד).

4. *Tzidduk HaDin* is not recited if the deceased was a child less than thirty days old. (יו״ד שמד:ד, גשר החיים טז:ו:ב).
5. *Tzidduk HaDin* is generally not recited on days when *Taḥanun* is not said (רמ״א יו״ד תא:ו) except for Erev Rosh Ḥodesh, Erev Ḥanukka, and Erev Purim. On those days, *Tzidduk HaDin* is recited, even after midday (ש״ך יו״ד תא ס״ק ג) . On the occasion of the burial of an "*adam gadol,*" *Tzidduk HaDin* may be recited on all days except for Ḥol HaMoed, the month of Nisan, Rosh Ḥodesh, Ḥanukka, and Purim (ט״ז או״ח תכ:ב).
6. It is customary in many communities not to recite *Tzidduk HaDin* when the interment occurs at night (רמ״א יו״ד תא:ו, גשר החיים טז:ו:ב). Other communities, however, do recite it even at night (חיים וברכה למשמרת שלום אות צ׳ לג).

KADDISH DEITḤADITA

If a *minyan* is present, the *Kaddish DeItḥadita* is recited by the mourners at the conclusion of the burial and the recitation of *Tzidduk HaDin.*

1. If no mourners are present, another person should recite this Kaddish in their stead (גשר החיים טז:ו:ג).
2. On days when *Taḥanun* is not recited the regular Mourner's Kaddish is recited.

SHURA

1. At the conclusion of the interment, two parallel lines are formed between which the mourners walk, receive comfort, and leave the cemetery. Some maintain the custom of beginning the line at a distance of at least four *amot* (6–8 feet) from the grave (גשר החיים טז:ז:ב).
2. As the mourners pass between the two lines, those present offer the words of comfort, *HaMakom yenaḥem etkhem*, etc.
3. A *shura* is not formed if the mourners are under the age of bar mitzva (גשר החיים טז:ז:ן).

4. A *shura* is formed even when the burial occurs on Ḥol HaMoed. Mourners who maintain the custom of removing leather shoes before passing through the *shura*, however, do not remove their shoes on Ḥol HaMoed (שמירת שבת כהלכתה סד:לא).

LEAVING THE CEMETERY

Washing Hands

1. Following the burial, it is customary to leave the cemetery via a different route (גשר החיים יד:כ).
2. Once outside the cemetery and before entering one's home, it is customary to wash one's hands (מג״א או״ח ד ס״ק כא). This custom applies to those who went to the cemetery as well as to those who were in the same room as the deceased at the funeral (פמ״ג א״א או״ח ד ס״ק כא).
3. While it is customary to wash three times, alternating between hands (משנה ברורה או״ח ד ס״ק לט), even washing once is sufficient (מג״א או״ח ד ס״ק יז).
4. Upon washing, each individual places the cup down and does not pass it directly to the next person (חיי אדם קנח:ל).
5. In Jerusalem it is customary not to dry one's hands after washing (בית לחם יהודה יו״ד שע״ו).

FUNERALS ON DAYS WHEN TAḤANUN IS NOT RECITED

(Rosh Ḥodesh, Ḥol HaMoed, rabbinic festivals, Erev Shabbat/Holidays after midday, and other special occasions)

1. EULOGIES: Mournful eulogies that "break one's heart" are not delivered. It is permissible, however, to deliver *divrei Torah* and speak of the inspiring actions of the deceased (חזון עובדיה ח"א עמ' רפח-רצא, נטעי גבריאל אבילות ח"א נב:ד).
2. KERIA: *Keria* is performed (יו"ד שמ:לא). In Israel, however, it is customary that only those in mourning for a parent tear *keria* on Ḥol HaMoed. Those in mourning for all other relatives delay the *keria* until after the conclusion of the festival (גשר החיים ד:לד).
3. KEL MALEI: The common custom is not to recite *Kel Maleh*. Instead, *Mikhtam LeDavid* (Psalm 16) is recited.
4. MAAMADOT: *Maamadot* are not performed.
5. TZIDDUK HADIN and KADDISH DEITḤADITA: *Tzidduk HaDin* and *Kaddish DeItḥadita* are not recited at the conclusion of the burial. In their place, *Mikhtam LeDavid* and the regular Mourner's Kaddish are said (גשר החיים טו:ו:ד). Erev Rosh Ḥodesh, Erev Ḥanukka, and Erev Purim are exceptions to this rule. On those days, *Tzidduk HaDin* and *Kaddish DeItḥadita* are recited even after midday (רמ"א יו"ד שמ:ו).
6. SHURA: At the conclusion of the burial a *shura* is formed to comfort the mourners.
7. SEUDAT HAVRAA: When a funeral is held on erev Shabbat or erev Yom Tov, the *seudat havraa* is not served after the ninth halakhic hour. (יו"ד שע"ח:ה, גשר החיים כ:ב:יא). On Rosh Ḥodesh and Hanukka a *seudat havraa* is served. On Purim the *seudat havraa* should include wine and meat (חזון עובדיה ח"א תצד). On Ḥol HaMoed the *seudat havraa* is served, but without the symbolic foods, i.e., hard-boiled eggs or lentils (גשר החיים כ:ב:י).

THE BURIAL SERVICE

Upon arrival at the cemetery, those present, aside from the mourners, who have not visited a cemetery for thirty days should recite the following paragraphs:

בָּרוּךְ Blessed are You, LORD, our God, King of the universe, Who formed you in judgment, Who nourished and sustained you in judgment, Who brought death on you in judgment, Who knows the number of you all in judgment, and Who in the future will restore you to life and maintain you in judgment. Blessed are You, LORD, Reviver of the dead.

אַתָּה You, my Master, are forever mighty, You are the Resurrector of the dead, with great power to save. He sustains the living with kindness, He resurrects the dead with great compassion, He supports those who are falling, He heals the sick, He sets the incarcerated free, and He fulfills what He has promised to those who sleep in the dust. Who is like You, O mighty One, and who can be compared to You, O King Who causes death and resurrects, and Who causes salvation to sprout? Trustworthy are You to resurrect the dead.

As the casket is carried to the graveside, the following paragraph is recited. The mode of recitation is dependent upon communal custom (See 227 for the halakhot).

יֹשֵׁב בְּסֵתֶר He who lives in the shelter of the Most High dwells in the shadow of Shaddai. I say of the LORD, "My refuge and stronghold, my God in whom I trust," for He will save you from the fowler's snare, from deadly plague. With His pinions He will cover you; beneath His wings you will find shelter; His loyalty is an encircling shield. You need not fear terror by night, nor the arrow that flies by day, nor the plague that stalks in darkness, nor disease that ravages at noon. A thousand may fall beside you, ten thousand at your right hand, but it will not come near you. You will only look with your eyes and see the punishment of the wicked. For you – "the LORD is my Refuge" – you have made the Most High your abode. No harm will befall you; no sickness will come near your home, (1)for He (2)will command (3)His angels (4)about you (5)to guard you (6)in all (7)your ways. *Ps. 91*

סדר הקבורה

Upon arrival at the cemetery, those present, aside from the mourners, who have not visited a cemetery for thirty days should recite the following paragraphs:

בָּרוּךְ אַתָּה יהוה אֱלֹהֵינוּ מֶלֶךְ הָעוֹלָם, אֲשֶׁר יָצַר אֶתְכֶם בַּדִּין, וְזָן וְכִלְכֵּל אֶתְכֶם בַּדִּין, וְהֵמִית אֶתְכֶם בַּדִּין, וְיוֹדֵעַ מִסְפַּר כֻּלְּכֶם בַּדִּין, וְהוּא עָתִיד לְהַחֲיוֹתְכֶם וּלְקַיֵּם אֶתְכֶם בַּדִּין. בָּרוּךְ אַתָּה יהוה, מְחַיֵּה הַמֵּתִים.

אַתָּה גִּבּוֹר לְעוֹלָם אֲדֹנָי, מְחַיֵּה מֵתִים אַתָּה, רַב לְהוֹשִׁיעַ, מְכַלְכֵּל חַיִּים בְּחֶסֶד, מְחַיֵּה מֵתִים בְּרַחֲמִים רַבִּים, סוֹמֵךְ נוֹפְלִים, וְרוֹפֵא חוֹלִים, וּמַתִּיר אֲסוּרִים, וּמְקַיֵּם אֱמוּנָתוֹ לִישֵׁנֵי עָפָר. מִי כָמוֹךָ בַּעַל גְּבוּרוֹת וּמִי דּוֹמֶה לָּךְ, מֶלֶךְ מֵמִית וּמְחַיֶּה וּמַצְמִיחַ יְשׁוּעָה, וְנֶאֱמָן אַתָּה לְהַחֲיוֹת מֵתִים.

As the casket is carried to the graveside, the following paragraph is recited. The mode of recitation is dependent upon communal custom (See 227 for the halakhot).

תהלים צא
יֹשֵׁב בְּסֵתֶר עֶלְיוֹן, בְּצֵל שַׁדַּי יִתְלוֹנָן: אֹמַר לַיהוה מַחְסִי וּמְצוּדָתִי, אֱלֹהַי אֶבְטַח־בּוֹ: כִּי הוּא יַצִּילְךָ מִפַּח יָקוּשׁ, מִדֶּבֶר הַוּוֹת: בְּאֶבְרָתוֹ יָסֶךְ לָךְ, וְתַחַת־כְּנָפָיו תֶּחְסֶה, צִנָּה וְסֹחֵרָה אֲמִתּוֹ: לֹא־תִירָא מִפַּחַד לָיְלָה, מֵחֵץ יָעוּף יוֹמָם: מִדֶּבֶר בָּאֹפֶל יַהֲלֹךְ, מִקֶּטֶב יָשׁוּד צָהֳרָיִם: יִפֹּל מִצִּדְּךָ אֶלֶף, וּרְבָבָה מִימִינֶךָ, אֵלֶיךָ לֹא יִגָּשׁ: רַק בְּעֵינֶיךָ תַבִּיט, וְשִׁלֻּמַת רְשָׁעִים תִּרְאֶה: כִּי־אַתָּה יהוה מַחְסִי, עֶלְיוֹן שַׂמְתָּ מְעוֹנֶךָ: לֹא־תְאֻנֶּה אֵלֶיךָ רָעָה, וְנֶגַע לֹא־יִקְרַב בְּאָהֳלֶךָ:

(1)כִּי (2)מַלְאָכָיו (3)יְצַוֶּה־(4)לָּךְ, (5)לִשְׁמָרְךָ (6)בְּכָל־(7)דְּרָכֶיךָ:

If words of eulogy are said at the cemetery, they should be said at this time, prior to the lowering of the casket.

The casket is lowered and covered with earth preferably until the grave is mounded, forming a tzurat ha'kever that encompasses the entire burial place.

Upon completion of the burial, the Tziduk HaDin below is recited.

On days when Taḥanun is not recited, *turn to page 222* *for Mikhtam LeDavid followed by the Mourner's Kaddish.*

THE ACCEPTANCE OF JUDGMENT

הַצּוּר The Rock, His work is whole, *Deut. 32*
and all His ways are justice.
A God of faith who does no wrong,
just is He and upright.

The Rock, perfect in every deed:
Who can say to Him,
"What have You done?"
He rules below and above.
He brings deals out death and grants life, *I Sam. 2*
casts down into Sheol and lifts up.

The Rock, perfect in every act:
Who can say to Him,
"Why do You so act?"
You who speak and act:
show us kindness we do not deserve,
and in the merit of the one who was bound like a lamb,
hear us and act.

Righteous in all His ways, the Rock who is perfect,
slow to anger and full of compassion,
please have pity and spare parents and children,
for Yours, Lord, are forgiveness and compassion.

If words of eulogy are said at the cemetery, they should be said at this time, prior to the lowering of the casket.

The casket is lowered and covered with earth preferably until the grave is mounded, forming a צורת הקבר *that encompasses the entire burial place.*

Upon completion of the burial, the צידוק הדין *below is recited.*

On days when תחנון *is not recited, turn to page 223 for* מִכְתָּם לְדָוִד *followed by* קדיש יתום.

צידוק הדין

הַצּוּר תָּמִים פָּעֳלוֹ דברים לב
כִּי כָל־דְּרָכָיו מִשְׁפָּט
אֵל אֱמוּנָה וְאֵין עָוֶל, צַדִּיק וְיָשָׁר הוּא:

הַצּוּר תָּמִים בְּכָל פֹּעַל, מִי יֹאמַר לוֹ מַה תִּפְעַל
הַשַּׁלִּיט בְּמַטָּה וּבְמַעַל.
מֵמִית וּמְחַיֶּה, מוֹרִיד שְׁאוֹל וַיָּעַל: שמואל א׳ ב

הַצּוּר תָּמִים בְּכָל מַעֲשֶׂה
מִי יֹאמַר לוֹ מַה תַּעֲשֶׂה
הָאוֹמֵר וְעוֹשֶׂה, חֶסֶד חִנָּם לָנוּ תַעֲשֶׂה
וּבִזְכוּת הַנֶּעֱקַד כְּשֶׂה
הַקְשִׁיבָה וַעֲשֵׂה.

צַדִּיק בְּכָל דְּרָכָיו הַצּוּר תָּמִים
אֶרֶךְ אַפַּיִם וּמָלֵא רַחֲמִים
חֲמָל נָא וְחוּס נָא עַל אָבוֹת וּבָנִים
כִּי לְךָ אָדוֹן הַסְּלִיחוֹת וְהָרַחֲמִים.

You are righteous, Lord, in bringing death and giving life.
In Your hand is the safekeeping of all spirits.
Far be it from You to erase our remembrance.
May Your eyes be open to us in compassion,
for Yours, Lord, are compassion and forgiveness.

If one lives for a year or a thousand years,
what does it profit him?
He shall be as if he had never been.
Blessed is the true Judge who brings death and gives life.

Blessed is He for His judgment is true,
and in His sight He surveys all.
He repays man in accord with his account and just desert,
and all must render acknowledgment to His name.

We know, Lord, that Your judgment is just.
You are just when You speak and fair when You judge.
It is not for us to criticize Your manner of judgment.
You are righteous, Lord, and Your laws are upright. *Ps. 119*

True Judge,
Judge of righteousness and truth:
Blessed is the true Judge
for all His judgments are righteous and true.

In Your hand is the soul of every living thing.
Your right hand and power are full of righteousness.
Have compassion on the remnant of the flock
of those who serve You,
and say to the angel [of death],
"Stay your hand."

צַדִּיק אַתָּה יהוה לְהָמִית וּלְהַחֲיוֹת
אֲשֶׁר בְּיָדְךָ פִּקְדוֹן כָּל רוּחוֹת, חָלִילָה לְּךָ זִכְרוֹנֵנוּ לִמְחוֹת
וְיִהְיוּ נָא עֵינֶיךָ בְּרַחֲמִים עָלֵינוּ פְקוּחוֹת
כִּי לְךָ אָדוֹן הָרַחֲמִים וְהַסְּלִיחוֹת.

אָדָם אִם בֶּן שָׁנָה יִהְיֶה, אוֹ אֶלֶף שָׁנִים יִחְיֶה
מַה יִּתְרוֹן לוֹ, כְּלֹא הָיָה יִהְיֶה
בָּרוּךְ דַּיַּן הָאֱמֶת, מֵמִית וּמְחַיֶּה.

בָּרוּךְ הוּא כִּי אֱמֶת דִּינוֹ, וּמְשׁוֹטֵט הַכֹּל בְּעֵינוֹ
וּמְשַׁלֵּם לְאָדָם חֶשְׁבּוֹנוֹ וְדִינוֹ, וְהַכֹּל לִשְׁמוֹ הוֹדָיָה יִתֵּנוּ.

יָדַעְנוּ יהוה כִּי צֶדֶק מִשְׁפָּטֶךָ
תִּצְדַּק בְּדָבְרֶךָ וְתִזְכֶּה בְּשָׁפְטֶךָ
וְאֵין לְהַרְהֵר אַחַר מִדַּת שָׁפְטֶךָ.
תהלים קיט צַדִּיק אַתָּה יהוה, וְיָשָׁר מִשְׁפָּטֶיךָ:

דַּיַּן אֱמֶת, שׁוֹפֵט צֶדֶק וֶאֱמֶת
בָּרוּךְ דַּיַּן הָאֱמֶת, שֶׁכָּל מִשְׁפָּטָיו צֶדֶק וֶאֱמֶת.

נֶפֶשׁ כָּל חַי בְּיָדֶךָ
צֶדֶק מָלְאָה יְמִינְךָ וְיָדֶךָ
רַחֵם עַל פְּלֵטַת צֹאן עֲבָדֶיךָ
וְתֹאמַר לַמַּלְאָךְ הֶרֶף יָדֶךָ.

Great in counsel, mighty in deed,
Your eyes are open to all of the ways of humans,
to give each one according to his ways,
to each according to the fruits of his actions. *Jer. 32*

Proclaiming that the LORD is upright.
He is my Rock, in whom there is no wrong. *Ps. 92*

The LORD has given, the LORD has taken.
May the LORD's name be blessed. *Job 1*

But He is merciful;
He forgives offense and does not destroy.
He suppresses His anger again and again
and never rouses His full fury. *Ps. 78*

On days when Taḥanun is not recited,
the following Psalm is recited in place of Tziduk HaDin.

מִכְתָּם לְדָוִד A mikhtam of David. Protect me, God, for in You I take refuge. I said to the LORD, "You are my Lord; My favor comes from none but You." As for the holy ones in the land, the mighty who were all my delight, may those who court other gods suffer many sorrows – I will not pour out their libations of blood; I will not bear their names on my lips. The LORD is my chosen portion and my cup. You direct my fate. A sweet heritage has fallen to my lot; my share is delightful to me. I will bless the LORD who has guided me; even at night, my conscience stirs me. I have set the LORD before me always; He is at my right hand; I shall not be shaken. Therefore my heart is glad, my spirit rejoices, and my body rests secure, for You will not abandon me to Sheol nor let Your devoted one see the Pit. You will teach me the path of life. In Your presence is fullness of joy; at Your right hand, bliss for evermore. *Ps. 16*

גְּדֹל הָעֵצָה וְרַב הָעֲלִילִיָּה ירמיה לב
אֲשֶׁר־עֵינֶיךָ פְקֻחוֹת עַל־כׇּל־דַּרְכֵי בְּנֵי אָדָם
לָתֵת לְאִישׁ כִּדְרָכָיו, וְכִפְרִי מַעֲלָלָיו:

לְהַגִּיד כִּי־יָשָׁר יהוה, צוּרִי וְלֹא־עַוְלָתָה בּוֹ: תהלים צב

יהוה נָתַן וַיהוה לָקָח, יְהִי שֵׁם יהוה מְבֹרָךְ: איוב א

וְהוּא רַחוּם, יְכַפֵּר עָוֹן וְלֹא־יַשְׁחִית תהלים עח
וְהִרְבָּה לְהָשִׁיב אַפּוֹ, וְלֹא־יָעִיר כׇּל־חֲמָתוֹ:

On days when תחנון *is not recited,*
the following Psalm is recited in place of צידוק הדין*.*

מִכְתָּם לְדָוִד, שָׁמְרֵנִי אֵל כִּי־חָסִיתִי בָךְ: אָמַרְתְּ לַיהוה, תהלים טז
אֲדֹנָי אָתָּה, טוֹבָתִי בַּל־עָלֶיךָ: לִקְדוֹשִׁים אֲשֶׁר־בָּאָרֶץ הֵמָּה,
וְאַדִּירֵי כׇּל־חֶפְצִי־בָם: יִרְבּוּ עַצְּבוֹתָם אַחֵר מָהָרוּ, בַּל־אַסִּיךְ
נִסְכֵּיהֶם מִדָּם, וּבַל־אֶשָּׂא אֶת־שְׁמוֹתָם עַל־שְׂפָתָי: יהוה,
מְנָת־חֶלְקִי וְכוֹסִי, אַתָּה תּוֹמִיךְ גּוֹרָלִי: חֲבָלִים נָפְלוּ־לִי
בַּנְּעִמִים, אַף־נַחֲלָת שָׁפְרָה עָלָי: אֲבָרֵךְ אֶת־יהוה אֲשֶׁר
יְעָצָנִי, אַף־לֵילוֹת יִסְּרוּנִי כִלְיוֹתָי: שִׁוִּיתִי יהוה לְנֶגְדִּי תָמִיד,
כִּי מִימִינִי בַּל־אֶמּוֹט: לָכֵן שָׂמַח לִבִּי וַיָּגֶל כְּבוֹדִי, אַף־בְּשָׂרִי
יִשְׁכֹּן לָבֶטַח: כִּי לֹא־תַעֲזֹב נַפְשִׁי לִשְׁאוֹל, לֹא־תִתֵּן חֲסִידְךָ
לִרְאוֹת שָׁחַת: תּוֹדִיעֵנִי אֹרַח חַיִּים, שֹׂבַע שְׂמָחוֹת אֶת־פָּנֶיךָ,
נְעִמוֹת בִּימִינְךָ נֶצַח:

Additional scriptural passages such as those listed below may be recited.

לַמְנַצֵּחַ To the lead singer – a psalm of the sons of Koraḥ. Hear this, all you peoples; listen, all dwellers of this world, low and high, rich and poor alike. My mouth will speak words of wisdom; my heart's utterance, understanding. I listen with care to a parable; I expound my theme to the music of the harp. Why should I fear when evil days come, when wicked deceivers surround me – those who trust in their wealth, who boast of their great riches? No person can ever redeem another or pay God the price of his release; the ransom of a life is costly; no payment will ever be enough to let him live forever, never seeing the grave. For all can see that wise men die and that the foolish and senseless all perish, leaving their wealth to others. They think their houses will last forever, their dwellings for all generations – they give their names to their estates, but a person, despite his wealth, cannot linger; he is like the beasts that perish. Such is the fate of the foolish, the end of those pleased with their own words – Selah. They go down to Sheol like sheep; death will be their shepherd. The upright will rule over them in the morning. Their forms will decay in Sheol, far from their noble mansions. But God will redeem my life from Sheol, for He will take me – Selah. Fear not when people grow rich, when their houses rise in esteem, for they will take nothing with them in death; their esteem will not descend with them. Though they counted themselves blessed in life, for people praise you when you prosper, they too will join the ranks of their ancestors, who will never see the light again. A person with wealth but without understanding is like the beasts that perish. *Ps. 49*

מִזְמוֹר לְדָוִד A psalm of David. Lord, who may dwell in Your tent? Who may live on Your holy mountain? The one whose ways are blameless, who does what is right, who speaks truth from the heart; the one who has no malice on his tongue, who does no wrong to his fellow, who does not cast a slur against his neighbor; the one who scorns those who are vile, who honors those who fear the Lord, who keeps an oath even when it hurts; the one who does not loan money for interest, who does not take a bribe against the innocent – anyone who acts thus will never be shaken. *Ps. 15*

Additional scriptural passages such as those listed below may be recited.

תהלים מט
לַמְנַצֵּחַ לִבְנֵי־קֹרַח מִזְמוֹר: שִׁמְעוּ־זֹאת כָּל־הָעַמִּים, הַאֲזִינוּ כָּל־יֹשְׁבֵי חָלֶד: גַּם־בְּנֵי אָדָם גַּם־בְּנֵי־אִישׁ, יַחַד עָשִׁיר וְאֶבְיוֹן: פִּי יְדַבֵּר חָכְמוֹת, וְהָגוּת לִבִּי תְבוּנוֹת: אַטֶּה לְמָשָׁל אָזְנִי, אֶפְתַּח בְּכִנּוֹר חִידָתִי: לָמָּה אִירָא בִּימֵי רָע, עֲוֹן עֲקֵבַי יְסוּבֵּנִי: הַבֹּטְחִים עַל־חֵילָם, וּבְרֹב עָשְׁרָם יִתְהַלָּלוּ: אָח לֹא־פָדֹה יִפְדֶּה אִישׁ, לֹא־יִתֵּן לֵאלֹהִים כָּפְרוֹ: וְיֵקַר פִּדְיוֹן נַפְשָׁם, וְחָדַל לְעוֹלָם: וִיחִי־עוֹד לָנֶצַח, לֹא יִרְאֶה הַשָּׁחַת: כִּי יִרְאֶה חֲכָמִים יָמוּתוּ יַחַד כְּסִיל וָבַעַר יֹאבֵדוּ, וְעָזְבוּ לַאֲחֵרִים חֵילָם: קִרְבָּם בָּתֵּימוֹ לְעוֹלָם מִשְׁכְּנֹתָם לְדוֹר וָדֹר, קָרְאוּ בִשְׁמוֹתָם עֲלֵי אֲדָמוֹת: וְאָדָם בִּיקָר בַּל־יָלִין, נִמְשַׁל כַּבְּהֵמוֹת נִדְמוּ: זֶה דַרְכָּם כֵּסֶל לָמוֹ, וְאַחֲרֵיהֶם בְּפִיהֶם יִרְצוּ סֶלָה: כַּצֹּאן לִשְׁאוֹל שַׁתּוּ מָוֶת יִרְעֵם, וַיִּרְדּוּ בָם יְשָׁרִים לַבֹּקֶר וְצוּרָם לְבַלּוֹת שְׁאוֹל מִזְּבֻל לוֹ: אַךְ־אֱלֹהִים יִפְדֶּה נַפְשִׁי מִיַּד שְׁאוֹל, כִּי יִקָּחֵנִי סֶלָה: אַל־תִּירָא כִּי־יַעֲשִׁר אִישׁ, כִּי־יִרְבֶּה כְּבוֹד בֵּיתוֹ: כִּי לֹא בְמוֹתוֹ יִקַּח הַכֹּל, לֹא־יֵרֵד אַחֲרָיו כְּבוֹדוֹ: כִּי־נַפְשׁוֹ בְּחַיָּיו יְבָרֵךְ, וְיוֹדֻךָ כִּי־תֵיטִיב לָךְ: תָּבוֹא עַד־דּוֹר אֲבוֹתָיו, עַד־נֵצַח לֹא יִרְאוּ־אוֹר: אָדָם בִּיקָר וְלֹא יָבִין נִמְשַׁל כַּבְּהֵמוֹת נִדְמוּ:

תהלים טו
מִזְמוֹר לְדָוִד, יהוה מִי־יָגוּר בְּאָהֳלֶךָ, מִי־יִשְׁכֹּן בְּהַר קָדְשֶׁךָ: הוֹלֵךְ תָּמִים וּפֹעֵל צֶדֶק, וְדֹבֵר אֱמֶת בִּלְבָבוֹ: לֹא־רָגַל עַל־לְשֹׁנוֹ לֹא־עָשָׂה לְרֵעֵהוּ רָעָה, וְחֶרְפָּה לֹא־נָשָׂא עַל־קְרֹבוֹ: נִבְזֶה בְּעֵינָיו נִמְאָס וְאֶת־יִרְאֵי יהוה יְכַבֵּד, נִשְׁבַּע לְהָרַע וְלֹא יָמִר: כַּסְפּוֹ לֹא־נָתַן בְּנֶשֶׁךְ וְשֹׁחַד עַל־נָקִי לֹא־לָקָח, עֹשֵׂה אֵלֶּה לֹא יִמּוֹט לְעוֹלָם:

מִזְמוֹר לְדָוִד A psalm of David. The LORD is my Shepherd; I lack nothing. *Ps. 23*
He lets me lie down in green pastures; He leads me beside still waters. He refreshes my soul, guiding me along the right paths for the sake of His name. Though I walk through the valley of the shadow of death, I fear no evil, for You are with me; Your rod and Your staff encourage me. You set a table before me in the face of my foes; You anoint my head with oil; my cup brims over. May only goodness and kindness follow me all the days of my life; let me live in the LORD's House for evermore.

On days when Taḥanun is not recited, the regular Mourner's Kaddish is recited at this point *(see page 248).*

For a male:

אֵל מָלֵא רַחֲמִים God, full of mercy, Who dwells on high, grant fitting rest beneath (*some say:* above) the protective wings of the Divine Presence, where the souls of the holy and pure ones – whose radiance is like that of the heavens – reside, to the soul of (*name of the deceased*) the son of (*father of the deceased*), who has gone to his eternal reward, insofar as I will make a charitable gift in memory of his soul, may the Garden of Eden be his resting place. For this reason may the ever-merciful One shelter the deceased under His protective wings forever, and may He bind his soul in lasting life. For the LORD will surely be his benefactor, so that he can rest in peace in his allotted place. And let us say, Amen.

For a female:

אֵל מָלֵא רַחֲמִים God, full of mercy, Who dwells on high, grant fitting rest beneath (*some say:* above) the protective wings of the Divine Presence, where the souls of the holy and pure ones – whose radiance is like that of the heavens – reside, to the soul of (*name of the deceased*) the daughter of (*father of the deceased*), who has gone to her eternal reward, insofar as I will make a charitable gift in memory of her soul, may the Garden of Eden be her resting place. For this reason may the ever-merciful One shelter the deceased under His protective wings forever, and may He bind her soul in lasting life. For the LORD will surely be her benefactor, so that she can rest in peace in her allotted place. And let us say, Amen.

מִזְמוֹר לְדָוִד, יהוה רֹעִי לֹא אֶחְסָר: בִּנְאוֹת דֶּשֶׁא יַרְבִּיצֵנִי, עַל־מֵי תהלים כג
מְנוּחוֹת יְנַהֲלֵנִי: נַפְשִׁי יְשׁוֹבֵב, יַנְחֵנִי בְמַעְגְּלֵי־צֶדֶק לְמַעַן שְׁמוֹ:
גַּם כִּי־אֵלֵךְ בְּגֵיא צַלְמָוֶת לֹא־אִירָא רָע, כִּי־אַתָּה עִמָּדִי, שִׁבְטְךָ
וּמִשְׁעַנְתֶּךָ הֵמָּה יְנַחֲמֻנִי: תַּעֲרֹךְ לְפָנַי שֻׁלְחָן נֶגֶד צֹרְרָי, דִּשַּׁנְתָּ
בַשֶּׁמֶן רֹאשִׁי, כּוֹסִי רְוָיָה: אַךְ טוֹב וָחֶסֶד יִרְדְּפוּנִי כָּל־יְמֵי חַיָּי,
וְשַׁבְתִּי בְּבֵית־יהוה לְאֹרֶךְ יָמִים:

On days when תחנון *is not recited, the regular* קדיש יתום *is recited at this point (see page 249).*

For a male:

אֵל מָלֵא רַחֲמִים, שׁוֹכֵן בַּמְּרוֹמִים, הַמְצֵא מְנוּחָה נְכוֹנָה תַּחַת (נ״א עַל) כַּנְפֵי הַשְּׁכִינָה, בְּמַעֲלוֹת קְדוֹשִׁים וּטְהוֹרִים, כְּזֹהַר הָרָקִיעַ מַזְהִירִים, לְנִשְׁמַת (פלוני בֶּן פלוני) שֶׁהָלַךְ לְעוֹלָמוֹ, בַּעֲבוּר שֶׁאֶתֵּן צְדָקָה בְּעַד הַזְכָּרַת נִשְׁמָתוֹ, בְּגַן עֵדֶן תְּהֵא מְנוּחָתוֹ. לָכֵן, בַּעַל הָרַחֲמִים יַסְתִּירֵהוּ בְּסֵתֶר כְּנָפָיו לְעוֹלָמִים, וְיִצְרוֹר בִּצְרוֹר הַחַיִּים אֶת נִשְׁמָתוֹ, יהוה הוּא נַחֲלָתוֹ, וְיָנוּחַ בְּשָׁלוֹם עַל מִשְׁכָּבוֹ, וְנֹאמַר אָמֵן.

For a female:

אֵל מָלֵא רַחֲמִים, שׁוֹכֵן בַּמְּרוֹמִים, הַמְצֵא מְנוּחָה נְכוֹנָה תַּחַת (נ״א עַל) כַּנְפֵי הַשְּׁכִינָה, בְּמַעֲלוֹת קְדוֹשִׁים וּטְהוֹרִים, כְּזֹהַר הָרָקִיעַ מַזְהִירִים, לְנִשְׁמַת (פלונית בַּת פלוני) שֶׁהָלְכָה לְעוֹלָמָהּ, בַּעֲבוּר שֶׁאֶתֵּן צְדָקָה בְּעַד הַזְכָּרַת נִשְׁמָתָהּ, בְּגַן עֵדֶן תְּהֵא מְנוּחָתָהּ. לָכֵן, בַּעַל הָרַחֲמִים יַסְתִּירֶהָ בְּסֵתֶר כְּנָפָיו לְעוֹלָמִים, וְיִצְרוֹר בִּצְרוֹר הַחַיִּים אֶת נִשְׁמָתָהּ, יהוה הוּא נַחֲלָתָהּ, וְתָנוּחַ בְּשָׁלוֹם עַל מִשְׁכָּבָהּ, וְנֹאמַר אָמֵן.

THE BURIAL KADDISH

Mourner: יִתְגַּדַּל Exalted and hallowed may God's great name be,
in the world that will in future be renewed,
reviving the dead
and raising them up to eternal life.
He will rebuild the city of Jerusalem
and in it reestablish His Temple.
He will remove alien worship from the earth
and restore to its place the worship of Heaven.
Then the Holy One, blessed be He,
will reign in His sovereignty and splendor.
May He reign in your lifetimes and in your days,
and in the lifetime of the whole house of Israel,
speedily and soon,
and say, Amen.

All: His great name be blessed forever and all time.

Mourner: Blessed and praised, honored, extolled,
glorified, adored and exalted above all
be the name of the Holy One,
blessed is He,
(*Between Rosh Hashana & Yom Kippur:* above and) beyond any
blessing, hymn, praise,
or expressions of consolation
that may be uttered in this world,
and say, Amen.

May abundant peace descend from heaven,
as well as life, for us and for all Israel,
and say, Amen.

May He Who makes peace in the highest heaven,
make peace for us, and for all Israel,
and say, Amen.

קדיש דאתחדתא

אבל: **יִתְגַּדַּל וְיִתְקַדַּשׁ שְׁמֵהּ רַבָּא** (קהל: אָמֵן)
בְּעָלְמָא דְּהוּא עָתִיד לְאִתְחַדָּתָא
וּלְאַחֲיָאָה מֵתַיָּא, וּלְאַסָּקָא יָתְהוֹן לְחַיֵּי עָלְמָא
וּלְמִבְנֵא קַרְתָּא דִירוּשְׁלֵם, וּלְשַׁכְלָלָא הֵיכְלֵהּ בְּגַוַּהּ
וּלְמֶעְקַר פֻּלְחָנָא נֻכְרָאָה מֵאַרְעָא
וְלַאֲתָבָא פֻּלְחָנָא דִשְׁמַיָּא לְאַתְרֵהּ
וְיַמְלִיךְ קֻדְשָׁא בְּרִיךְ הוּא בְּמַלְכוּתֵהּ וִיקָרֵהּ
בְּחַיֵּיכוֹן וּבְיוֹמֵיכוֹן וּבְחַיֵּי דְכָל בֵּית יִשְׂרָאֵל
בַּעֲגָלָא וּבִזְמַן קָרִיב, וְאִמְרוּ אָמֵן. (קהל: אָמֵן)

קהל ואבל: **יְהֵא שְׁמֵהּ רַבָּא מְבָרַךְ לְעָלַם וּלְעָלְמֵי עָלְמַיָּא.**

אבל: **יִתְבָּרַךְ וְיִשְׁתַּבַּח וְיִתְפָּאַר**
וְיִתְרוֹמַם וְיִתְנַשֵּׂא וְיִתְהַדָּר וְיִתְעַלֶּה וְיִתְהַלָּל
שְׁמֵהּ דְּקֻדְשָׁא בְּרִיךְ הוּא (קהל: בְּרִיךְ הוּא)
לְעֵלָּא מִן כָּל בִּרְכָתָא
/ בעשרת ימי תשובה: **לְעֵלָּא לְעֵלָּא מִכָּל בִּרְכָתָא**/
וְשִׁירָתָא, תֻּשְׁבְּחָתָא וְנֶחֱמָתָא
דַּאֲמִירָן בְּעָלְמָא, וְאִמְרוּ אָמֵן. (קהל: אָמֵן)

יְהֵא שְׁלָמָא רַבָּא מִן שְׁמַיָּא
וְחַיִּים, עָלֵינוּ וְעַל כָּל יִשְׂרָאֵל, וְאִמְרוּ אָמֵן. (קהל: אָמֵן)

עֹשֶׂה שָׁלוֹם/ בעשרת ימי תשובה: **הַשָּׁלוֹם**/ **בִּמְרוֹמָיו, הוּא יַעֲשֶׂה שָׁלוֹם עָלֵינוּ וְעַל כָּל יִשְׂרָאֵל, וְאִמְרוּ אָמֵן.** (קהל: אָמֵן)

On days when Taḥanun is not recited, the Mourner's Kaddish is said in place of the Kaddish DeIthḥadita

MOURNER'S KADDISH

Mourner: יִתְגַּדַּל Exalted and hallowed may God's great name be,
in the world He created as He willed.
May He reign in your lifetimes
and in your days, and in the lifetime
of the whole house of Israel,
speedily and soon,
and say, Amen.

All: May His great name be blessed forever and all time.

Mourner: Blessed and praised, honored, extolled,
glorified, adored
and exalted above all
be the name of the Holy One,
blessed is He,
(*Between Rosh Hashana & Yom Kippur:* above and) beyond
any blessing, hymn, praise,
or expressions of consolation
that may be uttered in this world,
and say, Amen.

May abundant peace descend from heaven,
as well as life, for us
and for all Israel,
and say, Amen.

May He Who makes peace in the highest heaven,
make peace for us,
and for all Israel,
and say, Amen.

On days when תחנון *is not recited,* קדיש יתום *is said in place of the* קדיש דאתחדתא

קדיש יתום

אבל: יִתְגַּדַּל וְיִתְקַדַּשׁ שְׁמֵהּ רַבָּא (קהל: אָמֵן)
בְּעָלְמָא דִּי בְרָא כִרְעוּתֵהּ
וְיַמְלִיךְ מַלְכוּתֵהּ
בְּחַיֵּיכוֹן וּבְיוֹמֵיכוֹן וּבְחַיֵּי דְכָל בֵּית יִשְׂרָאֵל
בַּעֲגָלָא וּבִזְמַן קָרִיב, וְאִמְרוּ אָמֵן. (קהל: אָמֵן)

קהל ואבל: יְהֵא שְׁמֵהּ רַבָּא מְבָרַךְ לְעָלַם וּלְעָלְמֵי עָלְמַיָּא.

אבל: יִתְבָּרַךְ וְיִשְׁתַּבַּח וְיִתְפָּאַר
וְיִתְרוֹמַם וְיִתְנַשֵּׂא וְיִתְהַדָּר וְיִתְעַלֶּה וְיִתְהַלָּל
שְׁמֵהּ דְּקֻדְשָׁא בְּרִיךְ הוּא (קהל: בְּרִיךְ הוּא)
לְעֵלָּא מִן כָּל בִּרְכָתָא
/בעשרת ימי תשובה: לְעֵלָּא לְעֵלָּא מִכָּל בִּרְכָתָא/
וְשִׁירָתָא, תֻּשְׁבְּחָתָא וְנֶחֱמָתָא
דַּאֲמִירָן בְּעָלְמָא, וְאִמְרוּ אָמֵן. (קהל: אָמֵן)

יְהֵא שְׁלָמָא רַבָּא מִן שְׁמַיָּא
וְחַיִּים, עָלֵינוּ וְעַל כָּל יִשְׂרָאֵל, וְאִמְרוּ אָמֵן. (קהל: אָמֵן)

עֹשֶׂה שָׁלוֹם/ בעשרת ימי תשובה: הַשָּׁלוֹם/ בִּמְרוֹמָיו
הוּא יַעֲשֶׂה שָׁלוֹם
עָלֵינוּ וְעַל כָּל יִשְׂרָאֵל, וְאִמְרוּ אָמֵן. (קהל: אָמֵן)

When taking leave of the deceased, one says:

לֵךְ Go in peace,
repose in peace,
and arise to your ultimate destiny
at the end of the days.

Upon leaving the burial site, all present other than the mourners form two rows facing each other through which the mourners walk. As the mourners pass, the following is said (*See pages 230–31 for the halakhot*)

הַמָּקוֹם May the Omnipresent
console you
among the other mourners
of Zion and Yerushalayim.

Some have the custom to pick blades of grass and throw them over their shoulders, saying:

וְיָצִיצוּ May they thrive in the towns *Ps. 72*
like field grass.
Remember that we are dust. *Ps. 103*

Upon leaving the cemetery and before entering one's home, it is customary to wash one's hands. (*See pages 231*).

בִּלַּע He will swallow up death forever; *Is. 25*
the Lord God,
He will wipe every tear from every face.
He will sweep His people's shame away from all the earth.
The Lord has spoken.

When taking leave of the deceased, one says:

For a Male:

לֵךְ בְּשָׁלוֹם, וְתָנוּחַ בְּשָׁלוֹם, וְתַעֲמוֹד לְגוֹרָלְךָ לְקֵץ הַיָּמִין.

For a Female:

לְכִי בְשָׁלוֹם, וְתָנוּחִי בְּשָׁלוֹם, וְתַעַמְדִי לְגוֹרָלֵךְ לְקֵץ הַיָּמִין.

Upon leaving the burial site, all present other than the mourners form two rows facing each other through which the mourners walk. As the mourners pass, the following is said (See pages 230–31 for the halakhot)

הַמָּקוֹם יְנַחֵם

אוֹתְךָ *for one male mourner*

אוֹתָךְ *for one female mourner*

אֶתְכֶם *for several mourners*

אֶתְכֶן *for several mourners, if all female*

בְּתוֹךְ שְׁאָר אֲבֵלֵי צִיּוֹן וִירוּשָׁלָיִם.

Some have the custom to pick blades of grass and throw them over their shoulders, saying:

תהלים עב / תהלים קג וְיָצִיצוּ מֵעִיר כְּעֵשֶׂב הָאָרֶץ: זָכוּר כִּי־עָפָר אֲנָחְנוּ:

Upon leaving the cemetery and before entering one's home, it is customary to wash one's hands. (See pages 231).

ישעיה כה בִּלַּע הַמָּוֶת לָנֶצַח, וּמָחָה אֲדֹנָי יֱהֹוִה דִּמְעָה מֵעַל כָּל־פָּנִים
וְחֶרְפַּת עַמּוֹ יָסִיר מֵעַל כָּל־הָאָרֶץ, כִּי יהוה דִּבֵּר:

HALAKHOT CONCERNING THE BEGINNING OF SHIVA AND THE SEUDAT HAVRAA

SHIVA

1. *Shiva* begins at the conclusion of the burial (i.e., once the grave is covered with earth) (יו״ד שעה:א). The mourner should make certain to perform an act of mourning (e.g., change to non-leather shoes or sit on a low stool) *l'khatḥila* by sunset, or *b'diavad* by the end of *bein hashmashot*, so that the day of burial will be counted as the first day of *shiva* (גשר החיים יט:ד:א-ב).
2. If the burial will be in another city, and the mourner is not traveling to the burial, *shiva* begins when the mourner "turns his face" i.e., stops escorting the deceased (יו״ד שעה:ב). If the cemetery is near the location where *shiva* will be observed, however, those who remain behind do not begin mourning until they are informed of the burial, or until they estimate that the burial has been completed (ערוה״ש יו״ד שעה:ז-ח).
3. If the mourner is not in the same city as the deceased and will not be traveling to the funeral, common practice in America is to begin *shiva* immediately upon the notification of death (שדי חמד ח״ח פאת השדה מערכת אבלות יד, אג״מ יו״ד ח״א סימן רנג).
4. In Israel, many do not begin *shiva* under any circumstance until the funeral has occurred (משיב דבר ח״ב סימן כו, פני ברוך סימן ח׳ הערה כג, יביע אומר יו״ד ח״ד סימן כח, ע״ע נפש הרב עמ׳ רנו).
5. Some authorities rule that a mourner who returns from accompanying the deceased to the burial in another city may join the mourners who have already begun sitting and conclude the *shiva* with them, even though the returnee's observed *shiva* will be shorter than seven days (רעק״א יו״ד שעה ד״ה ואם גדול). Other authorities maintain that the returning relative should continue to observe *shiva* for the full seven days (מסורת משה ח״ב יו״ד רס״ו).

6. In tragic situations when a body cannot be found, or the deceased is denied a timely burial, *shiva* begins as soon as the family despairs or can do nothing more to bury the deceased (יו״ד שמא:ד, שעה:ה-ו).
7. A candle should be lit in the *shiva* house throughout the week (כל בו על אבלות א:י).
8. The mourner neither dons *tefillin* on the day of the burial (יו״ד שפח:א) nor compensates for missed prayers [*tefillat tashlumin*]. The mourner should, however, recite the morning blessings [*Birkot HaShaḥar* and *Birkot HaTorah*] upon returning from the cemetery (גשר החיים יח:ב:ד).

SEUDAT HAVRAA

1. The first meal following the funeral is intended for the mourners and is known as the *seudat havraa*. Friends of the mourners should provide the food for the *seudat havraa* as an expression of concern for the mourners, and for the purpose of comforting them (לבוש יו״ד שעח:א).
2. If arrangements were not made, the mourners may eat their own food (ט״ז יו״ד שעח ס״ק א).
3. The meal often begins with foods symbolic of mourning, i.e., a hard-boiled egg or lentils, after which the mourner eats a regular meal (יו״ד שעח:ט, ש״ך יו״ד שעח ס״ק ח). Some communities serve wine at this meal (Rabbi Joseph Breuer, based on Sanhedrin 70a). Other communities serve both meat and wine at a *seudat havraa* so that the meal is considered a *seuda ḥashuva* (בשם הרב צבי שכטר).
4. The *seudat havraa* is not served at night if the funeral was held during the preceding day. If the funeral itself was conducted at night, however, a *seudat havraa* is served upon the mourner's return (פתחי תשובה יו״ד שעח ס״ק ב).
5. A *seudat havraa* is not served after the ninth halakhic hour on Friday afternoon or the eve of a holiday (יו״ד שעח:ג,ה).
6. While a mourner may participate in a *zimun* following a *seudat*

havraa, mourners may not join as part of a *minyan* for *Birkat HaMazon* (פתחי תשובה יו״ד שעט ס״ק).

7. If the funeral is conducted on Ḥol HaMoed, the mourners eat the *seudat havraa* while sitting on regular chairs (יו״ד תא:ד).

BIRKAT HAMAZON IN A HOUSE OF MOURNING

Leader Esteemed companions, let us say grace.

Others Blessed be the name of the Lord *Ps. 113*
from now and forevermore.

Leader Blessed be the name of the Lord
from now and forevermore. With your permission, my esteemed companions,
let us bless the One Who comforts mourners,
of Whose bounty we have partaken.

Others Blessed be the One Who comforts mourners,
of Whose bounty we have partaken
and through Whose goodness we live.

**People present who have not taken part in the meal say:*
*Blessed be the One Who comforts mourners,
and Whose name is blessed continually, forever and ever.

Leader Blessed be the One Who comforts mourners,
of Whose bounty we have partaken
and through Whose goodness we live.
Blessed be He, and blessed be His name.

BLESSING OF NOURISHMENT

בָּרוּךְ Blessed are You, Lord our God, King of the universe,
Who feeds the whole world in His goodness,
with grace, kindness, and mercy.
He gives food to all flesh, for His mercy endures forever.
Thanks to His great goodness we have never lacked what to eat.
For the sake of His great name may we never be short of food,
for He is the God Who feeds and sustains all, is good to all,
and provides food for all His creatures as created by Him.
Blessed are You, Lord, Who provides food for all.

ברכת המזון בבית האבל

Leader רַבּוֹתַי, נְבָרֵךְ.

Others יְהִי שֵׁם יהוה מְבֹרָךְ מֵעַתָּה וְעַד־עוֹלָם: תהלים קיג

Leader יְהִי שֵׁם יהוה מְבֹרָךְ מֵעַתָּה וְעַד־עוֹלָם:

בִּרְשׁוּת רַבּוֹתַי, נְבָרֵךְ מְנַחֵם אֲבֵלִים שֶׁאָכַלְנוּ מִשֶּׁלּוֹ.

Others בָּרוּךְ מְנַחֵם אֲבֵלִים, שֶׁאָכַלְנוּ מִשֶּׁלּוֹ וּבְטוּבוֹ חָיִינוּ.

**People present who have not taken part in the meal say:*

*בָּרוּךְ מְנַחֵם אֲבֵלִים, וּמְבֹרָךְ שְׁמוֹ תָּמִיד לְעוֹלָם וָעֶד.

Leader בָּרוּךְ מְנַחֵם אֲבֵלִים, שֶׁאָכַלְנוּ מִשֶּׁלּוֹ וּבְטוּבוֹ חָיִינוּ.

בָּרוּךְ הוּא וּבָרוּךְ שְׁמוֹ.

ברכת הזן

בָּרוּךְ אַתָּה יהוה אֱלֹהֵינוּ מֶלֶךְ הָעוֹלָם
הַזָּן אֶת הָעוֹלָם כֻּלּוֹ בְּטוּבוֹ
בְּחֵן בְּחֶסֶד וּבְרַחֲמִים
הוּא נוֹתֵן לֶחֶם לְכָל בָּשָׂר, כִּי לְעוֹלָם חַסְדּוֹ.
וּבְטוּבוֹ הַגָּדוֹל, תָּמִיד לֹא חָסַר לָנוּ
וְאַל יֶחְסַר לָנוּ מָזוֹן לְעוֹלָם וָעֶד
בַּעֲבוּר שְׁמוֹ הַגָּדוֹל.
כִּי הוּא אֵל זָן וּמְפַרְנֵס לַכֹּל וּמֵטִיב לַכֹּל
וּמֵכִין מָזוֹן לְכָל בְּרִיּוֹתָיו אֲשֶׁר בָּרָא.
בָּרוּךְ אַתָּה יהוה, הַזָּן אֶת הַכֹּל.

BLESSING FOR THE LAND

נוֹדֶה We thank You, LORD our God,
for the beloved, good, and spacious land
that You gave our fathers as an inheritance.
We thank You, LORD our God,
for bringing us out of the land of Egypt
and redeeming us from the house of bondage.
We thank You for Your covenant sealed in our flesh,
for Your Torah which You have taught us,
and for Your precepts that You made known to us.
We thank You also for the life, grace, and kindness
that You have graciously bestowed on us, and for the food we eat,
with which You nourish and sustain us continually,
every day, in every season, and at every hour.

On Ḥanukka:

עַל הַנִּסִּים [We thank You] for the miracles, the deliverance, and the triumphant victories and salvation, as well as wars which You wrought for our ancestors in those days at this season.

בִּימֵי מַתִּתְיָהוּ It happened in the days of Mattathias son of Johanan, the Hasmonean high priest, and his sons. Then the cruel Hellenist power rose up to force Your people Israel to forget Your Torah and transgress the commands of Your will. In that hour of their distress, You in Your great mercy rose to take up their cause and defend their rights. Meting out retribution You delivered the strong into the hand of the weak, the many into the hand of the few, the impure into the hand of the pure, the evil ones into the hand of the righteous, and the wicked into the hand of devotees of Your Torah. You thereby made for Yourself a great and holy name throughout Your world, as well as bringing about great deliverance and salvation for Your people Israel (known) to this day. Then Your children came to the Holy of Holies in Your house, cleared Your Temple, purified Your holy place, kindled lights in Your holy courts, and instituted these eight days of Ḥanukka to give thanks and sing praise to Your great name.

Continue with "For all these."

ברכת הארץ

נוֹדֶה לְּךָ, יהוה אֱלֹהֵינוּ
עַל שֶׁהִנְחַלְתָּ לַאֲבוֹתֵינוּ אֶרֶץ חֶמְדָּה טוֹבָה וּרְחָבָה
וְעַל שֶׁהוֹצֵאתָנוּ יהוה אֱלֹהֵינוּ מֵאֶרֶץ מִצְרַיִם
וּפְדִיתָנוּ מִבֵּית עֲבָדִים
וְעַל בְּרִיתְךָ שֶׁחָתַמְתָּ בִּבְשָׂרֵנוּ
וְעַל תּוֹרָתְךָ שֶׁלִּמַּדְתָּנוּ, וְעַל חֻקֶּיךָ שֶׁהוֹדַעְתָּנוּ
וְעַל חַיִּים חֵן וָחֶסֶד שֶׁחוֹנַנְתָּנוּ
וְעַל אֲכִילַת מָזוֹן שָׁאַתָּה זָן וּמְפַרְנֵס אוֹתָנוּ תָּמִיד
בְּכָל יוֹם וּבְכָל עֵת וּבְכָל שָׁעָה.

בחנוכה:

עַל הַנִּסִּים וְעַל הַפֻּרְקָן וְעַל הַגְּבוּרוֹת וְעַל הַתְּשׁוּעוֹת וְעַל הַמִּלְחָמוֹת שֶׁעָשִׂיתָ לַאֲבוֹתֵינוּ בַּיָּמִים הָהֵם בַּזְּמַן הַזֶּה.

בִּימֵי מַתִּתְיָהוּ בֶּן יוֹחָנָן כֹּהֵן גָּדוֹל חַשְׁמוֹנַאי וּבָנָיו, כְּשֶׁעָמְדָה מַלְכוּת יָוָן הָרְשָׁעָה עַל עַמְּךָ יִשְׂרָאֵל לְהַשְׁכִּיחָם תּוֹרָתֶךָ וּלְהַעֲבִירָם מֵחֻקֵּי רְצוֹנֶךָ, וְאַתָּה בְּרַחֲמֶיךָ הָרַבִּים עָמַדְתָּ לָהֶם בְּעֵת צָרָתָם, רַבְתָּ אֶת רִיבָם, דַּנְתָּ אֶת דִּינָם, נָקַמְתָּ אֶת נִקְמָתָם, מָסַרְתָּ גִּבּוֹרִים בְּיַד חַלָּשִׁים, וְרַבִּים בְּיַד מְעַטִּים, וּטְמֵאִים בְּיַד טְהוֹרִים, וּרְשָׁעִים בְּיַד צַדִּיקִים, וְזֵדִים בְּיַד עוֹסְקֵי תוֹרָתֶךָ, וּלְךָ עָשִׂיתָ שֵׁם גָּדוֹל וְקָדוֹשׁ בְּעוֹלָמֶךָ, וּלְעַמְּךָ יִשְׂרָאֵל עָשִׂיתָ תְּשׁוּעָה גְדוֹלָה וּפֻרְקָן כְּהַיּוֹם הַזֶּה. וְאַחַר כֵּן בָּאוּ בָנֶיךָ לִדְבִיר בֵּיתֶךָ, וּפִנּוּ אֶת הֵיכָלֶךָ, וְטִהֲרוּ אֶת מִקְדָּשֶׁךָ, וְהִדְלִיקוּ נֵרוֹת בְּחַצְרוֹת קָדְשֶׁךָ, וְקָבְעוּ שְׁמוֹנַת יְמֵי חֲנֻכָּה אֵלּוּ, לְהוֹדוֹת וּלְהַלֵּל לְשִׁמְךָ הַגָּדוֹל.

Continue with וְעַל הַכֹּל.

On Purim:

עַל הַנִּסִּים [We thank You] for the miracles, the deliverance, and the triumphant victories and salvation, as well as wars which You wrought for our ancestors in those days at this season.

בִּימֵי מָרְדְּכַי In the days of Mordekhai and Esther, in Shushan the capital, when the wicked Haman rose up against them, he sought to destroy, to kill, and to annihilate all the Jews, young and old, women and infants, in one day, the thirteenth day of the twelfth month, Adar, and plunder their possessions. In Your great mercy You nullified his counsel and subverted his designs, causing them to recoil on his own head so that he and his sons were hanged on the gallows. *Esther 3*

Continue with "For all these."

וְעַל הַכֹּל For all these blessings, Lord our God,
we thank You and bless You.
May Your name be blessed, in the mouths of all living beings,
continually, forever and ever.
As it is written,
"You shall eat and be satisfied, and bless the Lord your God *Deut. 8*
for the good land which He has given you."
Blessed are You, Lord, for the land and for the sustenance.

BLESSING FOR JERUSALEM

רַחֵם (נָא) Have pity (please,) Lord our God,
on Israel Your people, on Jerusalem Your city, and Zion
the dwelling place of Your glory,
on the royal house of David Your anointed,
and on the great and holy Temple
with which Your name is associated.
Our God, our Father,
shepherd us, sustain us, support us,
provide for all our needs,
maintain us, and, Lord our God,
give us immediate relief from all our troubles.

בפורים:

עַל הַנִּסִּים וְעַל הַפֻּרְקָן וְעַל הַגְּבוּרוֹת וְעַל הַתְּשׁוּעוֹת וְעַל הַמִּלְחָמוֹת שֶׁעָשִׂיתָ לַאֲבוֹתֵינוּ בַּיָּמִים הָהֵם בַּזְּמַן הַזֶּה.

בִּימֵי מָרְדְּכַי וְאֶסְתֵּר בְּשׁוּשַׁן הַבִּירָה, כְּשֶׁעָמַד עֲלֵיהֶם הָמָן הָרָשָׁע, בִּקֵּשׁ לְהַשְׁמִיד לַהֲרֹג וּלְאַבֵּד אֶת־כָּל־הַיְּהוּדִים מִנַּעַר וְעַד־זָקֵן טַף וְנָשִׁים בְּיוֹם אֶחָד, בִּשְׁלוֹשָׁה עָשָׂר לְחֹדֶשׁ שְׁנֵים־עָשָׂר, הוּא־חֹדֶשׁ אֲדָר, וּשְׁלָלָם לָבוֹז: וְאַתָּה בְּרַחֲמֶיךָ הָרַבִּים הֵפַרְתָּ אֶת עֲצָתוֹ, וְקִלְקַלְתָּ אֶת מַחֲשַׁבְתּוֹ, וַהֲשֵׁבוֹתָ לּוֹ גְּמוּלוֹ בְּרֹאשׁוֹ, וְתָלוּ אוֹתוֹ וְאֶת בָּנָיו עַל הָעֵץ. אסתר ג

Continue with וְעַל הַכֹּל.

וְעַל הַכֹּל, יהוה אֱלֹהֵינוּ
אֲנַחְנוּ מוֹדִים לָךְ וּמְבָרְכִים אוֹתָךְ
יִתְבָּרַךְ שִׁמְךָ בְּפִי כָּל חַי תָּמִיד לְעוֹלָם וָעֶד
כַּכָּתוּב: וְאָכַלְתָּ וְשָׂבָעְתָּ, וּבֵרַכְתָּ אֶת־יהוה אֱלֹהֶיךָ דברים ח
עַל־הָאָרֶץ הַטֹּבָה אֲשֶׁר נָתַן־לָךְ:
בָּרוּךְ אַתָּה יהוה, עַל הָאָרֶץ וְעַל הַמָּזוֹן.

ברכת ירושלים

רַחֵם (נָא), יהוה אֱלֹהֵינוּ
עַל יִשְׂרָאֵל עַמֶּךָ, וְעַל יְרוּשָׁלַיִם עִירֶךָ
וְעַל צִיּוֹן מִשְׁכַּן כְּבוֹדֶךָ, וְעַל מַלְכוּת בֵּית דָּוִד מְשִׁיחֶךָ
וְעַל הַבַּיִת הַגָּדוֹל וְהַקָּדוֹשׁ שֶׁנִּקְרָא שִׁמְךָ עָלָיו.
אֱלֹהֵינוּ, אָבִינוּ
רְעֵנוּ, זוּנֵנוּ, פַּרְנְסֵנוּ וְכַלְכְּלֵנוּ
וְהַרְוִיחֵנוּ, וְהַרְוַח לָנוּ יהוה אֱלֹהֵינוּ מְהֵרָה מִכָּל צָרוֹתֵינוּ.

Lord our God, do not make us dependent
on the gifts of people of flesh and blood,
or in need of their loans.
Rather let us depend only
on Your full, open, sacred, and bountiful hand,
so that we need never be embarrassed or humiliated.

נַחֵם Comfort, O Lord our God,
the mourners of Jerusalem
and those who mourn here.
Grant them consolation in their mourning
and gladness in their grief,
as it is said,
"As a mother comforts her son, so will I comfort you, *Is. 66*
and in Jerusalem you shall find comfort."
Blessed are You, Lord,
who brings comfort to Zion
through the rebuilding of Jerusalem.
Amen.

בָּרוּךְ Blessed are You, Lord our God, King of the Universe –
God our Father, our King, our Sovereign,
our Creator, our Redeemer, our Maker, our Holy One,
the Holy One of Jacob.
He is our Shepherd, Israel's Sheperd,
our living King who is good and does good,
the true God, the true Judge,
who judges righteously
and takes back souls in judgment.
He rules the world according to His will,
for all His ways are just,

וְנָא אַל תַּצְרִיכֵנוּ, יהוה אֱלֹהֵינוּ
לֹא לִידֵי מַתְּנַת בָּשָׂר וָדָם, וְלֹא לִידֵי הַלְוָאָתָם
כִּי אִם לְיָדְךָ הַמְּלֵאָה, הַפְּתוּחָה, הַקְּדוֹשָׁה וְהָרְחָבָה
שֶׁלֹּא נֵבוֹשׁ וְלֹא נִכָּלֵם לְעוֹלָם וָעֶד.

נַחֵם יהוה אֱלֹהֵינוּ אֶת אֲבֵלֵי יְרוּשָׁלָיִם
וְאֶת הָאֲבֵלִים הַמִּתְאַבְּלִים בָּאֵבֶל הַזֶּה.
נַחֲמֵם מֵאֶבְלָם וְשַׂמְּחֵם מִיגוֹנָם
כָּאָמוּר:
כְּאִישׁ אֲשֶׁר אִמּוֹ תְּנַחֲמֶנּוּ ישעיה סו
כֵּן אָנֹכִי אֲנַחֶמְכֶם וּבִירוּשָׁלַםִ תְּנֻחָמוּ:
בָּרוּךְ אַתָּה יהוה, מְנַחֵם צִיּוֹן בְּבִנְיַן יְרוּשָׁלָיִם.
אָמֵן.

בָּרוּךְ אַתָּה יהוה אֱלֹהֵינוּ מֶלֶךְ הָעוֹלָם
הָאֵל אָבִינוּ מַלְכֵּנוּ אַדִּירֵנוּ
בּוֹרְאֵנוּ גּוֹאֲלֵנוּ יוֹצְרֵנוּ קְדוֹשֵׁנוּ קְדוֹשׁ יַעֲקֹב
רוֹעֵנוּ רוֹעֵה יִשְׂרָאֵל
הַמֶּלֶךְ הַחַי, הַטּוֹב וְהַמֵּטִיב.
אֵל אֱמֶת, דַּיַּן אֱמֶת
שׁוֹפֵט צֶדֶק, לוֹקֵחַ נְפָשׁוֹת בְּמִשְׁפָּט
וְשַׁלִּיט בְּעוֹלָמוֹ לַעֲשׂוֹת בּוֹ כִּרְצוֹנוֹ
כִּי כָל דְּרָכָיו מִשְׁפָּט

and we are His people and His servants.
For everything, we are duty bound to acknowledge and bless Him.
May He who repairs the breaches in Israel,
repair this breach in us and grant us life and peace.
May He always bestow on us
grace, kindness, compassion, and all good things.
Of all that is good, may He never let us lack.

ADDITIONAL REQUESTS

הָרַחֲמָן May the Compassionate One
reign over us forevermore.

May the Compassionate One
be blessed in the heavens and on earth.

May the Compassionate One
be praised in every generation,
and glorified and honored among us for all time, eternally.

May the Compassionate One
maintain us with honor.

May the Compassionate One
break the yoke from our neck
and lead us upright to our land.

May the Compassionate One
send us great blessing on this household
and on this table at which we have eaten.

May the Compassionate One
send us the prophet Elijah –
may he be remembered for good –
to herald good tidings of redemption and consolation.

וַאֲנַחְנוּ עַמּוֹ וַעֲבָדָיו
וְעַל הַכֹּל אֲנַחְנוּ חַיָּבִים לְהוֹדוֹת לוֹ וּלְבָרְכוֹ.
גּוֹדֵר פִּרְצוֹת יִשְׂרָאֵל
הוּא יִגְדֹּר אֶת הַפִּרְצָה הַזֹּאת מֵעָלֵינוּ לְחַיִּים וּלְשָׁלוֹם.
הוּא יִגְמְלֵנוּ לָעַד חֵן וָחֶסֶד וְרַחֲמִים וְכָל טוֹב
וּמִכָּל טוּב לְעוֹלָם אַל יְחַסְּרֵנוּ.

בקשות נוספות

הָרַחֲמָן הוּא יִמְלֹךְ עָלֵינוּ לְעוֹלָם וָעֶד.

הָרַחֲמָן הוּא יִתְבָּרַךְ בַּשָּׁמַיִם וּבָאָרֶץ.

הָרַחֲמָן הוּא יִשְׁתַּבַּח לְדוֹר דּוֹרִים
וְיִתְפָּאַר בָּנוּ לָעַד וּלְנֵצַח נְצָחִים
וְיִתְהַדַּר בָּנוּ לָעַד וּלְעוֹלְמֵי עוֹלָמִים.

הָרַחֲמָן הוּא יְפַרְנְסֵנוּ בְּכָבוֹד.

הָרַחֲמָן הוּא יִשְׁבֹּר עֻלֵּנוּ מֵעַל צַוָּארֵנוּ
וְהוּא יוֹלִיכֵנוּ קוֹמְמִיּוּת לְאַרְצֵנוּ.

הָרַחֲמָן הוּא יִשְׁלַח לָנוּ בְּרָכָה מְרֻבָּה בַּבַּיִת הַזֶּה
וְעַל שֻׁלְחָן זֶה שֶׁאָכַלְנוּ עָלָיו.

הָרַחֲמָן הוּא יִשְׁלַח לָנוּ אֶת אֵלִיָּהוּ הַנָּבִיא זָכוּר לַטּוֹב
וִיבַשֶּׂר לָנוּ בְּשׂוֹרוֹת טוֹבוֹת יְשׁוּעוֹת וְנֶחָמוֹת.

הָרַחֲמָן May the Compassionate One bless –

When eating at one's own table, say
(include the words in parentheses that apply):
me, (my wife/husband, / my father, my teacher /
my mother, my teacher/ my children,)
and all that is mine,

A guest at someone else's table says
(include the words in parentheses that apply):
the head of this household, him (and his wife,
the head of this household / and his children,)
and all that is his,

Children at their parents' table say
(include the words in parentheses that apply):
my father, my teacher, (head of this household,)
and my mother, my teacher, (head of this household,)
them, their household, their children,
and all that is theirs.

For all other guests, add:
and all the diners here,

אוֹתָנוּ – together with us and all that is ours.
Just as our forefathers Abraham, Isaac, and Jacob were blessed
in all, from all, with all,
so may He bless all of us together with a complete blessing,
and let us say: Amen.

בַּמָּרוֹם In heaven may they invoke upon these people
and ourselves sufficient merit to ensure peace,
to bring blessing from the Lord,
and to have the God of our salvation treat us charitably.
May we find grace and good sense
in the eyes of God and man.

הָרַחֲמָן הוּא יְבָרֵךְ

When eating at one's own table, say (include the words in parentheses that apply):

אוֹתִי (וְאֶת אִשְׁתִּי / וְאֶת בַּעֲלִי / וְאֶת אָבִי מוֹרִי /
וְאֶת אִמִּי מוֹרָתִי / וְאֶת זַרְעִי) וְאֶת כָּל אֲשֶׁר לִי.

A guest at someone else's table says (include the words in parentheses that apply):

אֶת בַּעַל הַבַּיִת הַזֶּה, אוֹתוֹ (וְאֶת אִשְׁתּוֹ בַּעֲלַת הַבַּיִת הַזֶּה /
וְאֶת זַרְעוֹ) וְאֶת כָּל אֲשֶׁר לוֹ.

Children at their parents' table say (include the words in parentheses that apply):

אֶת אָבִי מוֹרִי (בַּעַל הַבַּיִת הַזֶּה)
וְאֶת אִמִּי מוֹרָתִי (בַּעֲלַת הַבַּיִת הַזֶּה)
אוֹתָם וְאֶת בֵּיתָם וְאֶת זַרְעָם וְאֶת כָּל אֲשֶׁר לָהֶם

For all other guests, add:

וְאֶת כָּל הַמְסֻבִּין כָּאן

אוֹתָנוּ וְאֶת כָּל אֲשֶׁר לָנוּ, כְּמוֹ שֶׁנִּתְבָּרְכוּ אֲבוֹתֵינוּ
אַבְרָהָם יִצְחָק וְיַעֲקֹב, בַּכֹּל, מִכֹּל, כֹּל
כֵּן יְבָרֵךְ אוֹתָנוּ כֻּלָּנוּ יַחַד בִּבְרָכָה שְׁלֵמָה
וְנֹאמַר אָמֵן.

בַּמָּרוֹם יְלַמְּדוּ עֲלֵיהֶם וְעָלֵינוּ זְכוּת
שֶׁתְּהֵא לְמִשְׁמֶרֶת שָׁלוֹם
וְנִשָּׂא בְרָכָה מֵאֵת יהוה וּצְדָקָה מֵאֱלֹהֵי יִשְׁעֵנוּ
וְנִמְצָא חֵן וְשֵׂכֶל טוֹב בְּעֵינֵי אֱלֹהִים וְאָדָם.

הָרַחֲמָן May the Compassionate One make us worthy of the Messianic Age and the life of the World to Come.
On weekdays: He Who gives great salvation *II Sam. 22*
/ *On Rosh Ḥodesh:* He Who is a tower of salvation /
to His king and shows kindness to His anointed,
to David and his descendants forever.
May He Who makes peace in the highest heaven
make peace for us and for all Israel,
and say, Amen.

יְראוּ Fear the Lord, you His holy ones, *Ps. 34*
for those who fear Him have no lack.
The young lions are poor and hungry,
but those who seek the Lord will not lack any good thing.
Give thanks to the Lord, for He is good, *Ps. 118*
for His loving-kindness is forever.
You open Your hand, *Ps. 145*
and You satisfy the desire of every living thing.
Blessed is the person who trusts in the Lord, *Jer. 17*
whose trust is in the Lord alone.
I was a young man and I have also grown old, *Ps. 37*
but I have not seen a righteous man forsaken
and his seed begging bread.
The Lord will give strength to His people. *Ps. 29*
The Lord will bless His people with peace.

הָרַחֲמָן הוּא יְזַכֵּנוּ לִימוֹת הַמָּשִׁיחַ וּלְחַיֵּי הָעוֹלָם הַבָּא
On weekdays מַגְדִּל/ *On* ראש חודש מִגְדּוֹל/ יְשׁוּעוֹת מַלְכּוֹ שמואל ב׳ כב
וְעֹשֶׂה־חֶסֶד לִמְשִׁיחוֹ, לְדָוִד וּלְזַרְעוֹ עַד־עוֹלָם:
עֹשֶׂה שָׁלוֹם בִּמְרוֹמָיו
הוּא יַעֲשֶׂה שָׁלוֹם עָלֵינוּ וְעַל כָּל יִשְׂרָאֵל
וְאִמְרוּ אָמֵן.

יְראוּ אֶת־יהוה קְדֹשָׁיו, כִּי־אֵין מַחְסוֹר לִירֵאָיו: תהלים לד
כְּפִירִים רָשׁוּ וְרָעֵבוּ
וְדֹרְשֵׁי יהוה לֹא־יַחְסְרוּ כָל־טוֹב:
הוֹדוּ לַיהוה כִּי־טוֹב, כִּי לְעוֹלָם חַסְדּוֹ: תהלים קיח
פּוֹתֵחַ אֶת־יָדֶךָ, וּמַשְׂבִּיעַ לְכָל־חַי רָצוֹן: תהלים קמה
בָּרוּךְ הַגֶּבֶר אֲשֶׁר יִבְטַח בַּיהוה ירמיה יז
וְהָיָה יהוה מִבְטַחוֹ:
נַעַר הָיִיתִי גַּם־זָקַנְתִּי תהלים לז
וְלֹא־רָאִיתִי צַדִּיק נֶעֱזָב וְזַרְעוֹ מְבַקֶּשׁ־לָחֶם:
יהוה עֹז לְעַמּוֹ יִתֵּן, יהוה יְבָרֵךְ אֶת־עַמּוֹ בַשָּׁלוֹם: תהלים כט

THE RABBINIC ROAD: CHALLENGES AND OPPORTUNITIES HAKAMAT MATZEVA

Grief changes over time, but not necessarily in predictable ways. After the passing of a loved one, the effect of time's passage on the mourning process is deeply personal.

- The *hakamat matzeva,* therefore, can be a transitional event fraught with both complex emotions and opportunities for healing. When approached by a family concerning a *hakamat matzeva,* the rabbi should initially review various options and formats available. He should stress that the primary obligation is to erect a proper monument, and that any accompanying ceremony is of secondary importance (see halakhot).
- Special attention should be given to the timing of the event. Days when *Taḥanun* is not recited should be avoided, and every effort should be made to ensure that the monument is in place within twelve months after the individual's passing, even if the ceremony may need to be delayed further.
- The rabbi should be clear in his reassurance that there is no right or wrong way for the unveiling to be conducted, and that the family should shape a ceremony that would be most meaningful to them and to the *niftar* (see halakha section for suggested inclusions, pages 272–73).
- The rabbi should meet with family members in preparation for the *hakamat matzeva,* with an eye toward determining their current state of mind and emotions. Among the issues the rabbi might seek to determine are: How have the mourners experienced the transition from acute to chronic absence? Can the moment of the *hakamat matzeva* become an important step in their bereavement journey?

HAKAMAT MATZEVA

THE OBLIGATION TO ERECT A MONUMENT

1. Erecting a monument over a person's grave is a time-honored tradition. It serves both as an indication of where the grave is located and as a source of honor to the deceased (גשר החיים פרק כח:א-ב).
2. Children have an obligation to erect a monument for a parent, even if there is no inheritance to cover its costs (אג"מ יו"ד ח"ד נ"ז:ה; ע"ע ערוה"ש שמח:ב). Similarly, a husband has an obligation to erect a monument for his wife (אבן העזר פט:א).
3. If there are no children to arrange for a monument, the heirs of the deceased must do so (יו"ד שמח:ב).
4. A monument may also be erected for a child, and even for a fetus, if that is the custom of the community (גשר החיים פרק כח א:ג).

WHEN IS A MONUMENT ERECTED

There are many different opinions as to the ideal time to erect a monument (בצל החכמה ח"ג סימן צז):

A. Immediately following *shiva* (גשר החיים כח:ב; כל בו על אבילות ח"א ה:ג:ב). This is a common practice among Sephardim (חזון עובדיה ח"א עמ' תנב). Others have the custom to build the foundation for a monument after *shiva* and then erect the monument at *sheloshim* (שו"ת מנחת אלעזר ח"ג סימן ל"ז).

B. Immediately following *sheloshim* (שו"ת מהר"ם בריסק ח"ב סימן כ"ט). This is the most common custom in Israel (הלכות אבילות - רי"צ רימון עמ' 59).

C. At the conclusion of the twelve months of mourning (אליה רבה או"ח רכ"ד:ז; ערוה"ש שעו:יא).

THE CEREMONY OF HAKAMAT MATZEVA

1. In pre-war Europe, it was unusual to have a formal gathering to mark a *hakamat matzeva*. Rather, the *ḥevra kaddisha* would

fulfill the family's obligations by placing a monument on the grave without a ceremony. If the placement coincided with a time the family was present (e.g., end of *shiva, sheloshim,* or *yud-bet ḥodesh*), *Tehillim* would be recited (אג"מ ח"ד יו"ד סימן סא:ג; ארחות רבינו ח"ד עמ' שכח).

2. Nevertheless, the custom has developed to dedicate a monument in the presence of family and friends, and to use that event to recite *Tehillim* and offer words of eulogy (כל בו על אבילות ח"א ה:ג:ז), followed by *Kel Maleh* and, if a *minyan* is present, to recite *Kaddish.*
3. Some authorities suggest it is appropriate to study *Mishnayot* at the cemetery during the *hakamat matzeva* (חיים וברכה למשמרת שלום ביה"ק אות יא).
4. If one has not been to a cemetery in the past thirty days, the blessing of *Asher Yatzar Etkhem BaDin* should be recited (או"ח רכד:יב).
5. In America, a custom has arisen to cover the monument with a cloth and to "unveil" it at the *hakamat matzeva* (*Jewish Way in Death and Mourning,* p. 195). Some authorities, however, oppose this "unveiling" as "pure nonsense" (*Madrikh* – Bulka, p. 179).
6. In some communities, after leaving the cemetery following the *hakamat matzeva* ceremony, it is customary for the family to host a meal in gratitude for performing this mitzva (כל בו על אבילות פרק ה ג:ז).

TIMING OF THE HAKAMAT MATZEVA

1. Because an integral part of the *hakamat matzeva* ceremony is a eulogy, or, at the very least, the reading of the inscription on the monument, both actions that evoke sorrow, the *hakamat matzeva* should not occur on days when *Taḥanun* is not recited (מנחת יצחק ח"ג סימן נא).
2. The *hakamat matzeva* should not occur within thirty days before Pesaḥ, Shavuot, or Sukkot (יו"ד שמז:א; לבושי מרדכי יו"ד ב ק"מ).
3. When necessary, there are authorities who permit the *hakamat matzeva* on days when *Taḥanun* is not said if no eulogies are recited. If the *hakamat matzeva* coincides with the end of *shiva,*

sheloshim, or the first *yahrzeit,* these authorities even permit a eulogy to be said within thirty days of a festival (שו״ת קנין תורה בהלכה ח״ב סימן קכב; דבר יהושע ח״ב סימן פ).

WHAT NEEDS TO BE ON A MATZEVA

1. Three key components should be included on a monument: the Hebrew name of the deceased; the date of death; and the abbreviation ת.נ.צ.ב.ה.
2. When writing the deceased's Hebrew name, Ashkenazim include the deceased's father's name (i.e., *ploni ben ploni*). Sephardim include the deceased's mother's name (גשר החיים כח:ג:א). Some communities include both the father's and mother's name (נטעי גבריאל הל׳ אבילות סו:ו).
3. In addition to the Hebrew name, some add the English (non-Jewish) name of the deceased. Many authorities forbid this practice (ציץ אליעזר ח״כ סימן יב; מהר״מ שיק יו״ד סימן קע״א). In communities where it is common to add the English name, however, it is not forbidden (*Jewish Way in Death and Mourning,* p. 191).
4. The Hebrew date of death should be written on the monument (גשר החיים כח:ג:ד). Many authorities forbid the inclusion of secular dates (מהר״ם שיק יו״ד קעא; פרי השדה ח״א סימן ג), while others permit it when it is the custom of the community (כל בו על אבילות פרק ה ג:ה; חיים וברכה למשמרת שלום – מצבה סימן פד).
5. Some include words of praise for the deceased or an appropriate quote. However, hyperbole and extensive praise are to be avoided (פני ברוך לו:ז). In fact, some authorities even eschew titles and other honorifics (מהר״ם שיק יו״ד קעא).
6. Following the inscription, the letters ת.נ.צ.ב.ה. are included (אוצר כל מנהגי ישורון אבילות סימן עב:יז; מהר״ם שיק יו״ד קעא).
7. It is inappropriate to spend large sums on a monument. It is, instead, a greater tribute to the deceased to buy books for a synagogue, or establish a free loan for the poor in his/her memory (חפץ חיים – אהבת חסד פרק טו).

ERECTING A MONUMENT

The service at erecting a memorial monument begins with appropriate readings, of which a few examples follow. In addition, some have the custom to recite the verses from Tehillim 119 which correspond to the deceased's name and the word Neshama. *See page 297 for chapter 119.*

אַשְׁרֵי־הָאִישׁ Happy is the one who does not walk in the counsel of the wicked, who does not stand on the path of sinners, who does not sit among the jeering cynics – instead, the LORD's teaching is all his desire, and he contemplates that teaching day and night. He is like a tree planted on streams of water yielding fruit in its season, its leaves never withering – all it produces thrives. Not so the wicked – they are like chaff blown away by the wind. Therefore, the wicked will not endure judgment, nor the sinners among the righteous crowd. For the LORD cares for the way of the righteous, while the way of the wicked will be lost forever. *Ps. 1*

מִזְמוֹר לְדָוִד A psalm of David. LORD, who may dwell in Your tent? Who may live on Your holy mountain? The one whose ways are blameless, who does what is right, who speaks truth from the heart; the one who has no malice on his tongue, who does no wrong to his fellow, who does not cast a slur against his neighbor; the one who scorns those who are vile, who honors those who fear the LORD, who keeps an oath even when it hurts; the one who does not loan money for interest, who does not take a bribe against the innocent – anyone who acts thus will never be shaken. *Ps. 15*

מִכְתָּם לְדָוִד A mikhtam of David. Protect me, God, for in You I take refuge. I said to the LORD, "You are my Lord; My favor comes from none but You." As for the holy ones in the land, the mighty who were all my delight, may those who court other gods suffer many sorrows – I will not pour out their libations of blood; I will not bear their names on my lips. The LORD is my chosen portion *Ps. 16*

סדר הקמת מצבה

The service at erecting a memorial monument begins with appropriate readings, of which a few examples follow. In addition, some have the custom to recite the verses from תהלים *119 which correspond to the deceased's name and the word* נשמה*.* *See page 297 for chapter 119.*

אַשְׁרֵי־הָאִישׁ אֲשֶׁר לֹא הָלַךְ בַּעֲצַת רְשָׁעִים, וּבְדֶרֶךְ חַטָּאִים תהלים א
לֹא עָמָד, וּבְמוֹשַׁב לֵצִים לֹא יָשָׁב: כִּי אִם בְּתוֹרַת יהוה חֶפְצוֹ,
וּבְתוֹרָתוֹ יֶהְגֶּה יוֹמָם וָלָיְלָה: וְהָיָה כְּעֵץ שָׁתוּל עַל־פַּלְגֵי מָיִם,
אֲשֶׁר פִּרְיוֹ יִתֵּן בְּעִתּוֹ וְעָלֵהוּ לֹא־יִבּוֹל, וְכֹל אֲשֶׁר־יַעֲשֶׂה
יַצְלִיחַ: לֹא־כֵן הָרְשָׁעִים, כִּי אִם־כַּמֹּץ אֲשֶׁר־תִּדְּפֶנּוּ רוּחַ:
עַל־כֵּן לֹא־יָקֻמוּ רְשָׁעִים בַּמִּשְׁפָּט, וְחַטָּאִים בַּעֲדַת צַדִּיקִים:
כִּי־יוֹדֵעַ יהוה דֶּרֶךְ צַדִּיקִים, וְדֶרֶךְ רְשָׁעִים תֹּאבֵד:

מִזְמוֹר לְדָוִד, יהוה מִי־יָגוּר בְּאָהֳלֶךָ, מִי־יִשְׁכֹּן בְּהַר קׇדְשֶׁךָ: תהלים טו
הוֹלֵךְ תָּמִים וּפֹעֵל צֶדֶק, וְדֹבֵר אֱמֶת בִּלְבָבוֹ: לֹא־רָגַל עַל־
לְשֹׁנוֹ לֹא־עָשָׂה לְרֵעֵהוּ רָעָה, וְחֶרְפָּה לֹא־נָשָׂא עַל־קְרֹבוֹ:
נִבְזֶה בְּעֵינָיו נִמְאָס וְאֶת־יִרְאֵי יהוה יְכַבֵּד, נִשְׁבַּע לְהָרַע וְלֹא
יָמִר: כַּסְפּוֹ לֹא־נָתַן בְּנֶשֶׁךְ וְשֹׁחַד עַל־נָקִי לֹא־לָקָח, עֹשֵׂה
אֵלֶּה לֹא יִמּוֹט לְעוֹלָם:

מִכְתָּם לְדָוִד, שָׁמְרֵנִי אֵל כִּי־חָסִיתִי בָךְ: אָמַרְתְּ לַיהוה, אֲדֹנָי תהלים טז
אָתָּה, טוֹבָתִי בַּל־עָלֶיךָ: לִקְדוֹשִׁים אֲשֶׁר־בָּאָרֶץ הֵמָּה, וְאַדִּירֵי
כׇּל־חֶפְצִי־בָם: יִרְבּוּ עַצְּבוֹתָם אַחֵר מָהָרוּ, בַּל־אַסִּיךְ נִסְכֵּיהֶם
מִדָּם, וּבַל־אֶשָּׂא אֶת־שְׁמוֹתָם עַל־שְׂפָתָי: יהוה, מְנָת־חֶלְקִי
וְכוֹסִי, אַתָּה תּוֹמִיךְ גּוֹרָלִי: חֲבָלִים נָפְלוּ־לִי בַּנְּעִמִים, אַף־

and my cup. You direct my fate. A sweet heritage has fallen to my lot; my share is delightful to me. I will bless the Lord who has guided me; even at night, my conscience stirs me. I have set the Lord before me always; He is at my right hand; I shall not be shaken. Therefore my heart is glad, my spirit rejoices, and my body rests secure, for You will not abandon me to Sheol nor let Your devoted one see the Pit. You will teach me the path of life. In Your presence is fullness of joy; at Your right hand, bliss for evermore.

For Ladies:

אֵשֶׁת־חַיִל An exemplary woman who can find? She is more valuable than pearls. *Prov. 31*

Her husband's heart trusts in her; he will lack no benefit.

She will repay his favors, not his insults, in all of her life's circumstances.

She searches for wool and flax, and her hands work adroitly.

She becomes like the merchant ships; she brings her bread from afar.

She rises while it is yet night; she gives sustenance to her household and portions to her maidservants.

When she sets her mind upon a field she buys it; with the fruits of her labor she plants a vineyard.

She girds herself with strength and vigorously exerts her limbs.

When she discerns that her wares are good, her lamp is not extinguished by night.

She sets her hands to the distaff, and her palms grasp the spinning rod.

She stretches out her palm to the poor and extends her hands to the needy.

She need not fear for her household because of snow, for her entire household is clothed in scarlet.

She makes bedcoverings for herself; linen and purple is her garment.

Her husband is well known in the city gates as he sits among the elders of the land.

She makes clothing and sells it and offers belts to the merchant.

Strength and beauty are her garment; she smiles as she faces the future.

נַחֲלָת שָׁפְרָה עָלָי: אֲבָרֵךְ אֶת־יהוה אֲשֶׁר יְעָצָנִי, אַף־לֵילוֹת יִסְּרוּנִי כִלְיוֹתָי: שִׁוִּיתִי יהוה לְנֶגְדִּי תָמִיד, כִּי מִימִינִי בַּל־אֶמּוֹט: לָכֵן שָׂמַח לִבִּי וַיָּגֶל כְּבוֹדִי, אַף־בְּשָׂרִי יִשְׁכֹּן לָבֶטַח: כִּי לֹא־תַעֲזֹב נַפְשִׁי לִשְׁאוֹל, לֹא־תִתֵּן חֲסִידְךָ לִרְאוֹת שָׁחַת: תּוֹדִיעֵנִי אֹרַח חַיִּים, שֹׂבַע שְׂמָחוֹת אֶת־פָּנֶיךָ, נְעִמוֹת בִּימִינְךָ נֶצַח:

For Ladies:

אֵשֶׁת־חַיִל מִי יִמְצָא, וְרָחֹק מִפְּנִינִים מִכְרָהּ: משלי לא
בָּטַח בָּהּ לֵב בַּעְלָהּ, וְשָׁלָל לֹא יֶחְסָר:
גְּמָלַתְהוּ טוֹב וְלֹא־רָע, כֹּל יְמֵי חַיֶּיהָ:
דָּרְשָׁה צֶמֶר וּפִשְׁתִּים, וַתַּעַשׂ בְּחֵפֶץ כַּפֶּיהָ:
הָיְתָה כָּאֳנִיּוֹת סוֹחֵר, מִמֶּרְחָק תָּבִיא לַחְמָהּ:
וַתָּקָם בְּעוֹד לַיְלָה, וַתִּתֵּן טֶרֶף לְבֵיתָהּ, וְחֹק לְנַעֲרֹתֶיהָ:
זָמְמָה שָׂדֶה וַתִּקָּחֵהוּ, מִפְּרִי כַפֶּיהָ נָטְעָה כָּרֶם:
חָגְרָה בְעוֹז מָתְנֶיהָ, וַתְּאַמֵּץ זְרוֹעֹתֶיהָ:
טָעֲמָה כִּי־טוֹב סַחְרָהּ, לֹא־יִכְבֶּה בַלַּיְלָה נֵרָהּ:
יָדֶיהָ שִׁלְּחָה בַכִּישׁוֹר, וְכַפֶּיהָ תָּמְכוּ פָלֶךְ:
כַּפָּהּ פָּרְשָׂה לֶעָנִי, וְיָדֶיהָ שִׁלְּחָה לָאֶבְיוֹן:
לֹא־תִירָא לְבֵיתָהּ מִשָּׁלֶג, כִּי כָל־בֵּיתָהּ לָבֻשׁ שָׁנִים:
מַרְבַדִּים עָשְׂתָה־לָּהּ, שֵׁשׁ וְאַרְגָּמָן לְבוּשָׁהּ:
נוֹדָע בַּשְּׁעָרִים בַּעְלָהּ, בְּשִׁבְתּוֹ עִם־זִקְנֵי־אָרֶץ:
סָדִין עָשְׂתָה וַתִּמְכֹּר, וַחֲגוֹר נָתְנָה לַכְּנַעֲנִי:
עוֹז־וְהָדָר לְבוּשָׁהּ, וַתִּשְׂחַק לְיוֹם אַחֲרוֹן:

She opens her mouth with wisdom, and the teaching of kindness is upon her tongue.
She watches over the conduct of her household, and she does not eat the bread of indolence.
Her children rise up and extol her; so does her husband praise her:
"Many women have excelled, but you have surpassed them all."
Charm is false and beauty – empty breath; a woman who fears the LORD, she is praiseworthy.
Commend her for the fruit of her hands, and let her deeds praise her in the city gates.

Words of eulogy are offered by the Rabbi, and when appropriate by representatives of the family and friends.

MEMORIAL PRAYERS

For a male:

אֵל מָלֵא רַחֲמִים God, full of mercy, Who dwells on high, grant fitting rest beneath (*some say:* above) the protective wings of the Divine Presence, where the souls of the holy and pure ones – whose radiance is like that of the heavens – reside, to the soul of (*name of the deceased*) the son of (*father of the deceased*), who has gone to his eternal reward, insofar as I will make a charitable gift in memory of his soul, may the Garden of Eden be his resting place. For this reason may the ever-merciful One shelter the deceased under His protective wings forever, and may He bind his soul in lasting life. For the LORD will surely be his benefactor, so that he can rest in peace in his allotted place. And let us say, Amen.

For a female:

אֵל מָלֵא רַחֲמִים God, full of mercy, Who dwells on high, grant fitting rest beneath (*some say:* above) the protective wings of the Divine Presence, where the souls of the holy and pure ones – whose radiance is like that of the heavens – reside, to the soul of (*name of the deceased*) the daughter of (*father of the deceased*), who has gone to her eternal reward, insofar as I will make a charitable gift in memory of her soul, may the Garden of Eden be her resting place. For this reason may the ever-merciful One shelter the deceased under His protective wings forever, and may He bind her soul in lasting life. For the LORD will surely be her benefactor, so that she can rest in peace in her allotted place. And let us say, Amen.

פִּיהָ פָּתְחָה בְחָכְמָה, וְתוֹרַת־חֶסֶד עַל־לְשׁוֹנָהּ:
צוֹפִיָּה הֲלִיכוֹת בֵּיתָהּ, וְלֶחֶם עַצְלוּת לֹא תֹאכֵל:
קָמוּ בָנֶיהָ וַיְאַשְּׁרוּהָ, בַּעְלָהּ וַיְהַלְלָהּ:
רַבּוֹת בָּנוֹת עָשׂוּ חָיִל, וְאַתְּ עָלִית עַל־כֻּלָּנָה:
שֶׁקֶר הַחֵן וְהֶבֶל הַיֹּפִי, אִשָּׁה יִרְאַת־יהוה הִיא תִתְהַלָּל:
תְּנוּ־לָהּ מִפְּרִי יָדֶיהָ, וִיהַלְלוּהָ בַשְּׁעָרִים מַעֲשֶׂיהָ:

Words of eulogy are offered by the Rabbi, and when appropriate by representatives of the family and friends.

תפילות אזכרה

For a male:

אֵל מָלֵא רַחֲמִים, שׁוֹכֵן בַּמְּרוֹמִים, הַמְצֵא מְנוּחָה נְכוֹנָה תַּחַת (נ״א עַל) כַּנְפֵי הַשְּׁכִינָה, בְּמַעֲלוֹת קְדוֹשִׁים וּטְהוֹרִים, כְּזֹהַר הָרָקִיעַ מַזְהִירִים, לְנִשְׁמַת (פלוני בֶּן פלוני) שֶׁהָלַךְ לְעוֹלָמוֹ, בַּעֲבוּר שֶׁאֶתֵּן צְדָקָה בְּעַד הַזְכָּרַת נִשְׁמָתוֹ, בְּגַן עֵדֶן תְּהֵא מְנוּחָתוֹ. לָכֵן, בַּעַל הָרַחֲמִים יַסְתִּירֵהוּ בְּסֵתֶר כְּנָפָיו לְעוֹלָמִים, וְיִצְרֹר בִּצְרוֹר הַחַיִּים אֶת נִשְׁמָתוֹ, יהוה הוּא נַחֲלָתוֹ, וְיָנוּחַ בְּשָׁלוֹם עַל מִשְׁכָּבוֹ, וְנֹאמַר אָמֵן.

For a female:

אֵל מָלֵא רַחֲמִים, שׁוֹכֵן בַּמְּרוֹמִים, הַמְצֵא מְנוּחָה נְכוֹנָה תַּחַת (נ״א עַל) כַּנְפֵי הַשְּׁכִינָה, בְּמַעֲלוֹת קְדוֹשִׁים וּטְהוֹרִים, כְּזֹהַר הָרָקִיעַ מַזְהִירִים, לְנִשְׁמַת (פלונית בַּת פלוני) שֶׁהָלְכָה לְעוֹלָמָהּ, בַּעֲבוּר שֶׁאֶתֵּן צְדָקָה בְּעַד הַזְכָּרַת נִשְׁמָתָהּ, בְּגַן עֵדֶן תְּהֵא מְנוּחָתָהּ. לָכֵן, בַּעַל הָרַחֲמִים יַסְתִּירֶהָ בְּסֵתֶר כְּנָפָיו לְעוֹלָמִים, וְיִצְרֹר בִּצְרוֹר הַחַיִּים אֶת נִשְׁמָתָהּ, יהוה הוּא נַחֲלָתָהּ, וְתָנוּחַ בְּשָׁלוֹם עַל מִשְׁכָּבָהּ, וְנֹאמַר אָמֵן.

MOURNER'S KADDISH

Mourner: יִתְגַּדַּל Exalted and hallowed may God's great name be,
in the world He created as He willed.
May He reign in your lifetimes
and in your days, and in the lifetime
of the whole house of Israel,
speedily and soon,
and say, Amen.

All: May His great name be blessed forever and all time.

Mourner: Blessed and praised, honored, extolled,
glorified, adored
and exalted above all
be the name of the Holy One,
blessed is He,
(*Between Rosh Hashana & Yom Kippur:* above and) beyond
any blessing, hymn, praise,
or expressions of consolation
that may be uttered in this world,
and say, Amen.

May abundant peace descend from heaven,
as well as life, for us and for all Israel,
and say, Amen.

Bow, take three steps back, as if taking leave of the Divine Presence, then bow, first left, then right, then center, while saying:

May He Who makes peace in the highest heaven,
make peace for us, and for all Israel,
and say, Amen.

Remain standing in pleace for a few seconds, then take three steps forward.

Those in attendance should place a pebble on the monument upon taking leave of the gravesite.

קדיש יתום

אבל: יִתְגַּדַּל וְיִתְקַדַּשׁ שְׁמֵהּ רַבָּא (קהל: אָמֵן)
בְּעָלְמָא דִּי בְרָא כִרְעוּתֵהּ, וְיַמְלִיךְ מַלְכוּתֵהּ
בְּחַיֵּיכוֹן וּבְיוֹמֵיכוֹן וּבְחַיֵּי דְכָל בֵּית יִשְׂרָאֵל
בַּעֲגָלָא וּבִזְמַן קָרִיב, וְאִמְרוּ אָמֵן. (קהל: אָמֵן)

קהל ואבל: יְהֵא שְׁמֵהּ רַבָּא מְבָרַךְ לְעָלַם וּלְעָלְמֵי עָלְמַיָּא.

אבל: יִתְבָּרַךְ וְיִשְׁתַּבַּח וְיִתְפָּאַר
וְיִתְרוֹמַם וְיִתְנַשֵּׂא וְיִתְהַדָּר וְיִתְעַלֶּה וְיִתְהַלָּל
שְׁמֵהּ דְּקֻדְשָׁא בְּרִיךְ הוּא (קהל: בְּרִיךְ הוּא)
לְעֵלָּא מִן כָּל בִּרְכָתָא
/בעשרת ימי תשובה: לְעֵלָּא לְעֵלָּא מִכָּל בִּרְכָתָא/
וְשִׁירָתָא, תֻּשְׁבְּחָתָא וְנֶחֱמָתָא
דַּאֲמִירָן בְּעָלְמָא, וְאִמְרוּ אָמֵן. (קהל: אָמֵן)

יְהֵא שְׁלָמָא רַבָּא מִן שְׁמַיָּא
וְחַיִּים, עָלֵינוּ וְעַל כָּל יִשְׂרָאֵל, וְאִמְרוּ אָמֵן. (קהל: אָמֵן)

Bow, take three steps back, as if taking leave of the Divine Presence, then bow, first left, then right, then center, while saying:

עֹשֶׂה שָׁלוֹם/ בעשרת ימי תשובה: הַשָּׁלוֹם/ בִּמְרוֹמָיו
הוּא יַעֲשֶׂה שָׁלוֹם
עָלֵינוּ וְעַל כָּל יִשְׂרָאֵל, וְאִמְרוּ אָמֵן. (קהל: אָמֵן)

Remain standing in pleace for a few seconds, then take three steps forward.

Those in attendance should place a pebble on the monument upon taking leave of the gravesite.

THE RABBINIC ROAD: CHALLENGES AND OPPORTUNITIES CONVERSION

The rabbi's role in a conversion to Judaism is to serve both as a gatekeeper - ensuring that the motivation of a conversion candidate is sincere, and as a facilitator – assisting a sincere convert in navigating the complex challenges ahead.

The establishment of the Geirus Protocols and Standards (GPS) network of *batei din* (see Halakha section) removes, in most cases, the rabbi's responsibility for the actual conversion and frees him from the occasional unwanted pressure (via congregants, communal leaders, or others) concerning particular conversions. Nevertheless, the rabbi plays a critical role, as sponsoring rabbi, educator, and advisor to conversion candidates.

- When dealing with prospective converts, the rabbi must remain keenly aware of the power imbalance inherent in the relationship. The candidate is completely dependent upon the rabbi for guidance and assistance through a process which often places the candidate's life on hold. The rabbi must be extremely careful to maintain a professional relationship with the candidate.
- At the initial meeting with a conversion candidate, the rabbi must convey the difficulties entailed in belonging to the Jewish people and accepting the mandates of halakha as described by the *Shulḥan Arukh* YD 268:1. There should neither be commitment to a particular timeline nor to a particular outcome. If the candidate is accompanied by a Jewish significant other, the expectation that this person must also commit to living according to halakha needs to be conveyed.
- If the rabbi is serving as "sponsoring rabbi," he should maintain regular contact with the candidate to monitor progress and deal

with any developing issues or concerns. GPS *batei din* provide a core reading list for conversion candidates. The rabbi can use this list as a guide for study.

- Critical to the prospective convert's education are the experiential opportunities offered by witnessing a Jewish home in action. The rabbi should arrange Shabbat and Yom Tov hospitality with members of the congregation.
- After the conversion is completed, the rabbi should maintain contact with the convert to ensure smooth entry into an appropriate community and to assist in dealing with any questions, issues, or challenges that may arise.

CONVERSION

1. The process of conversion is complex, and should only be entrusted to expert *dayanim* (יבמות מ״ז: ערוה״ש יו״ד רס״ח:ג). The Rabbinical Council of America, together with the Beth Din of America, have established a network of regional *batei din* to facilitate conversions that meet the highest halakhic standards and are accepted worldwide. These *batei din* follow the GPS (Geirus Policies and Standards) protocols (www.judaismconversion.org).
2. Members of a conversion *beit din* must at least be expert in the process of conversion, knowledgeable of the expectations of a convert, and capable of clearly communicating those expectations (אגרות משה יו״ד ח״א סימן קנ״ט, שו״ת מהר״ם שיק יו״ד סימן רמ״ח).
3. The *dayanim* should be present for all stages of the conversion process: *brit mila* (for male converts), acceptance of the mitzvot, and *tevila* (שו״ע יו״ד רסח:ג).
4. When performing a *brit mila* for a male convert, the *mohel* recites two *berakhot*. The first *berakha*, *Al HaMila*, is recited immediately prior to performing the *mila*. The *berakha* of *Boreh Peri HaGafen* is recited immediately afterward and is followed by the closing *berakha* of *Koret HaBrit* (שו״ע יו״ד רסח:ה, ט״ז רסח ס״ק י״ב).
5. If a male convert is already circumcised, the *mohel* performs *hatafat dam brit* and no *berakha* is recited (שו״ע יו״ד רסח:א). There are varying opinions among authorities as to precisely where the incision for *hatafat dam brit* is to be made. Common practice, however, is to make the incision on the *gid* near the *atara* (עיין ספר אוצר הברית ח״ב עמ׳ שמ״ב-שמ״ט).
6. When the conversion candidate is in the water of the mikva immediately prior to immersion, the *dayanim* should review with the conversion candidate: the key aspects of Jewish faith, some major and minor mitzvot, and the reward and punishment for the observance or violation of these mitzvot (שו״ע יו״ד רסח:ב). The

candidate must accept these responsibilities, without exception of even one mitzva or one *minhag* (אגרות משה יו״ד ח״ג סימנים ק״ו, וק״ח).

7. After immersing in the mikva, the convert recites the *berakha* of *Al HaTevila* (שו״ע יו״ד רס״ח:ב).
8. A female convert should wear a loose-fitting robe when immersing in the mikva, so that the *dayanim* can witness her full immersion while maintaining her modesty (שו״ת יביע אומר יו״ד ח״א סימן י״ט, כנס הדיינים תשע״ד הנהלת בתי הדין הרבניים - ירושלים עמ׳ נ״ו סעיף כח). In addition, once the *dayanim* have witnessed her full immersion, if they have the custom to remain in the room until they hear her *berakha,* they should move to a place where they no longer see her, wait to hear her *berakha,* and then leave the room so she can exit the mikva modestly (שו״ע יו״ד רס״ח:ב).
9. A child under the age of bar or bat mitzva (i.e., a *ger katan*) can be converted under the aegis of a *beit din,* on the basis of the principle of *zakhin le'adam shelo befanav* (שו״ע יו״ד רס״ח:ז). Nevertheless, the *beit din* must receive assurances from the parents that the child will be reared in an environment conducive to observance of mitzvot. According to GPS standards, the family must at least belong to an Orthodox synagogue within walking distance, commit to sending the child to a Jewish day school, and observe both *kashrut* and Shabbat (ע״ע אגרות משה אה״ע ח״ד סימן כו:ג, משפטי שאול ס״ס ל״ח, דעת כהן יו״ד קמ״ז).
10. Following a person's conversion, it is incumbent upon the community to extend an added measure of care to the convert; to the extent that the needs of the convert supersede the needs of other Jews (פרי מגדים אשל אברהם או״ח קנו:ב). This special care is called *ahavat hager* and is a positive mitzva from the Torah (רמב״ם הלכות דעות ו:ד, ערוה״ש או״ח קנ״ו:ח).

CONVERSION

If the prospective convert is a male, he is circumcised in the presence of the beit din. At that time, the following blessing is recited by the mohel:

בָּרוּךְ Blessed are You, LORD, our God, King of the universe, Who has sanctified us with His commandments, and has commanded us to circumcise converts.

If the convert has already been circumcised, then only a token covenantal extraction, called 'hatafat dam berit,' is made, and no berakhah is recited. After the circumcision, the following berakhot are recited over a full cup of wine:

בָּרוּךְ Blessed are You, LORD, our God, King of the universe, Who creates the fruit of the vine.

בָּרוּךְ Blessed are You, LORD, our God, King of the universe, Who has sanctified us with His commandments, and has commanded us to circumcise converts and to draw from them the covenantal blood, for without the covenantal blood, heaven and earth could not be sustained, as it is said, 'Only if I had no covenant with day and night, and if I had *Jer. 33* not established the laws of heaven and earth.' Blessed are You, LORD, Who establishes the covenant.

The one who recited the blessings then drinks from the cup of wine. After recovery from circumcision, the convert immerses in the mikva.

For the female convert, the main component of the conversion procedure following her embrace of Jewish belief and practice is immersion in the mikva.

Just prior to immersion, the beit din once again seeks the assurance of the convert (whether male or female) that immersion will be followed by full adherence to Jewish belief and practice. The immersion takes place in the presence of the beit din, who are especially attentive not to compromise the dignity of the immersing convert. The convert must be completely surrounded by the waters of the mikva, but can do this in a loosely fitting garment or covering that simultaneoustly preserves dignity and fulfills the halakhic requirements.

After immersion in the mikva, the following blessing is recited by the convert:

בָּרוּךְ Blessed are You, LORD, our God, King of the universe, Who has sanctified us with His commandments, and has commanded us about ritual immersion.

Following immersion, the convert is welcomed with a special prayer which includes the bestowal of a Jewish name. This prayer is cited in Nahalat Tzevi by HaRav Gedalyah Felder, p. 46

סדר הגיור

If the prospective convert is a male, he is circumcised in the presence of the בית דין*.*
At that time, the following blessing is recited by the מוהל*:*

בָּרוּךְ אַתָּה יהוה אֱלֹהֵינוּ מֶלֶךְ הָעוֹלָם
אֲשֶׁר קִדְּשָׁנוּ בְּמִצְוֹתָיו וְצִוָּנוּ לָמוּל אֶת הַגֵּרִים.

If the convert has already been circumcised, then only a token covenantal extraction, called הטפת דם הברית*, is made, and no* ברכה *is recited. After the circumcision, the following* ברכות *are recited over a full cup of wine:*

בָּרוּךְ אַתָּה יהוה אֱלֹהֵינוּ מֶלֶךְ הָעוֹלָם, בּוֹרֵא פְּרִי הַגָּפֶן.

בָּרוּךְ אַתָּה יהוה אֱלֹהֵינוּ מֶלֶךְ הָעוֹלָם, אֲשֶׁר קִדְּשָׁנוּ בְּמִצְוֹתָיו וְצִוָּנוּ
לָמוּל אֶת הַגֵּרִים וּלְהַטִּיף מֵהֶם דַּם בְּרִית, שֶׁאִלְמָלֵא דַם בְּרִית,
לֹא נִתְקַיְּמוּ שָׁמַיִם וָאָרֶץ, שֶׁנֶּאֱמַר: אִם־לֹא בְרִיתִי יוֹמָם וָלָיְלָה, ירמיה לג
חֻקּוֹת שָׁמַיִם וָאָרֶץ לֹא־שָׂמְתִּי: בָּרוּךְ אַתָּה יהוה, כּוֹרֵת הַבְּרִית.

The one who recited the blessings then drinks from the cup of wine.
After recovery from circumcision, the convert immerses in the mikva.

For the female convert, the main component of the conversion procedure following her embrace of Jewish belief and practice is immersion in the mikva.

Just prior to immersion, the בית דין *once again seeks the assurance of the convert (whether male or female) that immersion will be followed by full adherence to Jewish belief and practice. The immersion takes place in the presence of the* בית דין*, who are especially attentive not to compromise the dignity of the immersing convert. The convert must be completely surrounded by the waters of the mikva, but can do this in a loosely fitting garment or covering that simultaneoustly preserves dignity and fulfills the halakhic requirements.*

After immersion in the mikva, the following ברכה *is recited by the convert:*

בָּרוּךְ אַתָּה יהוה אֱלֹהֵינוּ מֶלֶךְ הָעוֹלָם
אֲשֶׁר קִדְּשָׁנוּ בְּמִצְוֹתָיו וְצִוָּנוּ עַל הַטְּבִילָה.

Following immersion, the convert is welcomed with a special prayer which includes the bestowal of a Jewish name. This prayer is cited in נחלת צבי *by HaRav Gedalyah Felder, p. 46*

For males:

אֱלֹהֵינוּ Our God and the God of our fathers, assure the continuing success of this convert whose name is called in Israel (*convert's Hebrew name*) son of our father Abraham and spread over him Your loving-kindness. Just as You have caused him to merit standing on the threshold and being protected under Your wings, so may You plant in his heart the love and awe of God, and open his heart with Your Torah. Guide him in the path of Your commandments to do Your will in order to find favor in Your eyes. Amen, thus may it be Your will.

For females:

אֱלֹהֵינוּ Our God and the God of our fathers, assure the continuing success of this convert whose name is called in Israel (*convert's Hebrew name*) daughter of our father Abraham and spread over her Your loving-kindness. Just as You have caused her to merit standing on the threshold and being protected under Your wings, so may You plant in her heart the love and awe of God, and open her heart with Your Torah. Guide her in the path of Your commandments to do Your will in order to find favor in Your eyes. Amen, thus may it be Your will.

It is fitting that following the completion of the conversion procedure, a male convert should don tallit and tefillin. Both male and female converts should recite the Shema affirmation of faith.

Hear, O Israel, the LORD is our God, the LORD is One. *Deut. 6*

Quietly: Blessed is the name of His glorious kingdom forever and ever.

וְאָהַבְתָּ You shall love the LORD your God with all your heart, and with all your soul, and with all your might. And these words which I command you this day shall be upon your heart. You shall teach them diligently to your children, speaking of them when you sit in your house and when you walk by the way, when you lie down and when you rise up. You shall bind them for a sign on your hand, and they shall be as *tefillin* between your eyes. And you shall write them upon the doorposts of your house and upon your gates. *Deut. 6*

Conversion is a joyous event, and should be celebrated in an appropriate, religiously meaningful fashion, such as by a Kiddush in shul or at a home, accompanied by fitting words of Torah by the convert and the supervising Rabbi.

For males:

אֱלֹהֵינוּ וֵאלֹהֵי אֲבוֹתֵינוּ, הַצְלַח נָא לַגֵּר הַזֶּה הַנִּקְרָא שְׁמוֹ בְּיִשְׂרָאֵל (שמו) בֶּן אַבְרָהָם אָבִינוּ, וּמְשֹׁךְ עָלָיו חַסְדֶּךָ. וּכְשֵׁם שֶׁזִּכִּיתָ אוֹתוֹ לְהִסְתּוֹפֵף וְלַחֲסוֹת תַּחַת כְּנָפֶיךָ, כֵּן תִּטַּע בְּלִבּוֹ אַהֲבָתְךָ וְיִרְאָתְךָ וְתִפְתַּח לִבּוֹ בְּתוֹרָתֶךָ, וְתַדְרִיכֵהוּ בִּנְתִיב מִצְוֹתֶיךָ וְלַעֲשׂוֹת רְצוֹנְךָ לְמַעַן יִמְצָא חֵן בְּעֵינֶיךָ. אָמֵן, כֵּן יְהִי רָצוֹן.

For females:

אֱלֹהֵינוּ וֵאלֹהֵי אֲבוֹתֵינוּ, הַצְלַח נָא לַגִּיּוֹרֶת הַזֹּאת שֶׁנִּקְרָא שְׁמָהּ בְּיִשְׂרָאֵל (שמה) בַּת אַבְרָהָם אָבִינוּ, וּמְשֹׁךְ עָלֶיהָ חַסְדֶּךָ. וּכְשֵׁם שֶׁזִּכִּיתָ אוֹתָהּ לְהִסְתּוֹפֵף וְלַחֲסוֹת תַּחַת כְּנָפֶיךָ, כֵּן תִּטַּע בְּלִבָּהּ אַהֲבָתְךָ וְיִרְאָתְךָ וְתִפְתַּח לִבָּהּ בְּתוֹרָתֶךָ, וְתַדְרִיכֶהָ בִּנְתִיב מִצְוֹתֶיךָ וְלַעֲשׂוֹת רְצוֹנְךָ לְמַעַן תִּמְצָא חֵן בְּעֵינֶיךָ. אָמֵן, כֵּן יְהִי רָצוֹן.

It is fitting that following the completion of the conversion procedure, a male convert should don טלית *and* תפילין*. Both male and female converts should recite the* שמע *affirmation of faith.*

דברים ו **שְׁמַע יִשְׂרָאֵל, יהוה אֱלֹהֵינוּ, יהוה ׀ אֶחָד:**

Quietly בָּרוּךְ שֵׁם כְּבוֹד מַלְכוּתוֹ לְעוֹלָם וָעֶד.

דברים ו וְאָהַבְתָּ אֵת יהוה אֱלֹהֶיךָ, בְּכָל־לְבָבְךָ וּבְכָל־נַפְשְׁךָ וּבְכָל־מְאֹדֶךָ: וְהָיוּ הַדְּבָרִים הָאֵלֶּה, אֲשֶׁר אָנֹכִי מְצַוְּךָ הַיּוֹם, עַל־לְבָבֶךָ: וְשִׁנַּנְתָּם לְבָנֶיךָ וְדִבַּרְתָּ בָּם, בְּשִׁבְתְּךָ בְּבֵיתֶךָ וּבְלֶכְתְּךָ בַדֶּרֶךְ, וּבְשָׁכְבְּךָ וּבְקוּמֶךָ: וּקְשַׁרְתָּם לְאוֹת עַל־יָדֶךָ וְהָיוּ לְטֹטָפֹת בֵּין עֵינֶיךָ: וּכְתַבְתָּם עַל־מְזֻזוֹת בֵּיתֶךָ וּבִשְׁעָרֶיךָ:

Conversion is a joyous event, and should be celebrated in an appropriate, religiously meaningful fashion, such as by a קידוש *in shul or at a home, accompanied by fitting words of* תורה *by the convert and the supervising Rabbi.*

מזמורי תהלים נבחרים
SELECTED PSALMS

ט לַמְנַצֵּחַ עַל־מוּת לַבֵּן מִזְמוֹר לְדָוִד׃ אוֹדֶה יהוה בְּכׇל־לִבִּי אֲסַפְּרָה
כׇּל־נִפְלְאוֹתֶיךָ׃ אֶשְׂמְחָה וְאֶעֶלְצָה בָךְ אֲזַמְּרָה שִׁמְךָ עֶלְיוֹן׃ בְּשׁוּב־
אוֹיְבַי אָחוֹר יִכָּשְׁלוּ וְיֹאבְדוּ מִפָּנֶיךָ׃ כִּי־עָשִׂיתָ מִשְׁפָּטִי וְדִינִי יָשַׁבְתָּ
לְכִסֵּא שׁוֹפֵט צֶדֶק׃ גָּעַרְתָּ גוֹיִם אִבַּדְתָּ רָשָׁע שְׁמָם מָחִיתָ לְעוֹלָם
וָעֶד׃ הָאוֹיֵב ׀ תַּמּוּ חֳרָבוֹת לָנֶצַח וְעָרִים נָתַשְׁתָּ אָבַד זִכְרָם הֵמָּה׃
וַיהוה לְעוֹלָם יֵשֵׁב כּוֹנֵן לַמִּשְׁפָּט כִּסְאוֹ׃ וְהוּא יִשְׁפֹּט־תֵּבֵל בְּצֶדֶק
יָדִין לְאֻמִּים בְּמֵישָׁרִים׃ וִיהִי יהוה מִשְׂגָּב לַדָּךְ מִשְׂגָּב לְעִתּוֹת
בַּצָּרָה׃ וְיִבְטְחוּ בְךָ יוֹדְעֵי שְׁמֶךָ כִּי לֹא־עָזַבְתָּ דֹרְשֶׁיךָ יהוה׃
זַמְּרוּ לַיהוה יֹשֵׁב צִיּוֹן הַגִּידוּ בָעַמִּים עֲלִילוֹתָיו׃ כִּי־דֹרֵשׁ דָּמִים
עֲנָוִים אוֹתָם זָכָר לֹא־שָׁכַח צַעֲקַת עניים׃ חׇנְנֵנִי יהוה רְאֵה עׇנְיִי מִשֹּׂנְאָי
מְרוֹמְמִי מִשַּׁעֲרֵי־מָוֶת׃ לְמַעַן אֲסַפְּרָה כׇּל־תְּהִלָּתֶיךָ בְּשַׁעֲרֵי
בַת־צִיּוֹן אָגִילָה בִּישׁוּעָתֶךָ׃ טָבְעוּ גוֹיִם בְּשַׁחַת עָשׂוּ בְּרֶשֶׁת־זוּ
טָמָנוּ נִלְכְּדָה רַגְלָם׃ נוֹדַע ׀ יהוה מִשְׁפָּט עָשָׂה בְּפֹעַל כַּפָּיו נוֹקֵשׁ
רָשָׁע הִגָּיוֹן סֶלָה׃ יָשׁוּבוּ רְשָׁעִים לִשְׁאוֹלָה כׇּל־גּוֹיִם שְׁכֵחֵי אֱלֹהִים׃
עֲנִיִּים כִּי לֹא לָנֶצַח יִשָּׁכַח אֶבְיוֹן תִּקְוַת ענוים תֹּאבַד לָעַד׃ קוּמָה יהוה
אַל־יָעֹז אֱנוֹשׁ יִשָּׁפְטוּ גוֹיִם עַל־פָּנֶיךָ׃ שִׁיתָה יהוה ׀ מוֹרָה לָהֶם
יֵדְעוּ גוֹיִם אֱנוֹשׁ הֵמָּה סֶּלָה׃

יג לַמְנַצֵּחַ מִזְמוֹר לְדָוִד׃ עַד־אָנָה יהוה תִּשְׁכָּחֵנִי נֶצַח עַד־אָנָה ׀
תַּסְתִּיר אֶת־פָּנֶיךָ מִמֶּנִּי׃ עַד־אָנָה אָשִׁית עֵצוֹת בְּנַפְשִׁי יָגוֹן בִּלְבָבִי
יוֹמָם עַד־אָנָה ׀ יָרוּם אֹיְבִי עָלָי׃ הַבִּיטָה עֲנֵנִי יהוה אֱלֹהָי הָאִירָה
עֵינַי פֶּן־אִישַׁן הַמָּוֶת׃ פֶּן־יֹאמַר אֹיְבִי יְכׇלְתִּיו צָרַי יָגִילוּ כִּי אֶמּוֹט׃

וַאֲנִי ׀ בְּחַסְדְּךָ בָטַחְתִּי יָגֵל לִבִּי בִּישׁוּעָתֶךָ אָשִׁירָה לַיהוָה כִּי
גָמַל עָלָי׃

כ לַמְנַצֵּחַ מִזְמוֹר לְדָוִד׃ יַעַנְךָ יהוה בְּיוֹם צָרָה יְשַׂגֶּבְךָ שֵׁם ׀ אֱלֹהֵי
יַעֲקֹב׃ יִשְׁלַח־עֶזְרְךָ מִקֹּדֶשׁ וּמִצִּיּוֹן יִסְעָדֶךָּ׃ יִזְכֹּר כָּל־מִנְחֹתֶךָ
וְעוֹלָתְךָ יְדַשְּׁנֶה סֶלָה׃ יִתֶּן־לְךָ כִלְבָבֶךָ וְכָל־עֲצָתְךָ יְמַלֵּא׃ נְרַנְּנָה ׀
בִּישׁוּעָתֶךָ וּבְשֵׁם־אֱלֹהֵינוּ נִדְגֹּל יְמַלֵּא יהוה כָּל־מִשְׁאֲלוֹתֶיךָ׃ עַתָּה
יָדַעְתִּי כִּי הוֹשִׁיעַ ׀ יהוה מְשִׁיחוֹ יַעֲנֵהוּ מִשְּׁמֵי קָדְשׁוֹ בִּגְבוּרוֹת יֵשַׁע
יְמִינוֹ׃ אֵלֶּה בָרֶכֶב וְאֵלֶּה בַסּוּסִים וַאֲנַחְנוּ ׀ בְּשֵׁם־יְהוָה אֱלֹהֵינוּ
נַזְכִּיר׃ הֵמָּה כָּרְעוּ וְנָפָלוּ וַאֲנַחְנוּ קַּמְנוּ וַנִּתְעוֹדָד׃ יְהוָה הוֹשִׁיעָה
הַמֶּלֶךְ יַעֲנֵנוּ בְיוֹם־קָרְאֵנוּ׃

כד לְדָוִד מִזְמוֹר לַיהוָה הָאָרֶץ וּמְלוֹאָהּ תֵּבֵל וְיֹשְׁבֵי בָהּ׃ כִּי־הוּא עַל־
יַמִּים יְסָדָהּ וְעַל־נְהָרוֹת יְכוֹנְנֶהָ׃ מִי־יַעֲלֶה בְהַר־יְהוָה וּמִי־יָקוּם
בִּמְקוֹם קָדְשׁוֹ׃ נְקִי כַפַּיִם וּבַר־לֵבָב אֲשֶׁר לֹא־נָשָׂא לַשָּׁוְא נַפְשׁוֹ נַפְשִׁי
וְלֹא נִשְׁבַּע לְמִרְמָה׃ יִשָּׂא בְרָכָה מֵאֵת יְהוָה וּצְדָקָה מֵאֱלֹהֵי יִשְׁעוֹ׃
זֶה דּוֹר דֹּרְשָׁו מְבַקְשֵׁי פָנֶיךָ יַעֲקֹב סֶלָה׃ שְׂאוּ שְׁעָרִים ׀ רָאשֵׁיכֶם
וְהִנָּשְׂאוּ פִּתְחֵי עוֹלָם וְיָבוֹא מֶלֶךְ הַכָּבוֹד׃ מִי זֶה מֶלֶךְ הַכָּבוֹד יהוה
עִזּוּז וְגִבּוֹר יהוה גִּבּוֹר מִלְחָמָה׃ שְׂאוּ שְׁעָרִים ׀ רָאשֵׁיכֶם וּשְׂאוּ
פִּתְחֵי עוֹלָם וְיָבֹא מֶלֶךְ הַכָּבוֹד׃ מִי הוּא זֶה מֶלֶךְ הַכָּבוֹד יְהוָה
צְבָאוֹת הוּא מֶלֶךְ הַכָּבוֹד סֶלָה׃

כח לְדָוִד אֵלֶיךָ יְהוָה ׀ אֶקְרָא צוּרִי אַל־תֶּחֱרַשׁ מִמֶּנִּי פֶּן־תֶּחֱשֶׁה
מִמֶּנִּי וְנִמְשַׁלְתִּי עִם־יוֹרְדֵי בוֹר׃ שְׁמַע קוֹל תַּחֲנוּנַי בְּשַׁוְּעִי אֵלֶיךָ
בְּנָשְׂאִי יָדַי אֶל־דְּבִיר קָדְשֶׁךָ׃ אַל־תִּמְשְׁכֵנִי עִם־רְשָׁעִים וְעִם־פֹּעֲלֵי
אָוֶן דֹּבְרֵי שָׁלוֹם עִם־רֵעֵיהֶם וְרָעָה בִּלְבָבָם׃ תֶּן־לָהֶם כְּפָעֳלָם

וּכְרֹעַ מַעַלְלֵיהֶם כְּמַעֲשֵׂה יְדֵיהֶם תֵּן לָהֶם הָשֵׁב גְּמוּלָם לָהֶם׃ כִּי
לֹא יָבִינוּ אֶל־פְּעֻלֹּת יְהוָה וְאֶל־מַעֲשֵׂה יָדָיו יֶהֶרְסֵם וְלֹא יִבְנֵם׃
בָּרוּךְ יְהוָה כִּי־שָׁמַע קוֹל תַּחֲנוּנָי׃ יְהוָה ׀ עֻזִּי וּמָגִנִּי בּוֹ בָטַח לִבִּי
וְנֶעֱזָרְתִּי וַיַּעֲלֹז לִבִּי וּמִשִּׁירִי אֲהוֹדֶנּוּ׃ יְהוָה עֹז־לָמוֹ וּמָעוֹז יְשׁוּעוֹת
מְשִׁיחוֹ הוּא׃ הוֹשִׁיעָה ׀ אֶת־עַמֶּךָ וּבָרֵךְ אֶת־נַחֲלָתֶךָ וּרְעֵם וְנַשְּׂאֵם
עַד־הָעוֹלָם׃

ל מִזְמוֹר שִׁיר־חֲנֻכַּת הַבַּיִת לְדָוִד׃ אֲרוֹמִמְךָ יְהוָה כִּי דִלִּיתָנִי וְלֹא־
שִׂמַּחְתָּ אֹיְבַי לִי׃ יְהוָה אֱלֹהָי שִׁוַּעְתִּי אֵלֶיךָ וַתִּרְפָּאֵנִי׃ יְהוָה הֶעֱלִיתָ
מִן־שְׁאוֹל נַפְשִׁי חִיִּיתַנִי מיורדי־בוֹר׃ זַמְּרוּ לַיהוָה חֲסִידָיו וְהוֹדוּ מִיָּרְדִי־
לְזֵכֶר קָדְשׁוֹ׃ כִּי רֶגַע ׀ בְּאַפּוֹ חַיִּים בִּרְצוֹנוֹ בָּעֶרֶב יָלִין בֶּכִי וְלַבֹּקֶר
רִנָּה׃ וַאֲנִי אָמַרְתִּי בְשַׁלְוִי בַּל־אֶמּוֹט לְעוֹלָם׃ יְהוָה בִּרְצוֹנְךָ
הֶעֱמַדְתָּה לְהַרְרִי עֹז הִסְתַּרְתָּ פָנֶיךָ הָיִיתִי נִבְהָל׃ אֵלֶיךָ יְהוָה
אֶקְרָא וְאֶל־אֲדֹנָי אֶתְחַנָּן׃ מַה־בֶּצַע בְּדָמִי בְּרִדְתִּי אֶל שָׁחַת
הֲיוֹדְךָ עָפָר הֲיַגִּיד אֲמִתֶּךָ׃ שְׁמַע־יְהוָה וְחָנֵּנִי יְהוָה הֱיֵה־עֹזֵר לִי׃
הָפַכְתָּ מִסְפְּדִי לְמָחוֹל לִי פִּתַּחְתָּ שַׂקִּי וַתְּאַזְּרֵנִי שִׂמְחָה׃ לְמַעַן ׀
יְזַמֶּרְךָ כָבוֹד וְלֹא יִדֹּם יְהוָה אֱלֹהַי לְעוֹלָם אוֹדֶךָּ׃

מט לַמְנַצֵּחַ לִבְנֵי־קֹרַח מִזְמוֹר׃ שִׁמְעוּ־זֹאת כָּל־הָעַמִּים הַאֲזִינוּ כָּל־
יֹשְׁבֵי חָלֶד׃ גַּם־בְּנֵי אָדָם גַּם־בְּנֵי־אִישׁ יַחַד עָשִׁיר וְאֶבְיוֹן׃ פִּי יְדַבֵּר
חָכְמוֹת וְהָגוּת לִבִּי תְבוּנוֹת׃ אַטֶּה לְמָשָׁל אָזְנִי אֶפְתַּח בְּכִנּוֹר
חִידָתִי׃ לָמָּה אִירָא בִּימֵי רָע עֲוֺן עֲקֵבַי יְסוּבֵּנִי׃ הַבֹּטְחִים עַל־
חֵילָם וּבְרֹב עָשְׁרָם יִתְהַלָּלוּ׃ אָח לֹא־פָדֹה יִפְדֶּה אִישׁ לֹא־
יִתֵּן לֵאלֹהִים כָּפְרוֹ׃ וְיֵקַר פִּדְיוֹן נַפְשָׁם וְחָדַל לְעוֹלָם׃ וִיחִי־עוֹד
לָנֶצַח לֹא יִרְאֶה הַשָּׁחַת׃ כִּי יִרְאֶה ׀ חֲכָמִים יָמוּתוּ יַחַד כְּסִיל וָבַעַר
יֹאבֵדוּ וְעָזְבוּ לַאֲחֵרִים חֵילָם׃ קִרְבָּם בָּתֵּימוֹ ׀ לְעוֹלָם מִשְׁכְּנֹתָם

לְדֹר וָדֹר קָרְאוּ בִשְׁמוֹתָם עֲלֵי אֲדָמוֹת: וְאָדָם בִּיקָר בַּל־יָלִין
נִמְשַׁל כַּבְּהֵמוֹת נִדְמוּ: זֶה דַרְכָּם כֵּסֶל לָמוֹ וְאַחֲרֵיהֶם ׀ בְּפִיהֶם
יִרְצוּ סֶלָה: כַּצֹּאן ׀ לִשְׁאוֹל שַׁתּוּ מָוֶת יִרְעֵם וַיִּרְדּוּ בָם יְשָׁרִים ׀
לַבֹּקֶר וצירם לְבַלּוֹת שְׁאוֹל מִזְּבֻל לוֹ: אַךְ־אֱלֹהִים יִפְדֶּה נַפְשִׁי וְצוּרָם
מִיַּד שְׁאוֹל כִּי יִקָּחֵנִי סֶלָה: אַל־תִּירָא כִּי־יַעֲשִׁר אִישׁ כִּי־יִרְבֶּה
כְּבוֹד בֵּיתוֹ: כִּי לֹא בְמוֹתוֹ יִקַּח הַכֹּל לֹא־יֵרֵד אַחֲרָיו כְּבוֹדוֹ: כִּי־
נַפְשׁוֹ בְּחַיָּיו יְבָרֵךְ וְיוֹדֻךָ כִּי־תֵיטִיב לָךְ: תָּבוֹא עַד־דּוֹר אֲבוֹתָיו
עַד־נֵצַח לֹא יִרְאוּ־אוֹר: אָדָם בִּיקָר וְלֹא יָבִין נִמְשַׁל כַּבְּהֵמוֹת
נִדְמוּ:

צא יֹשֵׁב בְּסֵתֶר עֶלְיוֹן בְּצֵל שַׁדַּי יִתְלוֹנָן: אֹמַר לַיהוה מַחְסִי וּמְצוּדָתִי
אֱלֹהַי אֶבְטַח־בּוֹ: כִּי הוּא יַצִּילְךָ מִפַּח יָקוּשׁ מִדֶּבֶר הַוּוֹת:
בְּאֶבְרָתוֹ ׀ יָסֶךְ לָךְ וְתַחַת־כְּנָפָיו תֶּחְסֶה צִנָּה וְסֹחֵרָה אֲמִתּוֹ:
לֹא־תִירָא מִפַּחַד לָיְלָה מֵחֵץ יָעוּף יוֹמָם: מִדֶּבֶר בָּאֹפֶל יַהֲלֹךְ
מִקֶּטֶב יָשׁוּד צָהֳרָיִם: יִפֹּל מִצִּדְּךָ ׀ אֶלֶף וּרְבָבָה מִימִינֶךָ אֵלֶיךָ
לֹא יִגָּשׁ: רַק בְּעֵינֶיךָ תַבִּיט וְשִׁלֻּמַת רְשָׁעִים תִּרְאֶה: כִּי־אַתָּה
יהוה מַחְסִי עֶלְיוֹן שַׂמְתָּ מְעוֹנֶךָ: לֹא־תְאֻנֶּה אֵלֶיךָ רָעָה וְנֶגַע
לֹא־יִקְרַב בְּאָהֳלֶךָ: כִּי מַלְאָכָיו יְצַוֶּה־לָּךְ לִשְׁמָרְךָ בְּכָל־דְּרָכֶיךָ:
עַל־כַּפַּיִם יִשָּׂאוּנְךָ פֶּן־תִּגֹּף בָּאֶבֶן רַגְלֶךָ: עַל־שַׁחַל וָפֶתֶן תִּדְרֹךְ
תִּרְמֹס כְּפִיר וְתַנִּין: כִּי בִי חָשַׁק וַאֲפַלְּטֵהוּ אֲשַׂגְּבֵהוּ כִּי־יָדַע שְׁמִי:
יִקְרָאֵנִי ׀ וְאֶעֱנֵהוּ עִמּוֹ־אָנֹכִי בְצָרָה אֲחַלְּצֵהוּ וַאֲכַבְּדֵהוּ: אֹרֶךְ יָמִים
אַשְׂבִּיעֵהוּ וְאַרְאֵהוּ בִּישׁוּעָתִי:

קיט אַשְׁרֵי תְמִימֵי־דָרֶךְ הַהֹלְכִים בְּתוֹרַת יהוה: אַשְׁרֵי נֹצְרֵי עֵדֹתָיו
בְּכָל־לֵב יִדְרְשׁוּהוּ: אַף לֹא־פָעֲלוּ עַוְלָה בִּדְרָכָיו הָלָכוּ: אַתָּה
צִוִּיתָה פִקֻּדֶיךָ לִשְׁמֹר מְאֹד: אַחֲלַי יִכֹּנוּ דְרָכָי לִשְׁמֹר חֻקֶּיךָ: אָז

לֹא־אֵבוֹשׁ בְּהַבִּיטִי אֶל־כָּל־מִצְוֺתֶיךָ׃ אוֹדְךָ בְּיֹשֶׁר לֵבָב בְּלָמְדִי
מִשְׁפְּטֵי צִדְקֶךָ׃ אֶת־חֻקֶּיךָ אֶשְׁמֹר אַל־תַּעַזְבֵנִי עַד־מְאֹד׃

בַּמֶּה יְזַכֶּה־נַּעַר אֶת־אָרְחוֹ לִשְׁמֹר כִּדְבָרֶךָ׃ בְּכָל־לִבִּי דְרַשְׁתִּיךָ
אַל־תַּשְׁגֵּנִי מִמִּצְוֺתֶיךָ׃ בְּלִבִּי צָפַנְתִּי אִמְרָתֶךָ לְמַעַן לֹא אֶחֱטָא־לָךְ׃
בָּרוּךְ אַתָּה יְהוָה לַמְּדֵנִי חֻקֶּיךָ׃ בִּשְׂפָתַי סִפַּרְתִּי כֹּל מִשְׁפְּטֵי־פִיךָ׃
בְּדֶרֶךְ עֵדְוֺתֶיךָ שַׂשְׂתִּי כְּעַל כָּל־הוֹן׃ בְּפִקֻּדֶיךָ אָשִׂיחָה וְאַבִּיטָה
אֹרְחֹתֶיךָ׃ בְּחֻקֹּתֶיךָ אֶשְׁתַּעֲשָׁע לֹא אֶשְׁכַּח דְּבָרֶךָ׃

גְּמֹל עַל־עַבְדְּךָ אֶחְיֶה וְאֶשְׁמְרָה דְבָרֶךָ׃ גַּל־עֵינַי וְאַבִּיטָה נִפְלָאוֹת
מִתּוֹרָתֶךָ׃ גֵּר אָנֹכִי בָאָרֶץ אַל־תַּסְתֵּר מִמֶּנִּי מִצְוֺתֶיךָ׃ גָּרְסָה
נַפְשִׁי לְתַאֲבָה אֶל־מִשְׁפָּטֶיךָ בְכָל־עֵת׃ גָּעַרְתָּ זֵדִים אֲרוּרִים
הַשֹּׁגִים מִמִּצְוֺתֶיךָ׃ גַּל מֵעָלַי חֶרְפָּה וָבוּז כִּי עֵדֹתֶיךָ נָצָרְתִּי׃ גַּם
יָשְׁבוּ שָׂרִים בִּי נִדְבָּרוּ עַבְדְּךָ יָשִׂיחַ בְּחֻקֶּיךָ׃ גַּם־עֵדֹתֶיךָ שַׁעֲשֻׁעָי
אַנְשֵׁי עֲצָתִי׃

דָּבְקָה לֶעָפָר נַפְשִׁי חַיֵּנִי כִּדְבָרֶךָ׃ דְּרָכַי סִפַּרְתִּי וַתַּעֲנֵנִי לַמְּדֵנִי
חֻקֶּיךָ׃ דֶּרֶךְ־פִּקּוּדֶיךָ הֲבִינֵנִי וְאָשִׂיחָה בְּנִפְלְאוֹתֶיךָ׃ דָּלְפָה נַפְשִׁי
מִתּוּגָה קַיְּמֵנִי כִּדְבָרֶךָ׃ דֶּרֶךְ־שֶׁקֶר הָסֵר מִמֶּנִּי וְתוֹרָתְךָ חָנֵּנִי׃
דֶּרֶךְ־אֱמוּנָה בָחָרְתִּי מִשְׁפָּטֶיךָ שִׁוִּיתִי׃ דָּבַקְתִּי בְעֵדְוֺתֶיךָ יְהוָה
אַל־תְּבִישֵׁנִי׃ דֶּרֶךְ־מִצְוֺתֶיךָ אָרוּץ כִּי תַרְחִיב לִבִּי׃

הוֹרֵנִי יְהוָה דֶּרֶךְ חֻקֶּיךָ וְאֶצְּרֶנָּה עֵקֶב׃ הֲבִינֵנִי וְאֶצְּרָה תוֹרָתֶךָ
וְאֶשְׁמְרֶנָּה בְכָל־לֵב׃ הַדְרִיכֵנִי בִּנְתִיב מִצְוֺתֶיךָ כִּי־בוֹ חָפָצְתִּי׃
הַט־לִבִּי אֶל־עֵדְוֺתֶיךָ וְאַל אֶל־בָּצַע׃ הַעֲבֵר עֵינַי מֵרְאוֹת שָׁוְא
בִּדְרָכֶךָ חַיֵּנִי׃ הָקֵם לְעַבְדְּךָ אִמְרָתֶךָ אֲשֶׁר לְיִרְאָתֶךָ׃ הַעֲבֵר חֶרְפָּתִי
אֲשֶׁר יָגֹרְתִּי כִּי מִשְׁפָּטֶיךָ טוֹבִים׃ הִנֵּה תָּאַבְתִּי לְפִקֻּדֶיךָ בְּצִדְקָתְךָ
חַיֵּנִי׃

וִיבֹאֻנִי חֲסָדֶךָ יְהֹוָה תְּשׁוּעָתְךָ כְּאִמְרָתֶךָ׃ וְאֶעֱנֶה חֹרְפִי דָבָר כִּי־
בָטַחְתִּי בִּדְבָרֶךָ׃ וְאַל־תַּצֵּל מִפִּי דְבַר־אֱמֶת עַד־מְאֹד כִּי לְמִשְׁפָּטֶךָ
יִחָלְתִּי׃ וְאֶשְׁמְרָה תוֹרָתְךָ תָמִיד לְעוֹלָם וָעֶד׃ וְאֶתְהַלְּכָה בָרְחָבָה
כִּי פִקֻּדֶיךָ דָרָשְׁתִּי׃ וַאֲדַבְּרָה בְעֵדֹתֶיךָ נֶגֶד מְלָכִים וְלֹא אֵבוֹשׁ׃
וְאֶשְׁתַּעֲשַׁע בְּמִצְוֺתֶיךָ אֲשֶׁר אָהָבְתִּי׃ וְאֶשָּׂא־כַפַּי אֶל־מִצְוֺתֶיךָ
אֲשֶׁר אָהָבְתִּי וְאָשִׂיחָה בְחֻקֶּיךָ׃

זְכָר־דָּבָר לְעַבְדֶּךָ עַל אֲשֶׁר יִחַלְתָּנִי׃ זֹאת נֶחָמָתִי בְעָנְיִי כִּי
אִמְרָתְךָ חִיָּתְנִי׃ זֵדִים הֱלִיצֻנִי עַד־מְאֹד מִתּוֹרָתְךָ לֹא נָטִיתִי׃
זָכַרְתִּי מִשְׁפָּטֶיךָ מֵעוֹלָם ׀ יְהֹוָה וָאֶתְנֶחָם׃ זַלְעָפָה אֲחָזַתְנִי
מֵרְשָׁעִים עֹזְבֵי תּוֹרָתֶךָ׃ זְמִרוֹת הָיוּ־לִי חֻקֶּיךָ בְּבֵית מְגוּרָי׃ זָכַרְתִּי
בַלַּיְלָה שִׁמְךָ יְהֹוָה וָאֶשְׁמְרָה תּוֹרָתֶךָ׃ זֹאת הָיְתָה־לִּי כִּי פִקֻּדֶיךָ
נָצָרְתִּי׃

חֶלְקִי יְהֹוָה אָמַרְתִּי לִשְׁמֹר דְּבָרֶיךָ׃ חִלִּיתִי פָנֶיךָ בְכָל־לֵב חָנֵּנִי
כְּאִמְרָתֶךָ׃ חִשַּׁבְתִּי דְרָכָי וָאָשִׁיבָה רַגְלַי אֶל־עֵדֹתֶיךָ׃ חַשְׁתִּי וְלֹא
הִתְמַהְמָהְתִּי לִשְׁמֹר מִצְוֺתֶיךָ׃ חֶבְלֵי רְשָׁעִים עִוְּדֻנִי תּוֹרָתְךָ לֹא
שָׁכָחְתִּי׃ חֲצוֹת־לַיְלָה אָקוּם לְהוֹדוֹת לָךְ עַל מִשְׁפְּטֵי צִדְקֶךָ׃
חָבֵר אָנִי לְכָל־אֲשֶׁר יְרֵאוּךָ וּלְשֹׁמְרֵי פִּקּוּדֶיךָ׃ חַסְדְּךָ יְהֹוָה מָלְאָה
הָאָרֶץ חֻקֶּיךָ לַמְּדֵנִי׃

טוֹב עָשִׂיתָ עִם־עַבְדְּךָ יְהֹוָה כִּדְבָרֶךָ׃ טוּב טַעַם וָדַעַת לַמְּדֵנִי כִּי
בְמִצְוֺתֶיךָ הֶאֱמָנְתִּי׃ טֶרֶם אֶעֱנֶה אֲנִי שֹׁגֵג וְעַתָּה אִמְרָתְךָ שָׁמָרְתִּי׃
טוֹב־אַתָּה וּמֵטִיב לַמְּדֵנִי חֻקֶּיךָ׃ טָפְלוּ עָלַי שֶׁקֶר זֵדִים אֲנִי בְּכָל־
לֵב ׀ אֱצֹּר פִּקּוּדֶיךָ׃ טָפַשׁ כַּחֵלֶב לִבָּם אֲנִי תּוֹרָתְךָ שִׁעֲשָׁעְתִּי׃
טוֹב־לִי כִי־עֻנֵּיתִי לְמַעַן אֶלְמַד חֻקֶּיךָ׃ טוֹב־לִי תוֹרַת־פִּיךָ מֵאַלְפֵי
זָהָב וָכָסֶף׃

יָדֶיךָ עָשׂוּנִי וַיְכוֹנְנוּנִי הֲבִינֵנִי וְאֶלְמְדָה מִצְוֺתֶיךָ: יְרֵאֶיךָ יִרְאוּנִי
וְיִשְׂמָחוּ כִּי לִדְבָרְךָ יִחָלְתִּי: יָדַעְתִּי יְהוָה כִּי־צֶדֶק מִשְׁפָּטֶיךָ וֶאֱמוּנָה
עִנִּיתָנִי: יְהִי־נָא חַסְדְּךָ לְנַחֲמֵנִי כְּאִמְרָתְךָ לְעַבְדֶּךָ: יְבֹאוּנִי רַחֲמֶיךָ
וְאֶחְיֶה כִּי־תוֹרָתְךָ שַׁעֲשֻׁעָי: יֵבֹשׁוּ זֵדִים כִּי־שֶׁקֶר עִוְּתוּנִי אֲנִי אָשִׂיחַ
וְיֹדְעֵי בְּפִקּוּדֶיךָ: יָשׁוּבוּ לִי יְרֵאֶיךָ וידעו עֵדֹתֶיךָ: יְהִי־לִבִּי תָמִים בְּחֻקֶּיךָ
לְמַעַן לֹא אֵבוֹשׁ:

כָּלְתָה לִתְשׁוּעָתְךָ נַפְשִׁי לִדְבָרְךָ יִחָלְתִּי: כָּלוּ עֵינַי לְאִמְרָתֶךָ לֵאמֹר
מָתַי תְּנַחֲמֵנִי: כִּי־הָיִיתִי כְּנֹאד בְּקִיטוֹר חֻקֶּיךָ לֹא שָׁכָחְתִּי: כַּמָּה
יְמֵי־עַבְדֶּךָ מָתַי תַּעֲשֶׂה בְרֹדְפַי מִשְׁפָּט: כָּרוּ־לִי זֵדִים שִׁיחוֹת אֲשֶׁר
לֹא כְתוֹרָתֶךָ: כָּל־מִצְוֺתֶיךָ אֱמוּנָה שֶׁקֶר רְדָפוּנִי עָזְרֵנִי: כִּמְעַט
כִּלּוּנִי בָאָרֶץ וַאֲנִי לֹא־עָזַבְתִּי פִקֻּדֶיךָ: כְּחַסְדְּךָ חַיֵּנִי וְאֶשְׁמְרָה
עֵדוּת פִּיךָ:

לְעוֹלָם יְהוָה דְּבָרְךָ נִצָּב בַּשָּׁמָיִם: לְדֹר וָדֹר אֱמוּנָתֶךָ כּוֹנַנְתָּ אֶרֶץ
וַתַּעֲמֹד: לְמִשְׁפָּטֶיךָ עָמְדוּ הַיּוֹם כִּי הַכֹּל עֲבָדֶיךָ: לוּלֵי תוֹרָתְךָ
שַׁעֲשֻׁעָי אָז אָבַדְתִּי בְעָנְיִי: לְעוֹלָם לֹא־אֶשְׁכַּח פִּקּוּדֶיךָ כִּי־בָם
חִיִּיתָנִי: לְךָ־אֲנִי הוֹשִׁיעֵנִי כִּי פִקּוּדֶיךָ דָרָשְׁתִּי: לִי קִוּוּ רְשָׁעִים
לְאַבְּדֵנִי עֵדֹתֶיךָ אֶתְבּוֹנָן: לְכָל־תִּכְלָה רָאִיתִי קֵץ רְחָבָה מִצְוָתְךָ
מְאֹד:

מָה־אָהַבְתִּי תוֹרָתֶךָ כָּל־הַיּוֹם הִיא שִׂיחָתִי: מֵאֹיְבַי תְּחַכְּמֵנִי
מִצְוֺתֶךָ כִּי לְעוֹלָם הִיא־לִי: מִכָּל־מְלַמְּדַי הִשְׂכַּלְתִּי כִּי עֵדְוֺתֶיךָ
שִׂיחָה לִי: מִזְּקֵנִים אֶתְבּוֹנָן כִּי פִקּוּדֶיךָ נָצָרְתִּי: מִכָּל־אֹרַח רָע
כָּלִאתִי רַגְלָי לְמַעַן אֶשְׁמֹר דְּבָרֶךָ: מִמִּשְׁפָּטֶיךָ לֹא־סָרְתִּי כִּי־אַתָּה
הוֹרֵתָנִי: מַה־נִּמְלְצוּ לְחִכִּי אִמְרָתֶךָ מִדְּבַשׁ לְפִי: מִפִּקּוּדֶיךָ אֶתְבּוֹנָן
עַל־כֵּן שָׂנֵאתִי ׀ כָּל־אֹרַח שָׁקֶר:

נֵר־לְרַגְלִ֥י דְבָרֶ֑ךָ וְ֝א֗וֹר לִנְתִיבָתִֽי׃ נִשְׁבַּ֥עְתִּי וָאֲקַיֵּ֑מָה לִ֝שְׁמֹ֗ר
מִשְׁפְּטֵ֥י צִדְקֶֽךָ׃ נַעֲנֵ֥יתִי עַד־מְאֹ֑ד יְ֝הוָ֗ה חַיֵּ֥נִי כִדְבָרֶֽךָ׃ נִדְב֣וֹת
פִּ֭י רְצֵה־נָ֣א יְהוָ֑ה וּֽמִשְׁפָּטֶ֥יךָ לַמְּדֵֽנִי׃ נַפְשִׁ֣י בְכַפִּ֣י תָמִ֑יד וְ֝תוֹרָתְךָ֗
לֹ֣א שָׁכָֽחְתִּי׃ נָתְנ֬וּ רְשָׁעִ֣ים פַּ֣ח לִ֑י וּ֝מִפִּקּוּדֶ֗יךָ לֹ֣א תָעִֽיתִי׃ נָחַ֣לְתִּי
עֵדְוֺתֶ֣יךָ לְעוֹלָ֑ם כִּֽי־שְׂשׂ֖וֹן לִבִּ֣י הֵֽמָּה׃ נָטִ֣יתִי לִ֭בִּי לַעֲשׂ֥וֹת חֻקֶּ֗יךָ
לְעוֹלָ֥ם עֵֽקֶב׃

סֵעֲפִ֥ים שָׂנֵ֑אתִי וְֽתוֹרָתְךָ֥ אָהָֽבְתִּי׃ סִתְרִ֣י וּמָגִנִּ֣י אָ֑תָּה לִדְבָרְךָ֥ יִחָֽלְתִּי׃
ס֣וּרוּ מִמֶּ֣נִּי מְרֵעִ֑ים וְ֝אֶצְּרָ֗ה מִצְוֺ֥ת אֱלֹהָֽי׃ סָמְכֵ֣נִי כְאִמְרָתְךָ֣ וְאֶֽחְיֶ֑ה
וְאַל־תְּ֝בִישֵׁ֗נִי מִשִּׂבְרִֽי׃ סְעָדֵ֥נִי וְאִוָּשֵׁ֑עָה וְאֶשְׁעָ֖ה בְחֻקֶּ֣יךָ תָמִֽיד׃
סָ֭לִיתָ כָּל־שׁוֹגִ֣ים מֵחֻקֶּ֑יךָ כִּי־שֶׁ֝֗קֶר תַּרְמִיתָֽם׃ סִגִ֗ים הִשְׁבַּ֥תָּ כָל־
רִשְׁעֵי־אָ֑רֶץ לָ֝כֵ֗ן אָהַ֥בְתִּי עֵדֹתֶֽיךָ׃ סָמַ֣ר מִפַּחְדְּךָ֣ בְשָׂרִ֑י וּֽמִמִּשְׁפָּטֶ֥יךָ
יָרֵֽאתִי׃

עָ֭שִׂיתִי מִשְׁפָּ֣ט וָצֶ֑דֶק בַּל־תַּ֝נִּיחֵ֗נִי לְעֹשְׁקָֽי׃ עֲרֹ֣ב עַבְדְּךָ֣ לְט֑וֹב
אַֽל־יַעַשְׁקֻ֥נִי זֵדִֽים׃ עֵ֭ינַי כָּל֣וּ לִישׁוּעָתֶ֑ךָ וּלְאִמְרַ֥ת צִדְקֶֽךָ׃ עֲשֵׂ֣ה
עִֽם־עַבְדְּךָ֣ כְחַסְדֶּ֑ךָ וְחֻקֶּ֥יךָ לַמְּדֵֽנִי׃ עַבְדְּךָ־אָ֥נִי הֲבִינֵ֑נִי וְ֝אֵדְעָ֗ה
עֵדֹתֶֽיךָ׃ עֵ֭ת לַעֲשׂ֣וֹת לַיהוָ֑ה הֵ֝פֵ֗רוּ תּוֹרָתֶֽךָ׃ עַל־כֵּ֭ן אָהַ֣בְתִּי
מִצְוֺתֶ֑יךָ מִזָּהָ֥ב וּמִפָּֽז׃ עַל־כֵּ֤ן ׀ כָּל־פִּקּ֣וּדֵי כֹ֣ל יִשָּׁ֑רְתִּי כָּל־אֹ֖רַח
שֶׁ֣קֶר שָׂנֵֽאתִי׃

פְּלָא֥וֹת עֵדְוֺתֶ֑יךָ עַל־כֵּ֝֗ן נְצָרָ֥תַם נַפְשִֽׁי׃ פֵּ֖תַח־דְּבָרֶ֥יךָ יָאִ֗יר מֵבִ֥ין
פְּתָיִֽים׃ פִּֽי־פָ֭עַרְתִּי וָאֶשְׁאָ֑פָה כִּ֖י לְמִצְוֺתֶ֣יךָ יָאָֽבְתִּי׃ פְּנֵה־אֵלַ֥י
וְחָנֵּ֑נִי כְּ֝מִשְׁפָּ֗ט לְאֹהֲבֵ֥י שְׁמֶֽךָ׃ פְּ֭עָמַי הָכֵ֣ן בְּאִמְרָתֶ֑ךָ וְֽאַל־תַּשְׁלֶט־
בִּ֥י כָל־אָֽוֶן׃ פְּ֭דֵנִי מֵעֹ֣שֶׁק אָדָ֑ם וְ֝אֶשְׁמְרָ֗ה פִּקּוּדֶֽיךָ׃ פָּ֭נֶיךָ הָאֵ֣ר
בְּעַבְדֶּ֑ךָ וְ֝לַמְּדֵ֗נִי אֶת־חֻקֶּֽיךָ׃ פַּלְגֵי־מַ֭יִם יָרְד֣וּ עֵינָ֑י עַ֝֗ל לֹא־שָׁמְר֥וּ
תוֹרָתֶֽךָ׃

צַדִּ֣יק אַתָּ֣ה יהוָ֑ה וְ֝יָשָׁ֗ר מִשְׁפָּטֶֽיךָ׃ צִ֭וִּיתָ צֶ֣דֶק עֵדֹתֶ֑יךָ וֶ֝אֱמוּנָ֗ה
מְאֹֽד׃ צִמְּתַ֥תְנִי קִנְאָתִ֑י כִּֽי־שָׁכְח֖וּ דְבָרֶ֣יךָ צָרָֽי׃ צְרוּפָ֣ה אִמְרָתְךָ֣
מְאֹ֑ד וְ֝עַבְדְּךָ֥ אֲהֵבָֽהּ׃ צָעִ֣יר אָנֹכִ֣י וְנִבְזֶ֑ה פִּ֝קֻּדֶ֗יךָ לֹ֣א שָׁכָֽחְתִּי׃
צִדְקָתְךָ֣ צֶ֣דֶק לְעוֹלָ֑ם וְֽתוֹרָתְךָ֥ אֱמֶֽת׃ צַר־וּמָג֥וֹק מְצָא֑וּנִי מִ֝צְוֺתֶ֗יךָ
שַׁעֲשֻׁעָֽי׃ צֶ֖דֶק עֵדְוֺתֶ֥יךָ לְעוֹלָ֗ם הֲבִינֵ֥נִי וְאֶֽחְיֶֽה׃

קָרָ֣אתִי בְכָל־לֵ֭ב עֲנֵ֥נִי יהוָ֗ה חֻקֶּ֥יךָ אֶצֹּֽרָה׃ קְרָאתִ֥יךָ הוֹשִׁיעֵ֑נִי
וְ֝אֶשְׁמְרָ֗ה עֵדֹתֶֽיךָ׃ קִדַּ֣מְתִּי בַ֭נֶּשֶׁף וָאֲשַׁוֵּ֑עָה לדבריך יִחָֽלְתִּי׃ (לִדְבָרְךָ֥)
קִדְּמ֣וּ עֵ֭ינַי אַשְׁמֻר֑וֹת לָ֝שִׂ֗יחַ בְּאִמְרָתֶֽךָ׃ ק֭וֹלִי שִׁמְעָ֣ה כְחַסְדֶּ֑ךָ
יְ֝הוָ֗ה כְּמִשְׁפָּטֶ֥ךָ חַיֵּֽנִי׃ קָ֭רְבוּ רֹדְפֵ֣י זִמָּ֑ה מִתּוֹרָתְךָ֥ רָחָֽקוּ׃ קָר֣וֹב
אַתָּ֣ה יהוָ֑ה וְֽכָל־מִצְוֺתֶ֥יךָ אֱמֶֽת׃ קֶ֣דֶם יָ֭דַעְתִּי מֵעֵדֹתֶ֑יךָ כִּ֖י לְעוֹלָ֣ם
יְסַדְתָּֽם׃

רְאֵה־עָנְיִ֥י וְחַלְּצֵ֑נִי כִּֽי־תֽ֝וֹרָתְךָ֗ לֹ֣א שָׁכָֽחְתִּי׃ רִיבָ֣ה רִ֭יבִי וּגְאָלֵ֑נִי
לְאִמְרָתְךָ֥ חַיֵּֽנִי׃ רָח֣וֹק מֵרְשָׁעִ֣ים יְשׁוּעָ֑ה כִּֽי־חֻ֝קֶּ֗יךָ לֹ֣א דָרָֽשׁוּ׃ רַחֲמֶ֣יךָ
רַבִּ֣ים ׀ יהוָ֑ה כְּֽמִשְׁפָּטֶ֥יךָ חַיֵּֽנִי׃ רַ֭בִּים רֹדְפַ֣י וְצָרָ֑י מֵ֝עֵדְוֺתֶ֗יךָ לֹ֣א נָטִֽיתִי׃
רָאִ֣יתִי בֹ֭גְדִים וָאֶתְקוֹטָ֑טָה אֲשֶׁ֥ר אִ֝מְרָתְךָ֗ לֹ֣א שָׁמָֽרוּ׃ רְ֭אֵה כִּֽי־
פִקּוּדֶ֣יךָ אָהָ֑בְתִּי יְ֝הוָ֗ה כְּֽחַסְדְּךָ֥ חַיֵּֽנִי׃ רֹאשׁ־דְּבָרְךָ֥ אֱמֶ֑ת וּ֝לְעוֹלָ֗ם
כָּל־מִשְׁפַּ֥ט צִדְקֶֽךָ׃

שָׂ֭רִים רְדָפ֣וּנִי חִנָּ֑ם ומדבריך פָּחַ֥ד לִבִּֽי׃ שָׂ֣שׂ אָ֭נֹכִי עַל־אִמְרָתֶ֑ךָ (וּ֝מִדְּבָרְךָ֗)
כְּ֝מוֹצֵ֗א שָׁלָ֥ל רָֽב׃ שֶׁ֣קֶר שָׂ֭נֵאתִי וָאֲתַעֵ֑בָה תּוֹרָתְךָ֥ אָהָֽבְתִּי׃ שֶׁ֣בַע
בַּ֭יּוֹם הִלַּלְתִּ֑יךָ עַ֝֗ל מִשְׁפְּטֵ֥י צִדְקֶֽךָ׃ שָׁל֣וֹם רָ֭ב לְאֹהֲבֵ֣י תוֹרָתֶ֑ךָ
וְאֵֽין־לָ֥מוֹ מִכְשֽׁוֹל׃ שִׂבַּ֣רְתִּי לִֽישׁוּעָתְךָ֣ יהוָ֑ה וּֽמִצְוֺתֶ֥יךָ עָשִֽׂיתִי׃
שָֽׁמְרָ֣ה נַ֭פְשִׁי עֵדֹתֶ֑יךָ וָאֹהֲבֵ֥ם מְאֹֽד׃ שָׁמַ֣רְתִּי פִ֭קּוּדֶיךָ וְעֵדֹתֶ֑יךָ כִּ֖י
כָל־דְּרָכַ֣י נֶגְדֶּֽךָ׃

תִּקְרַ֤ב רִנָּתִ֣י לְפָנֶ֣יךָ יהוָ֑ה כִּדְבָרְךָ֥ הֲבִינֵֽנִי׃ תָּב֣וֹא תְּחִנָּתִ֣י לְפָנֶ֑יךָ

כְּאִמְרָתְךָ הַצִּילֵנִי׃ תַּבַּעְנָה שְׂפָתַי תְּהִלָּה כִּי תְלַמְּדֵנִי חֻקֶּיךָ׃ תַּעַן
לְשׁוֹנִי אִמְרָתֶךָ כִּי כָל־מִצְוֺתֶיךָ צֶּדֶק׃ תְּהִי־יָדְךָ לְעָזְרֵנִי כִּי פִקּוּדֶיךָ
בָחָרְתִּי׃ תָּאַבְתִּי לִישׁוּעָתְךָ יְהוָה וְתוֹרָתְךָ שַׁעֲשֻׁעָי׃ תְּחִי־נַפְשִׁי
וּתְהַלְלֶךָּ וּמִשְׁפָּטֶךָ יַעְזְרֻנִי׃ תָּעִיתִי כְּשֶׂה אֹבֵד בַּקֵּשׁ עַבְדֶּךָ כִּי
מִצְוֺתֶיךָ לֹא שָׁכָחְתִּי׃

קכא שִׁיר לַמַּעֲלוֹת אֶשָּׂא עֵינַי אֶל־הֶהָרִים מֵאַיִן יָבֹא עֶזְרִי׃ עֶזְרִי מֵעִם
יְהוָה עֹשֵׂה שָׁמַיִם וָאָרֶץ׃ אַל־יִתֵּן לַמּוֹט רַגְלֶךָ אַל־יָנוּם שֹׁמְרֶךָ׃
הִנֵּה לֹא־יָנוּם וְלֹא יִישָׁן שׁוֹמֵר יִשְׂרָאֵל׃ יְהוָה שֹׁמְרֶךָ יְהוָה צִלְּךָ
עַל־יַד יְמִינֶךָ׃ יוֹמָם הַשֶּׁמֶשׁ לֹא־יַכֶּכָּה וְיָרֵחַ בַּלָּיְלָה׃ יְהוָה יִשְׁמָרְךָ
מִכָּל־רָע יִשְׁמֹר אֶת־נַפְשֶׁךָ׃ יְהוָה יִשְׁמָר־צֵאתְךָ וּבוֹאֶךָ מֵעַתָּה
וְעַד־עוֹלָם׃

קכח שִׁיר הַמַּעֲלוֹת אַשְׁרֵי כָּל־יְרֵא יְהוָה הַהֹלֵךְ בִּדְרָכָיו׃ יְגִיעַ כַּפֶּיךָ כִּי
תֹאכֵל אַשְׁרֶיךָ וְטוֹב לָךְ׃ אֶשְׁתְּךָ ׀ כְּגֶפֶן פֹּרִיָּה בְּיַרְכְּתֵי בֵיתֶךָ בָּנֶיךָ
כִּשְׁתִלֵי זֵיתִים סָבִיב לְשֻׁלְחָנֶךָ׃ הִנֵּה כִי־כֵן יְבֹרַךְ גָּבֶר יְרֵא יְהוָה׃
יְבָרֶכְךָ יְהוָה מִצִּיּוֹן וּרְאֵה בְּטוּב יְרוּשָׁלִָם כֹּל יְמֵי חַיֶּיךָ׃ וּרְאֵה־בָנִים
לְבָנֶיךָ שָׁלוֹם עַל־יִשְׂרָאֵל׃

קל שִׁיר הַמַּעֲלוֹת מִמַּעֲמַקִּים קְרָאתִיךָ יְהוָה׃ אֲדֹנָי שִׁמְעָה בְקוֹלִי
תִּהְיֶינָה אָזְנֶיךָ קַשֻּׁבוֹת לְקוֹל תַּחֲנוּנָי׃ אִם־עֲוֺנוֹת תִּשְׁמָר־יָהּ אֲדֹנָי
מִי יַעֲמֹד׃ כִּי־עִמְּךָ הַסְּלִיחָה לְמַעַן תִּוָּרֵא׃ קִוִּיתִי יְהוָה קִוְּתָה נַפְשִׁי
וְלִדְבָרוֹ הוֹחָלְתִּי׃ נַפְשִׁי לַאדֹנָי מִשֹּׁמְרִים לַבֹּקֶר שֹׁמְרִים לַבֹּקֶר׃
יַחֵל יִשְׂרָאֵל אֶל־יְהוָה כִּי־עִם־יְהוָה הַחֶסֶד וְהַרְבֵּה עִמּוֹ פְדוּת׃
וְהוּא יִפְדֶּה אֶת־יִשְׂרָאֵל מִכֹּל עֲוֺנוֹתָיו׃

קלג שִׁיר הַמַּעֲלוֹת לְדָוִד הִנֵּה מַה־טּוֹב וּמַה־נָּעִים שֶׁבֶת אַחִים גַּם־

יַ֥חַד׃ כַּשֶּׁ֤מֶן הַטּ֨וֹב ׀ עַל־הָרֹ֗אשׁ יֹרֵ֗ד עַֽל־הַזָּ֥קָן זְקַֽן־אַהֲרֹ֑ן שֶׁ֝יֹּרֵ֗ד
עַל־פִּ֥י מִדּוֹתָֽיו׃ כְּטַל־חֶרְמ֗וֹן שֶׁיֹּרֵד֮ עַל־הַרְרֵ֪י צִ֫יּ֥וֹן כִּ֤י שָׁ֨ם ׀ צִוָּ֣ה
י֭הוה אֶת־הַבְּרָכָ֑ה חַ֝יִּ֗ים עַד־הָעוֹלָֽם׃

TEHILLIM INDEX

For additional resources visit the RCA website
www.rabbis.org/hamadrikh